AMERICAN GOVERNMENT

Second Edition

Robert A. Heineman, Ph.D.
Alfred University

Steven A. Peterson, Ph.D.
Alfred University

Thomas H. Rasmussen, Ph.D.
Alfred University

McGraw-Hill, Inc.

New York   St. Louis   San Francisco   Auckland   Bogotá   Caracas
Lisbon   London   Madrid   Mexico City   Milan   Montreal   New Delhi
San Juan   Singapore   Sydney   Tokyo   Toronto

American Government

16 17 18   DOH   15 14 13

ISBN: 0-07-028215-3

Sponsoring Editor: Jeanne Flagg
Production Supervisor: Elizabeth Strange
Editing Supervisor: Patty Andrews

Library of Congress Cataloging-in-Publication Data

Heineman, Robert A.
   American government / Robert A. Heineman, Steven A. Peterson,
Thomas H. Rasmussen.—2nd ed.
      p.   cm.
   Includes bibliographical references (p.   ) and index.
   ISBN 0-07-028215-3
   1. United States—Politics and government.   I. Peterson, Steven A.
II. Rasmussen, Thomas H.   III. Title.
JK274.H34   1995
320.473—dc20   94-38881
                                                         CIP

Robert A. Heineman received his B.A. degree from Bradley University and his Ph.D. from The American University. He has held governmental positions at the national, state, and local levels and is currently professor of political science and director of the master's program in community services administration at Alfred University. He is the author of *Authority and the Liberal Tradition* and co-author of *The World of the Policy Analyst*. He has published various articles and reviews in the field of American politics.

Steven A. Peterson is professor of political science at Alfred University. He received his Ph.D. from the State University at Buffalo. He has published widely in such journals as *Journal of Politics, American Journal of Political Science, Administration & Society,* and *Political Psychology*. He has authored or co-authored books on state and local politics, policy analysis, gerontology, and political behavior. His areas of interest are American politics, judicial process, political behavior, biopolitics, and applications of postmodern theory to the study of politics.

Thomas H. Rasmussen is professor of political science at Alfred University. After receiving his B.A. degree from Earlham College and his Ph.D. from Syracuse University, he taught for three years in Africa at the University of Zambia. He is coauthor of two books and has published many articles in the fields of comparative politics and environmental policy.

Preface

This introduction to the institutions and processes of American government and politics is an inexpensive alternative to the longer textbooks that cover these subjects in greater detail. We are gratified that the first edition was so well received by users in need of a brief introduction to American government and politics. This revised second edition gives us the opportunity to update the material and to include the findings of recent scholarship.

The organization of this book follows that of the major texts. Individual chapters focus on the federal framework and the constitutional background; the processes of representation including public opinion, political parties and interest groups; and the formal governmental institutions of the presidency, Congress, the courts, and the bureaucracy. Later chapters describe the public policy process and examine the evolution of policy in the areas of civil rights and liberties, political economy, and foreign policy.

In writing this book, we have kept in mind three primary considerations. First, we have attempted to provide essential factual information about American government and politics. Second, we have tried to give historical depth to this material. Third, we have introduced the reader to those concepts we feel are most useful in interpreting the facts of American politics. No solutions to political issues are provided here, and no single theoretical approach is employed. This book offers the reader essential information about the political system and some basic conceptual tools for making judgments about political issues.

As a general framework, this book uses three commonly accepted perspectives or theories about the relative power of political leaders and citizens. The democratic perspective emphasizes that the people who elect leaders should be able to hold them accountable. The elitist perspective maintains that political institutions are inevitably dominated by a few who make decisions without much effective popular control. The pluralist interpretation suggests that the various interests in society mobilize resources to influence policy in areas that directly concern them. How these interpretations apply to American government and politics will be discussed throughout this book.

This text has been a joint effort among Professors Heineman, Peterson, and Rasmussen. Professor Rasmussen has served as coordinator and liaison with the publisher. He is responsible for chapters 1, 9, 10, 13, and 15. Professor Heineman has written chapters 3, 7, 8, 11, and 14. Professor Peterson's responsibility has been chapters 2, 4, 5, 6, and 12. Writing and revising this book has been a challenge and reward for all of us. In view of our widely varying theoretical perspectives, this book also may be a tangible indication of the value of the pluralist model in the academic world.

Robert A. Heineman
Steven A. Peterson
Thomas H. Rasmussen

Acknowledgments

The authors are most grateful to many people whose cooperation and support made timely completion of this revised edition possible. Special thanks go to our spouses, Alice Heineman, Bettina Franzese and Margaret Byrd Rasmussen. They have busy lives of their own as parents and working professionals, yet they generously provide us with constant encouragement, support, and sense of perspective. We gratefully acknowledge their many contributions to our well-being while we have been writing about American government and politics.

The stylistic and substantive good sense of Jeanne Flagg, our editor at McGraw Hill, has improved this edition. Her words of encouragement also made our work easier, and we are indebted to her. Professor Russell D. Renka of Southeast Missouri State University reviewed an initial draft of the manuscript and offered many perceptive, helpful suggestions that we have been able to incorporate into our revisions. Michael O'Grady and Warren Emerson also provided useful advice. Any errors and shortcomings that remain are, of course, our responsibility. Susan Meacham and Karen Mix cheerfully and competently helped with the technical details of preparing this second edition.

We also thank several generations of very fine Alfred University students who have studied American government and politics with us in introductory and advanced courses. Their stimulating questions and observations have helped us refine our understanding of American politics. Without them, we would never have written this book.

Contents

CHAPTER 1

Politics in a Changing Society

In 200 years America has been transformed from a primarily agrarian society to an industrial society. In 1790 most people lived on farms and provided for their own needs; today most people live in cities or suburbs and earn their living providing goods and services for other people.

One of the constants of American life over these 200 years has been government. Government affects our lives from the day we are born to the day we die. Government supports health clinics that provide prenatal care to some expectant mothers, inspects baby food for wholesomeness and accurate labeling, and bans the marketing of unsafe toys. Government operates the schools in which we learn, builds the highways on which we drive, and regulates the television we watch. Government provides for the common defense, which may require military conscription for many young people in times of international crisis and war.

Government supplies police and fire protection in our communities. Government provides financial assistance to the very young, the very old, the handicapped, and others who cannot maintain a minimal standard of living for themselves and their families. Government cushions the impact of crises for workers who lose their jobs, homeowners struck by floods or hurricanes, and farmers faced with falling grain prices. Government organizes a social security system, subsidizes the heavy medical needs of the aging, and licenses funeral homes. Truly, government is an important part of our lives from cradle to grave.

Chapter 1 surveys changes in the role of government in society over 200 years and introduces democratic, elitist, and pluralist perspectives on American political life. After describing the constitutional and federal framework of American government in Chapters 2 and 3, the book examines ways citizens participate in politics. Americans typically disagree about how much the government should do, and their efforts to influence government decisions are the stuff of politics. People who share a point of view join interest groups and support political parties. Public opinion polls record what citizens think about important policy issues. In regularly held elections, voters register their approval or disapproval of their elected officials. These political institutions are discussed in Chapters 4 through 7.

Government embodies those institutions established in the Constitution which define and carry out policies affecting how Americans live their lives. Congress passes laws and raises taxes. The president establishes priorities and, with the Cabinet and White House staff, supervises the work of some 3 million civilian employees who do the federal government's work. In the courts, judges penalize individuals who assault or cheat others and ensure that the actions of the president and Congress are consistent with the spirit of the Constitution as it has evolved over time. How these institutions work is discussed in Chapters 8 through 11.

Of course, the institutions of American government and politics cannot be separated as neatly as they are in the chapters of a book. Institutions work together (or against each other) in addressing the important public policy issues of our day. The dynamics of the policy process are explored in Chapters 12 through 15.

Although government is one of the constants of American life, its role is constantly changing. The Founding Fathers could not foresee that one day government would regulate business, manage the economy, or administer a social security system, but now it is generally accepted that government should perform these tasks. They could not imagine the rapid development of computer and telecommunications technology and all that it implies in terms of jobs and social changes. The better we understand how our political institutions have responded to social changes in the past, the better we can judge how government might respond to future social changes.

The Role of Government in Human Affairs

To resolve the political issues of today and tomorrow wisely, we need to think about what government should do and how well government does its work. Does the government provide peace and safety for its citizens, defending society from external enemies and enforcing laws which deter citizens from physically attacking or stealing from other citizens? Does the government promote a more equal distribution of well-being by alleviating extreme poverty, taxing rich people more heavily than poor people, and granting all citizens access to schooling and adequate housing? Does the government permit the people meaningful control over their rulers by holding free and fair elections, allowing a political opposition to organize and campaign, and guaranteeing citizens basic freedoms of speech, press, and worship?

The majority of the governments around the world do not perform any of these tasks particularly well. Many people have the misfortune to live under governments which are ineffective, corrupt, and cruel. The industrialized democracies of Europe and North America probably do best, although the United States lags behind many societies in providing a more equal distribution of material resources. Americans accept levels of chronic poverty and homelessness which are not tolerated in democratic Western Europe.[1]

Most Americans would not willingly live under a different kind of government. Given this broad support for the institutions of government, however, Americans still debate sharply the proper role of government in society. One important issue is how large a role government should play in economic and social life.

Laissez-Faire Government

The idea that government should play a limited role in human affairs developed in seventeenth-century England when reformers advocated a society in which individuals would be free to live their lives as they saw fit, with few restraints imposed by sovereign and church. At the time, absolute monarchs had the power and prestige to define their own priorities without any meaningful control from the people they ruled. Absolute monarchs claimed to rule as the representatives of God on earth, and as their subjects had to obey the will of God, so they had to obey the will of the sovereign. Monarchs ruled as they chose, unchecked by their subjects. The rulers made the laws, executed the laws, and settled disputes over application of the law. A monarch's successor was always a close relative, usually the eldest son. Rulers could tax their people and spend the revenues much as they pleased. They reserved the right to tell subjects how to worship. Monarchs controlled economic activity, selling the right to produce or trade important products to favorites and punishing any subject who challenged the royal monopoly.[2]

Citizens in seventeenth-century England challenged absolute monarchy and expressed several principles that became the foundation of laissez-faire government:

The principle of no taxation without representation—those who pay the taxes are entitled to have a say in how they are spent.

The principle of parliamentary sovereignty—the chief executive, whether monarch or president, governs as long as the elected representatives of the people agree that that person may govern.

The principle of individual freedom—individuals shall be free to think, speak, and worship as they see fit.

The principle of self-interest—individuals may choose where to reside, how to earn a living, and what life-style to lead, according to personal preference.

The principle of limited power—political rulers have limited responsibilities. That government is best which governs least, and governmental activities should be performed at the local level whenever possible.

The Founding Fathers who wrote our Constitution in 1789 accepted these principles. During the 1800s, Americans generally thought that society was best served if the government played a very limited role in economic and social life. Individual Americans transformed abundant natural resources into a highly productive agriculture. In the cities, factories produced more and better products. Most government services were supplied at the state and local levels. Beyond sheriff, judge, and schoolhouse, government provided few services, and individuals made their own way. At the national level, government activities were largely military in nature. Government soldiers pushed Mexico out of Texas, crushed the secessionist South in the Civil War, and decimated Native American populations who resisted white settlers moving into their lands.

Activist Government

By the end of the nineteenth century, reformers began to doubt that laissez-faire government was the best way to promote individual freedom and well-being. The Constitution gave individuals an important measure of control over their government, but now individual freedom was threatened from a new and unexpected quarter: the large industrial corporation. Put simply, individuals as workers and consumers could not compete on equal terms with corporate power, and the new industrial magnates grew rich and powerful at the expense of average farmers and workers. Many industries came to be dominated by one firm, which could charge very high prices. If only one railroad served a farm town, for example, the railroad could charge farmers a high price to transport grain and make a large profit.

Workers often had to labor for low wages under poor working conditions. A contract fair to both employer and employee can be reached only if the two parties have approximately equal power. However, workers often had to accept what the employer offered, and women and children often worked long hours in unsafe factories for pennies. Industries dumped their untreated wastes into the nation's waters and skies and laid off workers during periodic business slumps, causing great family hardship.[3]

By the 1890s, reformers proposed that the role of government should be expanded to check abusive corporate power and to protect the interests of individual workers and consumers. Reformers began to work for legislation to curb monopoly power in steel, railroads, oil, and other industries. The government regulated the packaging and sale of food and drugs to consumers in 1906 after a muckraking journalist, Upton Sinclair, exposed unsanitary practices in the meat-packing industry.[4]

Conservationists prevailed upon government to develop an extensive national park system in order to protect the land from thoughtless, short-sighted ranchers and mining companies. Important political reforms included extending the right to vote to women; providing for the direct election of judges and minor political officials; and introducing the referendum, which allowed citizens to vote directly on policy issues.

After the Great Depression of 1929 stalled economic activity and threw one-fourth of the labor force out of work, Americans in unprecedented numbers became convinced that laissez-faire government and an unmanaged capitalist economy did not work. Franklin Delano Roosevelt won a landslide victory in the presidential election of 1932 and swept a reform-minded Congress into office too. In the following years, the role of the federal government was much expanded. The National Labor Relations Act supported the right of workers to join unions and to bargain with their employers. The Social Security Act gave workers a monthly income after retirement. The Agricultural Adjustment Act sought to protect farmers from devastating falls in the prices of their crops. The Securities and Exchange Commission (SEC) began to regulate financial institutions.[5]

Increased Support for Government Involvement

For more than 40 years following Roosevelt's first election, the federal government played an active and expanding role in society. In the area of civil rights, the federal government acted to discourage discrimination on the basis of race, creed, or gender. In 1948, Harry S. Truman signed an executive order banning racial discrimination in the armed forces. In 1954, the Supreme Court declared racially segregated schools to be unconstitutional. In 1964, Congress enacted the Civil Rights Act, which prohibited discrimination in any public or private institution on the basis of race, religion, or national origin. In 1972, the Equal Employment Opportunity Act was passed to combat race and gender discrimination in employment.

Other government programs sought to provide everyone with a decent material standard of living, including a reasonable standard of food, clothing, shelter, and medical care and some protection from unemployment and the cares of old age. To promote greater socioeconomic equality, the government made available food stamps and housing subsidies, unemployment insurance and social security, scholarships, and work-training programs.

By the late 1970s, about 9 percent of American economic production and about 47 percent of the federal budget were devoted to social security, Medicare, food stamps, and other social welfare programs. These social spending programs did much to ease the burden of poverty in America; about 40 percent of social welfare spending went to persons with incomes below the official poverty line. However, when the income from social welfare programs is added to earned household income, 11 percent of American families still live below the poverty line. Without the income from government social welfare programs, 21 percent of American families would live in poverty.[6]

President Reagan and the Role of the Federal Government

Exactly how far government should go in promoting freedom from discrimination and guaranteeing an adequate material standard of living has become a matter of considerable dispute. To what extent does the Constitution require that governments, schools, and employers not discriminate against women or members of racial or religious minorities? Should government provide special scholarships and require affirmative action hiring programs to compensate for past discrimination? Should we as a society spend more on federal programs which redistribute income from the relatively well-off to the poor?

During his 1980 presidential election campaign, Ronald Reagan launched a sharp attack on the principle that the federal government should play an ever-expanding role in economic and social life. As President, Reagan fought for cuts in domestic spending programs, sponsored cuts in the income tax, slashed the budgets of federal regulatory agencies, and turned over responsibility for some government programs to the states. In the area of civil rights, the Reagan administration affirmed the values of community and tradition. If the community consensus is that religious values should be taught in the schools, homosexuality discouraged, and the values of home and family cherished, these community standards should be respected. Government should not defend unpopular atheists or homosexuals against the unfriendly actions of the majority culture.[7]

Political debate has continued over these issues during the administrations of moderate Republican George Bush (1988–1992) and moderate Democrat Bill Clinton, elected in 1992. Are activist or laissez-faire principles likely to prevail? The answer depends on how Americans think government should respond to continuing social change. It also depends on who is most successful at building political support for particular policies. Because the American political system is complex, skilled observers often disagree about the relative power of those who participate in the game of politics. In the next section we examine three perspectives on who shapes policy choices in American politics and government.

Perspectives on Power

Power is the ability to get someone to do your bidding, even if that person does not want to. Of enduring interest in politics is the power relationship between the rulers (whether a hereditary monarch, a military group, or popularly elected officials) and the citizens whom they rule. How much control do Americans have over their government? How much control should they have? In seeking to answer these questions, defenders and critics of American government and politics have developed three theories about power in American political life.

Democratic theory asks to what extent the people actually govern themselves and exercise control over their elected leaders. *Elitist theory* maintains that in any society a wealthy, prestigious, powerful minority occupies key political positions and makes important policy decisions without much control by the people. *Pluralist theory* observes that citizens have much influence on political issues of great interest and importance to them but little influence on other issues. These three theories—democratic, elitist, and pluralist—are sets of ideas which help us organize and interpret our political experience.

Democratic Theory

From a democratic perspective, the important political issue is how effectively the people control their leaders. How much control citizens in a democracy actually have is a matter of some debate. The word "democracy" comes from the Greek word *demos* and means "rule by the people." In ancient Athens, interested citizens met in the city square to discuss and resolve public issues, approaching the democratic ideal of rule by the people. Subsequent generations of political philosophers were inspired by the idea that the people should participate actively in their own governance.[8]

In larger societies, citizens tend to participate less fully in political life. In contemporary America the people rule only in the minimal sense that they choose those who rule over them. Issues in industrial society are complex, and most citizens have neither the time nor the inclination to study them carefully. Participation in politics is often limited to passing judgment on the overall performance of officials in occasional elections. Indeed, most citizens cannot recall the names of their representatives in Congress. At best, the participatory democratic model is an ideal to be worked toward, not an accurate description of political reality in contemporary America.[9]

Democracy in Practice

In practice, American citizens do have considerable control over their leaders, certainly in comparison with the authoritarian regimes so common in the world. In many societies, political power is based on armed might, and would-be rulers literally fight it out to determine who will govern and for what purpose. Because the military has most of the weapons, colonels and generals make and break governments or establish military dictatorships. In the United States, the military has remained under civilian control, and political battles have been fought with ballots, not bullets. In comparison with other societies, American elections are free, political parties compete, and civil liberties are respected.

Attempts to gain a political advantage by circumventing the checks and balances provided in the Constitution have met with much disfavor. In 1937, President Franklin Roosevelt proposed to increase the number of Supreme Court justices from nine to fifteen so he could pack the Court with liberal justices. Although Roosevelt was at the peak of his popularity, his plan was widely criticized and quietly withdrawn.[10]

The experiences of other countries show that it is one thing to write a constitution giving people some meaningful control over their rulers and quite another to establish a democratic government in actual practice. In Latin America, states throwing off the yoke of Spanish rule in the 1820s and 1830s modeled their new constitutions on the U.S. Constitution. Important provisions were ignored, however, and a small landowning aristocracy dominated politics. The military frequently overthrew civilian politicians and suspended the constitutions. Similarly, England and France sought to encourage democratic parliamentary forms of government in their Asian and African colonies after World War II, but in most cases, noncompetitive elections, erosion of basic freedoms, and periods of military rule prevailed. Citizens exercised very little control over their rulers.

In the 1970s, fewer than 30 of the world's 150 political systems could be classified as democratic, although many more have had short periods of democratic governance.[11] In the 1990s, most African, Asian, and Latin American nations are experimenting with democratic elections. An important reason this came about was the collapse of authoritarian communist rule in the Soviet Union and Eastern Europe. The fall of communism revealed that the sacrifice of freedom and the lack of any significant popular control of political leaders was not justified. Certainly authoritarian regimes failed to create efficient economies or just social systems. How many of these democratic experiments will end in creation of successful, enduring democracies remains to be seen.

Preconditions for Stable Democracy

Since citizens have won a substantial measure of control over their rulers in so few societies, it is important to ask when democratic political institutions are likely to succeed. The ruled have a better chance to keep control over their rulers in a free market economy, for the government then does not control production units such as factories or decide whom one works for, what job one works at, or where one lives.

Also important is the freedom to associate with others. In the United States, people belong to many social groups which are not controlled by the government but which do seek to influence the decisions of political leaders. On behalf of their members, churches speak out on abortion and school prayer issues, trade unions champion full-employment policies, the American Legion and Veterans of Foreign Wars build pride in a militarily strong America, and the Sierra Club works to preserve our nation's natural resources from economic development and our environment from industrial pollution.

People must also agree to resolve their differences within the framework of political institutions and to play by the political rules of the game. That means extending to all a fair chance to become part of the majority which makes political decisions and recognizing that minimal rights of small and unpopular minorities must be respected. Political factions may be tempted to seize power by force of arms and to distribute the fruits of victory to their followers. Democratic institutions require a spirit of bargaining and accommodation with one's political opponents.[12]

This willingness to settle for half a loaf and to recognize the essential minimum demands of political opponents is impossible when ethnic conflicts are allowed to fester and deepen into murderous hatred. Ethnic antagonism in Bosnia, in the former Soviet republics, in Sudan, and Somalia creates a hostile climate in which people are unlikely to have confidence in democratic political institutions.

With the important exception of the Civil War, political leaders in the United States and their supporters have adhered to the rules of the political game as defined in the Constitution for 200 years. In few societies would a presidential candidate defeated by a few percentage points wish his victorious opponent well and retire to private life, as routinely happens in American politics.

As you read about government and politics, think about the quality of American democracy. To what extent do the people hold their political leaders accountable? How responsive are elected officials to the wishes of their constituents?

Elitist Theory

Elitists build upon the observation that a few people in society monopolize resources and wield influence. A professional politician, a full-time employee of an interest group, and a wealthy campaign contributor are more powerful than an 18-year-old worker in a fast-food restaurant, a single parent working 40 hours a week while raising two children, or a millionaire whose passions are watching professional sports and collecting antique cars.

The fundamental insight of elitism is that within any political group, 99 percent of the members are bystanders while the other 1 percent make decisions. The work and outputs of Congress are structured by the leaders, not by rank-and-file members. In political parties, an elite few choose a short list of acceptable candidates, write platforms, and define party positions on important issues. The agenda of interest groups is controlled by group leaders. Ordinary party members make campaign contributions and support party candidates, but the basic decisions are made by the elite few.

Elitists are persuaded that on the national level, a small group, perhaps 7000 individuals, dominates political life. This political elite includes top advisers to the president, key members of Congress, opinion-shaping print and television journalists, highly placed corporation officers, and lawyers and bankers to whom elected political figures listen.[13]

Characteristics of Elite Rule

When observers argue that elites dominate American political life, they are likely to note several characteristics of elite rule.

Attention to the Big Issues.   The ruling minority guides the general direction of American politics, defines the terms of political debate, makes the major decisions about the role of government in society, and shapes the contours of economic policy. Many specific details are not worked out by the elite because these details are not important enough to merit their concern. The elite may not care whether the Air Force gets a new plane or the Navy gets a new carrier as long as military preparedness is maintained. And the elite may not care whether the Republican or Democratic candidate is elected president, as long as the elite can control the nominating process. Members of the elite make sure that both political parties put up candidates of similar social and occupational backgrounds and life experiences.

Members of the political elite work hard to control the agenda for political discussion, a process which E. E. Schattschneider calls the "mobilization of bias."[14] In his view, the problem is not that the elite and the non-elite argue about political issues and the elite few always win; the problem is that the members of the elite control the agenda by deciding what the issues are. The average citizen does not have the time or the energy, the interest, or the knowledge to become familiar with complex public issues. Because the people are incapable of understanding and resolving public issues, democracy is an impossible dream and the elite few dominate politics by default.

Competition Within the Elite.   Frequently, members of the elite are divided among themselves. For example, doctors no longer have a free hand in formulating health care policy. Other health care providers, including insurance companies, hospitals and nursing homes, drug manufacturers, and other health care support professionals, demand to be heard. And corporations alarmed at soaring health care costs challenge the dominance of medical professionals in shaping the health care system. Average Americans who are the patients and who pay most of the bill will not have much say.[15]

Intra-elite competition is an important source of social change. The role of government in society changes as elites adapt to a new environment. In post–Civil War America, the new industrial elites favored limited government and low taxes, but they also expected the federal government to subsidize railroad construction and subjugate native Americans. In the early 1900s, corporations advocated expanded federal regulation to protect established firms. Thus, established meat-packers favored that government inspect meat plants to protect the reputation of the industry from unscrupulous new entrants. Similarly, railroads favored rate regulation to protect the industry from price wars.[16]

Circulation of the Elite.   Members of the elite move into and out of elite status regularly. In the nineteenth century, an industrial elite challenged the older commercial elite, and in the 1930s, labor leaders and ethnic leaders joined the ranks of the elites. Early elites were largely white Anglo-Saxon Protestant males; in recent decades, increasing numbers of Catholics, Jews, blacks, and women have been admitted into the ranks of the elite.

Informal Rule.   The political elite rule informally in that they do not rent office space, have a letterhead, or develop a specific agenda.

Criticism of Elite Domination

Most observers of politics who believe that a political elite dominates also believe that elite rule is not in the best interests of the people. Among the most influential early critics of elitism were Karl Marx and C. Wright Mills. Writing in nineteenth-century Europe, Karl Marx saw that the industrial revolution was creating an all-powerful industrial and commercial elite (the bourgeoisie) whose power rested in their control of capital, the means of producing economic wealth.[17] The bourgeoisie created a political elite to serve its interests. Marx denied that political leaders were powerful in their own right—they were, he thought, little more than a tool of the dominant class, which derived its power from control of the economy. While Marx saw the growing power of the economic elite, Mills broadened the elite to include key national political leaders, shapers of the public opinion, and presidents of prominent universities and other social institutions.[18]

The followers of Marx and Mills today argue that the elite has successfully turned the middle class against the poor so the wealthy can set the main policy course without interference. The middle classes direct their political efforts against affirmative action programs and social welfare spending which benefit the poor, while they ignore tax loopholes and the privileges of the rich. As always, the system benefits the rich; the distribution of income among the rich, the middle class, and the poor has not changed appreciably over the last 50 years.

Contemporary critics of elitism also are disturbed that Americans are given material affluence and mind-deadening entertainment in exchange for surrender of the right to participate in setting priorities. They argue that the middle class has been bought off with bread and circuses—material affluence and high-technology entertainment. Sadly, they say, we do not experience the joys of creative political participation beyond the pale rituals of watching television news nightly and casting an occasional ballot.

Average citizens are content with their lot, say the critics, because the elite deceives them successfully. Rather than resenting the wealth of the powerful, members of the middle class envy the rich as they read *People* magazine and watch *Lifestyles of the Rich and Famous* on television. "With a little luck, initiative, and energy, I too can become rich and famous," thinks the average American. "You are the loser in an unfair game," thinks elitism's critic, "and you don't even know it."

The Argument for Elite Rule

Not all students of politics believe that elite rule is undesirable. Supporters of elitism argue that, paradoxically, a political democracy works better if the people play a rather limited role because the members of the elite are more committed to democratic values than are the masses. The masses, they say, are more easily prejudiced and more inclined to compromise the civil liberties of unpopular religious, ethnic, and political minorities.[19]

Also, mass political apathy and inattentiveness to public issues indicate general satisfaction with the policies of an elite-dominated system. People become actively concerned with political issues when they are discontented, and discontented people may follow antidemocratic demagogues. For example, in 1933, many Germans supported Hitler, who promptly destroyed the democratic institutions of the Weimar Republic. Alternatively, the discontented may try to secede from the political system, as Southerners did over the issues of northern economic domination and the spread of slavery in 1861.

A Weakness of the Elitist Perspective

Proving false the idea that a small group dominates political life is difficult because any decision can be interpreted as the work of a self-serving elite. For example, if government raises taxes that hit average people hard, such as the social security payroll tax or a tax on energy, elites are making the decision in their own interest. If government raises the progressive income tax on high-income earners, elites are buying popular support for the elite-dominated political system.

And what if a member of the elite advocates policies which favor nonelite groups? Ted Kennedy is a highly publicized, wealthy senator from Massachusetts; he is also an articulate spokesman for the poor. Is he disqualified as a member of the elite because he advocates social welfare favorable to the poor? Or do we say that members of the elite are united only on the important issues and that since they are divided on helping the poor, helping the poor is not an important issue? Such reasoning makes it impossible to disprove the existence of a unified elite.

As you read about American government and politics, look for evidence supporting or refuting the claims of Marx, Mills, and their contemporary followers that an elite dominates our political life.

Pluralist Theory

Pluralist theory seeks the middle ground between democratic theory, which emphasizes that the citizens effectively control their leaders and participate significantly in their own governance, and elitist theory, which asserts that a few thousand people monopolize political power independent of any significant mass control.[20]

From a pluralist perspective, American politics is an amalgam of many largely autonomous policy subsystems, each consisting of different influential actors addressing specific issues. For example, farmers and farm groups influence agricultural policy; soldiers and weapons manufacturers tend to dominate military policy; doctors, hospitals, and pharmaceutical companies tend to shape health care policy.

The principal architect of pluralist theory, Robert Dahl, describes the American political system as a "polyarchy," which means "rule by the many."[21] He agrees with elitists that few people participate in the making of decisions, but he objects to the idea that a small power elite dominates. He agrees with democratic theorists that the masses exert considerable influence and that decision makers must be responsive to the people if they expect to remain in office. Pluralists, like democrats, draw our attention to elections and public opinion, interest groups, and political parties. These representative institutions allow people to control their rulers. In a well-functioning democracy, the executive, legislative, and judicial branches are responsive to these representative institutions.

Types of Political Resources

Pluralist theory maintains that power is widely distributed because many different kinds of resources—organization, expertise, money, numbers, and time and effort—can be converted into power on specific issues.

Organization.   While individuals have neither the time nor the energy to persuade public officials, they can and do join interest groups. Their $25 membership fee helps pay the salary and expenses of a full-time professional who will urge public officials to support the viewpoint of group members. The activities and effectiveness of interest groups are discussed in Chapter 7.

Expertise.   Public officials often want to know the probable consequences of a proposed policy. To learn how well a defensive shield against missiles will work, they will talk with strategic experts, engineers, and physicists. To slow the spread of acquired immune deficiency syndrome (AIDS), politicians and administrators will listen to the views of doctors and AIDS patients. Many Americans develop useful expertise on the job or through their life experiences.

Money.   Citizens can convert their money into political influence. By financing a candidate's election campaign, a contributor may gain a chance to meet with the candidate and express his or her point of view. Since money is essential in democratic politics, wealthy individuals have more clout than poor people do.

Numbers.   In a democracy, political leaders must win the votes of citizens to remain in office. Mindful that the next election is coming up, politicians are careful not to alienate their supporters. The media conduct public opinion polls regularly on important political issues, and politicians read the results with interest. Public opinion and elections are discussed in Chapters 4 and 6.

Time and Effort.   A few citizens are active in politics beyond occasionally discussing issues with friends and voting in elections. They may work on behalf of candidates in election campaigns, write letters to their representatives or to a local newspaper, and participate in demonstrations to underline the importance of an issue. In the pluralist view, many citizens have significant power on one issue but very little on other issues. Farmers shape agriculture policy but have little influence on health care or transportation policy. Fundamentalist Christians are influential in the abortion debate but have little influence on immigration policy or protectionism and free trade issues. Organized labor speaks effectively about policies to reduce the unemployment rate but has little voice in setting standards for nuclear plant safety.

The Argument for Pluralism

Pluralists are generally satisfied that government institutions respond to the people's perceptions of what policies are needed. No major groups in society are denied a voice in the policy matters of greatest interest to them, and most interests can muster enough political clout to adjust policy to their liking. The system is responsive, and on controversial issues it encourages compromise. While no one is completely satisfied, compromise produces policies with which most can live.

A Critique of Pluralism

Some critics of American government and politics are profoundly dissatisfied with a pluralist political system dominated by a dense network of self-interested groups. Politics dominated by special interests pressing self-serving claims which government is unable to resist is called interest group liberalism.[22] Special interests are powerful enough to prevent government policymakers from pursuing the common good. Consider the following examples:

The textile or shoe industry seeks tariff protections which will raise prices to consumers and invite retaliation by other nations.

Farmers seek subsidies for their peanut, tobacco, and milk production.

Opponents of nuclear power plants challenge and delay design and construction, raising costs dramatically.

Handicapped persons seek access ramps in all public buildings at tax-payer expense.

The National Rifle Association (NRA) successfully opposes gun-control restrictions which most people favor.

Pro-choice and antiabortion groups are fundamentally opposed and find no common ground for compromise.

These examples suggest that government institutions often fail to resist special-interest pleading. Public policies meet the needs of parochial special interests but work against the interests and preferences of the majority. Hyperpluralism diminishes the quality of public life. For example, the entrenched power of well-established economic interests contributes to economic stagnation. Groups threatened by foreign competition, regional decline, or technological obsolescence defend their vested interest in the status quo rather than adapt to changing technology and competition from low-cost producers. Such groups expect government to insulate them from the forces of change, but slower growth hurts everyone in the long run.[23]

Also, social divisiveness replaces a spirit of accommodation and compromise. Members of single-interest groups, such as the NRA and pro-choice and antiabortion groups, believe passionately in their single cause. Complete victory is their goal. They are reluctant to moderate their demands in order to find an alternative which the majority can support. The activities of equally intense pro-choice and antiabortion groups lead to stalemate. Government cannot find an acceptable solution to major national problems.

Another problem is that the true preferences of society are distorted when intense minorities dominate the policy-making process. A majority may prefer some form of gun control, but elected officials know that opposing gun control will win the votes of NRA members. Supporting gun control will not earn them votes, since gun control supporters are less passionate and typically evaluate a candidate's position on many issues. Therefore, the intense minority wins and the cooler majority loses.

Finally, our political system affords special-interest groups too many opportunities to achieve their policy objectives. Within Congress, the complicated process by which a bill becomes a law provides many opportunities to kill or modify unfavorable policies. To prevent a proposed law from being passed, an unhappy interest group needs to control the decision-making process at only one point. Disgruntled groups make extensive use of the courts to delay and obstruct. Environmental groups sue the Environmental Protection Agency to require industries to install expensive pollution control equipment. Religious groups bring local school districts into court to prevent sex education or the teaching of evolution. In our federal system, federal, state, and local governments must cooperate to implement many policies. If special interests are displeased with decisions made in Washington, they can continue the fight at state and local levels. A government responsive to its citizens addresses issues of common concern and crafts a package of policies acceptable to a broad cross section of the people. In a political system dominated by self-serving interest groups, government cannot do its job.

How well the American political system is working depends on what we expect it to do. That is why democratic, elitist, and pluralist theories are celebrated by some and criticized by others.

Within democratic theory, some writers advocate more individual participation in political life and closer citizen control over elected officials. Others believe that the masses are inclined to take a short-run, selfish position and follow unscrupulous, colorful demagogues who promise them impossible dreams. In this view, if people confine their political participation to voting and entrust political decision making to an elite committed to democratic institutions and values, it is best to leave well enough alone.

Within elitist theory, critics condemn domination by a political elite, while defenders believe that common people are well served to choose an elite to govern on society's behalf. Defenders of elitist theory are more concerned that excessive popular interference will hamstring the government's ability to act decisively in the public interest.

Within pluralist theory, defenders are pleased that most groups in society can influence the decisions of greatest importance to them. Critics complain that the proliferation of self-interested groups has created a stalemate society in which our political leaders lack the authority to make necessary social decisions. Such leaders, they say, cannot balance the budget or strengthen our competitive position abroad without incurring the wrath of powerful social groups.

Recommended Reading

Robert A. Dahl: *Dilemmas of Pluralist Democracy: Autonomy vs. Control,* Yale University Press, New Haven, 1982.

Theodore Lowi: *The End of Liberalism,* Norton, New York, 1979.

C. Wright Mills: *The Power Elite*, Oxford University Press, New York, 1956.

Mancur Olson: *The Rise and Decline of Nations: Economic Growth, Stagflation and Social Rigidity*, Yale University Press, New Haven, 1983.

Carole Pateman: *Participation and Democratic Theory*, Cambridge University Press, Cambridge, England, 1970.

Kenneth Prewitt and Alan Stone: *The Ruling Elites: Elite Theory, Power, and American Democracy*, Harper & Row, New York, 1973.

CHAPTER 2

The Founding Fathers

Time Line

1690	John Locke's *Second Treatise of Civil Government* is published
1700s	Commonwealthmen (radical Whig) writing catches on in the colonies, heightening suspicion of the English government
1773	Tea Tax is levied
1774	First Continental Congress
1776	Declaration of Independence
1781	Articles of Confederation approved
1787	Constitutional Convention is held in Philadelphia
1789	The first year of government under the United States Constitution

In 1787, fifty-five distinguished Americans met in Philadelphia to draft the Constitution, a document which has served the United States for 200 years.

The Founding Fathers were influenced by European debates over the nature of government, by the evolution of parliamentary sovereignty in England, and by their own political experience in the thirteen colonies. The Constitution was the product of heated debate about the proper relationship between people and their government. This chapter presents some of the central issues, summarizes the contents of the Constitution, and offers several interpretations of the Founding Fathers' motives.

Background of the New Republic

To understand the origins of the United States Constitution, one must go back in time from 1787 and consider the European political debates over the nature of government and the relationship between the people and their government. One also must look at the English experience and, even more, at the Americans' interpretations of the English "constitution." Finally, one must take into account the political forms with which the Americans were most familiar: how the colonies and then the states were governed. A brief consideration of these subjects makes the debates in the Constitutional Convention in Philadelphia more comprehensible. So, too, does such an examination render more clearly the disputes between the Federalists (those who supported the proposed Constitution after the 1787 Convention) and the anti-Federalists (those who disagreed with the proposed Constitution). At the outset, it is critical to note that a key issue in the enterprise is the relationship between the people and their government. The proper nature of representation lies at the root of the debate over the Constitution.

Some scholars who study the Constitution believe that great philosophical ideas governed the formulation of that document. Others view the Founding Fathers in Philadelphia as representing narrow economic interests. Were the gentlemen who gathered in Philadelphia an assembly of "demigods," as argued by Thomas Jefferson? Were they a narrow elite defending their personal-property interests, as historian Charles Beard has alleged? Or were they hardworking, pragmatic democratic politicians, as John Roche has asserted? None of these portrayals is accurate standing alone. As this chapter develops, questions such as these will be addressed in an attempt to provide a deeper understanding of the founding of the United States of America under the Constitution.

European Political Thought

A long tradition asserts that people should have a significant role in their own governance. As early as Aristotle's *Politics,* one can find an argument in favor of democracy as the practically (although not ideally) most virtuous form of government. Marsiglio of Padua (1280–1343), in his *Defensor Pacis,* asserted:

> The legislator, or prime and proper cause of law, is the people or body of citizens, or *its more weighty part* [emphasis is by the authors]. . . . The more weighty part, I say, takes into consideration the number and quality of persons in that community for which the law is enacted.

The part of this quotation with emphasis added has been seized upon by some political thinkers as an early argument for majority rule.

In 1579, French dissenters published the *Vindiciae contra Tyrannos,* which contended that the king is in fact a representative of the people and draws his power from them. The *Vindiciae,* at one point, says:

> In a commonwealth, commonly compared to a ship, the king holds the place of pilot, the people in general are owners of the vessel, obeying the pilot, whilst he is careful of the public good; as though this pilot neither is nor ought to be esteemed other than servant to the public.

These various sources all emphasize one singular point—the citizenry, in some form, is sovereign, whether through direct democracy or through some form of representation.

Locke

One idea accepted by some of the leading figures in the Constitutional Convention was that political society represented a kind of social contract in which, at some point, citizens had consented to live under a certain political structure. A theorist commonly deemed important for the American Revolution and the Constitution because of his social-contract theory of government is John Locke. He is sometimes referred to as the "philosopher of the American Revolution," a title that would no doubt have dismayed him. Locke began by assuming that before people entered civil society, they had lived in a state of nature. Life in that environment was not totally unpleasant. However, inconveniences existed. For instance, if two people disagreed over a matter, how was the issue to be resolved? Without any authoritative source of decision making, such as government, resolution of such disputes would be uncertain.

As a result of the inconveniences of life in the state of nature, people created a social contract by which they called into being civil society; once this society was formed, the people then further contracted to create government. Government acted to protect people's liberties—especially the right to property. Each citizen was viewed as the recipient of a set of natural rights owed to that person by the mere fact that the individual was human. Government, as Locke is normally understood, is to be limited so that it does not infringe on the natural rights of citizens. If government oversteps its bounds, then the people have the right of revolution, that is, the right to overthrow the old regime and replace it with a new one which will better protect their natural rights.

The most salient points for the American founding from Locke's *Second Treatise of Civil Government* (1690), then, are a belief in natural rights, the consent of the governed (through the social contract), limited government, the primacy of property rights, and the right to revolt against the repressive government. While there remains considerable controversy over how important Locke really was for the Revolutionary War's justification and the debates over the Constitution, ideas similar to his were common currency in the colonies before the Revolution and in the period prior to the Constitutional Convention.

Locke's ideas fall within what is called the liberal tradition. As a general perspective, liberalism emphasizes individualism, property rights, freedom, and equality of opportunity, ideas clearly present in Locke's work.[1]

Harrington

Another idea weighing heavily in the debates of 1787 was the proper structure for the proposed government. James Harrington's book, *Commonwealth of Oceana* (1656), was well known in the New World. Two points made in that volume are of special significance. The first is Harrington's contention that "government . . . is an art whereby a civil society of men is instituted and preserved upon the foundation of common right or interest; or it is the empire of laws, and not of men." Second, Harrington stated that to safeguard a government of laws against the arbitrary usurpation of power on behalf of the few, a balanced government (i.e., one in which the different classes of citizens all have some representation in government) is necessary. He advocated a structure of government in which power would be divided among three distinct units: (1) a senate of intellectual aristocrats who would debate proposed laws; (2) a people's body to follow the counsel of the senate and approve the proposals; and (3) a magistracy, answerable to the people, to execute the laws. This combination of offices, he felt, should protect an empire of law.

Harrington was cited enthusiastically in the Constitutional Convention of 1787 and was referred to approvingly by other leading figures of the day, such as John Adams. In addition, colonial charters in the Carolinas, New Jersey, and Pennsylvania were based on such principles.

Montesquieu

To prevent abuse of power by government, Locke also called for some division of power. A legislative branch would make laws; an executive branch would carry out internal or domestic laws; and a federative branch would exercise powers of war and peace, treaty making, and activities conducted outside the country's boundaries. Especially significant in this regard was the French thinker Baron Charles-Louis de Secondat de Montesquieu, whose *The Spirit of Laws* (1748) was much noted in the transactions in Philadelphia in the steamy summer months of 1787. Montesquieu raised an argument for balanced government that was translated by the Founding Fathers into a call for a separation of powers in government. Montesquieu admired the English unwritten "constitution" and believed that one reason for the great liberties of the English people was balanced government. He went on to claim that in every government there were three powers—legislative, executive, and judicial (focusing on matters of law). Montesquieu observed:

> When the legislative and executive powers are united in the same person, or in the same body of magistrates, there can be no liberty; because apprehensions may arise, lest the same monarch or senate should enact tyrannical laws, to execute them in a tyrannical manner. . . .
> There would be an end of everything, were the same man or the same body, whether of the nobles or of the people, to exercise those three powers, that of enacting laws, that of executing the public resolutions, and of trying the causes of individuals.

One cannot claim that the words of these various thinkers were directly responsible for the structure of the Constitution of 1787. The Founding Fathers' actual experiences with their own institutions of government in the colonial era and under the Articles of Confederation (the constitution that governed the United States during the Revolutionary War and until the 1787 Constitution was ratified) were important, as was their understanding of the English "constitution." Nonetheless, the ideas of these European thinkers were part of the working vocabulary of politics for the Founding Fathers.

The Development of Representative Institutions in England

In the thirteenth century, English kings found that they could not finance their foreign policy and conduct affairs of state without augmenting their funds from other sources. In 1254, King Henry III was warring in France and desperately needed additional money to continue the war. Consequently, he called for a meeting of the knights of the realm. Each county was to select representatives to a parliament to discuss how much money would be raised (if any) to be transmitted to the king. In 1265, another parliament was called; this time not only knights but also citizens and free men of the cities and boroughs were summoned. In 1295, Edward I organized one more parliament. To this gathering were called the lords, two knights from each county, two citizens from each city, and two representatives from each borough. The summons given to the bishops by the king included the phrase "What touches all should be agreed by all." Those attending the parliament were to have full and sufficient authority to act on behalf of those whom they represented.

By 1603, practically, the consent of a now official Parliament was necessary for the king to act. Its role was to advise and consent. Early on, then, representation was deemed vital in England to justify raising revenues for government. Indeed, "taxation without representation" was considered inappropriate. As time went on, the representatives came to have greater input into a wider variety of policies, such as responses to personal petitions from individuals, settling grievances, and deciding on administrative and broader policy matters. By 1688, with the "Glorious Revolution," Parliament had for all intents and purposes become the central actor in English politics. For a long time, then, some form of representation in a legislative body was part of the governing process in England. This long heritage was part of the background of the colonists in the new world at the time of the American Revolution and, later, at the Constitutional Convention.

The Americans found key elements in the unwritten English "constitution":

1. Meaningful representation—by which English citizens had at least an indirect role in government.

2. Limited government—the sense that leaders could not exercise power in tyrannical fashion, the belief that there were real limits on what governments could do.

3. The primacy of the common law—which would protect individuals from arbitrary government power (recall Harrington's claim that governments should be empires of law and not of men).

The Colonial Experience

Two features of the colonists' experience are especially important to understand in the rush toward revolution and, later, in the debate over the proposed Constitution in 1787: the influence of the English radical thinkers and the colonial political and social structure.

The English Radical Whigs

As to the first, it seems clear that the so-called radical Whigs or Commonwealthmen in England were widely read and appreciated by the colonists—much more so than in the writers' home country. The key point raised by these thinkers was that there was a conspiracy afoot in England to destroy the English "constitution." With this destruction would come tyranny and repression, the end of the freedoms so closely associated with England at that time. The culprits were those political leaders (and opposing factions) who were trying to enhance their power and fortune. Robert Walpole, a prime minister of the period, was singled out for criticism by the radical press during his administration (1721–1742).

The Political Structure of the Colonies

The experiences of the colonists with their own political institutions tended to reinforce the near paranoia nurtured by the Whigs. In prerevolutionary America, the legislature (especially the lower house) was often set against the governor, who was appointed in England. The crown governors had great powers on paper (such as a veto over colonial legislation, the power to dissolve the lower house in a colony, and authority to appoint or dismiss judges). At the same time, the colonial assemblies held the power of the purse, that is, the right to raise revenues for government functions. This created a great weapon against the governors, who had to bargain with the colonists' representatives for funding.

The result was tension and conflict. The colonists interpreted conflict in terms of the writings of the radical Whigs. As such, the colonists were convinced that the conflict proved that the governors and their superiors in England were trying to abridge the colonists' freedoms. The colonists responded by placing greater faith in their representatives, especially in the lower houses of the colonial assemblies. First, they advocated and were successful in increasing the number of representatives as new towns developed. This increased the degree to which colonists' views were presented in the assemblies. Second, to prevent governors from using corrupt means, such as bribery, to get cooperation from representatives, colonists adopted the technique of "instruction." The people of a town, in essence, *instructed* their representatives how they should vote on matters before the assemblies. This made it difficult for governors to control the representatives. Thus Americans developed confidence in the representative legislature as a bulwark of freedom.[2]

Whom did the leading thinkers in the colonies most look to when they debated their future course of action? Locke and Enlightenment thinkers as well as radical Whigs were cited frequently in the debate over independence. However, in political pamphlets published from 1760 until 1805, a period which embraces the Revolution, the Declaration of Independence, and the Constitution, Montesquieu was most cited, followed by Blackstone (a chronicler of the English common law). Well behind in total number of citations were Locke, Hume, Plutarch, Trenchard and Gordon, Pufendorf, and Cicero, to mention some of the better-known names.

In addition, the Bible was, far and away, the single most cited source (as opposed to individual political thinkers). In the 1780s, the decade in which the Constitution was authored, the Bible was the most cited general source; Enlightenment thinkers were second and Whigs third, although the Bible was not cited much from 1787 to 1788 during the debates surrounding the Constitution.[3]

The Social Structure of the Colonies

Historian Jackson Turner Main has examined financial records of the Revolutionary period to ascertain what the social structure was across the thirteen colonies.[4] He contends that several clearly defined classes emerge. First, between one-third and two-fifths of the men were in a lower class. These numbers include black slaves, white servants, and landless laborers hired by property owners. Those in the lower classes had little income or wealth. Nonetheless, most of their needs were met, and there were good prospects for white lower-class individuals to advance into a "middling" range.

The middle class was predominantly made up of small farmers, artisans, and professionals (doctors, ministers, teachers). Members of this class generally lived comfortably. The vast bulk of white men (70 percent) can be placed here. Finally, there was an upper class (perhaps 10 percent of the white male population), composed of large landowners, commercial traders, and very successful professionals. The upper class lived very well. It was more difficult to move from "middling" status to becoming one of the "better sort" than it was to progress from the lower class to the middle class. The 10 percent in the upper class probably accounted for 50 percent of the income received by individuals in the colonies.

While there seems to have been movement toward greater inequality before the Revolution, the War for Independence apparently halted this trend momentarily. Main says that

> the consequences are to be seen particularly in the greater ease with which men could enter the urban elite, the rising standard of living especially among farmers, the declining significance of titles . . . and the comparable democratization of the officer class. All of these were much more pronounced in the North.[5]

Revolution and Confederation

The Declaration of Independence

The conflicts between governors and legislatures fed the distrust reinforced by the ideas of the radical English thinkers. Add to this the series of taxation measures imposed on the colonies after the French and Indian War

(1754–1763), and we begin to see the serious move toward independence. However, the colonies did not demand complete independence right away; they drifted toward it through several stages.

The first response to the perception that England was overstepping its bounds was the claim that the colonies ought to be represented in the English Parliament. Benjamin Franklin argued that if the colonies were granted an equitable delegation in Parliament, the result would be a relaxation of tension and, in fact, a stronger bond between the colonies and the mother country. However, passage of the Stamp Act, a direct tax on all colonial transactions, prodded colonial leaders to abandon this position.

The second phase was development of the claim that there was a difference between external and internal taxation. External taxation meant that Parliament could regulate trade among the different colonies of the empire, including the American colonies. However, internal taxation, that is, direct taxes levied against the colonies and their inhabitants, could be authorized only by the colonial legislatures, not by Parliament. After the 1773 Tea Tax was enacted, this phase ended.

Finally, the colonists drew on the philosophical view that all humans possess certain rights that cannot be trampled on by the government. James Wilson, one of the leading legal minds in the colonies, said:

> All men are, by nature, equal and free: no one has a right to any authority over another without his consent: all lawful government is founded on the consent of those who are subject to it: such consent was given with a view to ensure and to increase the happiness of the governed, above what they could enjoy in an independent and unconnected state of nature. The consequence is, that the happiness of the society is the first law of every government.[6]

This was a potentially explosive doctrine, for if colonists came to see England as violating their basic rights, revolution could be easily justified.

England took stricter action still against the colonies, including efforts by the English military to seize the munitions of the colonial militia outside Boston. The battles of Lexington and Concord led to the final break. By the summer of 1776, the decision to declare independence was made by the Second Continental Congress. On June 7, Richard Henry Lee of Virginia introduced the motion that "these United Colonies are, and of right ought to be, free and independent states." To draw up a justification for independence, the Second Continental Congress appointed a committee of John Adams, Benjamin Franklin, Thomas Jefferson, Robert Livingston, and Roger Sherman.

On July 4, 1776, the Second Continental Congress formally adopted this Declaration of Independence, authored largely by Jefferson. The introduction to this document was theoretical; the remainder of the Declaration was a recitation of the allegedly wicked acts of King George III that led the colonists to break with England.

The first two substantive paragraphs summarize a belief in people's basic rights ("life, liberty, and the pursuit of happiness"). They also claim that if government fails to protect these, the people have the right to revolt against it and create a new government. Jefferson's ideas bear a considerable resemblance to Locke's theory. Whether or not the Declaration of Independence is a common restatement of Locke or, more generally, of the Enlightenment (there is debate over this matter), its major points were considered the common sense of the matter.[7]

After independence was declared, the states began to draw up new constitutions. For the most part, these provided for legislative dominance, since these representative bodies were seen as protectors of the people's rights and instruments for carrying out the citizens' will.

The Articles of Confederation

The Second Continental Congress assigned a committee the task of drawing up a structure for the national government in 1776. In 1777, the Congress agreed to the Articles of Confederation. This first American constitution needed to be approved by all thirteen states. The last, Maryland, ratified the Articles in 1781. The name of the new government was to be the United States of America. The document allowed each side to retain "its sovereignty, freedom and independence."

The major institution of government was the national Congress. Each state had one vote—all were equally represented, although each state could send between two and seven delegates. The major difficulty of governing the country under the Articles of Confederation was the weakness of the central government. For instance, the Congress could request revenues from the states to fund national programs, but sometimes the states simply did not comply. Moreover, routinely, the states did not provide the amount called for. Hence the very basic ability of the national government to fund its activities was subject to the willingness of the states to pay their share. There also was such distrust of a standing national army that the military force of the United States was extraordinarily weak. As a result, British forts continued to operate within the territorial boundaries of the new nation after the peace treaty with England was concluded. Further limiting the central government, states reserved the right to place tariffs on imports from other states. Interstate commerce was hobbled as a result, as states sometimes took part in trade wars.

After the successful conclusion of the Revolutionary War, the interest of many representatives in Congress waned, as the sense of immediate danger from England declined. One unfortunate result was declining attendance, such that by 1784 quorums became harder to attain and little business could be transacted. As new delegate to Congress James Manning informed a colleague, "Matters highly interesting to this Confederacy; and indeed I think to the Question whether the federal government shall long exist, are now before Congress, and there are not states sufficient to transact the necessary Business."[8]

An additional problem with Congress under the Articles of Confederation was that membership turned over rapidly, thus preventing development of institutional memory and a stable leadership structure. The state assemblies, in contrast, had less turnover and manifested greater ability to get things done as stable leadership structures evolved.[9]

The Articles of Confederation were not a complete failure, however. After all, the War for Independence was won and a peace treaty had been signed under this first American constitution. The Northwest Ordinance was passed, providing for the development of the Northwest Territory and the future admission of new states carved from it into the United States.

Also worth noting is that under the Articles there was, to some extent, a transfer of political power from the "better sort" (the wealthy, well-born men who had been politically dominant in the colonies before the Revolution) to the "middling" class (professionals, artisans, and yeoman farmers). Under the Articles, the proportion of representatives in the state legislature who were what today is called middle class increased after the Revolution, at the expense of the "better sort" (or what today is called the upper class). This seems associated with the discontent many eminent persons felt toward the governing process.[10]

At both the state and national levels, the legislatures were the supreme governing bodies. This was in large part a reaction against the royal governors' alleged usurpation of power before the Revolution. People believed that legislative supremacy was the best way to preserve freedom.

The Road to the Constitutional Convention

The Call for Change

The problems associated with the Articles of Confederation led some leaders to call for changes in the document (amending the Articles required unanimous support). A conference at Mount Vernon in 1785 sought to settle a number of disputes involving trade between Virginia and Maryland. Delegates were sufficiently encouraged by the results of this meeting to desire a larger one to deal with the problems of governing under the Articles of Confederation. A convention was scheduled for Annapolis in 1786. All the states were asked to send delegates to discuss regulation of interstate commerce. Few states sent representatives. Those who attended, though, resolved to petition Congress to sponsor a convention to amend the rules under which the United States operated.

Shays' Rebellion

While there was some skepticism in a number of states over calling such a convention, the problems with the Articles were widely recognized, and many leading figures of the day agreed that some revisions were needed. Shays' Rebellion that winter was the final element that led to a convention being authorized for Philadelphia. Shays' Rebellion was a short-lived expression of despair by debtor farmers in western Massachusetts. They organized and moved to shut down courts in that state to prevent foreclosure on their lands by the banks. The rebellion was easily quashed, but it emphasized the weakness of the national government, which had no forces to deal with such a disturbance.

The Constitutional Convention

The Founding Fathers: A Portrait

Demographics

The Founding Fathers—the 55 men who gathered in Philadelphia in the summer of 1787—were by no means typical Americans of the day. They were a group of powerful political figures, much better educated than the average American and well-to-do by the standards of the time. A few were among the wealthiest men in the United States, such as George Washington and Robert Morris. Most were from coastal regions and from cities, even though the vast bulk of Americans lived in rural areas. The delegates to the Constitutional Convention numbered in their ranks some of the ablest and best leaders in the country. George Washington, Benjamin Franklin, James Madison, Alexander Hamilton, Roger Sherman, and James Wilson were among the most capable men around. Few of the major figures of the time were absent. Patrick Henry was selected as a delegate, but he did not attend because he "smelt a rat," fearing that it was foreordained that a strong national government would be created to replace the Articles. Samuel Adams and John Hancock were not there either. Nor did Thomas Jefferson or John Adams attend, since both were abroad.

Political Beliefs

The basic sources of knowledge and ideas that animated debates in the Constitutional Convention were (1) the Founding Fathers' understanding of the English "constitution"; (2) their experience with the colonial and state governments as well as with the Articles of Confederation; (3) the legal and political heritage stemming from England; and (4) the ideas of such thinkers as Locke, Harrington, and Montesquieu.

Basic political views were shared by the bulk of delegates to the Constitutional Convention. For one thing, they distrusted human nature. As James Madison said in *Federalist 51* (one of a series of essays published in New York to aid ratification of the Constitution in 1788 and coauthored with John Jay and Alexander Hamilton), "If men were angels, no government would be necessary." He followed up this statement, however, by declaring that, in fact, people were not angels. They pursued their own interests and could use power to advance their own goals and abuse the rights of others. At one point, *Federalist 63* concluded that "there are particular moments in public affairs, when the people, stimulated by some irregular passion, or some illicit advantage, . . . may call for measures which they themselves will afterwards be the most ready to lament and to condemn."

Delegates also saw property as an important right to be protected by government. Many felt that this was the preeminent purpose of government. There was a general spirit of "republicanism," that is, a support for some kind of representative government with the people playing a role in selecting their leaders. While some delegates, such as Alexander Hamilton and Gouverneur Morris, had aristocratic or monarchist tendencies, even they believed that some significant element of popular representation was necessary. Overall, support for a popular role was conditional; few of the delegates trusted the masses to exercise direct control over government (James Wilson was one exception). They chose to have the people's will "refined" through the mature judgment of their representatives.

The Constitutional Convention Begins

The Virginia Plan

The delegates from Virginia arrived as a group before the others. They put the time to good use by devising a plan to introduce at the opening of the Convention. In this way, they would control the agenda. The Virginia Plan, largely written by James Madison, was introduced by Governor Edmund Randolph when enough states' delegations had arrived in Philadelphia to begin business. George Washington was selected to chair the convention.

The Virginia Plan called for a two-house legislature, with both houses having proportional representation. The number of representatives from each state was to be determined by the state's population. For instance, if one state had twice as many citizens as another, it would have two times the number of representatives in both houses. This scheme was advantageous for states with larger populations, since they could control decisions in the Congress. There was also a roughly drawn provision calling for the national legislature to "negative all laws passed by the several states, contravening in the opinion of the National Legislature the articles of Union." This would establish that, in cases of dispute between state and national law, the national power would be supreme.

The New Jersey Plan

The small states were not pleased. They countered with the New Jersey Plan, calling for a one-house Congress in which each state would have equal representation. This, of course, went against the Virginia Plan. Interestingly enough, the New Jersey Plan, which plainly claimed that it was designed merely to revise the Articles of Confederation, contained an even more clearly defined supremacy clause, which later became part of the new Constitution. This clause stated that all acts and treaties of the national government would be the "supreme law of the respective States," overriding any state laws or constitutions that were in disagreement.

Votes taken on the two plans early in the convention led to the defeat of the New Jersey Plan. The lineup in favor of proportional representation tended to show Massachusetts, Pennsylvania, and Virginia (large states) joining with North Carolina, South Carolina, and Georgia. (A common view among the delegates was that the southern states would have greater populations than the northern states in the future.) The New Jersey Plan was supported by New York (whose delegation was controlled by opponents of a strong national government), New Jersey, Delaware, Maryland, and Connecticut (the latter four being small states). New Hampshire's delegates did not arrive until later, and Rhode Island never did send delegates.[11]

The Connecticut Compromise

Although the large states had the votes, they also knew that the small states would not agree to a Constitution in which their votes would be swamped in Congress. After much turmoil, a compromise that had been floating around for some time began to look more attractive. The Connecticut Compromise, authored by Roger Sherman, advocated a two-house Congress, with one body's representation based on population and the other's grounded in equal representation of each state. After several delegates fortuitously left the Convention, the large-state bloc lost its dominance. A crucial tie vote led to a committee being formed to develop a proposal. This turned out to be a version of the Connecticut Compromise. At this point, the states lined up solidly behind it. The issue of representation that had threatened the Constitution was now resolved.[12]

Major Decisions

Separation of Powers

In the early stages of the Convention, most delegates expected a Constitution providing clear legislative dominance (both the Virginia and New Jersey plans featured Congress appointing the executive). As time went on, though, delegates became uncomfortable with one branch being so dominant. Support began to develop for a separation of powers.

The Founding Fathers drew upon Montesquieu and other thinkers to justify this. They argued that legislative power (lawmaking), executive power (carrying out the laws), and judicial power (interpreting and applying laws to cases) should be separated into three branches of government. The logic was that if these powers were located in one branch, that body might wield power in a tyrannical way and abridge the rights of citizens.

Checks and Balances

However, mere separations of powers was not enough. The different branches also would need checks on one another; hence, the principle of checks and balances.

The president can veto an act of Congress (a check on that branch) and appoints justices to the Supreme Court (a check on the judiciary). In turn, Congress can override the president's veto and can impeach the president. Congress, through the Senate's power to consent to presidential nominees to the judiciary, also has a check on the Supreme Court. In addition, Congress has the power to impeach and remove justices from office. The judicial branch's checks are not as clearly laid out in the Constitution. Practice (and the words of some of the Founding Fathers) are the basis of the judiciary's power of judicial review, that is, the authority to declare unconstitutional acts of Congress and the president which violate the terms of the Constitution.

The logic for this mechanical structuring and counterbalancing of the branches is made plain by James Madison in *Federalist 51*:

> The great security against a gradual concentration of the several powers in the same department, consists in giving to those who administer each department, the necessary constitutional means, and personal motives, to resist encroachments of the others. The provision for defense must in this,

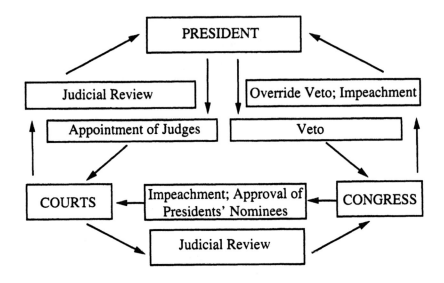

Fig. 2.1   Checks and Balances

as in all other cases, be made commensurate to the danger of attack. Ambition must be made to counteract ambition.

Thus, the original enchantment with legislative dominance had begun to erode in favor of separation of powers and checks and balances. Those who wanted strict separation included representatives from New Hampshire, Massachusetts, North Carolina, South Carolina, and Georgia. States lining up behind the more fluid checks and balances were Connecticut, New Jersey, Pennsylvania, Delaware, Maryland, and Virginia.[13]

Federalism

Another important characteristic of the Constitution is federalism, most simply defined as the division of power between state and national governments with considerable authority granted to each level of government. Practically, the Founding Fathers had to allow much power to reside in the states or the people would not have allowed the Constitution's approval. Indeed, some of the delegates in Philadelphia would have embraced a Constitution placing sole power at the national level. Nonetheless, such a program would have been politically unfeasible. Citizens (and many of their leaders) had loyalties to their own states and would not have accepted the dismantling of states' power.

Slavery

An issue important to states with widespread slavery was the status of that "peculiar institution." The Constitution recognized slavery, treated slaves as property, and called for fleeing slaves to be returned to the state from which they escaped. The document allowed continued importation of slaves (at least until 1808).

Other Rights and Powers

The Constitution also addressed several fundamental deficiencies of the Articles of Confederation:

1. It gave the power to control interstate commerce to Congress; states could no longer regulate trade with their fellow states.

2. Its supremacy clause gave any actions properly enacted under the Constitution supremacy over any state's constitution and laws.

3. It empowered the national government to raise revenues directly, rather than relying on requests to individual states.

4. It gave the national government the sole right to regulate commerce with other nations; no longer would each state be in a position to carry on its own foreign trade policy separate from the other states.

Provisions of the Constitution

Article I

The first article defines the structure and powers of the legislative branch. It calls for a Senate (the states are equally represented, with each state electing two senators) and a House of Representatives (each state's delegation size is based on the state's population—the greater the population, the more representatives).

Basic powers are outlined in Sections 7 and 8. Section 7 provides for revenue (tax) bills to originate in the House; it also allows Congress to override a presidential veto by a vote of two-thirds of the members in each house. Section 8 lists a long array of legislative powers (such as control over interstate commerce, authority to declare war, and power of taxation). The final paragraph gives Congress the power "to make all laws which shall be necessary and proper for carrying into Execution the foregoing Powers." This is commonly known as the elastic clause. The first article is the longest in the Constitution, reflecting the belief of the Founding Fathers that Congress would be the dominant branch.

Article II

The second article speaks to executive power, vested in the president. It lays out the method of electing a president and vice president and impeaching the president. The second article is quite brief, not speaking in great detail of the powers of the executive. It provides for executive power over the military (as commander in chief) and treaty making and permits the president to appoint high government officials (federal judges and foreign ambassadors).

Article III

The third article defines the role of the Supreme Court and allows Congress to create a lower court system. It specifies those cases over which the federal courts have jurisdiction (or the power to hear a case).

Article IV

States must honor the public acts and proceedings of other states according to the first section of this article. The second section calls for citizens of each state to have the privileges of citizens of all the states and allows for extradition of prisoners from one state to another. This article also provides for admission of new states into the Union and guarantees a republican form of government for each state.

Article V

The procedure for addition of amendments to the Constitution is spelled out here.

Article VI

Debts contracted before the Constitution's adoption were to continue as valid. This article's second paragraph contains the Supremacy clause, which states that "this Constitution and the Laws of the United States which shall be made in Pursuance thereof; and all Treaties made, or which shall be made, under the Authority of the United States, shall be the supreme Law of the land." That is, the Constitution, federal law, and treaties are superior to the states' constitutions and laws.

Article VII

The approval of nine states puts the Constitution into operation, according to this article.

Reflections

Upon examining the structure of the Constitution and the debates surrounding its formulation in Philadelphia, we see that the Founding Fathers preferred a "messy" system of government (for want of a better term) rather than one facilitating authoritative decision making. Separation of powers, checks and balances, and federalism, when added together, create the conditions for gridlock and for making it difficult to take quick action routinely. The conditions are ripe for much negotiation and bargaining and compromising in order to get things done, across levels of government and across branches of government.

The end result, however, would seem to increase the odds against tyranny coming about; the Founding Fathers had feared the rise of tyranny if there were one central power source within the system. In current debates, then, many of those who want to alter the constitutional balance to increase "efficiency" of government, that is, reducing the odds of gridlock taking place, fundamentally misunderstand the desires of the Founding Fathers and the system which they constructed.

The Founding Fathers: An Economic Elite or Democratic Politicians?

Charles Beard's Thesis

Charles Beard's *An Economic Theory of the Constitution of the United States*[14] created a great stir upon its publication in 1913. Beard claimed that the Constitution was an undemocratic document drawn up and ratified in an undemocratic way for the benefit of a personal-property elite. He argued that personal-property interests (public securities, shipping and manufacturing interests, money loaned at interest—in general, capital) were adversely affected under the Articles of Confederation. As a result, personal-property interests bypassed the existing rules of government to create a new order that would accommodate their interests.

Inflationary policy pursued in states such as Rhode Island punished those who lent money (banks). Poor farmers would take out a loan and then, after the state legislature passed "easy money" laws, pay back the loan to the bank in less valuable, inflated dollars. While this was advantageous to the debtor farmers, it was just as surely harmful to other economic interests. As a result, safeguards were built into the new Constitution to protect property interests; for example, only the national government was allowed to coin money.

The Constitution was ratified in a novel departure from the amending process under the Articles of Confederation, which called for unanimity. The Constitution would go into effect with the approval of nine states. Thus, according to Beard, there was an "end run" on the Articles of Confederation. Furthermore, says Beard, many farmers were disenfranchised because of property restrictions; thus many people were unable to express their views toward the Constitution.

Critics of Beard

Later analyses indicate that Beard simply is wrong. Forrest McDonald notes, for example, that those delegates who refused to sign the Constitution were a veritable all-star team of personal-property holders.[15] According to Beard, however, such people should have been advocates. McDonald points out in addition that a large proportion of the political factions and regions within each state were represented at the Convention. For example, Hamilton represented the Schuyler faction from New York, while Lansing and Yates stood for the Clinton faction. Thus two of the major contending political forces were accounted for in Philadelphia. One could hardly say that the deck was stacked in advance in favor of any single interest. Votes in the Convention itself did not seem to be related to the individual delegate's personal versus real property (land) holdings.

Robert Brown authored another powerful critique of Beard.[16] He attacks Beard on several fronts. First, he contends that no single economic interest of personal property spearheaded the Constitution. Actual patterns of support for the Constitution—in the Convention and later in the states' ratifying processes—did not correspond to a simple breakdown of real property versus personal property.

Was the Constitution put into operation undemocratically? Brown reports that the franchise among white American free men was widespread indeed. He examines the historical evidence and finds extraordinarily broad voting rights among adult free white men in states as diverse as New Hampshire and New York. Furthermore, the debates in the Convention show that

> Being practical politicians, the Convention delegates recognized that they had to write a Constitution which would meet the approval of the electorate. Perhaps the most convincing evidence for the wide extent of

democracy was the constant concern in the Convention for what the people would or would not accept.[17]

This does not mean that economic factors had no impact. Many scholars acknowledge that economic factors did play an important role. However, Beard's thesis is not correct, and any explanation must be more complex than his argument about real and personal property.

The Founding Fathers as Democratic Politicians

Another influential perspective is that the Founding Fathers were practical democratic politicians. John Roche has contended that the delegates were not about to go back to their home states with a document that could not receive support from the people.[18] There was continual reference in the debates in Philadelphia to what the people would or would not accept in a new government. The delegates, as practical people, readily compromised on key issues, such as allocating representatives among the various states. One difficulty with the strong form of this argument, however, is that there was not the degree of consensus on basic issues that Roche claims; rather, there were some fundamental ideological conflicts between the delegates. Roche contends that ideology was of little significance given the practical nature of the democratic politicians. In addition, he downplays too much the economic influences at work during the constitutional debate.

Jackson Turner Main has demonstrated that the anti-Federalists (those who opposed the proposed Constitution) tended to come from noncommercial areas (living away from the shores and the rivers, since waterways were dominant transportation routes by which goods could enter into the stream of commerce). Furthermore, they tended to be strongly influenced by the radical Whigs and were uneasy about strong government as a consequence. On the other hand, Federalists (supporters of the document) generally came from commercial areas and were more sanguine about a more energetic national government.[19]

The Ratification Battle

Drawing up a Constitution agreeable to the delegates of eleven states was difficult enough (New York did not have a quorum because two of its three delegates were opposed and left the Convention in the middle of its work; Rhode Island, of course, did not send any delegates at all). There remained the political task of securing the approval of nine states.

When the Convention finally finished its business, the Constitution was sent to each state for ratification (or approval). States organized special ratifying conventions; when nine states approved the document, it would go into effect. Some states ratified quickly. In others, debate was dramatic and the issue was in doubt until the final vote took place. In the end, however, the Federalists (those who favored adopting the Constitution) triumphed over the anti-Federalists (opponents of the proposed Constitution).

Advantages of the Federalists

It appears that the numbers in the two camps were rather even. What, then, accounts for the Federalists' overwhelming success? They had a number of important resources:[20]

1. The support of George Washington, whose prestige among Americans cannot be overemphasized.

2. Their superior political organization (Federalists cooperated across the states; they had developed a well-oiled political organization).

3. Their control of the newspapers in some states (such as Pennsylvania), which, as a result, allowed them to shape what people would read about the debates (needless to say, anti-Federalist positions would be little publicized).

4. Their deflection of the major issue of the anti-Federalists—the lack of a Bill of Rights in the Constitution—was met by promises to add a Bill of Rights after the Constitution went into effect.

5. The sheer eminence of the Federalist leaders (while there were important opponents of the Constitution, such as Patrick Henry in Virginia, Elbridge Gerry in Massachusetts, and George Clinton in New York, the glittering array of supporters outshone even those luminaries).

6. The agreement by most that the Articles of Confederation had to be changed because of their deficiencies.

Points of Debate

Although the Federalists had the advantages, the debate over the proposed framework for a new government was important in that it focused attention on significant elements of that new government and clarified for later generations the assumptions underlying the Constitution.

Representation

One key point separating the contending parties was their differing views of the nature of representation. The Federalists tended to distrust the people more than their opposition did. Consequently, they favored what is often called the trustee or Burkean orientation toward representation. The trustee believes that he or she is selected to exercise mature judgment and conscience in decision making. The trustee does not accept the idea that he or she simply must reflect what constituents want. For instance, Gouverneur Morris, a leading Federalist, said that "the best course that could be taken would be to leave the interests of the people to the representatives of the people." James Madison, in *Federalist 63,* said:

> To a people as little blinded by prejudice, or corrupted by flattery, as those whom I address, I shall not scruple to add, that such an institution [as the Senate, with longer terms for its members] may be sometimes necessary, as a defense to the people against their own temporary errors and delusions. As the cool and deliberate sense of the community ought, in all governments, and actually will, in all free governments, ultimately prevail over the views of its rulers; so there are particular moments in public affairs, when the people, stimulated by some irregular passion, or some illicit advantage, or misled by the artful misrepresentation of interested men, may call for measures which they themselves will afterwards be the most ready to lament and condemn. In these critical moments, how salutary will be the interference of some temperate and respectable body of citizens, in order to check the misguided career, and to suspend the blow mediated by the people against themselves, until reason, justice, and truth can regain their authority over the public mind?

In other words, a Senate with a long term will be able to examine issues dispassionately and make mature judgments—not responsive directly to the "momentary whim" of the populace—just as would be expected from trustees.

Anti-Federalists were more likely to take the delegate or mandate perspective. Here a representative is obliged to act for the people as they would themselves, that is, to do what the people expect of him or her. One way of accomplishing this was to demand term limitations of those who hold office, a position of the anti-Federalists that foreshadows the contemporary debate about term limits for Congress (see Chapter 8). Luther Martin, for example, argued two centuries ago in classic anti-Federalist fashion that a representative

> ought to vote in the same manner that his constituents would do . . . provided his constituents were acting in person, and had the same knowledge

and information as himself: and therefore that the representative ought to be dependent upon his constituents, and answerable to them; that the connection between the representatives and the represented ought to be as near and as close as possible.[21]

In general, anti-Federalists distrusted power. In that sense, they were, as historian Cecilia Kenyon put it,[22] "men of little faith," being pessimistic about the ability of people to use power properly. Federalists, while themselves fearful of abuses of power, felt that government could be structured to check tyrannical uses of power. One way of doing this, in Madison's words, was to "set ambition against ambition." Separation of powers and checks and balances were means of accomplishing this.

Federalist 10

Madison's *Federalist 10* is one effort to defend a large-scale republic. The anti-Federalists feared that a faction (a group of self-interested people) would seize control of the strong national government and curtail citizens' liberties. Madison argued that a large republic could actually safeguard freedoms. He begins by noting that "the latent causes of faction are thus sown in the nature of man" and that "the most common and durable source of factions has been the various and unequal distribution of property."

To prevent a single faction from exercising tyrannical power, a large republic was in order. Madison contended:

The two great points of difference between a democracy and a republic are, first, the delegation of the government, in the latter, to a small number of citizens elected by the rest; secondly, the greater number of citizens, and greater sphere of country, over which the latter may be extended.

The effect of the first difference is, on the one hand, to refine and enlarge the public views, by passing them through the medium of a chosen body of citizens, whose wisdom may best discern the true interest of the country. . . . Under such a regulation, it may well happen that the public voice, pronounced by the representatives of the people, will be more consonant to the public good, than if pronounced by the people themselves.

. . . The other point of difference is, the greater number of citizens, and extent of territory, which may be brought within the compass of republican, than of democratic government; and it is this circumstance principally which renders factious combinations less to be dreaded in the former, than in the latter. The smaller the society, the fewer probably will be the distinct parties and interests composing it; the fewer the distinct parties and interests, the more frequently will a majority be found of the same party; and the smaller the number of individuals composing a majority, and the smaller the compass within which they are placed, the more easily will they concert and execute their plans of oppression. Extend the sphere, and you take in a greater variety of parties and interests; you make it less probable that a majority of the whole will have a common motive to invade the rights of other citizens; or if such a common motive exists, it will be more difficult for all who feel it to discover their own strength, and to act in unison with each other.

In this remarkable passage, two important themes relative to the Federalist versus anti-Federalist debate emerge. The first is the call for a trustee-style representative to moderate the people's occasional poor judgment; the second is the advocacy of larger republics as a way to minimize the odds that any single group will take over the machinery of government for its own selfish ends.

The Bill of Rights

One concrete contribution of the anti-Federalists was the impetus to add a Bill of Rights to the Constitution. Many were fearful of government under the proposed Constitution having too much power and suppressing the people's freedom. To counter this telling criticism, the Federalists offered to add a Bill of Rights upon adoption of the Constitution. Once they advanced this proposition, considerable opposition melted away. Indeed, shortly after the new republic began business under the Constitution, the Congress drew up a Bill of Rights which it then transmitted to the states for their approval. Finally, ten of these (the first ten amendments to the Constitution) were ratified, the Bill of Rights as people know it today.

Constitutional Change

The Constitution can change through a variety of mechanisms. The three most important are amendment, judicial interpretation, and actual practice.

Amendment

The process of amending the Constitution, according to Article V, includes the following routes:

1. Two-thirds of each house of Congress will propose an amendment which is then subject to ratification by three-quarters of the states' legislatures or by conventions in three-quarters of the states (Congress decides which will be in operation).

2. The legislatures of two-thirds of the states will call for a convention to propose amendments which will be subject to ratification in the same manner as above.

Thus far, no amendment has been approved in the second manner. Twenty-seven amendments have been added through the first path, the last being accepted in 1992 (Congress shall not be able to change its pay until after the intervention of an election). Among the more significant are the First Amendment (guaranteeing freedom of speech, religion, and press), the Fourth Amendment (protecting against illegal government searches and seizure of one's effects), the Fifth Amendment (prohibiting being forced to testify against oneself), the Sixth Amendment (guaranteeing right to counsel), the Thirteenth Amendment (abolishing slavery), the Fourteenth Amendment (guaranteeing to blacks due process and equal protection of the law), the Fifteenth Amendment (giving former slaves the right to vote), the Sixteenth Amendment (allowing a federal income tax), the Nineteenth Amendment (giving women the right to vote), and the Twenty-sixth Amendment (giving 18-year-olds the right to vote).

Judicial Interpretation

Another, informal, way of altering the Constitution is judicial interpretation. For instance, there is no clearly stated power of judicial review (the power of a court to strike down a law as unconstitutional), but the Supreme Court in *Marbury v. Madison* (1803) inferred the existence of this power. Thereafter, it has been generally accepted that the courts indeed have this authority. Courts' decisions, then, can change the Constitution's meaning.

Actual Practice

Finally, actual practice can affect the Constitution's meaning. At the origin of the republic, political parties were feared. People felt that parties divided the citizenry and led to domestic disturbances. The Constitution itself does not mention parties at all. Yet, over time, these organizations have become central actors in American politics.

Democratic theorists emphasize the concern of the Founding Fathers for providing the citizens with real input into their national government, for example, through their election of members of the House of Representatives. They contend that the records of the debates in the Constitutional Convention testify to the concern of the delegates with the people's will. Democratic theorists observe that the American enterprise, begun with the Constitution, is the culmination of the philosophical tradition, begun with Aristotle, that the people should rule.

Elite theorists come to a different conclusion. They see the Founding Fa-

thers as an elite of their day—not typical of average Americans at all. Even if personal-property concerns did not motivate the Founding Fathers, it is clear that economic factors were involved. The fact is that many Americans were not in favor of the Constitution, and the sheer political might of the Federalists' organization carried the day. Elitists argue that it is not coincidence that the Constitution was written at a time when the "middling" class was beginning to gain political power at the expense of the better sort.

Finally, pluralists see James Madison's Federalist 10 *as a kind of theoretical wellspring for their perspective. Madison's view that politics is about the clash of contending interests lies at the heart of current pluralist theory. It is probably relevant that the bulk of the political factions (or groups) of the day were represented in Philadelphia. This can be interpreted as saying that the Constitution itself was the result of pluralistic politics at work, with accommodation of competing interests, multiple centers of power, and distinct factions each gaining something from the new government as a result of the bargaining process.*

Recommended Reading

Bernard Bailyn: *The Ideological Origins of the American Revolution,* Harvard University Press, Cambridge, Mass., 1967.

Charles A. Beard: *An Economic Interpretation of the Constitution of the United States,* Macmillan, New York, 1913; reprint 1935.

Christopher Collier and James Lincoln Collier: *Decision in Philadelphia,* Ballantine Books, New York, 1986.

Alexander Hamilton, James Madison, and John Jay: *Federalist Papers,* various editions.

Calvin C. Jillson: *Constitution Making: Conflict and Consensus in the Federal Convention of 1787,* Agathon Press, New York, 1988.

Jackson Turner Main: *The Antifederalists,* University of North Carolina Press, Chapel Hill, 1961.

Forrest McDonald: *We The People,* University of Chicago Press, Chicago, 1958.

Garry Wills: *Inventing America,* Vintage Books, New York, 1978.

CHAPTER 3

The Federal System:
Structure and Dynamics

Time Line

1862	Enactment of the Morrill Act providing for land grants to states for institutions of higher education in agriculture and technology
1913	Passage of Sixteenth Amendment providing for federal income tax
1914	Enactment of Smith-Lever Act establishing the Agricultural Extension Service, the first modern grant-in-aid program
1923	Supreme Court holds federal grant-in-aid programs immune from judicial challenge
1929	Beginning of Great Depression and increase in federal aid to states and localities
1933–1937	Many New Deal initiatives ruled unconstitutional by Supreme Court under dual federalism doctrine

1937	Supreme Court abandons dual federalism doctrine and withdraws it as limit on economic policy
1953	Kestnbaum Commission is established to examine effects on federal system of growth in federal programs
1962	In *Baker v. Carr* (369 U.S. 186), the Supreme Court declares that federal courts have jurisdiction over malapportioned state legislatures
1965	Passage of Voting Rights Act provides first effective protection for black voting rights
1963–1968	Great Society expansion of categorical grant-in-aid programs
1969–1976	Nixon-Ford movement toward greater grant flexibility with establishment of general revenue sharing and increase in block grants
1981–1988	Reagan administration slows domestic spending, ends general revenue sharing, and increases use of block grants

Federalism is a form of government in which power is distributed between two levels of government within the same geographic territory. Thus, in the United States, most citizens are subject to both a state government and the national government. A unitary system of government, in contrast, concentrates all power at the national level. In a nation such as France, all power stems from Paris; local or regional units of government are creations of the central government and serve as administrative units of the national government. There are advantages and disadvantages to federal systems and to unitary systems. Either may be democratic, although it is difficult to envision a federal system being totalitarian.

This chapter sets forth the framework of American federalism and examines some of the relationships that have evolved within it. The Constitution defines the basic elements of the federal system; judicial interpretation has served to keep these elements in a working balance. The spending power of the national government has been a significant factor influencing the evolving dynamics of federalism. Political parties, too, have played a role; they have enhanced the power of the states and have provided the energy for advancing policies at both the national and state levels. The chapter concludes with a brief look at relations among the states and among local governments.

The Federal System: An Overview

The federal system differs markedly from the confederation that preceded the Constitution. The Articles of Confederation provided for a national governmental system that gave the states supremacy. The national Congress was a meeting place for representatives of the states. No effective action could be taken without unanimous consent of the states. The national government could act only with state approval. The key distinction between the national government under the Articles of Confederation and that under the Constitution is that the latter can act directly on individual citizens while the former could not. It is this difference that allows the national government under the Constitution to be powerful. As most citizens are aware, if the national government wishes to raise an army or to collect taxes, it will contact them directly. This was not possible under the Articles of Confederation.

The basic structure of American federalism provided in the Constitution does not encourage a highly coordinated or efficient approach to government, but it does allow democratic government to function over a society of tremendous diversity. Moreover, it allows the heterogeneity and freedom that give strength to American democracy. Constitutional interpretation, political change, demographic movement, economic growth, and the clash of policy views have modified and elaborated this framework. At issue has been a balance of power between state and national governments that has shifted back and forth throughout American history.

The federal system is often described in terms of national, state, and local governments. In a sense, this is functionally correct: there are national, state, and a wide variety of local governments in the United States. In terms of power, however, this description is misleading. There are only two sources of government power in the United States: the national government and the states. All local governments derive from state power. Cities, towns, and counties are created by states and can be eliminated by states. They have no power independent from that given to them by the state governments. Moreover, under the standard of legal interpretation known as Dillon's rule, state grants of power to its subdivisions are to be interpreted narrowly in favor of the state.[1]

Constitutional Framework

The Constitutional Document

The Constitution spells out the basic structure of American federalism. It specifically limits the national government to the powers given to it therein. The national government is, however, supreme in this area of power.

As described in the Tenth Amendment, states may exercise powers that do not conflict with acts of the national government or that are not prohibited by the Constitution. Unlike the national government, the states possess police powers, that is, powers that are inherent in a government's duty to act for the health, welfare, morals, and safety of its citizens. Following the language of the Tenth Amendment, these powers are often called the "reserved powers" of the states. The states are protected in a number of ways from being threatened as states by the national government. The Constitution provides that a state's representation in the Senate may not be changed without its consent. A state may not be partitioned or merged with another state against its will. Furthermore, the Constitution may not be amended without ratification by three-quarters of the states.

Judicial Interpretation

Supreme Court interpretations of the meaning of constitutional clauses and of the extent of national power have played an integral role in the development of American federalism. In the early years of the Constitution, the states continued to believe that they retained the autonomy they had under the Articles of Confederation. They were reluctant to concede power to a national government. In this respect, the role of the Supreme Court was crucial. Although the Court's interpretations of the extent of national power have varied, it has consistently maintained the supremacy of its decisions and of national law over state power.

The Marshall Court

The Supreme Court, under Chief Justice John Marshall from 1800 to 1835, used its interpretations of the Constitution to place national power on solid legal footing. In addition to being a good jurist, Marshall was an able politician. Under his guidance, the Court confronted numerous state challenges to national power by deftly maneuvering to deal with only one or two obstreperous states at a time. In this fashion, the Court could bring the weight of other states along with its judicial reasoning to bear on dissident states.

At the same time, the Marshall Court was interpreting the delegated powers of Congress broadly. Congress's power over commerce among the states was given an expansive interpretation in *Gibbons v. Ogden* (1824),[2] and in *McCulloch v. Maryland* (1819)[3] the Court construed the "necessary and proper" clause of the Constitution as granting additional power to Congress. In the *Gibbons* case, New York had given Ogden, a former partner of Gibbons, a monopoly over steamboat traffic in New York state. Gibbons, who had a federal license to ply his steamboat trade from New Jersey to New York City, claimed that this authority overrode the state monopoly. The Court agreed with Gibbons that in the area of commerce among the states, congressional power supersedes state power. The *McCulloch* decision was the culmination of struggles between state banking interests and those supporting a national bank. Maryland imposed a heavy tax on any banks not chartered by the state, which, of course, was aimed directly at the branch of the national bank in Maryland. The Supreme Court gave an expansive definition of Congress's right to implement powers delegated to it in the Constitution and declared unconstitutional state attempts to limit this authority through taxation.

Dual Federalism

The Supreme Court has not, however, always been a strong supporter of national power. During the period from approximately 1875 to 1937, the Court developed the constitutional doctrine of dual federalism as a limit on Congress's power to regulate corporate property. Under this doctrine, the Tenth Amendment was interpreted as defining the boundaries of national power. The powers reserved to the states were seen as posing barriers at the state lines to the exercise of national power. Thus, attempts by Congress to regulate child labor in the states were thwarted by the Supreme Court's use of the dual federalism doctrine. A narrow majority of the Court argued that manufacturing is a local activity whose control was reserved to the states by the Tenth Amendment. Congress's delegated powers, whether those of commerce or taxation, could not intrude into this area of activity to regulate the employment of children.[4] During the first third of the twentieth century, the dual federalism doctrine was a serious limitation on national power.

Decline of Dual Federalism

The beginning of the end of the dual federalism doctrine was the election of Franklin Delano Roosevelt to the presidency in 1932. At first the Court continued to have the upper hand. Most of Roosevelt's New Deal measures were ruled unconstitutional by the Court, many under the dual federalism doctrine. With his reelection in 1936 by a huge majority, however, the President focused on the Court. His threat to pack the Court, which is related in detail in Chapter 11, moved that body to reexamine its approach to national power. The result was that the dual federalism doctrine as a limit on national power was laid to rest. Since 1937, the Supreme Court has been extremely reluctant to overturn any exercise of congressional power in the area of economic and social regulation.[5] Consequently, the national government has been able to extend its power dramatically. This extension of national power reached its apex under Lyndon Johnson and his Great Society efforts to change America.

State Power Today

Today the Court continues to defer to the exercise of national power. In terms of national-state relationships, the only times such power comes under extensive scrutiny by the Court are when that power appears to threaten the functions of states as states.[6] In *New York v. United States* (1992),[7] the Supreme Court again asserted the importance of the Tenth Amendment in defining the allocation of power within the federal system. In the Low-Level Radioactive Waste Policy Amendments of 1985, Congress had required that states take title to hazardous nuclear waste at a waste generator's request if the state has not established disposal sites by the deadline provided in the statute. The Supreme Court held this to be an unconstitutional extension of Congress's power. It declared that even though the states had agreed to allow Congress to act in this fashion, it could not do so. In this instance, the Court was especially concerned that the states were hiding behind a congressional mandate to shield themselves from having to take responsibility for the politically difficult task of disposing of nuclear waste.

While granting wide discretion to national power in the areas of economic and social policy, the Court also has become more deferential to the exercise of state power where individual liberties are involved. Unlike the Warren Court, for example, the Burger Court and Rehnquist Court have been more willing to allow states to enact measures defining individual rights. The states may not, of course, define rights more restrictively than the boundaries set by the Supreme Court. But they are free to define them more expansively, and in states with high courts more liberal than the Supreme Court, individuals may have greater protections than those provided by the Supreme Court or the courts in other states. Thus, in keeping with the policy preferences of Presidents Nixon, Ford, and Reagan, the Court has countenanced a greater flexibility and freedom in state policy initiatives.

The Evolution of Fiscal Federalism

The Grant-in-Aid Policy

While expansion of the national government's delegated powers has proceeded at a rapid pace since 1937, the power of the national government to spend for the general welfare has been an instrument of national policy since at least the middle of the nineteenth century. In this regard, the grant-in-aid has been a device often used for implementing national goals at the state and local levels. Through the grant-in-aid procedure, the national government makes funds available to governments that meet specified standards.

Perhaps the first modern grant-in-aid program of significance was the Morrill Act of 1862, in which Congress made land grants available to states that established agricultural and technical colleges. These land-grant colleges have since grown into major universities throughout the United States.

Grants-in-Aid Become Established

The grant-in-aid approach to expanding national power gained momentum in the twentieth century for several reasons. First, the enactment of the Sixteenth Amendment allowing the national government to levy an income tax supplied that government with an enormous source of income that the states could not hope to match. Second, the Smith-Lever Act of 1914 establishing the agricultural extension service provided a prototype for later grants-in-aid.[8] It established national standards that had to be satisfied, and it required matching funds from state and local governments. Third, in 1923 in the companion cases of *Frothingham v. Mellon* and *Massachusetts v. Mellon*,[9] the Supreme Court held that grants-in-aid are immune from judicial challenge. Thus, while other national programs and efforts at regulation were being ruled unconstitutional by a conservative Supreme Court, grant-in-aid programs were free from such attacks.

It should be noted parenthetically at this point that these early decisions were modified somewhat by *Flast v. Cohen* (1968),[10] in which the Court held that when a grant-in-aid program appears to contravene a specific prohibition of the Constitution, a taxpayer may have standing to sue to challenge that program. This doctrine has been narrowly applied, however, and other than in cases questioning programs that appear to aid the establishment of religion, it has not had an effect on grant-in-aid projects.

The New Deal

The Great Depression led to an expansion of government aid programs. At its beginning, the national government simply made millions of dollars of aid available to the states to help the unemployed. Later, these programs were given specific functions. Those grant-in-aid programs which survived the New Deal were the basic entitlement grants providing assistance to the blind, the disabled, and dependent children.

The Kestnbaum Commission

During the years after World War II, some new grant-in-aid programs were established, but their number was not large. Nonetheless, suggestions that the states might be threatened by the increase in national programs caused President Eisenhower concern. In response to his urging, Congress in 1953 authorized the establishment of the Commission on Intergovernmental Relations (usually termed the Kestnbaum Commission after Meyer Kestnbaum, its chair) to examine the state of the federal system. Generally, the commission found that a healthy diversity remained in the federal system. As a result of the interest in intergovernmental relations and the respect given to the work of the Kestnbaum Commission, the Advisory Commission on Intergovernmental Relations was established in 1959. This agency conducts studies of the changing relationships between the national government and state and local governments and is the source of much valuable information in this respect.

The Great Society

The activities of the Johnson administration revived concern that the fiscal power of the national government would seriously weaken state governments as important governmental units. With his Great Society program, Lyndon Johnson sought to remake American society, and one of the primary tools for this was the grant-in-aid. The number of federal grant-in-aid programs has been estimated at 29 in 1945. This number reached 181 by 1964 and more than doubled under the Johnson administration to approximately 387 in 1968.[11] Today there are almost 600 grant-in-aid programs, with a huge proportion of these originating in the Great Society programs or later amendments to those programs. In the words of Kenneth T. Palmer, "The effect of the work of the Eighty-ninth Congress [1965–1966] was to diffuse grants-in-aid throughout the domestic functions" of government.[12] In this respect, the Johnson administration was truly a watershed in the history of fiscal federalism. Its heavy use of grants-in-aid continues to have political ramifications throughout the American political system.

Through grant-in-aid programs, the Johnson administration provided funds for education, housing, health, employment, and the poor. It was this latter area that raised the most controversy and had the greatest effects on the federal system. In its "war on poverty" effort headed by the Office of Economic Opportunity, the Johnson administration channeled funding directly to the disadvantaged. It specifically avoided using traditional state and local social service agencies and established federal field agencies at local levels. The intent was to create constituencies of the poor who would be responsible for guiding programs intended to aid them and who would be politically active in protecting those programs.[13]

The effects of the Johnson administration's efforts on the federal system deserve detailed comment. Clearly, the Johnson people assumed the political viability of a pluralistic model of democracy in which programs survive because they build constituency support among the people whom they serve. The Johnson administration chose to construct such constituencies by design.

The contribution of these programs to alleviating poverty remains a matter of debate among social scientists. Their ramifications for federal relationships receive more general agreement.

First, these programs did not mesh well with other national programs at local levels. There was often competition and misunderstanding between them and traditional social service efforts undertaken by social security offices and the Labor Department, for example. Second, the local community action agencies and boards organized to implement the antipoverty programs created political bases of power separate from the traditional urban party organizations. Furthermore, these agencies had considerable amounts of money to spend. Governors and mayors saw their traditional party structures threatened by this new development, and Congress, responding to their concerns, eventually gave local officials more power over the community action agencies. Third, an exceptionally important spinoff of this new organizational activity at the local level was increased participation by blacks in urban politics. Fourth, the mechanism used heavily by the Johnson administration was the categorical grant-in-aid. (All but two of the 387 grant-in-aid programs in 1968 were categorical.) This approach funneled money to specific targets for specific purposes. It allowed localities little discretion in how the money was to be used. Administrators at the national level saw this as a way to protect minorities and the disadvantaged. State and local officials, on the other hand, resented this extension of national regulations and power into the local level.

Reaction Against National Power

The years since the Great Society have witnessed a fairly consistent reaction against the centralization of policy at the national level. The challenge has been to find ways to deliver federal financial assistance to the states and localities without being heavy-handed.

"Marble-Cake" Federalism

In the period following World War II, Morton Grodzins described the federal system as a "marble cake."[14] He argued that the tendency had been to view the federal system as a kind of three-layered cake with functions and relationships neatly divided and distinguishable. But this was not accurate. Programs often intermixed functions and funding from national, state, and local levels in a marble-cake type of arrangement.

"Picket-Fence" Federalism

Later, the activities and extensive use of categorical grants-in-aid under the Great Society led to depiction of intergovernmental relations as picket-fence federalism. The argument here was that categorical grants were so encumbered with regulations and so specialized that the programs they funded resembled fence pickets that extended from the national to the local level. Deil S. Wright suggests that at least eleven identifiable general functional areas—highways, welfare, education, hospitals, mental health, libraries, airports, urban renewal, agriculture, vocational education, and public housing—met this description.[15] These programs were implemented by experts or professionals, such as social workers, teachers, and engineers, whose power was bolstered both by their expertise and by federal regulations. One result of this dominance of programs by experts was that from the national level to the local level these people interacted among themselves more easily than they interacted with elected officials, who were supposed to be their bosses.

Other Problems with Categorical Grants-in-Aid

There were other problems with categorical grants-in-aid that caused concern for local government officials. These grants led to what was labeled "hardening of the categories." Grants formulated at the national level could not take into account the variety of circumstances and needs at the local level. A city might need funds for more libraries, but if national funds were available for parks, the city's officers would find themselves pressured to apply for the money that was available. Libraries would be lost in the shuffle as city resources and priorities were oriented toward receiving money for parks. This is simply a hypothetical example, but the point is that the use of categorical grants-in-aid tended to cause local governments to skew their priorities toward the national definitions of need.

Categorical grants-in-aid also favored those governments which could obtain good grantspeople, individuals skilled in obtaining monies. Many rural areas were simply left out of the competition for funds because they had no databases or people capable of putting together a respectable grant request.

Finally, the requirements attached to categorical grants-in-aid caused continuing difficulties for state and local governments. These requirements had to be met in order to receive funds. However, there was no guarantee that the national government would not attach other requirements later. For example, long after state governments had become heavily dependent on federal highway funding, the national government decided to require states to raise the drinking age to 21 or give up portions of their funds.

Private institutions that receive federal funding also feel the burden of these kinds of mandates. One of the more controversial proposals in this respect was President Nixon's suggestion that colleges and universities with students receiving federal aid—a category including almost all such institutions—be required to allow federal agents on campus to monitor student unrest. Fortunately, this idea was rather quickly discarded by Congress.

States Gain in Political Capacity

Much of the impetus behind the categorical grant-in-aid approach had been the belief that the states could not be trusted to be responsible or equitable with funds. Serious problems were caused by the rural dominance of state legislatures, which discouraged concern with the problems of urban areas and with more effective government generally, and by electoral discrimination against blacks in the southern states. However, during the 1960s, several events occurred that enhanced the status of the states. One of these was federal court intervention in the districting of state legislatures. The Supreme Court's standard of "one person, one vote" forced the state legislatures to reapportion. The result was that urban and suburban areas for the first time received their fair share of representation in the nation's state legislatures. Another important event was the enactment of the 1965 Voting Rights Act, which gave blacks in the South effective voting power. This newly acquired power soon was reflected in local, state, and national elections. Finally, many states revamped their governmental structures to make them more efficient. State experiments with approaches to environmental control, health care, and tax policy began to serve as models for national action.

Fiscal Flexibility: Nixon through Reagan

Beginning with the Nixon administration, the national government became more sensitive to state and local concerns that they were being dominated by national fiscal prowess. President Nixon responded to state demands for more policy flexibility with more flexible federal grants.

General Revenue Sharing

General revenue sharing, enacted in the State and Local Assistance Act of 1972, was the most innovative of the Nixon proposals. Under this approach, states and localities received a portion of the federal income taxes that their citizens paid. These funds had few strings attached and left the states and localities wide latitude in how the funds could be spent. The rationale for this funding was that the national government was returning to these political units some of the revenue that it took from them with the income tax.

Special Revenue Sharing

This period also saw the institution of what was called special revenue sharing. Special revenue sharing was similar to what was later called block grants. Under special revenue sharing, a number of categorical grants were combined into funding for a general area in an attempt to reduce the diversity of regulations and the policy fragmentation that had been created by the tremendous growth in categorical grants-in-aid. For example, Urban Renewal, Model Cities, and other urban grants were combined into a general program for community development.

Block Grants

The Johnson administration had begun to respond to pleas for greater flexibility in federal funding with block grant programs under the Partnership in Health Act of 1966 and the Law Enforcement Assistance Administration established in 1968. Under Presidents Nixon and Ford, this trend continued. Three major new block grant programs were initiated: the 1973 Comprehensive Employment and Training Act (CETA) and in 1974 the Community Development Block Grant Program and Title XX of the Social Security Act, which provided funds for social welfare programs. Generally, these programs achieved their goal of giving more discretion to state and local governments. A less positive development was that those disadvantaged segments of society which had been protected by the regulations accompanying categorical grants-in-aid were under the new approach more dependent on the decisions of state and locally elected officials. The result was a tendency for the funding from these programs to drift toward the less disadvantaged but more politically articulate portions of the community.[16] The CETA program in particular received a great deal of criticism in this respect, and in 1978, the Carter administration tightened the eligibility requirements in an attempt to direct funds to the most needy. Finally, under the Reagan administration, CETA was replaced by the Job Training Partnership Act of 1982. This act retained local discretion in the use of funding but focused the program more heavily on training and employment in the private sector.

The Reagan administration approached the use of block grants in a somewhat more calculating fashion than had the Nixon administration, with the primary goals of lessening federal domestic spending and giving the states more control over spending. President Reagan was concerned that despite efforts to consolidate federal funding, expenditures and the number of grant programs had continued to increase. Between 1967 and 1980, the number of federal grant programs grew from an estimated 379 to 539.

Throughout his administration, Reagan worked at cutting federal domestic spending and merging specialized grant programs into block grants, but his most significant attack on the proliferation of grant-in-aid programs came early in his administration in the Omnibus Budget Reconciliation Act of 1981. This measure consolidated 54 categorical grant programs into 9 block grants. Thus, in 1991, the total number of federal grant programs remained about the same as in 1980 (approximately 557 as compared to 539), although total spending for them had risen sharply; and, while Reagan's use of block grants had some effect on the structure of federal aid, 80 to 90 percent of grants remained categorical in form. Although President Reagan had hoped that the use of block grants-in-aid would weaken the constituencies supporting specific programs, these interests remained powerful obstacles to further reduction in the number of federal programs and provided continuing support for increased funding for established programs.

Opposition to the "New Federalism"

Opposition to Reagan's "new federalism" developed quickly, however. State officials liked the lessening of federal regulations and the greater latitude they had in spending the funds in the new block grant programs.[17] Arkansas Governor Bill Clinton spoke for many other state chief executives when he told President Reagan, "Whether we agree with you or not, we all admit that you've made us more important."[18] However, under the Reagan administration, the price of this increased importance was less money, and state officials vigorously opposed the decrease in federal funds that accompanied the change in grant format. Moreover, local officials, who had often developed close relationships with federal funding sources, now found themselves dependent on their state governments for less funds. State and local officials also were unhappy when general revenue sharing was terminated as part of the Reagan administration's efforts to reduce federal spending. General revenue sharing was never popular with Congress, basically because members of Congress received no personal credit for dispensing the funds. When spending cuts had to be made, general revenue sharing was one of the more vulnerable programs, even though many cities had become heavily dependent on the funding.

Disruption of Established Political Relationships

President Reagan liked the increased autonomy that block grants provided the states, but he also understood that block grants weakened vested political interests that continually pushed for increased funding. With fewer requirements to be met for receiving funds, there was less need in national agencies for specialists whose primary responsibilities focused on one narrow program. Categorical grants-in-aid encouraged the proliferation of such specialists and tied them to the clientele being served and to the congressional committees and subcommittees funding and authorizing the programs. These relationships became cozy triangles, or subgovernments, that as almost self-sustaining political entities could be important obstacles to presidential policy and direction. Block grants, however, undermined these relationships by eliminating the specialization in programs, thus removing the incentive for specialized political interest support.

The move from categorical grants-in-aid to greater use of block grants also disrupted established political relationships at the level of local politics. The Johnson administration had encouraged the participation of citizens in the making of funding decisions at the local level. Many of the new federal programs required locally elected boards for this purpose. The ideal of local democracy has, of course, been important to many American thinkers. In practice, however, it was difficult in most urban areas to arouse much interest at all in the elections of these federally mandated boards. The result was that these boards were often elected by a handful of citizens. It would be hard to argue that such boards were very representative. Nonetheless, they created constituencies for the categorical grant-in-aid programs with which they were involved, and they became part of the local policy process where their interests were concerned. When, however, the categorical grant-in-aid programs were melded into block grants, the existence of these boards at the local level was threatened, as was their continued funding. Local officials were then faced with irate citizens, some of whom were both vociferous and nasty. In this respect, national policy decisions had direct and difficult policy ramifications for local governments.[19]

An Era of National Fiscal Duress

A ballooning federal budget deficit and increasing voter resistance to higher taxes played an important role in determining the contours of fiscal federalism under the Bush and Clinton administrations. Facing these factors, Presidents Bush and Clinton were simply unable to continue to offer federal funds as incentives for major new policy initiatives. Those new grant programs that were enacted during the Bush administration were quite small in comparison to the huge amounts that were required for established health and welfare grant programs such as Medicaid and Aid to Families with Dependent Children (AFDC).[20] Thus, the search for new approaches for dealing with national problems began to turn toward revised relationships with the states. An example of this orientation was the Family Support Act of 1988, passed in the last year of the Reagan administration. This legislation relied heavily on giving the states greater flexibility in trying to move individuals off welfare, allowing states to offer limited fiscal incentives to keep two-parent families together and financial and technological assistance in helping to trace the fathers of those children on welfare. President Clinton's efforts to reform the health care system also reflected the need to draw on greater state cooperation, reduce federal paperwork requirements, and insist that private enterprise bear a greater share of the financial burdens. Within this new context, it seems clear that new federal initiatives on the scale of the Great Society are simply out of the question and that the states will continue to be important sources of new policy ideas.

Both block grants-in-aid and categorical grants-in-aid remain important forms of federal assistance to states and localities. Some of these are project grants; they are awarded on the basis of applications made for them. Others are allocated according to formulas or eligibility. AFDC and Medicaid, for example, are entitlement programs under which people become eligible for funds based on formulas. If individuals meet the criteria established by statute or administrative regulation, they are legally entitled to the benefits of the program.

Cooperative Federalism

American federalism is a much more informal, cooperative, marble-cake kind of system than judicial decisions or discussions of fiscal relationships alone might indicate. Professional associations offer opportunities for government people from the various levels of the federal system to interact at conferences and to share ideas through journals and other publications. These associations are especially important in setting standards of conduct and in encouraging new approaches to problems. Also, many national agencies look to the personnel at the state and local levels for effective implementation of their programs. In law enforcement generally, cooperation among various governmental units is essential to the successful prosecution of crime.

Grodzins used the Federal Bureau of Investigation (FBI) as an example of a federal agency that is heavily dependent on local law enforcement organizations for information. At the same time, he pointed out, the FBI provides training and other services to local law enforcement people.[21] The use of computer networking and improved databases has made such cooperation even more effective in law enforcement.

Intergovernmental Relations Among States and Localities

While the interplay between the national government and the states tends to dominate the dynamics of the American federal system, other governmental interrelationships also play a role in constructing policies that will affect citizens.

State-State Relations

The Constitution contains several clauses intended to facilitate interaction among the states and protect individuals moving from state to state. In Article IV, Section 1, the Constitution requires that "Full Faith and Credit shall be given in each State to the public Acts, Records, and judicial Proceedings of every other state." This "full faith and credit" clause is an attempt to ensure that the records of one state will be respected and accepted by other states. Section 2 of Article IV proclaims that "The Citizens of each State shall be entitled to all Privileges and Immunities of Citizens in the several States." In *Toomer v. Witsall*, 334 U.S. 395 (1948), the Supreme Court interpreted this clause as being "designed to insure a citizen of State A who ventures into State B the same privileges which the citizens of State B enjoy." From court decisions over time, these privileges appear to include at a minimum the rights to travel freely, to hold and dispose of property, and to engage in business ventures.

States have cooperated with each other to deal with common problems. One form of cooperation, the interstate compact, requires the approval of Congress. Interstate compacts have been useful in enabling states to work with regional problems in areas such as environmental pollution and transportation and to overcome difficulties in other areas such as law enforcement and child support, where individuals use state boundaries to their advantage. Interstate compacts formally obligate their signatories to honor the commitments they have made.

States also derive significant benefits from less formal cooperation. Officials from neighboring states may exchange ideas on innovative approaches to problems. Over the years, meetings among state officials on regional and national bases have encouraged the exchange of ideas and allowed for the communication of concerns and problems. In many instances, these meetings have been sponsored by associations of state officers that act throughout the year as clearinghouses for information on matters of common concern.[22]

Local-Local Relations

Local governments also interact through associations and more informally. Through councils of government (COGs), local leaders in many regions will meet to discuss common concerns and to develop approaches toward mutual problems. This can foster more coordinated action among local governments. However, COGs have no enforcement mechanisms, and the refusal of some local leaders to live up to agreements that have been reached can frustrate efforts to maintain coordinated action in an area. Another area of joint action among local government officials has been lobbying higher levels of government for assistance. Officials at both national and state levels have faced increasing pressure from organized lobbying by local governments.

Competition

Of course, competition can easily replace cooperation as the mode of interaction among states and among local governments. The perennial efforts by governments to attract industry to their jurisdictions often generate intense competition. New industry can offer more jobs for local residents and increase the tax base for government, making life more pleasant for everyone in an area. Unfortunately, this competition often leads governments to provide tax breaks and other inducements that may in the long run be harmful to their financial health and encourage industries to move to lower-cost environments, with the result that one area is harmed by another's temporary good fortune.

The federal system has evolved in response to changing views of the proper role of government. Where forceful government action of some magnitude has been seen as necessary, such as during the Great Depression or during the Johnson administration's efforts to alleviate poverty, national power has gained. Until the Nixon and Reagan presidencies, the growth of national power had been the dominant trend in twentieth-century federal relations. Today, there is a definite shift toward placing more responsibilities on state governments.

Several strong forces have helped to shape the contours of federalism. Especially influential throughout history has been the attitude of the Supreme Court toward the powers of the national government and the states. The use of grants-in-aid has enabled the national government to use its tremendous financial resources to influence state and local governments. And the considerable increase of informal and formal cooperation among national and state and local government officials has provided reciprocal benefits to the parties involved. Finally, the political parties, with their power bases at the state and local levels, remain important checks on national power.

The shifts of power in the dialogue between the national government and the states and localities have been accompanied by assumptions about democracy and pluralism and charges of elitism. Those who favor the return of greater power to the states argue that these governments are closer to the people and thus more responsive to their needs. Others, however, have seen the extension of national power, especially through the use of categorical grants-in-aid, as a means of ensuring that disadvantaged segments of the population at the local level are protected. Through the use of categorical grants-in-aid, the Johnson administration aimed directly at expanding group power and the boundaries of pluralism. This dramatic and obvious attempt to utilize national power and resources to manipulate the political system, in turn, provided am-

munition for those who maintain that American public policy is determined by the powerful few.

Recommended Reading

In addition to the following books, *Intergovernmental Perspective*, published quarterly by the Advisory Commission on Intergovernmental Affairs in Washington, D.C., contains valuable current information on intergovernmental relations.

Thomas J. Anton: *American Federalism and Public Policy*, Random House, New York, 1989.

Timothy J. Conlan: *New Federalism*, Brookings Institution, Washington, D.C., 1988.

Robert Jay Dilger, ed.: *American Intergovernmental Relations Today*, Prentice-Hall, Englewood Cliffs, N.J., 1986.

Thomas R. Dye: *American Federalism*, Lexington Books, Lexington, Mass., 1990.

Morton Grodzins: *The American System*, Transaction, New Brunswick, N.J., 1983.

Arnold M. Howitt: *Managing Federalism*, Congressional Quarterly Press, Washington, D.C., 1984.

Laurence J. O'Toole, Jr., ed.: *American Intergovernmental Relations*, Congressional Quarterly Press, Washington, D.C., 1985.

William H. Riker: *Federalism*, Little, Brown, Boston, 1964.

Deil S. Wright: *Understanding Intergovernmental Relations*, 3d ed., Brooks/Cole, Pacific Grove, Calif., 1988.

Joseph Francis Zimmerman: *Federal Preemption*, Iowa State University Press, Ames, Iowa, 1991.

CHAPTER 4

Public Opinion and the Media

Scholars have found it hard to agree on a definition of public opinion. One way of looking at it is this: Public opinion is people's evaluations and understanding of politics in general and their views on specific political issues of the day. This straightforward, if simplistic, definition serves as a useful starting point. This chapter considers methods of studying public opinion, what Americans believe about politics, political participation in the United States, and the role of the media in influencing public opinion.

Studying Public Opinion

How can we find out what American public opinion is? The most common means of studying it is by questionnaire. To put it plainly, if you want to know what people think about politics, you ask them. This is the essential reason for conducting survey research, and students of public opinion have many data sources on which to call. One of the most important is the University of Michigan's Survey Research Center (SRC), whose Center for Political Studies publishes the National Election Studies series. In each presidential election and each midterm congressional election, the SRC carries out interviews with 1500 to 2500 Americans. Results are shared with the larger academic community. These interviews provide a rich source of information on what Americans think about politics.

The University of Michigan studies are a model of what survey research should look like. They are well structured to ensure the validity of the findings. Key stages involved in such studies are sampling and questionnaire construction.

Sampling

If one is interested in an accurate reading of public opinion at a particular point in time, one must aim for a probability sample. Each individual in the population being studied must have an equal chance of being selected to respond to the questionnaire. One obvious way to do this is to use a random sample. For instance, every person in the population being studied would have his or her name placed in a very large hat. The researcher would then pull names out of the hat, something like televised lottery drawings, producing a simple random sample. In practice, however, other, more sophisticated probability sampling techniques are used when dealing with large populations.

One characteristic of sampling that makes no sense to many people is that a rather small number of interviews can yield a fairly precise estimate of public opinion. If one uses a probability sample, a survey of 1500 people would produce results that are normally accurate 95 percent of the time to within 3 percent of the actual value in the entire population. For example, if 55 percent of a sample of 1500 American citizens said that they planned to vote for a Republican candidate for president, one could infer that this estimate is within 3 percent of the total electorate's actual views—that is, the real figure in the population is between 52 and 58 percent. This is normally as fine-tuned an estimate as one would want. Thus, it would be a waste of money and energy to interview more people.

Questionnaire Construction

Some politicians send mail questionnaires to their constituents. Some of these questionnaires provide extraordinarily good examples of biased wording. An item that reads "Do you think that President Clinton should stand up against the North Korean government over nuclear weapons or should we let them become the dominant power in the region to carry out their evil plans?" is not going to register people's real attitudes about American policy toward North Korea. The question is badly biased. So would be a question that reads "Do you agree with the Democratic party that we should do something about millions of Americans going to bed each night hungry?" In developing a questionnaire, one must ensure that the questions are not slanted and that the wording will be understandable to all. (Some refer to this second principle as

KISS—"Keep it simple, stupid.") To ask a question like "Are there deleterious consequences of the American policy in Bosnia?" is going to cause problems. Many people simply do not know what the word "deleterious" means.

Public Opinion Polling

Public opinion polling has become important in politics. A public official will sometimes hire a polling consultant to ascertain public opinion on an issue concerning him or her. During elections, candidates often have a pollster on their campaign staff to determine what public opinion is, what voters think of the candidate, and so on. Newspapers and TV network news programs sponsor public opinion surveys to provide news; they report on the results of these surveys to reveal what Americans are thinking.

What Americans Believe: Political Orientations

A word is in order about the basic consensus that exists on political values. The political views of Americans tend to be liberal, in that Americans support private property, self-reliance, free enterprise, freedom, equality of opportunity, achievement motivation, and individualism.[1] Americans take these values for granted and do not seriously question them. Furthermore, this tradition is supported by the poor as well as by the wealthy, by the working class as well as by the upper class. From 1940 to the present, approval of this perspective has remained consistent and high. Donald Devine has remarked that "the liberal tradition has the widespread support necessary for a consensual political culture."[2] This ultimately enhances the American system's stability, since few people disagree with the values underlying it.

Among the most significant types of political beliefs held by Americans are what are called political orientations, that is, general evaluations of politics. Some of the more important are support for democratic values, trust in government, political efficacy, ideology, political involvement, and postmaterialism. Each of these is considered in the following paragraphs. Another key orientation, party identification, is discussed in Chapters 5 and 6.

Democratic Values and Rules of the Game

Americans agree on certain general democratic rules of the game. When asked "Should every citizen have an equal chance to influence government policy?" or "Should the minority be free to criticize majority decisions?" or "Should people in the minority be free to try to win majority support for their opinions?" Americans overwhelmingly say "Yes." This indicates consensus on general democratic principles. This consensus has remained consistent from the 1950s until now.

In the 1950s, people also were asked if atheists, communists, or blacks should be able to exercise such freedoms. In these instances, consensus broke down, with many Americans saying that such then unpopular groups should not be allowed freedom of speech and other democratic rights. Educated and politically active people were much more tolerant than the mass public.[3] In the 1970s and later, survey research revealed that the public had become much more tolerant toward these groups. This suggests that the public has become more supportive of democratic values as applied to specific cases.

This greater tolerance may be an illusion, however, for evidence from a national survey and from a survey in Minneapolis–St. Paul indicates that the level of tolerance has not really changed—only the targets of intolerance. Americans are not as intolerant of blacks, atheists, and communists now as they were in the 1950s, but they have replaced these groups as targets of their intolerance with others (such as homosexuals, radical political groups, and pro-choice or antiabortion groups). Thus people seem as intolerant now; it is just that they are intolerant toward different groups and more tolerant of those focused on in the 1950s.[4]

If the masses are intolerant, how is democracy to be preserved? One common answer is that leaders are the true repository of democratic values, such as tolerance for unpopular groups. However, another important study suggests that leaders may not be so democratic. In the 1950s, state government legislation passed to repress communists in terms of their ability to run for office or their opportunity to be employed by government was much more affected by elite intolerance than by mass intolerance toward communists. This surely indicates that the public should not necessarily be sanguine about the commitment of political leaders to democratic norms.[5]

Ideology

One way of ascertaining ideology is to ask if people are liberal or conservative. While Americans are liberal in the general sense discussed earlier,[6] they disagree on the proper interpretation of the ideology. To confuse matters, the polar positions in this dispute within a basic liberalism are referred to as "liberals" and "conservatives." In the American context, liberals are more oriented toward social change, government involvement in regulating the economy, and government acting to assist the disadvantaged. Conservatives are more likely to support the status quo and to wish for less government intrusion in the economy. Moderates are those who see themselves in the "middle of the road" between the other two.

Recent data indicate that there have not been great sea changes over time in the relative popularity of liberalism versus conservatism on economic issues in the American public, although a modest conservative turn preceded Ronald Reagan's accession to office and his early years as president. In terms of "life-style" ideology, there has been a consistent liberalizing trend when the last 50 years are considered, although that trend has slowed or stopped within the past decade or so.[7]

Within these broad trends, we find more finely grained oscillations. One study reports that the public experienced more liberal "moods" in the early 1960s (the peak of liberalism in the period from 1956 to 1988), 1968, 1972, and an increasing liberalism beginning in 1986. On the other hand, the public mood became more conservative in 1966, modestly so in 1969, and most conservative in 1980.[8] The Republican party caught the conservative public mood in 1980, with Reagan's victory. In 1960, Kennedy mirrored the liberal mood. The difference was that Kennedy was too timid and did not make use of the liberal mood in the public to press for advancement of some of his policy choices, whereas Reagan took full advantage and used his modest electoral mandate to leverage considerable change in a conservative direction. Bill Clinton won the presidency during a liberalizing moment in the public mood, but a cautious Congress and the extant large deficits in the federal budget projected over the ensuing years, coupled with the large and growing national debt, hampered his efforts to ride the liberal wave.

It appears that people born after 1946 tend to be somewhat more liberal than those born earlier. From this position, at least one scholar has argued that there will be a continuing, over-time, slow liberalization among the public, as baby boomers and their children replace earlier generations who are more conservative.[9] However, the historic pattern of ebbs and flows in the public mood, discussed above, suggests that there will be continuing oscillations in the future (perhaps against a somewhat more liberal base of comparison).

Ideology in terms of liberal versus conservative has real political effects. Liberals are more often Democrats, and conservatives are more often Republicans. Liberals tend to support more liberal candidates for office, and conservatives tend to support more conservative candidates.

What shapes the level of conservatism or liberalism for the public at large? One study discovers that changes in aggregate ideological preferences over time tend to be associated with changes in national economic conditions. Expectations of an improving economy produce greater liberalism in the public at large, and anticipation of poorer economic tidings goes with more conservative orientations with respect to domestic policy.[10]

Trust in Government

During the 1950s, Americans expressed high levels of trust in their government. However, beginning in 1964, that trust began to deteriorate. Throughout the 1970s, the decline continued. This trend apparently began as a result of civil rights laws enacted in the early 1960s. Many whites were unhappy about such laws as the Civil Rights Act of 1964 and the Voting Rights Act of 1965. Many blacks at first became more positive about government, as one might predict. However, they too began to report less trust in government shortly thereafter. Presumably, they concluded that no dramatic changes in their lives occurred after passage of these bills and, hence, that their faith in government had been misplaced.

It is likely, then, that dissatisfaction with civil rights legislation triggered the decline in trust. Thereafter, public disagreement over what should be done in Vietnam and the Watergate scandal and "stagflation" all fueled continuing decline.[11] Starting in the early 1980s, faith in government began to increase once more, particularly among whites. This appears to have been due to the upbeat mood associated with the presidency of Ronald Reagan. The level of confidence should not be overstated, however. The level of trust is still only about half what it was in the 1950s.[12] If national political tides become more positive, the pool of support ought to rise further. Of course, if major new problems crop up, especially with the economy, one would expect trust to recede further.

Political Efficacy

Political efficacy is an individual's sense that he or she can influence government and that government will respond to that person. In the 1950s and early 1960s, two-thirds of Americans disagreed with the statement "People like me don't have any say about what government does." In 1968, this number dropped significantly, as more Americans felt less influential in politics. The lowered efficacy continued throughout the 1970s and into the 1980s. Watergate and "stagflation"—with the accompanying doubts about leaders' responsiveness and capabilities—appear to have shaped these responses. In 1984, efficacy had rebounded close to the levels of the 1950s. This signals the greater faith of Americans in their political effectiveness and government's responsiveness.[13]

Political Involvement

How interested people are in politics and the extent of the information they have about politics indicate political involvement. In the Survey Research Center's National Election Studies, people have been asked from 1960 to the present if they follow government and public affairs. According to this index, interest was generally higher in the 1970s than in the 1960s. This may reflect a heightened interest in general public affairs because of the important issues of the 1970s—Vietnam to Watergate to "stagflation." Other measures of political interest—caring who wins elections and following campaigns in newspapers—indicate less interest in the 1970s. Lesser interest in elections might result from the sense that problems remained after elections, so a "What's the use?" feeling could have developed. This is consistent with low trust and efficacy.

A final measure of political interest is how often individuals read newspapers. The General Social Survey, administered to a sample of Americans each year by the National Opinion Research Center (NORC) out of Chicago, shows that people's regular reading of newspapers declined from 1967 to 1988.[14] A part of this, of course, is that Americans have come to use television more and more over this same period. However, in the end, Americans will become less well informed about politics, since television news can transmit only a fraction of the news that newspapers can.

Americans have typically been characterized as not possessing a great amount of political information. High proportions (more than 50 percent) of citizens cannot say what two countries were involved in the Strategic Arms Limitation Treaty (SALT) talks in 1979, how long a term members of the U.S. House of Representatives serve, who their congressional representative in the House is, or who their two U.S. senators are.[15]

Civic Duty

Generally, civic duty is a person's belief that he or she ought to be involved in politics and vote. The standard way of measuring this belief has been to ask people during interviews whether they agree with statements such as "If a person doesn't care how an election comes out, then that person shouldn't vote in it" or "A good many local elections aren't important enough to bother with." It is important to be aware of civic duty, since those with a greater sense of responsibility are more apt to vote and participate in other ways in politics. In comparison with other orientations considered in this section, civic duty has remained stable over time.[16]

Postmaterialism

Another political orientation is the extent to which one can be considered either materialist or postmaterialist. People growing up in times of scarcity, it is contended, develop materialist attitudes. These individuals are interested in attaining basic survival needs—food, shelter, clothing. As a result, they come to see government as responsible for providing these. On the other hand, those who mature in times of abundance, such as have generally existed in the United States since World War II, take economic and material needs for granted; postmaterialists come to see government as responsible for facilitating self-expression.

Younger people and those who grew up in wealthier homes are more likely to be postmaterialists. Politically, they support women's rights, antipoverty programs, environmentalism, the antinuclear movement, and life-style freedom. They are also less apt to accept traditional values. Religion may be of little importance in their lives. They tend to accept homosexuality and sexual permissiveness, and they prefer more lenient divorce laws. Materialists are most likely to accept the traditional values.[17] Postmaterialists are slowly closing the gap on the number of materialists—younger people, having grown up in rather good economic times, are more likely to be postmaterialist than their elders. If the economy is healthy over the next decade or so (and there is disagreement about the likelihood of that), an inexorable movement toward postmaterialism will occur, although postmaterialists are now nowhere near a majority—even among the young. If the economy turns sour for a protracted period, postmaterialism is likely to decline.

Economic Decline and Political Behavior: A Bleak Future?

A number of important commentators contend that the American economy is stagnating and may well remain sluggish or even decline over the long run.[18] This is occurring, according to some scholars, as a result of large federal budget deficits, increasing competition for international trade, an end to the formerly healthy annual increases in the real income of families, too great an investment in defense spending over a lengthy period rather than in the domestic economy, and slow strangulation of the economy as special-interest groups influence decision makers to build protection for themselves into the law (thus making the economy less efficient as market principles are undermined). If the future actually becomes as grim as the "gloom and doomers" say, what implications will follow for public opinion and political behavior?

As inflation rises, people become less optimistic about their personal futures and the future of the United States and its economy.[19] Voting based on social class may increase in a faltering economy. M. Stephen Weatherford observes that "there is a tendency for worsening conditions to be associated with higher levels of status polarization, while improved conditions go with lower levels of class voting."[20]

A thorough exploration of the effects of individual economic adversity on vote turnout, using 1974 Census Bureau data, shows that self-reported financial decline reduces the odds of a person's turning out for elections. So too does recent unemployment and being in poverty. Examination of data from 1896 to 1980 indicates that economic problems depress overall turnout rates. Moreover,

> Unemployment and other economic adversities are extremely stressful, causing loss of self-esteem, pride, and self-confidence; depression; and other more serious mental disorders.[21]

These consequences collectively lead to diminished turnout. People are more preoccupied with their own problems, and politics takes a backseat. As John Ostheimer and Leonard Ritt put it, "When a person experiences economic adversity his scarce resources are spent on holding body and soul together—surviving—not on remote concerns like politics."[22]

Economic traumas have other effects. Accompanying the belief that one's economic fortunes are sinking are an increased sense of the world as meaningless, political distrust, and less confidence in governmental leadership and basic American institutions. Some speculate that this may have potentially dire effects, leading to a weakening of attitudes supporting democracy. Sustained periods of economic decline, then, might considerably undermine democratic values.[23]

Sources of Political Orientations

Political Socialization

Political socialization is the process by which people learn about politics. It is ongoing; basic orientations are subject to change throughout a person's life cycle—from birth to death.[24] Because political learning begins very early in life, much attention has been focused on the agents of socialization for children.

The Agents of Political Socialization for Children

The family is a primary force. In the home, children learn which party their parents identify with and often come to see themselves as being loyal to the same party. The family does not mold children's views on specific issues, nor does it provide children with a wealth of facts about the American political system. What it does is help to shape children's general orientations about politics, such as trust and efficacy.

The school fills in factual gaps and adds to children's political knowledge. Schools also tend to transmit a society's dominant values to the young. Education has other effects as well. Students who can take part in discussions about politics in the classroom—especially among more affluent students—tend to be more politically efficacious. Extracurricular involvement in high school is tied to greater efficacy and participation.

Media increasingly play a role in political learning; they are dealt with in a later section of this chapter.

Other Factors in Political Socialization

Experiences faced by people in their everyday lives also affect political views—from childhood through adulthood, once more indicating that political socialization is a lifelong process. For instance, becoming a mother—but not becoming a father—tends to reduce the level of political participation in state and national politics, probably simply because the mother must spend so much time parenting that state and national politics take a back seat.[25] Being afflicted with poor health appears to reduce extent of political participation.[26] Those who are more involved in their place of worship tend to be more conservative in their political views—especially with respect to life-style issues.[27]

Political generation can be a factor in socialization as well. One study finds that those who were part of the sixties generation (that is, they came of political age in the 1960s) have tended to remain somewhat distinct over time in their political views, for instance, remaining more liberal on life-style issues.[28]

Demographic Sources of Political Orientations

Individuals' personal and social characteristics have an effect on what they think about politics. Most basic are education, income and social status, age, and gender.

Education profoundly influences people's political orientation. People who are more educated are more tolerant and supportive of democratic values, more sophisticated in their political conceptualizations, more politically efficacious (that is, they feel that they can affect politics and that government officials will listen to them), and more involved in politics. They are also more likely to have a strong sense of civic duty and to have postmaterialist values.

Income and social status affect political orientation in a similar manner. Higher social status is associated with greater ideological sophistication and support for democratic values, trust in government, political efficacy, political involvement, and civic duty. Children from wealthier families tend to be more postmaterialist.

A person's age has some relationship to that person's political perspectives. Older people are more apt to be materialist and more involved in politics. They are also more conservative on some issues, although the relationship is a complex one.

One's gender can affect public opinion. Studies show that women are less efficacious, less cynical about politics, and less involved. To illustrate some gender differences in issue positions, women generally support government assistance for the disadvantaged.

Public Opinion and Policy

People's views on the issues and their ideological preferences are not merely interesting academic subjects. The policies of democratic governments are often influenced by expression of public opinion. There is ample evidence to suggest that public opinion affects judicial decisions,[29] congressional rollcall voting,[30] and the actions of state governments.[31]

One illustrative study of the courts' responsiveness to public opinion looks at U.S. Supreme Court decisions over a broad period of time. Thomas Marshall gathered national poll results on 110 different issues that could be matched against specific Supreme Court rulings from the 1930s to 1986. He found that 62 percent of the Court's rulings were consistent with majority preference as expressed in public opinion polls.[32] Thus, the Supreme Court, often thought of as beyond politics, appears to respond to public opinion. The 62 percent figure is similar to that derived for congressional responsiveness to citizens' views.[33] However, the linkage between public opinion and Supreme Court decisions has apparently been weakened considerably by the unbroken string of conservative appointments beginning with Richard Nixon's presidency—at least up to Clinton's appointment of Ruth Bader Ginsburg in 1993. Because of these appointments, the Court has drifted away from mainstream public opinion in a more conservative direction,[34] in that sense losing touch with the public mood.

In a study of responsiveness to public opinion at the state level, Gerald Wright and his colleagues drew on CBS/*New York Times* surveys conducted in all 50 states between 1976 and 1982. These polls included a question asking about the respondents' liberalism or conservatism. The investigators simply created from answers to this question an overall measure of ideology for each state, based upon the responses of individual citizens in those states. The level of liberalism was compared with actual policies enacted by each state and measured in terms of "policy liberalism" (such as greater educational spending per pupil, more concern with consumer protection, easier Medicaid eligibility, and the like). Public opinion was highly correlated with states' actual policies.[35]

Perhaps the most substantial effort to establish that public opinion affects government decisions is a study by Benjamin Page and Robert Shapiro, based on poll results from 1935 to 1979.[36] Looking at polling questions asked during this period, the investigators identified issues of the day on which people's views subsequently changed noticeably. The investigators discovered 357 such issues. Additionally, they gathered information on changes in policy by the U.S. Supreme Court, Congress, and state governments. Then they checked to see if government policies changed as public opinion shifted. Overall, there was congruence 66 percent of the time within a year after public opinion was altered. That figure increases to 90 percent correspondence if the time frame is lengthened beyond one year. A number of factors seem to influence the effects of public opinion. For one, the bigger the shift in the public's views, the greater and more rapid is the change in policy. While opinion and policy are congruent for the federal courts and Congress, congruence is even more pronounced in state governments. If public opinion shifts in a more liberal direction, government is more responsive than if the change is conservative.

Thus, public opinion seems to make a difference. However, the question remains: Is public opinion itself manipulated by an elite? This is discussed later in the chapter in the section entitled "The Media and Politics."

Political Participation

Dimensions of Participation

Political participation refers to people's actions that are designed to have some effect on government. Scholars recognize two different species of activity—conventional and unconventional.

Conventional Activity

Actions within this category are what most people think of as participation.

Voting in Elections. This is the most common political activity. In their study carried out in 1967, Sidney Verba and Norman Nie found that 72 percent of people reported voting in the 1960 and 1964 presidential elections (this figure is higher than the turnout really was in those elections because of the well-known tendency of people to overreport their voting turnout).[37] This 1967 study serves as a baseline against which to compare more recent information on Americans' political behavior later in this section.

Campaigning. Another type of political action is campaign activity. This includes trying to persuade others to vote for a certain candidate, actively working for a party or candidate, attending political meetings, giving money to a party or candidate, and being a member of a political club. About 29 percent of Americans were so engaged in 1967.

Communal Activity. Twenty-eight percent reported this type of participation, which includes working with others to solve a local problem, membership in a problem-solving community organization, and contacting public officials as part of a group. This is basically action based on cooperation among different people to pursue a common goal.

Contacting. Particularized contacting, carried out by about 14 percent of the citizenry in 1967, occurs when people as individuals contact a political official to try to get him or her to do something to benefit them.

When Americans were surveyed in 1987 to compare their political participation levels with those from the 1967 study, some very interesting changes had occurred. People reported voting less in 1987 than in 1967; they increased their contributions of money to a campaign or cause; they became more aggressive in terms of communal participation.[38] It appears as if people came to think that they were better off using their money or group action as a lever to get government to respond rather than depending upon the vote.

Mix of Conventional Participatory Activities

Americans can be categorized in terms of the mix of their participatory acts. Figure 4.1 summarizes these findings from the Verba and Nie study. Inactives are hardly involved, other than occasionally voting. And they are the most numerous type of participant (22 percent). Voting specialists rank second (21 percent); these people vote regularly but do little else. Communalists are a numerous lot, too (20 percent). These persons engage in communal actions and vote but are largely inactive in campaign activities. Campaigners (15 percent) participate extensively in campaigns and vote; on the other hand, they are inactive in communal behavior. Parochial participants are few in number (4 percent); they are not involved in campaigns or communal affairs, although they do vote regularly. Their participation in politics seems keyed to taking initiative to benefit their own personal lives. The last class consists of complete activists (11 percent). As the term suggests, these are people characterized by their regular involvement in all the conventional activities.

Unconventional Activities

A distinct form of action not covered to this point is participation in such unconventional activities as political demonstrations, protest meetings, violent protest, disobeying laws, and the like. While such behavior is intended to influence officials, it takes place outside normally accepted channels. Verba and Nie, unfortunately, did not examine unconventional behavior. There are no figures to be compared with conventional participation. However, indirect evidence suggests that people in general are less likely to select this behavior

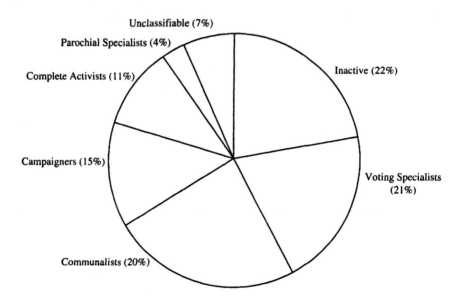

Fig. 4.1   Categories of Political Participation

than they are conventional ones as a way to influence government. Younger people and blacks are more likely to engage in unconventional activity as a tactic than other groups. Over time, unconventional activities appear to have become more acceptable to the general population.[39]

Who Participates?

Conventional Participation

Both social and political factors increase the odds of people participating in politics.

Social Factors.   Those who are higher in social status, with more income, more education, and greater organizational involvement (membership and leadership in nonpolitical groups), are more likely to participate in politics. So too are those who have deeper roots in the community in terms of length of residence. People who have developed a group consciousness (black consciousness, feminist consciousness, or age consciousness, for instance) are more active. Among the least active are the young and the unmarried. In general, men participate more in politics than women do, although in terms of turnout in elections it seems there is now no difference.

Political Factors.   Political orientation can shape the likelihood of political activism. Citizens who are interested in politics, who have higher information levels, and who identify with specific political parties are more likely to participate. A sense of political efficacy also goes with participation. An individual with a strong sense of civic duty, the belief that one should be active in politics, is going to participate more. Finally, postmaterialist individuals are more active.

The Socioeconomic Model.   One simple way of linking social and political factors together is illustrated in Figure 4.2 This is called the socioeconomic model. The higher in social status a person is, the greater are the odds that he or she will feel more efficacious, be interested in politics, and have a sense of civic duty. These orientations, in turn, push the individual toward participation in politics.

Other factors come into play as well. For instance, among black Americans, living in a city which has a black mayor appears to lead to a sense of "empowerment," which, in turn, elevates the level of political participation.[40] And when political leaders (candidates and incumbents and other party officials) emphasize citizen involvement, the people seem to respond by actually

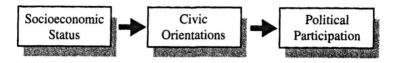

Fig. 4.2   Linking of Social and Political Factors

participating more. Thus, political elites can serve to elevate levels of activism by encouraging the public.[41]

Unconventional Participation

Taking part in demonstrations—whether violent or nonviolent—is a typical example of what political scientists label unconventional behavior. People so involved have many of the same characteristics as those who are most active in conventional forms of political behavior. For example, persons likely to be part of a demonstration are the more educated; they are more socially active and more tied into social networks; they are more involved in politics, politically efficacious, and postmaterialistic. Young men are somewhat more prone to take part.

The Effects of Political Participation on Policy

Fundamental to political participation is the conviction that getting involved actually does—or at least can—make a difference. According to Verba and Nie, this is not naive faith; participation, they argue, does affect decision makers—but not always with the result that one might initially expect.

Assume that political leaders wish to know what the public thinks on an issue. Two strategies for accomplishing this are the polling strategy and the participation strategy.

By using the polling strategy, the leader finds out the peoples' interests through a public opinion interview of a probability sample of citizens within his or her constituency. What the leader obtains is an accurate snapshot of constituents' views at that particular point in time. By using the participation strategy, the political leader gets an idea of citizens' wishes by their communications to him or her (whether by vote, letters and telegrams, or talks with individuals or groups). The first strategy, polling, is extremely expensive; thus the second is more likely to be used.

Do these two strategies yield the same interpretations of what public opinion actually is? One way to find out is to compare the distribution of policy preferences of the population as a whole as determined by a survey research questionnaire with that part of the population which participates most in politics.[42] When people were asked about serious problems which faced them, three areas emerged: welfare, income, and education. On welfare—by which the researchers mean problems in obtaining adequate housing or employment or in paying for medical care—almost a third of the people sampled indicated that they had such a problem. However, if only the most participant respondents were considered, as would be the case if the participation strategy were followed, only a fifth of the respondents thought that they had a welfare problem. This suggests that the intensity of the welfare issue would be underplayed if leaders derived constituency needs from the participation strategy.

On the other hand, a leader attending to participants would most likely find more concern about education than exists in the general population. Thus a distortion occurs:

> It would seem that the leader who used the participation strategy would be less sensitive to the existence of severe personal economic problems in the society than would the leader who used the polling strategy. And the more narrowly he limited the population he observed—if he were attuned only to the most active 5 percent of the population, for instance—the more such personal economic problems would be obscured. Participation makes some problems more visible and others less so.[43]

The next question that must be addressed is the extent to which leaders actually follow the participation strategy. In fact, citizen participation does appear to have some influence on leaders. Overall, the views of leaders tend to be like the view of highly participatory citizens, even when taking into account individuals' social and economic backgrounds. Ultimately, then, the data show that it makes a difference if citizens participate. It also matters who participates. As Verba and Nie conclude:

> The fact that the participation input comes from a small and unrepresentative sample makes a difference in how leaders respond. Participation is a powerful mechanism for citizen control, but how that mechanism works depends on who participates.[44]

Indeed, some cities have instituted explicit schemes to build citizen participation into the local decision-making process. An exploration of the impact of such systems in five cities—Birmingham, Dayton, Portland, San

Antonio, and St. Paul—suggests that creation of direct channels of communication between citizens and their local leaders (elected officials plus top bureaucrats) can reduce the bias discovered by Verba and Nie. Surveys of residents, elected officials, and bureaucrats in those five cities suggest that "concurrence" (agreement on the issues of the day between public officials and citizens) is higher in cities with as opposed to those without such participative structures. Thus, conscious efforts to link citizens and their government appear to produce more responsive local governments.[45]

The Media and Politics

People spend vast amounts of time watching television, reading newspapers and newsmagazines, listening to the radio, and seeing movies. The mass media surround them and engulf them each day. For most people, the media provides ears and eyes to the world; they serve as a means of surveillance.

Many books have been written on media and politics. However, an examination of American public opinion without considering the media would be incomplete. This section explores briefly the structure of American media, the impact of the media on public opinion, and how mass media can be used by leaders to affect the views of Americans.

Media Structure

The media that have the most important effects on public opinion are probably television and newspapers. What is sometimes referred to as the "inner ring" of media organizations includes the news departments of the three television networks, CNN, the two wire services (Associated Press and United Press International), and certain major newspapers (the *New York Times,* the *Wall Street Journal,* and the *Washington Post*). Political officials in Washington are very attentive to these media, and many of them play to the media to get publicity for themselves and their policies.

Other media tend to pick up stories from the inner ring. The image of crusading newspapers developing their own stories is somewhat misleading. "Pack journalism" often describes how news is covered, with reporters following one another's lead in a kind of follow-the-leader game, with the inner ring having the greatest influence. Going along with this is a decline in newspaper competition. Fewer and fewer large cities have competing newspapers, so that citizens have less and less choice about what they will read.

Some theorists who believe that an elite rules the United States have combined these two pieces of information to argue that the media are centralized in a few hands and that news is shaped by a few media leaders. This opens up the possibility that the elite can shape the messages transmitted by the media to the masses. In this way, the elite can "brainwash" the people into believing that the social and political system is democratic even though, in reality, elitism best describes the system. Of course, many other analysts disagree with this contention.

The Media and Public Opinion

The Media and the Young

In the past, the key agents of political learning for children were seen as the family and the school. The media were not taken into serious account. Now, that neglect has diminished. One reason is the nearly unbelievable amount of time the young spend in front of television sets.

One study looked at the effects of media exposure on 760 fifth and sixth graders in 1973.[46] The target of this investigation was the effects of "media use" (defined as exposure to news media) on support for political parties, support for elections, political action (wearing a campaign button or talking to people about an election), and political knowledge. The results? Media use by these children produces higher levels of political knowledge, greater support for the electoral process, less support for the political parties (perhaps because of negative portrayals of parties by the news media), and greater political participation. Generally, though, researchers assume that pre-high-school students are not as affected as their elders.

Adolescents seem to be heavily affected by the media. Some evidence indicates that adolescents use the media as a political resource more than they use their own parents or their school. Several different studies speak to the importance of media for adolescents' political learning. For example, heavy media users differ from light users. A 1974 study of 1000 Pennsylvania high-school students categorized 39 percent of the sample as heavy news media users and 22 percent as light users. Heavy users, it turned out, had greater political awareness and were more politically participant.[47]

Watching entertainment programs on television also can affect adolescents' political views. In Providence, Rhode Island, 619 adolescents interviewed in 1980 were found to spend, in the aggregate, quite a bit of time watching television crime shows (for example, *CHIPS, Quincy, Vega$,* and *Hart to Hart*). The more a person watched such programming, the less was that person's support for civil liberties. The impact was greater for older respondents. This seems to be a function of the distorted views of crime and the criminal justice system presented in television shows.[48]

The Media as the Bearers of Bad News

Adults, too, are significantly affected by the media. Some scholars have argued that news media in general produce negative views of American politics among citizens. Probably the best-known argument is the contention that television news takes a negative and critical stance toward politics, producing "videomalaise," cynicism, and a lowered sense of efficacy.[49] This is conceivable because of the kinds of stories network television news tends to emphasize. However, other studies do not indicate that television news (or other sources, for that matter) is particularly negative in its coverage of American politics. It may be that news media, by objective reporting of *real* problems, makes people aware that these problems do exist. Hence consumers of news become more cynical because many governmental efforts to solve problems simply fail. The media act as the bearers of bad news.[50]

Agenda Setting by the Media

Another media impact is agenda setting, the process by which certain issues come to be identified as important and worthy of government action. That there are agenda-setting effects seems well established. For example, in the 1968 presidential election, voters' viewpoint on the important issues of the day seemed to reflect media emphases. Generally, media spotlighting of issues leads to issues being noticed and can, although there are no guarantees, influence people to see these issues as worthy of action.

To illustrate, consider the following rather simple experiment.[51] People were divided into four groups to take part in this study. Each group saw common news items, actually run on the network evening news. In addition, the three experimental groups saw some additional news segments added to this basic package of stories that all people saw. One group watched stories on the simulated evening news which emphasized defense weaknesses; another group saw a newscast with environmental stories replacing defense stories; a third group saw inflation stories instead. The fourth, the control group, saw the basic package of news stories without any additional segments emphasizing a certain issue. Comparisons of viewers' responses on questionnaires before and after seeing the sequences over a four-day period indicated that those who saw the defense and environmental stories came to rank these as more important over the time span studied; this represents an agenda-setting effect.

The Priming Effect

Related to this is the so-called priming effect, in which greater media emphasis on an issue leads members of the public to take what they have learned from this coverage and use it in another context. For example, during Reagan's presidency, widespread media coverage of the Iran-contra affair led people to use this information to evaluate the president's performance. The impact was more pronounced among those with less political information to begin with.[52]

Leaders' Use of Media

Elites use the media to advance their interests. Presidents, for example, often work to make media coverage more positive by trying to win the favor of reporters, shaping the flow of news from the executive agencies to emphasize good publicity and "hide" bad news, devising attractive photo opportunities, and arranging work schedules to produce better odds for favorable media coverage. The White House has an elaborate communications organization, which suggests the perceived importance of the media for a president. Presidents can shape media coverage through news releases, briefing, backgrounds, appearances by top spokespersons on news programs (such as *Meet the Press*), so-called leaks, news conferences, and televised broadcast speeches. The latter two call for somewhat more attention.

If one looks at presidential news conferences from the 1920s through the 1970s, certain patterns emerge. With the advent of television, news conferences have become less frequent and less regular, perhaps because any mistake made will be witnessed immediately by a large number of citizens. Potential damage is greater and damage control more difficult. When problems arise, presidential news conferences become more irregular. There is avoidance behavior, particularly on foreign policy matters.[53] Conferences are used less, then, when problems for the president are most likely to be highlighted.

A cataloging of major broadcast presidential speeches from 1949 to 1980 also produces evidence of presidential use of the media in the interest of the administration. Such addresses are most likely to occur with significant shifts in presidential popularity. If popularity goes up, it seems that presidents try to boost it further; if it declines, addresses seem to be designed to stop the sag. Positive events (taking credit) and negative events (damage control or, in foreign affairs, "rallying around the flag") also increase the odds of an address. Major addresses are less likely with increases in unemployment or inflation or if military activity increases. More to the point, such strategies may have some impact.

Lyn Ragsdale observes that "the occurrence of a presidential speech has a significant positive effect on levels of presidents' public support."[54] On average, a major broadcast speech produces a 3 percent boost in popularity. Thus, presidents may be able to manipulate their popularity ratings via the media. When a president's popularity is high (50 percent or greater approval), his rhetoric can influence Americans' views on major policy issues of the day. In this way, a president can exercise real leadership over public opinion. On the other hand, less popular presidents seem unable to mobilize support for their policy preferences.[55]

Congress also uses the media—especially for the benefit of its individual members. Extensive in-house media facilities are available for members of the House of Representatives. For instance, recording studios are available for use by incumbents. Members take advantage of this as well as of their franking privileges to build links with the folks back home. Many suggest that such facilities have contributed considerably to incumbents' success rates in elections.

Democratic theorists can find comfort in several observations in research: the citizenry believes itself politically capable and has greater faith in the political system now than it had during the 1970s; Americas' sense of civic duty remains rather high; and public opinion seems to have a real impact on public policy, just as political participation does.

Elitists might counter by pointing out that political leaders can use the media to influence, perhaps to manipulate, public opinion. Further, the more educated and the wealthier are more participant in politics and hence are more likely to influence decision makers. Thus, the linkage between citizens and their representatives is strongest for the "haves."

Pluralists would argue that different groups with their respective interests must be taken into account by leaders. As Chapter 5 indicates, the political parties try to build coalitions of group support. As a result, the myriad groups in society will have their voices represented through their political parties.

Recommended Reading

M. Margaret Conway: *Political Participation in the United States,* 2d ed., Congressional Quarterly Press, Washington, D.C., 1991.

Doris Graber: *Mass Media and American Politics,* 4th ed., Congressional Quarterly Press, Washington, D.C., 1993.

William G. Mayer: *The Changing American Mind,* University of Michigan Press, Ann Arbor, 1992.

Benjamin I. Page and Robert Y. Shapiro: *The Rational Public,* University of Chicago Press, Chicago, 1992.

Steven J. Rosenstone and John Mark Hansen: *Mobilization, Participation, and Democracy in America,* Macmillan, New York, 1993.

Roberta Sigel, ed.: *Political Learning in Adulthood,* University of Chicago Press, Chicago, 1989.

CHAPTER 5

Political Parties

Time Line

1790s–1815	Federalists versus Jeffersonian Democrat-Republicans
1830s–1850s	Whigs versus Democrats
1860–present	Democrats versus Republicans
1860–1896	Republicans marginally dominant
1896–1932	Republicans clearly dominant
1932–1964	New Deal realignment with Democrats dominant
1964–present	Dealignment? A new party era?

Political parties have been a prominent feature of American politics since near the beginning of the republic. For much of American history, parties have been viewed as important actors in linking citizens and their leaders. This chapter begins by discussing the nature and functions of American political parties, follows with a brief history of these parties, and outlines the role of parties in the electorate and with government officials and party organization itself. Are

America's parties disintegrating? Are they becoming more vital? Do they have a future? The chapter concludes by addressing these questions.

What Is a Political Party?

What is the exact nature of political parties? A host of definitions have been advanced over time, but the most common is, simply, that a political party is an organization that sponsors and supports candidates for office under its label.

The Three Components

American parties have three components, each of which plays a significant role.

Party in the Electorate. Within the electorate the party is made up of the people who identify with one of the parties and feel a sense of loyalty to it. Their links with the party are rather passive, and their party work is often no more strenuous than voting for its candidates.

Party Organization. This component includes the active party workers, from precinct captains to ward leaders to county chairperson to the state central committee to the national party committee. Party organization is the formal party structure.

The Party in Government. In government, the party is composed of candidates who have won their elections under a party label. The major examples at the national level are the president and members of Congress. These elected officials are generally the most visible spokespersons for their party.

Functions of Political Parties

Political parties have a variety of functions, as listed below:

1. They serve as linkage institutions. By this, scholars mean that the party helps to link the people with government and its policies. By choosing one party's candidate over another's, a majority of voters indicate where they want government policy to go, since the parties stand for (at least somewhat) different principles. Thus, by their support, the voters can influence the direction of policy.

2. They recruit candidates to run for office.

3. They provide a convenient label (the party's name and whatever else might symbolize the party to the voter) to attach to candidates to differentiate them.

4. To some extent, they educate the public by urging people to vote and by providing campaign materials that describe candidates and their political views and promises.

5. They help resolve conflict. There are myriad groups in society, each with its own priorities. Parties try to draw support from many groups; to do so, they must advance conciliatory positions. By taking more moderate positions, they stand to alienate smaller numbers of voters.

Basic Characteristics of American Political Parties

1. The United States has a two-party system. Most democracies are not structured in this way; France and Italy, for instance, have multiparty systems with many competing parties. A number of factors have been advanced to explain why the United States has two dominant parties. Some political commentators point to the common beliefs shared by party leaders and followers. They say that there has always been a basic consensus on the values of liberalism (recall the discussion in Chapter 4). Hence, two moderate parties with the ability to negotiate and compromise are, so it is claimed, a logical consequence.

However, the most powerful explanation is the nature of elections. The method of electing officials in the United States is basically the single-member district with a plurality vote (whoever gets the most votes wins—even if there is no majority). This system works against smaller parties, as statistical analyses of different democratic countries show.[1] Why is this the case?

To understand this system's impact, consider an alternative system for selecting officials—proportional representation. In this case, if a national legislature were being elected, a party—let's call it the Republicrat party—would receive, in one form of the system, seats in the legislature in proportion to the votes that the party received. Hence, if the Republicrats got 10 percent of the popular vote, they would earn 10 percent of the seats in the legislature (if 100 seats were at stake, the party would get 10 percent of these, or 10 seats). Thus, receiving only 10 percent of the popular vote still translates into the Republicrats having representation in the legislature. Proportional representation systems encourage smaller parties.

On the other hand, the single-member-district system can discourage small parties. The Republicrats, let us assume, still have 10 percent popular support in the electorate, Republicans 45 percent and Democrats 45 percent. That support, however, is scattered throughout 100 districts, each of which elects one representative. The Republicrats, if their support is 10 percent per district, will gain *no* representatives, since either Republicans or Democrats will have enough votes to win every district. In the end, the Republicrat voter wastes his or her vote by supporting the Republicrat candidate. Thus the voter will end up casting a ballot for either a Republican or a Democrat, who can win, rather than a Republicrat, who cannot win.

Still another factor favoring the strength and endurance of a two-party system is the nature of our election laws. Designed by officials of the two major parties (no coincidence!), these election laws make it difficult for third parties to even get their candidates on the ballot. For instance, some states demand a very large number of signatures on a petition before allowing a minor party to have its candidates placed on the ballot. This makes it quite unlikely that this party will find its candidates' names placed before the voting public.

2. Parties in the United States are pragmatically oriented. They tend to advance moderate positions; they are not rigidly ideological (debate is intense *within* the party over what its positions ought to be); and they appeal to many groups to gain support. Parties offer positions designed to appeal to a fairly wide spectrum of American political opinion. The Democrats have many conservative loyalists. There are also some relatively liberal Republican officeholders, such as Senator Robert Packwood. The parties, then, are accommodative, since they attempt to address a wide array of interests. And when they are perceived as *not* being open to a variety of views, they may lose support. This appears to have happened to the Republicans in the 1992 elections, when many voters saw them as responding only to the most conservative elements in the Republican party—and, hence, as being out of step with some mainstream opinions.[2]

3. Parties in the United States are not structurally centralized. Consequently, the party leaders find it a problem to discipline officeholders who do not go along with them. In votes in Congress, there are usually defectors who vote with members of the other party. For example, many conservative Democrats in the House of Representatives bolted the party leadership's position and supported President Reagan's budget in the early 1980s (the defectors were called "boll weevils"). Yet, it is very rare when a party will punish one of its members for so straying. One recent instance of penalizing a member of Congress for breaking with the party occurred in 1983. The Democratic leadership moved to take Representative Phil Gramm's seat on the House Budget Committee away from him because of his active support of President Reagan's budget against the party's po-

sition. However, these comments about loose party centralization should be read while keeping in mind evidence that party leadership in the U.S. House of Representatives has actually become stronger in recent years.[3]

The History of American Parties

Political factions had been prominent in the states under the Articles of Confederation (see Chapter 2). These were often referred to as parties. At the time of the Constitutional Convention, few American leaders had a favorable view of these organizations. Historian Richard Hofstadter calls their orientation "anti-party."[4] Alexander Hamilton and James Monroe, among the most negative toward political party, believed that parties were evil, reflecting the efforts of special interests to gain control of government for their own selfish goals. They felt that the norm for any society should be consensus on its goals and the rules of the game; this would produce peace and tranquility for that society. A party—in their view—represented minority interests working against the larger public interest. Hence party competition was a sign of disease in a political society—and must somehow be suppressed.

This line of reasoning is, in fact, typical of that of many developing countries. For example, after Zimbabwe achieved its independence, the party gaining control shortly thereafter tried to stamp out opposition parties. The new government's justification was that opposition parties bespoke plots to damage the country. Its position is very close to that of Hamilton and Monroe, who were, after all, leaders in a developing country in the 1790s. Despite this distaste for party, parties did indeed emerge in the 1790s.

Of course, the other antiparty position, exemplified by James Madison, was more moderate. Madison believed, too, that party had negative effects. However, as noted in *Federalist 10,* he felt that its harmful consequences could be controlled through representation and a larger republic encompassing more disparate perspectives.

Federalists and Jeffersonian Democrat-Republicans

These two parties became contenders for power in the mid-1790s as Hamilton and his followers found themselves at odds with Jefferson, Madison, and their like-minded colleagues. The Federalists, with Hamilton and John Adams as early spokesmen, stood for a pro-England, anti-France foreign policy and a more active federal government, one involved in supporting business and manufacturing interests.

The Jeffersonian Democrat-Republicans were less hospitable toward England and leaned toward France. They also opposed the somewhat more supportive stance of the Federalists toward manufacturing and commerce. The Jeffersonians were the party of the yeoman farmer, whereas the "better sort" were more likely to be Federalists.

What happened to those, the anti-Federalists, who had fought against the Constitution's approval? Many Americans were in this camp; what happened to them in the first party era? While anti-Federalists were not a political party as such during the ratification battles, they did become a part of the Federalist/Democratic-Republican system. They became allies of supporters of the Constitution (such as Madison), who were opposed to the policies of Hamilton and the Federalist party, to provide the backbone of the Jeffersonian party.[5]

The two parties competed fairly evenly for a couple of elections, but after 1800, the Federalists faded badly and were essentially dead as a party by 1815. This ended the first party era. After the demise of the Federalists, the heirs of Jefferson were the only party organization left. The term "Era of Good Feeling" (1816–1824) referred to the lack of party contention, not to the amicability of politics.

Whigs versus Democrats

Andrew Jackson's victory over John Quincy Adams in the 1828 presidential election was the catalyst leading to the rise of the second party era. The opposition to Jackson grew quickly and precipitated the rise of the Whig party to challenge Jacksonian Democrats. The Whigs were not a direct successor of the Federalists; its leaders were not old Federalists, and its organization had no ties to the Federalists. The Whigs were a very pragmatic party, based on a broad coalition of interests opposed to Jacksonian policies and to Jackson himself.

To the extent that the Whigs had a policy orientation, it was more nationalistic and business-oriented (as opposed to agriculture-oriented). The Whigs did court mass support, however. They ran war heroes for president (such as William Henry Harrison and Zachary Taylor) who had little experience and had few previously widely known political views. The two parties were competing on a national level by 1840. Party organization and political campaigning became recognizable in today's terms. If an American today were transported back to the Martin Van Buren–William Henry Harrison election of 1840, he or she would be familiar with the way the Democrats and Whigs conducted their campaigns.

The rise of race and slavery as issues in the 1850s precipitated the breakup of the Whig party. As a broad accommodationist party, the Whigs could not handle the sectional conflict over the issue of permitting slavery in the western territories, which broke out in the 1850s. The only question was what new party would replace them. Free-Soilers? Know-Nothings? Or a party originating in (take your pick) Ripon (Wisconsin), Angelica (New York), or Friendship (New York)—the Republicans?

The Long-Running Road Show: Democrats versus Republicans

The Republican party became the new rival of the Democrats and was marginally dominant from 1865 to 1896. Abraham Lincoln's victories in 1860 and 1864 signaled the beginning of this period, during which major changes took place in the United States. Perhaps most significant were industrialization and urbanization. Power moved from agriculture to business in the economic sphere. Regional conflict remained—the industrializing Northeast against the farmers of the South, the West, and the Midwest.

The Republicans were more supportive of industry, the Democrats of agriculture. By 1896 the Democratic party had become dominated by agricultural interests, which were increasingly disenchanted with being left in the wake of rapid industrialization. William Jennings Bryan electrified the Democratic presidential convention of 1896 with his "Cross of Gold" speech, which called for a policy favoring the small farmers. He won the nomination, only to be defeated in the election by William McKinley. From 1896 to 1932, the Republicans were clearly the dominant party.

Between 1928 and 1936, another massive change occurred, as the Republicans—cursed with the almost unimaginable dislocations caused by the Great Depression—saw new voters, children of immigrants, blacks, and the working class move toward support of the opposition Democrats. The Democrats, with Franklin Roosevelt's victories in 1932 and 1936, entrenched themselves as the new majority party.

In the New Deal era, the Democrats stood for what is called the positive state, the use of government power to help the disadvantaged and powerless and the working class and the belief that such power ought to be used for the good of the public. They supported civil rights of blacks (at least northern Democrats did). The Republicans remained more supportive of business interests and generally fought to reduce government regulation of the private sector.

Has the United States entered or is it entering yet another party era? Are the Republicans becoming the new majority party? Or does the victory of Bill Clinton in 1992 presage a return to the dominance of the New Deal Democratic coalition? These are frequently raised questions, and ones that will be addressed in detail in later sections.

Critical Elections

A few elections (or election periods) in American history have drastically altered the balance of power in American politics. These are called critical elections, of which there are two distinct types—converting and realigning.

Types of Critical Elections

Realigning Elections.   The most dramatic elections are those in which a majority party sinks to minority status (or disappears altogether) and the underlying voter coalitions change. The years 1928 to 1936 form one such realigning period. A realigning election sees coalitions of party loyalists altered and a different party—either the minority party or a new party—coming to dominance. This situation nicely describes the beginnings of the New Deal era.

Converting Elections.   In this type of election, the majority party stays dominant, but the parties' coalitions change. In 1896, the Republican base changed to include residents of industrial cities. The key feature in such elections is the alteration of party coalitions. At the time of critical elections, changes normally follow as new issues come to the fore that demand new policy approaches.[6]

Critical elections are often thought of as happening abruptly. However, this need not be the case. V. O. Key, Jr., spoke of "secular realignment," in which the change process could take place over a lengthy time period:

> A secular shift in party attachment may be regarded as a movement of the members of a population category from party to party that extends over several presidential elections and appears to be independent of the peculiar factors influencing the vote at individual elections. . . . A movement that extends over a half century is a more persuasive indication of the phenomenon in mind than is one that lasts less than a decade.[7]

Conditions Leading to Critical Elections

Research points to three kinds of contributors to critical elections: new issues arising, incompetent party leadership, and external factors (such as the rise of media and public opinion polling).

New Issues.   One of the most common assumptions made in theorizing about critical elections is that one party (and it is normally the dominant one) becomes "out of step" with the times. New issues arise and the party is unable to adapt to these altered circumstances. The Democrats were dominant up until the Civil War as a more agriculturally oriented party. As industrialization reshaped the nation, the party began to lose sway over the electorate, for it was increasingly unable to speak to the new needs created by America's industrial revolution.

Incompetent Party Leadership.   Party leaders can be inept and contribute to realignment. One can speak of the "intelligence of parties" in terms of adapting to the electoral environment.[8] More adaptive parties, presumably, are more likely to be successful in elections. If a party's leadership were to "lose touch" with the voters, then that party would be at risk of falling behind in party competition.

External Factors.   Elements from the larger society can affect the odds of critical elections taking place. For instance, consider the use of public opinion polling. Now that parties' and candidates' use of this tool has become so widespread, the likelihood of critical elections occurring has diminished greatly, since a party has no excuse now to fall out of step with public opinion.[9] Consider, too, the level of information among the electorate about an election. In the past, realignment was primarily due to people not voting because they lacked information. Now, with the advent of television, with presidential debates commonly taking place, and with more investigative reporting, voters have much more information available to them, and hence realignment becomes less probable.[10]

Case Study: 1896

The McKinley-Bryan struggle illustrates the *converting election.* Republicans maintained their dominance, but underlying party coalitions changed dramatically. Some parts of the electorate, formerly Democratic supporters from rural areas, "dropped out" as they saw their political power erode and ceased voting as regularly for their party. Thus, the Democrats lost strength in one of their key constituencies.[11] At the same time, some urban blue-collar workers came to support the Republican party, out of fear of Bryan's—and the Democrats'—perceived lack of empathy with urban and industrial issues.[12] Thus, a shrinking of the electorate along with changes in party affinities produced a critical election.

Case Study: 1928–1936

1932 is looked at as the quintessential *realigning election.* Here, the majority Republicans were thrashed and became the minority party for many decades to come; party coalitions changed considerably, with urban areas, ethnics, and blacks moving predominantly into the Democratic Party.[13] However, the picture is not quite so clear. For one thing, 1928 (and even before) is when much of the realignment actually occurred.[14] For another, we find a combination of "mobilization" toward the Democratic party: (1) those not previously attached to either party, such as those just coming of voting age or those who had not voted before even though otherwise eligible to do so, and (2) "conversion," Republicans moving into the Democratic party permanently as well as vice versa.

One argument seems to make sense of the various data. Mobilization toward the Democratic party began in the mid-1920s, the culmination coming with Al Smith's unsuccessful run for the presidency as a Democrat in 1928. In 1932 and 1936, we find conversion becoming the dominant mechanism for change in the party universe. Thus, even though people often speak of the 1932 realignment, the process probably took place over more than a decade (perhaps meeting minimal requirements of a secular realignment), with different dynamics accounting for change in different elections.

Reflections on the Idea of Critical Elections

Some analysts believe that the whole idea of critical elections is not very fruitful, since there have been so few such elections. Indeed, much literature has focused on the emergence in 1932 of a new Democratic majority party, and some authors have used this as the basis for developing a complex theory of realignment. But this was just one election! Hence, although the concept of critical elections might be useful to sensitize people to sometimes dramatic changes in party dynamics, it probably should not be taken as seriously as it has been over time.[15]

Party in the Electorate

Party identification is one of the most important political orientations: it helps to shape candidate evaluation and actual voting behavior. Although it tends to be rather stable, there have been important changes from time to time, and the future of the party in the electorate is unclear.

Party System Support

One way of looking into the future of the party in the electorate is to consider the trends in people's support for a party system in the first place. Do people see parties as vital institutions that ensure responsive government? Or might they judge parties to be ineffective and actual causes of government problems? A study by Jack Dennis finds that the positive feelings of American citizens for their political party system declined greatly from the 1960s to about 1980. In the 1980s, people seemed to think that parties were not so bad after all. However, the level of approval of the party system was not up to what it was in the early 1960s (parties had recovered only about a third of their loss by 1984). Dennis believes that the more recent positive feelings toward the party system may be due to a change in the political atmosphere of the 1980s. He says that "the improved level of party system legitimation [that is, people's support for the party system] may also have something to do with the less politically traumatic 'era of good feelings' that has accompanied, in the public mind, the Reagan incumbency."[16] As long as the political arena featured approval of the Reagan administration and its successors, then positive feelings for the parties would be expected to at least continue or even to grow.

What has been the record with respect to Dennis's prediction since 1984? Later in the decade, while parties were surely not loathed by the American people, they had not recaptured their once great support, either.[17]

Party Identification

Central to the party in the electorate is party identification. If there were ever to be a hall of fame for questionnaire items, the Survey Research Center's indicator of partnership would be a charter member: "Generally speaking, do you usually consider yourself as a Republican, a Democrat, an Independent, or what?"

Basic trends are clear up to 1984. The number of Independents has increased dramatically—from 22 percent of those interviewed by the Survey Research Center in 1952 to 34 percent in 1984. The proportion of the electorate calling themselves Democrats (adding together weak and strong identifiers) has declined over time, from 47 percent in 1952 to 37 percent in 1984. Republican identification had been declining from 1952 to 1980, but it bounced back in 1984. The gap between Democrats and Republicans dwindled to 9 percent in 1984 (37 percent Democrats versus 28 percent Republicans), from 20 percent in 1952. By 1988, the gap had become 7 percent (35 percent Democrats as opposed to 28 percent Republicans).[18]

The increase in the number of Independents over time has been interpreted as implying that party has become less important to the electorate and as marking the decline of party significance. This may be a premature assessment. The number of Independents has been declining in the years since 1984. Also, the gap between the two parties in terms of how many citizens line up behind each has declined. The resurgence of the Republican party has signaled to some a realignment (to be discussed more extensively in a later section).

However, the increase in Independents over time may be illusory. A substantial proportion of those who call themselves Independent, when pressed by interviewers, will concede that they lean toward either the Republican or Democratic parties. These so-called independent leaders actually behave much like partisans; that is, Democratic leaners seem to behave pretty much like those people who call themselves Democrats without being prodded to do so.[19] From 1952 through 1960, an average of 8 percent of the electorate defined itself as pure Independent (not leaning one way or another); by 1990, that figure had risen to an eight-year average of 11 percent. From 1952 to 1960, Independent leaners averaged about 14 percent of the electorate; from 1984 to 1990, that figure had risen considerably—to 24 percent. Thus, the greatest increase in the number of Independent voters has been among the ranks of the leaners—who appear to be "closet" partisans in the first place.

What factors affect the proportion of Democrats versus Republicans in the electorate at large? First, economic conditions of the previous year and a half (ascertained by an index of consumer sentiment) are associated with "macropartisanship"; as consumer sentiment becomes more pessimistic, people begin shifting away from the party in power. Second, presidential approval plays a role. As support for the president increases, so, too, does support for the president's party, as people begin to shift toward it. However, people have short memories! Shifting of party support due to presidential approval reflects only the previous quarter's evaluations by the people. Thus, consumers' views of economic conditions have a longer-lasting, more enduring impact than presidential approval.[20]

Party Coalitions

The New Deal coalition was at the heart of Democratic partisan support for many decades. There is much talk about its disintegration today. Nonetheless, the traditional bases of party support continue to hold—even though they are much weakened. Robert Axelrod's analysis of coalition support shows that the most loyal supporters of the Democratic party are blacks, the poor, and residents of central cities. Catholics and southerners have become quite a bit less loyal over the past 30 years, and union loyalty has dropped somewhat. To compound the Democratic party's problems, its most tenacious supporters do not represent large proportions of the total population.[21]

In the meantime, Republicans win a majority of voters who are nonpoor, white, nonunion, Protestant, Northern, and non–central city. Moreover, there are substantial numbers of such people among the populace. In addition, Republicans are continuing to make inroads among white southerners. As Axelrod observed:

> The advantages for the Republicans and the problems for the Democrats are deeper than the personalities of their respective candidates in 1984,

and are reflections of basic trends cutting across the traditional cleavages in the American population.[22]

Party Leaders and Followers

In 1957 and 1958, party leaders (about 3200 delegates from the Republican and Democratic national party conventions) and followers (almost 1500 American citizens) filled out questionnaires addressing the extent to which leaders and the rank-and-file party members shared political views. Leaders clearly differed, suggesting that there was a real distinction in the parties' perspectives. On issue after issue, Republican leaders were more conservative and Democratic leaders were more liberal. On the other hand, the followers tended to be more similar and lacked the striking differences found in the comparison of leaders. The Republican rank and file was actually closer to the Democratic leaders than to the Republican leaders, indicating that the Democratic leadership was more in tune with the mass party loyalists.[23]

In 1972 and 1976, the tides of public opinion had shifted, and now the rank and file of both parties tended to be nearer the Republican than the Democratic leadership. This may be saying that in the 1970s the Democratic leadership was losing touch with its rank-and-file party identifiers.[24]

In 1980, another study was carried out. Party leaders were defined as a sample of delegates to the two parties' 1980 presidential conventions, county chairs, state party chairs, and members of the Republican and Democratic National Committees. Citizens' views were ascertained by responses in several national surveys completed in 1980. This time, Democratic leaders ranked from moderate (county chairs) to liberal (the most liberal were delegates to the convention), whereas Republican leaders were quite homogeneous—and conservative. The mass identifiers also were different from one another, with more liberals and moderates in the Democratic ranks and more conservatives dominating the Republican rank and file. Even among Democratic identifiers, though, 42 percent called themselves conservative. At the party elite level, there were marked differences between the competing parties.

Among the masses, neither set of party leaders was clearly representative of the partisan identifiers. On social issues (such as the Equal Rights Amendment), both Republican and Democratic identifiers were much closer to the Democratic than the Republican leadership. On economic issues (cutting government spending and services), a fairly straightforward pattern emerged. Republican elites were more conservative, then came the Republican identifiers, then the Democratic identifiers, and, finally, the Democratic leaders as least conservative (actually, as liberal). Generally, Democratic followers were closer to their leaders than Republican followers were to their party elites. With defense expenditures, Republican leaders and followers were very similar, and Democratic identifiers were much closer to Republican leaders than to Democratic ones.[25] Analogous findings come from a comparison of nominating convention delegates and the electorate as a whole in 1988.[26]

What does all this mean? It seems that the two parties' elites have become more distinct over time, often teetering on the edge of losing touch with their constituents. Perhaps this is why Michael Dukakis, despite some advantages over George Bush, lost in 1988; he may not have been perceived as in the mainstream as a result of Bush's election campaign. And, in 1992, Bill Clinton was seen by Democrats as moderate, thus positioning himself more closely to the center of the Democratic rank and file.

The Republican party has come back from the brink of being a noncompetitive party to approaching parity with the Democrats. The old Democratic New Deal coalition is fraying. This package of changes may portend a major change in partisan politics—or it may not. This issue deserves fuller attention and will be discussed later in this chapter.

Party Organization

The Party Organization

On paper, the party organization for Democrats and Republicans is impressive. The foot soldier at the base of local organization is the precinct captain or committeeperson. This person's role is to get out the vote for the party on election day, although many really do very little. The next layer is likely to be the town or village committee (in rural areas) or the city or ward committee (in urban areas). Next is the county central committee, headed by the county chair. The county chair is normally the most important local political official, responsible for campaign strategy, fund-raising, and the dispensing of patronage (non–civil service jobs given to loyal party supporters).

The state party committee membership is selected from districts throughout the state (for example, congressional districts or counties). Normally, the state committee selects a state chair who is largely responsible for the ongoing work of the state party.

At the apex of this party pyramid is the national party committee. Members are selected to represent the various states. The national committee selects a national party chair, who, with his or her staff, administers party business on a day-to-day basis. Normally, the president handpicks a party chair who is routinely approved by the national committee. The presidential candidates in election years designate who the national chair will be. When a party loses the presidential race, its committee has a freer hand in selecting a chair later on.

The Decline of Party Organization

Despite having what look like well-defined organizational structures, the parties' organizations have often been described as weak and fragmented. Local parties can have much autonomy from their state central committee, and state and local organizations are not normally "under the thumb" of their national committees.

The most common view is that state and local party organizations are weaker than they used to be—and that the national organization has generally never been very powerful. The decline of state and local organization is due to several factors. One is the use of primary elections to select party candidates for office. This effectively removes the party's control over nominations for elective office, and as a result, those who are elected end up being less beholden to the party organization. One can now be nominated for and elected to office with little or no help from the party organization. Candidates use the media and their own set of supporters to win votes in the primary election; then they can use the same strategy to win office. Consequently, the party in government (elected officials and candidates) is often independent of the party organization.

Another blow to state and local organizations has been the increasing number of jobs under civil service protection. With fewer patronage jobs available to reward party loyalists, the ability of the party organizations to maintain a loyal cadre of workers is reduced.

Finally, at the local level, many positions are unfilled, especially at the precinct level. Moreover, many party workers are quite inactive. This means that rather few people are going to be doing any party work.

Party Organization Resurgence?

The prevailing picture of party organization is rather bleak. However, recent evidence suggests that party organizations may be reviving at all levels—local, state, and national.

Local Parties

One survey of county chairs throughout the United States reports that from 1964 to 1980 county parties were doing more in a number of areas. The local organizations became more active in raising money, distributing campaign literature, arranging political events, and sponsoring registration drives. Both the Republican and Democratic parties have become organizationally stronger at the local level. The local parties are still not well-oiled machines, though. There is minimal staffing and not a great deal of budgetary support; often there is even no permanent party headquarters.[27]

State Parties

When state organizations are compared from the 1950s and 1960s up to 1980, similar evidence for stronger parties emerges. Most states have developed a permanent headquarters with full-time leadership and a more professional staff. Party budgets have increased dramatically, and as one consequence, state organizations sponsor many more programs. Some of these focus on elections, such as helping to fund candidates' campaigns, providing services to candidates (for example, polls), and recruiting candidates to run for office. State organizations also have increased organization-building activities. They sponsor polls, publish newsletters, and work on developing party issue positions.[28] While both Republican and Democratic state party organizations got stronger up until 1970, improvements in Democratic organizations ceased about then. Meanwhile, Republican state organizations have continued their revitalization into the 1980s.

National Parties

The national committees, especially the Republicans, are playing larger roles.[29] In addition to the Republican National Committee, both the Senate and the House Republican Campaign Committees have been active. For instance, in the 1980 elections these three committees raised $100 million. They cooperated with one another in gaining these funds and in spending them. These organizations provided campaign contributions to candidates for national and state offices. The committees used something of a "triage" model, providing support for candidates who needed it and who had a chance to win. Less support went to sure winners and sure losers. In the long run, this might make the party in government more beholden to the Republican party organization. The Republican committees also organized a national advertising campaign on behalf of Republican candidates ("Vote Republican for a change"), sponsored get-out-the-vote drives for the local party organizations, and organized fund-raising activities to help state party organizations.

The Democrats have lagged greatly behind the Republicans at the national party level, even though the gap has narrowed.[30] They have been able to raise less money and provide fewer services to Democratic candidates and state and local party organizations.

The Electoral Impact of Party Organization

A party organization working to get its voters to turn out in an election makes a real difference. One study found that activities by party organizations accounted for about 7 percent of the vote in selected statewide and national elections in 1984.[31] Other research suggests that vigorous efforts by a local party organization can affect between 4 percent and 20 percent of the votes cast for different offices.[32] Thus the strength and vitality of state and local party organizations can have a significant impact on election outcomes.

Party in Government

The party in government is the set of public officials elected under a party's banner and the influence of the party on these officials' behavior. The trend in the party in government over the past several decades is increased strength, largely at the expense of the party organization.

Some scholars decry the greater independence of the party in government from the party organization. Many would prefer a model of government referred to as responsible parties or party government. Political party organizations would develop a comprehensive set of issue positions (perhaps guided by an overarching ideological framework). They would insist that the candidates they sponsor for office work to advance their programs once elected. The party organization would discipline those who broke rank, thus ensuring cohesiveness (that is, members of the party in government voting together).

Advocates of responsible parties believe that this system, if put into operation, would make government decision making more principled, since legislators' votes, for example, would be determined by a coherent ideological framework. Interest-group lobbying or the need to curry favor with constituents by devoting great amounts of time to running errands for the folks back home (such as investigating why a person's social security check did not arrive on time) would be less influential. This would add an element of rationality to the policy process and would render government much more likely to enact policies in accord with the majority's wishes.

This situation, obviously, does not exist in the United States. On roll-call votes in the Senate and the House of Representatives, many legislators break from their party's position. The parties tend to advance an array of policy positions designed to appeal to heterogeneous groups within their coalition. This can lead to an incoherent program, as different promises are made to different groups with little regard for how well they fit together as a package.

And, of course, elected officials are relatively independent of their party organization. Many build their own campaign organizations apart from the official party organization. The new style of campaigning describes the increasingly typical way of getting elected. Candidates have their own set of campaign workers who are loyal to them and not necessarily to the party organization. Candidates can generate their own campaign funds and are not particularly dependent upon funds from the party, making those running for office less beholden to the party organization. Increasingly, campaigns are media-oriented, with professional consultants working with candidates to get them elected, all apart from the party machinery. In the end, the party in government cannot be effectively guided by the party organization.

This is even more the case for incumbents (elected persons already in office) who desire reelection. Incumbents engage in errand-running activities for their constituents (such as trying to take care of people's problems with government and bringing federal money into their districts). This leads the voters to reward the incumbents by supporting them in the next election. Once more, elected officials can build a base of support independent of the party organization.

Still, party is an important factor in the public lives of elected officials. The best way to predict how a member of Congress will vote on a bill is still his or her party affiliation. Since 1968, the extent of party cohesion (a majority of Democrats voting against a majority of Republicans) has risen in Congress.[33] This may signal an enhanced role of party in decision making in the national legislature. One need only note the Senate and House Republicans' remarkable unity in opposing the budget proposals advanced by President Bill Clinton in 1993. As well, party members align strongly together within committees in their votes, with some slight strengthening of party loyalty evident in recent years.[34] And, as noted earlier, party leadership in the House of Representatives is much stronger than it was two decades ago. Even federal judges' decisions are related to their party background.

Thus, although the party in government is hardly controlled by the party organization, as supporters of the responsible-party view would like, party is a key consideration in the behavior of elected officials. This at least says that party continues to play a role for government leaders.

Toward Party Realignment?

1964 and 1968 as Possible Realigning Years

Some claim that 1964 (or even 1968) was a critical election year in the United States, one in which race was the issue restructuring political coalitions. The logic for this contention can be outlined thus:[35]

1. From the 1940s until 1964, Republicans were more moderate and Democrats were more conservative in House of Representatives and Senate votes on civil rights bills. After 1964, Democrats in Congress became more moderate to liberal than Republicans.

2. Voters accurately perceived this change.

3. After 1964, new Republican identifiers became more conservative and new Democrats more liberal on racial issues.

This response by voters to changes in congressional behavior could help to explain the defection from the Democrats of blue-collar workers and southern whites, since both groups are more conservative on racial issues. This seems to be part of a two-stage process. First, southern whites came to see themselves as less Democratic (party identification as a Democrat weakens, fewer vote for Democratic presidential candidates, support of Republican candidates in subpresidential races increases). This is dealignment, where party becomes less relevant and important as a guide for the citizenry. A major reason for this change was the rapid loss of Democratic identification in young southern white voters (much of which occurred between 1964 and 1968). However, Democratic identification has weakened among older voters as well. Thus, this first stage involves weakening of Democratic party bonds in the south.

In the second stage, southern whites shifted toward Republican identification. In 1980 and 1981, for instance, dramatic shifts toward the Republican party occurred among whites in Florida. The key group, once more, was younger voters, with some older conservative/segregationist Democrats joining the rush.

In addition, many white southerners seem to carry a kind of dual identification. They see themselves as Republicans in national elections (presidential and congressional) and as Democrats in state and local elections. This dual identification began in earnest in 1964.

Performance-Based Voting

Thus, 1964 to 1968 were important elections. Race was an important part of the answer as to why change has occurred. So too was dissatisfaction with Democratic presidential performance. However, there is disagreement over what these findings mean. First, recall the earlier discussion which concluded by noting that some analysts do not believe that the concept of realignment or critical elections means very much. Second, party loyalties have been generally weakening. Martin Wattenberg refers to the alleged realignment as "hollow."[36] Evidence suggests that much of the gain in Republican identification was performance-based, a function of Ronald Reagan's success as president. Note that in 1992 George Bush, saddled with voters' perceptions that he was not a particularly skillful president, found voters deserting him and swinging toward Bill Clinton.

Political parties are becoming less salient and less important to voters. In an increasingly candidate-centered age, party does not have the same value as a cue for the electorate as it used to. Furthermore, the greatest shift from Democratic to Republican identification seems to be centered in the least educated, the least interested, and the least informed politically and, consequently, the most volatile in their views.[37] Results of the 1988 and 1992 elections further suggests the importance of performance-based voting, as we shall see in Chapter 6.

The Role of the Media

The media play a significant role in the declining relevance of party. Because media campaigns are often undertaken by candidates these days, party is becoming less important to aspirants for elective office. Data gathered during the 1978 congressional elections indicate that as media spending increases, party becomes less salient to the voters and the candidates themselves become more so. Candidates are becoming electoral entrepreneurs working for themselves and seeing party as secondary.

Media affect voters' behavior in other ways. Many people view television as the most trustworthy and dependable source of news. Unfortunately, reliance on television as a news source limits viewers' ability to distinguish candidates' positions, and, hence, leads to a reduction in voter turnout rates, since those who cannot see differences between candidates are less likely to vote. The lower levels of interest and information associated with television dependence are reducing the ability of Americans to judge parties and candidates. This, in turn, may render the electorate more volatile.

Future election outcomes may depend more on the short-term forces of candidate evaluation and specific issues than on the long-term force of party identification. Wattenberg notes:

> Even if the Republican surge is a long-lasting one, it will be of limited importance as long as partisanship in the electorate continues to decline. . . . The candidate-centered age will be with us for a long time to come, regardless of whether the next political era will be a Democratic or Republican one.[38]

Divided Government

Earlier, the concept of responsible-party government was discussed. Underlying this is the assumption that one party controls all branches of government. However, it is manifestly clear that divided government is the nature of the current party system. Since 1952, the Republicans have usually controlled the presidency and the Democrats Congress. In the 20 national elections since then (presidential elections plus midterm congressional elections), 7 have resulted in unified government and 13 in divided party control. In 1992, the country returned, at least temporarily, to unified government. But this rather rare unity is unlikely to continue unless voters see President Clinton as successful.

Furthermore, state government is divided, with one party having the governorship and the other a majority in one or the other state legislative houses. From 1946 to 1990, the percentage of unified state governments (both houses plus the governorship in one party's hands) has declined from 85 percent to just under 45 percent. Another symbol of divided government is the common occurrence of one U.S. Senator from a state being Republican and the other a Democrat. In 1946, about 30 percent of the states had a split-party Senate delegation; in 1990, that figure was almost 45 percent.[39] Why have these changes come about, and what do they mean? Chapter 6 discusses this in somewhat greater depth.

Democratic theorists emphasize the linkage function of parties and note how party helps to organize alternatives for voters to facilitate their choice on election day. A plurality of the electorate selects its leaders, who, in turn, reflect the basic party views approved by voters. This should lead to policies broadly reflective of the public's preferences.

Elitists would counter that there is little difference between the parties ("tweedledum-tweedledee") and that both parties are firmly in the mainstream liberal tradition, offering little meaningful choice to voters. Further, both parties are beholden to major powerful interests for financing. In the end, parties dance as the strings are pulled by elite puppeteers.

Pluralists contend that each party is composed of a coalition of interests. Much bargaining and negotiation take place among them to produce party positions that give each of the various constituent groups something of value. In this way, the interests of a multitude of people are taken into account by the parties' desire to gain backing.

Recommended Reading

Paul Allen Beck and Frank Sorauf: *Party Politics in America,* 7th ed., HarperCollins, New York, 1992.

John F. Bibby: *Politics, Parties, and Elections in America,* 2d ed., Nelson-Hall, Chicago, 1992.

Walter Dean Burnham: *Critical Elections and the Mainsprings of American Politics,* Norton, New York, 1970.

Everett Carll Ladd, Jr.: *American Political Parties,* Norton, New York, 1970.

Martin P. Wattenberg: *The Decline of American Political Parties,* 2d ed., Harvard University Press, Cambridge, Mass., 1986.

CHAPTER 6

Voting and Elections

If there is any single institution that both scholars and the mass population consider central for democracy it is elections. The United States has a near mania for them; it is unlikely that any other country has so many. Not only do Americans have the opportunity to elect officials to numerous offices at all levels of government, in some states they can also take part in a special type of election known as a recall, *to remove elected officials from office. In addition, some states provide for* initiative; *if enough signatures are obtained by petition, that issue can be put on a ballot. Once the proposal is on the ballot, the citizens will have the chance to vote for or against it in a* referendum. *The referendum allows citizens to make laws directly.*

The ideal civics textbook model of a citizen is the issue-oriented voter. This person examines the positions of competing candidates on the issues of the day and then votes for the one closest to his or her own views. Most political scientists do not believe that this accurately describes American voters. Weighing against this characterization, they point out, are citizens' low levels of political information, the importance of a person's habitual party identification, and the relative lack of interest in politics.

This chapter examines the structure of elections and the nature of the electorate, presidential and congressional election politics, and some basic issues involved with the American electoral process. The final section considers what elections can say about where power lies in the United States.

The Electorate

Changes in the Electorate

Over time, the American electorate has expanded greatly. In the early years of the republic, adult white men were the eligible electorate; some free black men in northern states were also able to vote. Property requirements in some states further reduced the franchise. In the early third of the nineteenth century, property requirements were loosened, increasing further the right to vote.

The Fifteenth Amendment to the Constitution, approved in 1870, specifically granted the franchise to recently freed black slaves. Some decades after this, southern states moved to restrict blacks from voting, using methods ranging from beatings to literacy tests. Over time, though, the Supreme Court and, later, Congress took initiatives to restore the constitutional right of blacks to vote. The Voting Rights Acts of 1965 had a particularly dramatic effect on black voter turnout in the South. This law called for U.S. government registrars to enter counties with a persistent record of thwarting black voters to register blacks. Shortly after the act went into effect, black voter turnout rates jumped significantly.

Although some states allowed women to vote, it was only in 1920, with the passage of the Nineteenth Amendment, that American women as a group were empowered to vote. This further expanded the size of the electorate. Finally, in 1971, the Twenty-sixth Amendment lowered the voting age to 18.

Who Votes?

Considerable data have been generated to describe the types of people most likely to vote in general elections. Major forces shaping likelihood of voting are education, income, age, government employment, region, and minority status.

Those with more years of education participate in elections at a noticeably higher rate, as do the wealthier. Age has a less clear-cut impact. Looking at the simple relationship between age and voting, we find that turnout goes up until the sixties and drops off thereafter. If, however, we take into account the fact that older Americans are less educated, then the statistics show that turnout rates continue to increase until people enter their late seventies.

Government employees are quite a bit more likely to vote than people in other lines of work, perhaps because their jobs may be at stake. People living in the South vote at lower rates than people elsewhere in the United States.

Minorities, including blacks and Hispanics, turn out less in general elections. Currently, there is no difference in voting rates between men and women.[1]

People's political views have a modest impact on turnout rates, even when education and income are taken into account. Republicans are somewhat more likely to vote than Democrats; conservatives or liberals are more likely to vote than moderates. Generally, on their basic political positions, those who vote are similar to the entire population. There is no particular bias.

Recent Trends in Voter Turnout

Turnout rate in presidential elections declined markedly from 1960 to 1988, from about 63 percent to about 50 percent. In 1992, that figure rebounded to 55 percent. Why did turnout decrease steadily only to rise somewhat in 1992? One argument has it that the decline is primarily due to the failure to vote of low-income whites, who have been dropping out of the electorate faster than those who are financially better off. Howard Reiter contends that the poor are turned off or alienated from politics, believing that the system is not responsive to them.[2] However, this does not appear to be the major factor in turnout decline.

Another perspective points to the effects of two factors—the declining strength of party identification and lowered feelings of political efficacy.[3] The stronger one's partisan support, the more likely one is to vote. As Americans' identification with the parties weakened throughout the 1960s and 1970s, so, too, did their turnout. This accounts for about one-quarter of the decline in voting rates. In addition, the belief among Americans that government would respond to them declined. As this aspect of political efficacy declined, so did turnout. If you do not think that government will respond to you, why vote? This trend explains about one-half the decline in presidential election turnout over a 20-year period.

These explanations of the 1960 to 1988 voter turnout decline are in terms of an individual's likelihood to vote. Several characteristics of elections themselves are important in shaping overall turnout rates. First among these is the type of election. Presidential elections produce the highest turnout of all, doubtless because of the extensive media coverage and attendant interest generated. Midterm congressional elections tend to run about 10 percent lower in turnout rates. Primaries lead to the lowest turnout.

Second, if competition between the candidates is great, more people vote. If, on the other hand, one candidate is a runaway leader, turnout tends to drop. Third, registration laws have an impact. Some states make it easier to register to vote than others. For instance, in those states with evening and weekend hours and minimal residency requirements (the amount of time one has to reside in an election district before becoming eligible to vote), larger proportions of citizens actually vote.

A fourth element is the effort of parties and groups to mobilize voters to participate in elections. For instance, from 1956 through 1988, if a party contacted a voter, that increased the odds of that person turning out by about 8 percent.[4]

Evidence indicates that the bulk of the decline in turnout from the 1960s through 1988—about 90 percent of the 11 percent drop—can be accounted for by lower "mobilization" as parties and groups put less emphasis on getting out the vote and presidential elections became less competitive. Other factors contributing to the decline were a younger electorate, weakened social involvement, declining sense of political efficacy, and loosened bonds with the political parties. Easing of voter registration and increasing educational levels worked to increase turnout, but their effects were swamped by those contributing to the decline.

Why the rebound in 1992? Mobilization seems important. The race for president was competitive—with the added spice of a popular third-party candidate in Ross Perot. Also, the parties and groups appeared to put extra emphasis on getting people to vote. Finally, of course, voters seemed to care about the election, with change as the mantra in many people's minds.

The Structure of Elections

The path to elected office has two central obstacles—getting nominated and getting elected.

Getting Nominated

Before getting elected to office, one must become a candidate. This ordinarily means having to win a political party's nomination. Normally, incumbents are nominated with little opposition. If no incumbent is interested in the nomination, then the struggle to get the party's label for the general election is more spirited.

The Primary

The basic method for nominating candidates is the primary. A primary is a type of election in which voters select one from among all contenders for a nomination. The primary has weakened the party organization, since a candidate can gain nomination under a party label if he or she garners enough votes in the primary. Consequently, one can become a party's nominee without the party organization's support. This renders candidates less beholden to the organization.

The primary began as a reform to "democratize" the nomination process around the turn of the century. However, relatively few voters turn out, and those who do are not necessarily typical of party supporters as a whole. Other problems may crop up, too. Candidates hostile to a party's positions may get nominated under the party banner; primaries may produce candidates who can get the support of nonrepresentative primary voters but who are unpopular with the general rank and file; primary contests between candidates may be so heated that the party's chances of winning the general election decline as bitterness remains. This type of nasty contest is called a divisive primary.

Getting Elected

The Campaign

Once a person is nominated for office, he or she campaigns to gain enough support to win the general election. Campaigns can be exciting, with debates, flashy advertising, speeches, and parades. However, as a rule, campaigns do not convert voters, that is, influence them to change their candidate preference. They are more likely to reinforce people's preexisting preferences or activate people who may have been thinking about supporting the candidate into actually doing so.

Rules of the Election Game

On election day, citizens troop to the polls to cast their vote, using the Australian (secret) ballot.

Single-Member Districts. The elections for the national legislature in the United States feature single-member districts, in which one person is elected from a particular district. This technique of selecting representatives strongly militates against success by a third party,[5] as discussed in Chapter 5.

One Person, One Vote. Another important rule of the election game is "one person, one vote." In *Wesberry v. Sanders* (1964), the U.S. Supreme Court decided that the number of voters in different congressional districts in a state ought to be as equal as possible. This means that each person's vote has the same weight as that of each person in other districts. Prior to this decision, there could be, for instance, 100,000 people in one district and 50,000 in another in the same state. An individual's vote in the second district would be worth twice that of a person in the first district.

Gerrymandering.   Nonetheless, parties can still try to draw district lines in such a way as to benefit their candidates. According to the Constitution, the states define district boundaries for seats in the U.S. House of Representatives. After a census, these boundaries may have to be redrawn to comport with the "one person, one vote" rule. If a party controls both houses of the legislature and the governorship, its officials might construct districts in such a way as to benefit candidates of that party. Such a practice is called gerrrymandering. For example, if a Democratic incumbent were in a "marginal" district (one in which his or her margin of victory was habitually low) and the state's officials were mainly Democrats, then the state legislature might add to the district an area from a neighboring district that is heavily Democratic and move a Republican area to another district. The House member would now be in a safe district. There are limitations on gerrymandering—drawing district lines for partisan gain—but a resourceful legislature can benefit one party, although the impact is often overestimated.[6] Currently, gerrymandering on a partisan basis is mostly designed to help incumbents (an incumbent-protection policy).

Occasionally, one finds strange bedfellows in the battle over gerrymandering. After the 1980 census, the Republican National Committee supported a suit brought by Indiana Democrats against Indiana Republicans for improperly redistricting; simultaneously, the Republicans brought suit in California against the Democrats for precisely the same reason. In the court battle, the California Republicans and Indiana Democrats were, in effect, allied against the Indiana Republicans and California Democrats.

The "New Style" in Campaigning

At one time, the party organization was the central actor in campaigns. The party workers would canvass their precincts, wards, and neighborhoods to get out the vote on behalf of the party's candidates. In return, the candidates who won would be beholden to the party organization.

Such is no longer the case. In the "new style" of campaigning, which began in the 1960s, the focus is on the candidate, *not* the party. The candidate is a kind of electoral entrepreneur, creating his or her own organization and generating his or her own support—perhaps completely independent of the party organization under whose banner the candidate is running. In a real sense, candidates now rent a campaign. They hire professional campaign consultants, public relations experts, media specialists, pollsters, and advertising people. An entire industry of campaign consultants awaits, eager and willing to be hired by candidates.

The campaign is based on marketing concepts, just as are efforts to sell cereal, deodorants, or panty hose. Researchers conduct polls to determine prospective voters' interests, what voters want in a candidate, and how citizens evaluate different candidates. Then, a campaign is tailored to the specific "market" identified by the research. The media become the most important carriers of candidates' messages in the new style—not the party faithful as before.

The new style has been defended as a more efficient way of getting information to the voters. Some claim that it enhances democracy by forging tighter links between voters and candidates. The people running for office try to find out the voters' concerns and then address those concerns. In this sense, linkage is strengthened.

However, there are problems. For one thing, the new style is expensive (for example, buying television time quickly gobbles up huge chunks of campaign funds). For another, it may, as some critics fear, lead to a cynical packaging of candidates, with little care for getting the voters to know the real person behind the candidate. In the end, the new style may be decried as manipulative. It seems clear that the party organization has suffered considerably at the hands of the new style. What the party can provide is less valued now, so candidates invest less energy in supporting that organization.

Presidential Elections

Presidential elections feature three key steps: party nomination, the campaign for votes in the general election, and the electoral college.

Party Nominations: Primaries, Caucuses, and Conventions

To get the nomination, technically, a presidential candidate must win a majority of delegates at the presidential nominating convention convening the summer before the general elections (the election itself is held on the first Tuesday after the first Monday in November). Each state is allotted a set of delegates to vote for presidential candidates (the formula is different for Republicans and Democrats).

The two means by which delegates are selected in the state are the primary and the caucus.

Primaries

Those states with primaries provide for citizens to vote in a party primary for one candidate or another (the method by which this is done varies considerably across primary states). Normally, a person must be a registered voter of one of the parties to vote in its primary—the closed primary—although other states allow a person to vote in either party's primary—the open or blanket primary. The votes are tallied and delegates are allocated from the state to the different candidates.

One question is how democratic the primaries actually are. A variety of evidence indicates that turnout is lower in primaries than in the general election. In 1976, about 29 percent of the voting-age population voted in primaries, whereas about 54 percent of the eligible electorate turned out for the Carter-Ford election. Data from other years show that turnout rates in primaries are only about half of those for the actual election.

Furthermore, primary voters are somewhat atypical of the rank and file in general. Those who take part in primaries tend to be middle- and upper-income citizens, more educated, and more strongly attached to their party. Scholars once thought that those who voted in primaries are more strongly liberal or strongly conservative and are more motivated to vote than moderates or slightly liberal or conservative people. That is, Republican candidates would have to appeal to the conservative population and Democratic candidates to liberal constituents, all of which would have distorted the nomination process by underweighing the moderate elements of both parties.[7] However, more recent evidence indicates that there are no significant ideological differences between primary voters and rank-and-file party members.[8]

Caucuses

Caucuses provide a second mechanism for selecting delegates. One common approach is this: (1) party members meet at the local or precinct level to select delegates to a county convention; (2) a county convention selects delegates to a state convention; (3) the state delegation selects delegates to the national nominating convention.

The key for a candidate to do well in caucus states is to have his or her supporters turn out at the local level to ensure that delegates supporting the candidate are selected to the county convention. A good organization is necessary to get out the voters at the local level.

Participants at local-level caucuses are unrepresentative of the parties' rank and file. In 1976, only about 2 percent of the eligible electorate took part in the caucuses. Those who are involved are more likely to be middle- or upper-class, strongly partisan, and very ideological.[9]

Democratic "Superdelegates"

In 1982, the Democratic party added a new wrinkle to the presidential selection process—the addition of "superdelegates" to the convention roster. Among these superdelegates, allocated to the different states, are governors, big-city mayors, members of Congress, and state party chairs. These people will act as unpledged delegates at the convention, although they may well in actual fact be committed to one candidate or another. In 1984, the superdelegates went predominantly for Walter Mondale, turning a rather narrow victory in primaries and caucuses into a convincing victory in the convention. Thus, it now seems possible—although probably not very likely—for a candidate to win the nomination who receives fewer delegates via caucuses and primaries but wins the great bulk of the superdelegates,[10] although normally the outcome has been decided by the primary and caucus routes well before the convention.

The Nominating Convention

The convention itself has less significance than it used to in carrying out its primary function—selecting a presidential candidate. Now a majority of delegates normally are pledged to a single candidate before the conventions begin. The conventions are not without value, though. The two parties get considerable free media coverage because networks and newspapers define conventions as news.

The Political Campaign: Presidential and Congressional

The Campaign Organization

Once the parties' candidates are named for the presidency or for Congress, the campaign begins in earnest. The employment of a solid campaign organization is crucial. Key personnel might include a campaign manager, who helps organize and carry out an overall campaign strategy; a fund raiser, who gathers funds on a full-time basis; a lawyer, who advises the campaign on what is demanded by the complex campaign finance laws; consultants, such as media advisors, pollsters, and public relations experts, who provide advice for devising and carrying out a successful campaign strategy; an advance person, who makes arrangements so that candidates get to where they are supposed to be; and the general staff, including policy advisors and researchers who help candidates come up with concrete policy proposals and can "dig up dirt" on opponents and their positions.

Campaign Expenditures

Campaigns cost money—and the new style of campaigning with its emphasis on media has a voracious appetite. Campaign expenditures have increased faster than inflation in recent years. To prevent abuses in raising money for campaigns, Congress passed the Federal Election Campaign Act of 1971 and several amendments thereafter, with the 1974 amendments being the most central. This act includes the following provisions:

1. *Disclosure reports.* Candidates and campaign committees must file detailed reports outlining sources of funds and where money is spent.

2. *A presidential campaign fund.* Taxpayers check a box on their income tax returns if they wish to have $3 of their taxes go into a general campaign fund to be allocated among eligible presidential candidates.

3. *Federal funding of presidential campaigns.* Candidates can receive money from the campaign fund, up to 50 percent of their expenses in prenomination campaigning and 100 percent for the general election. In return, candidates must limit total spending to a certain amount stipulated by the law. Candidates who do not use federal funds may spend unlimited amounts.

4. *Creation of a Federal Election Commission.* This body oversees the law to make sure that its requirements are observed by the candidates.

5. *Approving the creation of political action committees (PACs).* Previous laws prohibited corporations and unions from directly contributing money to campaigns. Now, such organizations can create PACs to raise and disburse funds to parties and candidates.

The results of the reform laws are fairly clear. Greater monitoring of where candidates get money and how they spend it reduces the odds of corruption, since all monies have to be accounted for. The reforms have slowed the increase in spending on presidential elections. Finally, and most unexpectedly, PACs have exploded in number. Many more organizations and groups formed PACs than had been anticipated, and they now provide a major portion of campaign contributions, a fact which has led to much controversy.

Do campaign contributions affect government officials' decisions? One study suggests that PACs can influence roll-call votes of U.S. representatives.[11] Members of the House who received contributions from PACs tended to become more supportive of PACs' positions on legislation. The effect was most pronounced for those who had been relatively neutral before. It is not proper to infer that the votes were bought, however. What probably happened was that the PACs "bought" access to the legislator, who, out of courtesy to a supporter, allowed PAC representatives to make their case directly to him or her. Information can be persuasive; hence, this access increases the chances of a member of Congress coming to support the group. One factor diminishing the impact of contributions was that PACs generally supported those who already voted for their interests rather than those who were neutral. Significantly, the great bulk of contributions went to incumbents.

Moneyed interests may also influence Congress in other ways. For instance, it appears that interest-group lobbying may affect committee work by members of Congress more than do the voters themselves.[12]

Media and Campaigns

Media, including advertising, newspaper endorsements, and televised debates, are important forces in elections.

Advertising. Generally, ads reinforce preexisting preferences; few people change their minds because of advertising. This is especially so in presidential elections. More important, advertisements may provide potential voters with knowledge about the candidates. In fact, Thomas Patterson and Robert McClure found that televised presidential ads gave more information on issue positions to voters than did television newscasts.[13] The latter tends to focus on the "horse race" aspects of elections and ignore issues and candidate qualifications. Television ads may even help diminish the knowledge gap between the most and least informed voters.

In congressional elections, television advertising also has an important role to play. The more that people are exposed to ads, the greater is their knowledge of the candidate being "sold," the greater is their interest in the campaign, and the more likely they are to come to like the candidate being advertised. Candidate advertising also helps set the election agenda; issues emphasized in commercials tend to be issues voters come to deem as most important. Incumbents can spend more money on television advertising; hence they receive a further advantage over challengers. Ads have greater impact if they are repeated often and are entertaining. However, last-minute television programs paid for by parties or candidates affect more voters' choices. Tactically, then, a last-minute television blitz in a close election can make a difference.[14]

Media Endorsements. Normally, the Republican candidates for president receive more newspaper endorsements than Democratic candidates. The candidate being endorsed receives a modest boost in support (although if competition exists in a newspaper market and different papers endorse different candidates, there is no net change). In congressional elections, endorsements affect the vote indirectly, by raising a candidate's name recognition. Since to know a candidate is to like him or her, endorsements translate into votes.[15]

Televised Debates. Six presidential campaigns have featured televised debates—1960, 1976, 1980, 1984, 1988, and 1992. While the debates may not change the course of an election, they do have an impact on voters.

1. Debates may enhance or diminish candidates' images. John F. Kennedy no longer was seen as too young and inexperienced in 1960; Ronald Reagan's performance in 1980 helped dispel the notion that he could not keep facts straight; Michael Dukakis's dispassionate rendering

of what he would do if his wife were murdered hurt his image in the 1988 election; Bill Clinton came across as the overall debate winner in 1992, dispelling some doubts that people had about him.

2. Debates can yield higher information levels. Studies of the 1976 and 1984 debates conclude that viewers learned more about the candidates and had a clearer sense of the differences between them. Debates also seem to stimulate political discussion, as they did in 1960.

Not surprisingly, viewing debates diminishes the knowledge gap between the most and least informed citizens. Those who followed politics least in 1976 gained the greatest amount of information about the candidates; those who read papers regularly and already had elevated levels of information learned much less.

Data suggest that the major effects on voters' choices are reinforcement and activation; little conversion takes place.[16]

People's preexisting candidate preferences shape their judgments of who won or lost a debate. For instance, in 1980, individuals believed that their preferred candidate won.[17] An exception to this is 1984's first debate. Ronald Reagan did very badly, as even his supporters recognized. Nonetheless, voter preferences remained relatively unchanged.

The Electoral College

In presidential elections, voters do not directly elect the winner. Rather, their votes select electors, who, in turn, select the president. Each state is allotted a set of electors equal to the number of senators (2) plus the number of representatives from that state. The largest states consequently have the greatest weight, with California holding the most (54). Lightly populated Alaska and Wyoming have 3 electoral votes each. The Twelfth Amendment to the Constitution details the process. Electors meet in their home state and note their votes for president and vice president. Since selection of electors is on a winner-take-all basis, the electors' vote from the state is unanimous. The results are sent to Washington, where the president of the Senate counts the electoral votes. Whichever slate wins a majority is named the winner.

What if there is no majority? The House of Representatives steps in to choose a president. Each state casts one vote, so its delegation meets to decide for whom to cast that state's vote. The candidate who gets a majority (26) of all the states becomes president. A similar process works in the case of a vice president, except that here the Senate selects the winner. Each senator casts his or her vote, and the person receiving the majority (51) of all senators' support becomes vice president.

Today a candidate must receive 270 electoral votes to gain the necessary majority. The last time an election went to the House of Representatives was 1824, when John Quincy Adams defeated Andrew Jackson. Close contests in 1960, 1968, and 1976 led some to fear that there would be no clear victor in the electoral college; however, in each of those elections a majority emerged for the winning candidate.

For presidential candidates, the electoral college shapes campaign strategy. One has to "go where the ducks are," the most populous states. Indeed, presidential candidates do spend more time in such states than in the less populated ones.

What Shapes Voters' Choices?

Presidential Elections

The Three-Factor Explanation of Voting

The standard approach to analyzing voter choice is to weigh the long-term force of *party identification* (called long-term because it tends to persist in individuals from election to election) against the short-term forces of *issue positions* and *candidate evaluation* (called short-term because they can change from election to election).

In the 1950s, party identification was the dominant force shaping individuals' voting choices. However, its importance has declined since then. By the middle 1960s, issue voting began to increase. Issue voting refers to voters' examination of the issue positions of candidates and comparison of those with their own stance. Such voters select the candidate who ranks closest to their own views. Issue voting in elections from 1952 to the present peaked in 1972, but it seems to have declined since then. In fact, in 1984 many voted for Ronald Reagan despite their policy/issue disagreement with him. The third factor, candidate evaluation, has been a powerful force all along.

The Six-Factor Explanation of Voting

A more recent approach to explaining how people vote considers candidates' past performance (retrospective evaluations), their likely future performance, their past issue positions, their future policy stands, their attributes (such as personal integrity), and the voter's party identification. With these six factors, as Miller and Borelli contend, one can statistically examine what is most important for predicting voter's choices at the polls.[18]

How has this six-factor approach worked in recent presidential elections?

1980.   Jimmy Carter gained votes from party identification (there were more Democrats than Republicans) and perceived candidate attributes (voters were uncertain about Reagan's command of facts and his age, for instance).

On other factors, Ronald Reagan had the advantage over President Carter. Most significant of all factors was retrospective performance. Simply, voters felt that Carter had not done a good job. On the remaining factors, Reagan enjoyed some advantage over Carter. Reagan reflected a more conservative mood among the public, although his mandate was only modest. He did receive 51 percent of the popular vote (Jimmy Carter and third-party candidate John Anderson split the rest)—but 49 percent of the American people who bothered to vote did *not* support him.

In the final analysis, 1980 represents a rejection of Jimmy Carter by voters on the grounds of his perceived poor record as president and a reflection of a conservative mood (to end shortly thereafter).[19] Reagan was not viewed in particularly positive terms. One could conclude that the outcome was to a considerable extent "ABC"—"Anyone but Carter."

1984.   Oddly enough, in 1984, only one of the six factors operated in President Reagan's favor—retrospective performance. Americans evaluated Reagan's past performance very positively and Walter Mondale's very negatively (voters associated him with what they saw as a flawed Carter presidency—Mondale, after all, had been Carter's vice president).

All the other factors worked on Mondale's behalf. Voters' party identification (again, 1984, more people defined themselves as Democrats than as Republicans) was most important. Next was retrospective policy; voters indicated that they were not enchanted with Reagan's policies. They felt that he had moved too far toward conservatism, and this yielded an electoral benefit for Mondale. With prospective policy, voters had a mild preference for Mondale's future policy proposals over Reagan's. The conservative mood that had peaked in 1980 had begun receding by 1982, and Reagan was no longer in complete tune with this change in mood.[20] Least influential of all was prospective performance, for which Mondale, by the tiniest amount, was preferred over Reagan. Consequently, although Reagan benefited from only one item, retrospective performance, approval of his work (and disapproval of Mondale's performance as associated with Carter) was enough to provide a resounding victory.

Miller and Borrelli conclude by noting of 1984:

> While Reagan received the most positive evaluation for retrospective performance of any incumbent president during the past three decades, he was also the most negatively assessed on the retrospective policy dimension. The preponderance of 19 percent more negative than positive comments regarding the policies he enacted during his first term in office represents, by all historic comparisons, an astounding rejection of his con-

servative program. No other presidential candidate, incumbent or challenger, received such a clearly negative appraisal from the public of either past or prospective policies. Yet he was reelected to the office in a landslide. How did that happen?

Contrary to much speculation . . . that landslide victory cannot be accounted for by Reagan's supposedly overwhelming personal appeal. No doubt Reagan received predominantly positive evaluations for his strong leadership and charismatic style . . . , but that appeal was offset by the public perception that he lacked compassion and was unconcerned and uninformed about much of what went on in government. . . .

Reagan's popular appeal rests on his past performance and success in office, rather than his personal characteristics or conservative policies, as the media have tried to suggest.[21]

1988. By 1988, the mood in America, as reported in Chapter 4, was rapidly becoming more liberal—yet George Bush defeated Michael Dukakis. How could this be? It appears that Dukakis had the advantage primarily in two areas: party identification (more Americans called themselves Democrats than Republicans, but by a smaller margin than prior to the Reagan years) and candidate attributes (Bush was seen as cool and distant and removed from the affairs of ordinary people). On the other hand, Bush's single greatest strength was retrospective performance. People associated him with the Reagan administration, and they still evaluated the former president's performance positively. Although the mood of the country was moving to the left, people felt Bush's positions to be closer to theirs than were Dukakis's. The "Willie Horton" ad, for example, reinforced many people's sense that Dukakis was out of step on the issue of crime. Prospectively, the mood was becoming more liberal, but Dukakis was unable to take advantage of this.[22]

1992. This election has some similarities to that of 1980. At least one element of this election might be referred to as the "ABB" ("Anyone but Bush") effect. One analyst was uncharitable enough to refer to George Bush as "the most ineffective person to occupy the White House since the creation of the modern presidency by Franklin Roosevelt."[23] This kind of commentary suggests that retrospective performance would *not* play in favor of the Republicans this time around. Kathleen Frankovic simply notes that "1992 turned out to be a very simple election. It was a referendum on the incumbent president—and George Bush lost."[24]

In this election, despite his encounters with stories of marital infidelity and draft evasion, Bill Clinton was viewed more positively than either George Bush or Ross Perot in terms of his personal attributes; Clinton "caught the wave" of the more liberal mood (introducing a mandate quality into the election results, much as with Ronald Reagan in 1980); Clinton was closer to the American people on the issues that the public wanted addressed (prospective policy); Clinton gained a slight advantage on party identification.[25] This election was, in two key respects, similar to that in 1980: first, retrospective performance evaluations torpedoed an incumbent president; second, the challenger better captured the public's ideological mood. Thus, in both elections, performance ("What have you done lately?") and ideology (the public's mood) played a role. Both elections can be seen as laying the groundwork for rather weak mandates—but mandates nonetheless.

Third-Party Presidential Voting

Sometimes, of course, Americans vote for neither the Republican nor the Democratic candidate for president. Why would people seemingly throw away their vote for a candidate who has normally no chance of wining? Voting for a third-party candidate is hardly a common event. Still, Eugene McCarthy received 756,691 votes in 1976; John Anderson won 5,720,000 in 1980; David Bergland (Libertarian party) had 228,314 in 1984; Ron Paul (Libertarian) garnered 432,179 votes in 1988; H. Ross Perot (United We Stand) picked up an astonishing 19,741,048 in 1992. The electorate's perception that the two major parties are not addressing major problems goes with increased voting for third-party candidates in the 50 American states. More populous states have lower levels of third-party voting; closer contests for president reduce third-party voting.[26]

Congressional Elections

As with presidential elections, both short- and long-term forces influence voting choices in congressional elections. Especially with respect to the House of Representatives, incumbency must be accorded great weight. Voters have less information about Senate races than presidential races, however, and even less about contests for the House of Representatives. Congressional elections are just not that important to them. In 1972, for instance, 63 percent of a sample of Americans said they cared a lot about the presidential election—but only 39 percent cared a lot about congressional races.

It is to be expected, then, that issues are not as important in congressional races as in presidential elections. Issues have only half the impact in elections for the House as for president (the Senate ranks in between). Candidate evaluations play a limited role, too. When voters are asked what they do or do not like about House candidates, perceptions of personal characteristics (especially trustworthiness and competence) were found to weigh very heavily—more so than for senatorial or presidential contenders. Since House incumbents work so hard to gain the trust of their constituents, this is hardly a surprising finding.

A key variable influencing people's votes in congressional elections is party identification. Voters tend to rank candidates sharing their party label more positively than those under the opposition's banner. However, over time, an increasing number of voters have "defected" from their party identification to support the other candidate. Why? It seems that defecting is tied to voter support for incumbents. Many people are willing to vote against their party if the incumbent represents the other party. This incumbency effect is less pronounced in the Senate than in the House, although it still exists.

Incumbents, especially in the House, have much higher name recognition than their opponents. Most analysts of Congress conclude that to know anything about a candidate is to like him or her, so, consequently, incumbents have a huge built-in advantage. In the House, challengers of incumbents are generally not well known. One result is 90 percent or better reelection success rates for House incumbents—even in a year like 1992, in which there was said to be an "anti-incumbency" mood. The reelection rate is lower for Senate incumbents, apparently because their challengers are more likely to have considerable name recognition (such as former governors).[27]

What leads to the incumbency effect? Two primary causes are normally identified: errand running for constituents and bringing back to the district federal funding for projects that will benefit the constituency. However, the picture is probably not quite this simple.

Incumbents often act as errand runners for their constituents, carrying out "casework" to help people with problems. For example, if a citizen on social security does not get his or her check on time, that person may contact the House member. The representative (or, more likely, an assistant), in turn, contacts the Social Security Administration to see what has gone wrong. Finally, the agency responds to the congressional inquiry and mails the check out. The result is one happy constituent who will now supposedly support the incumbent. An astonishing number of people ask for help from their representatives; one survey finds that 22 percent of those interviewed claim to have requested assistance from their representatives. Moreover, 28 percent said that they had heard of others who had asked for help.[28] Evidence indicates that casework does increase victory margins[29]—but perhaps not in as straightforward a way as many believe.

Members of Congress also can try to bring federal dollars and jobs into their districts through "pork barrel" legislation and then claim credit for this bounty. One common means of "bringing home the pork" is to get support for the U.S. Army Corps of Engineers, which builds dams, widens river channels, and constructs flood-control projects. Winning and losing elections (especially for House incumbents) is largely a local event, based on how good an errand runner, "pork" provider, and credit claimer the incumbent is.

However, the success of incumbents is probably not due directly to this hard work on behalf of constituents.[30] They scare off strong challengers by bringing home the pork, by errand running, by publicizing (advertising) their good deeds for the district. Incumbents also build up large campaign war chests. As a result, incumbents tend to face weak challengers with low name recognition, who serve as "cannon fodder" for the incumbent. Potentially strong challengers decide to wait for another time, when conditions are ripe for winning. After all, why endanger a promising career by running against an incumbent who has a satisfied constituency and formidable electoral financial resources?

In addition, there appears to be a party effect—with Republicans generally offering less attractive and weaker candidates to challenge incumbents than do the Democrats. Here may be one hidden reason for the continuing Democratic hegemony in the House of Representatives.[31] Indeed, some Republican winners may not easily learn how to play the game of casework and district attentiveness—thus reducing their odds of reelection.

U.S. senators, for example, tend to vote their own way until the two years before their reelection quest; then they moderate their positions in order to gain electoral support.[32] However, southern Republican conservatives elected for the first time to the Senate in 1980 did not moderate their positions and did not carry out any significant casework—and they went down in flames in 1986.[33] Other Republican conservatives, such as New York's Alphonse D'Amato (known as "Pothole Al" for his virtuosity as a caseworker), who learned the casework lessons, went on to successful reelection. A related point: Republican members of the U.S. House of Representatives tend to retire from that body sooner than their Democratic counterparts. Thus, incumbency is less of a resource for the House Republicans as a whole than for their Democratic peers.[34]

There is some role for national concerns in congressional elections; they are not solely local events. If voters judge the country's economic condition as bad, incumbents of the president's party will lose some support; in some cases, this translates into defeat.[35] Some evidence suggests that if voters believe that the president is generally not doing a good job, they tend not to vote for candidates of the president's party in midterm elections. This also adds a national component to congressional elections.[36]

Divided Government: The Voters' Choice?

As we noted in Chapter 5, in recent decades the norm has been a government divided between Democrats controlling Congress and Republicans holding the White House. Indeed, Bill Clinton's election as a Democrat with a Democratic Congress appears unusual in these times. Is there any sensible explanation in terms of voter behavior for divided government's having been so common in recent years?

One argument is quite straightforward: It is *not* gerrymandering; it is *not* simply casework; it is *not* presidential approval or disapproval; it is *not* coattails; it is *not* just the bursting campaign war chests of incumbents. Rather, it is political. As Gary Jacobson, a leading congressional election scholar, has put it, "You can't beat somebody with nobody."[37] And Republicans tend to field poor-quality challengers against Democratic incumbents.

Furthermore, the voters may be leery of entrusting full control of government to either party. While they see Republicans as more frugal and as wanting to put the lid on tax increases, they also see Republicans as not particularly concerned about ordinary citizens and as likely to cut popular programs. At the same time, they see Democrats as apt to tax and spend—but also to defend the programs that they like. In fact, according to this argument, Americans see both parties as too far from the middle of the road. Hence, one solution is to create gridlock—to elect the Republican candidate for president to restrain excessive Democratic taxing and spending, but to counter by electing Democrats to control Congress in order to prevent draconian Republican cuts in programs. Is this asking too much of the voters? The evidence is certainly not yet clear, but this is one argument that merits consideration.[38]

What are the consequences of divided government? David Mayhew's research suggests that divided government per se does not seem to reduce the amount of innovative policy-making enacted by the national government.[39] Other research indicates that when one party controls the presidency and the other Congress, Supreme Court decisions are apt to be more moderate in civil liberties and civil rights decisions, suggesting that divided government leads to more moderate justices being appointed.[40]

Why, then, did voters end their romance with divided government in 1992? To a large extent, theirs was a retrospective performance evaluation of George Bush—and they did not like what he had done for them lately. Also, Bill Clinton did appear to catch the ideological mood of the public better than George Bush did. And, perhaps, voters became somewhat tired of what the media kept referring to as "gridlock."

Voting, Elections, and Public Policy

Do elections influence government decisions? To do so, several conditions would have to be met:

1. Candidates must take different positions on the issues of the day. If the candidates held the same views, it would make little difference who was elected.

2. Candidates have to try to carry out their campaign promises. If candidates do not, then those who vote for them on the basis of those promises will not have their preferences enacted.

3. Voters must be able to discern differences between candidates and vote on the basis of issue positions.

Differences between Candidates

An often heard comment is that "there ain't a nickel's worth of difference" between candidates or between parties. This can be called the "tweedledum-tweedledee" perspective. One argument on its behalf comes from the work of Anthony Downs.[41] Figure 6.1 summarizes Down's logic. If one assumes that most voters are ideologically moderate, then rational parties (or candidates) will take the middle-of-the-road position, where the votes are. This results in parties (or candidates) promulgating similar positions. Others point out that candidates will take ambiguous positions on controversial issues to gain support without arousing opposition. For instance, both Hubert Humphrey and Richard Nixon advocated "peace with honor," an ambiguous position, in Vietnam in 1968. Thus, American voters were unable to distinguish between the two men on what the citizens saw as the most important issue of the day.[42]

However, other evidence suggests that there are often discernible differences between candidates. Certainly Ronald Reagan did not adopt middle-of-the-road positions in his quest for the presidency. More generally, in presidential elections, it seems that there are predictable divergences between the two parties' platform promises. For example, Republicans tend to point toward better management of government, Democrats toward a pro-labor, sympathetic social welfare position.[43]

Carrying Out Campaign Promises

Sometimes candidates, on being elected, do not carry out their promises. John Kennedy proposed to close the "missile gap" with the Soviet Union—a very difficult promise to carry out given that there was no missile gap (unless,

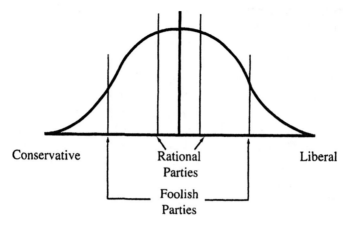

Fig. 6.1   Source: Anthony Downs, An Economic Theory of Democracy, *Harper & Row, New York, 1957.*

of course, one notes that the United States had a substantial advantage over the Soviet Union)! Lyndon Johnson claimed that he would not introduce American troops into Vietnam in large numbers when, in fact, he and his advisors were planning to do exactly that. More recently, Jimmy Carter and Ronald Reagan both asserted that they would balance the federal budget (although this is probably not so much a broken promise as one beyond their ability to fulfill). George Bush wanted people to read his lips—"No new taxes." Bill Clinton assured the middle class that they would receive a tax reduction.

Statistically, however, the evidence indicates that promises are generally redeemed. One study reports that in presidential elections, the party winning the presidency carries out 75 percent of its promises and ignores only about 10 percent. Indeed, even the losing party is able to carry out a reasonable proportion of its promises.[44]

Voters' Ability to Vote on the Basis of Differences

Voters also have a responsibility if elections are to guide public policy. One requirement is that they be aware of candidates' positions on the issues. As described in Chapter 4 and in previous sections of this chapter, this criterion is, at best, only partially met. In presidential elections, as we have seen, voters tend to know something of basic issues; with House races, there is little issue awareness. Yet if a presidential incumbent is running for reelection, voting is likely to be based on "approval"—not issues. Although the electorate was moving in a rather more conservative direction by 1980, that was only part of the reason that Ronald Reagan won. Ironically, in 1984, the president won big even though the public disagreed with his policy positions.

In House of Representative contests, where incumbency is a key factor, there seems to be rather little issue content. One can hardly blame the voter, by the way, for not doing a lot of issue voting in congressional races. After all, representatives serve as errand runners, bearers of "pork," and the like. If incumbents tend not to emphasize issues, the electorate cannot be expected to do so. Indeed, in Senate elections, incumbents become much more moderate in their roll-call voting in the two years before the election—as if trying to "curry favor" with the voters, effectively "tricking" them,[45] thus making effective issue voting that much more difficult!

So What?

Do elections make a difference? Evidence indicates that the national economy is influenced. From 1950 to 1983, when a Democrat resided in the White House, unemployment rates were lower; a Democratic Congress goes with greater transfers in income from the better-off to the less well-off. The overall effect is a reduction in the income gap between rich and poor.[46] In those years in which there is a Democratic president and the number of nonsouthern Democrats in Congress increases due to electoral fortunes, social spending is stimulated.[47] Since World War II, we find that when Republicans control the White House, inflation seems to decline, as the administration places more concern on keeping the economy from overheating, whereas unemployment tends to decline with Democratic administrations, as they speak to the interests of their electoral base.[48]

Elections are considered to be one prerequisite for representative democracy. That elected officials so assiduously court voters in the United States is one measure of the significance of elections. Two of the three requirements for the vote to serve as a guide to policy seem fairly well met, thereby supporting the idea that elections can be democratic instruments.

Elite theorists can point to the type of people who become candidates— upper-middle-class or upper-class, well-educated, white men. Those who run for office and hold office are not typical of Americans at large. Further, the voters who select candidates in primaries (and presidential caucuses) tend to be from higher strata and atypical of the larger citizenry.

Pluralists point out that candidates try to build coalitions large enough to attain electoral success. They seek the support of different groups.

Recommended Reading

Angus, Campbell, Philip E. Converse, Warren E. Miller, and Donald Stokes: *The American Voter*, Wiley, New York, 1964.

V. O. Key, Jr.: *The Responsible Electorate*, Vintage Books, New York, 1966.

Richard G. Niemi and Herbert F. Weisberg, eds.: *Classics in Voting Behavior*, Congressional Quarterly Press, Washington, D.C., 1993.

Richard G. Niemi and Herbert F. Weisberg, eds.: *Controversies in Voting Behavior*, 3d ed., Congressional Quarterly Press, Washington, D.C., 1993.

Steven J. Rosenstone and John Mark Hansen: *Mobilization, Participation, and Democracy in America*, Macmillan, New York, 1993.

Raymond A. Wolfinger and Steven J. Rosenstone: *Who Votes?* Yale University Press, New Haven, 1980.

handwritten notes in top margin:

— mischief —> dangerous

— no one is writing about this in a flattering way (except *Federalist*)

— regulating is challenging

CHAPTER 7

Political Interest Groups

In many ways, organized interests have become the dynamic element in the political process in the United States. In the past they have been seen primarily as lobbyists before the legislature or the agencies of the executive branch. Today, however, their influence extends throughout the governmental process—from the election of candidates through judicial decision making. This chapter discusses the ideas that underly the justifications and, more recently, the criticisms of interest-group influence. It then presents some concepts for a better understanding of group behavior, describes common tactics of groups, and provides examples of current groups.

In a pluralistic, democratic society where freedom of association is encouraged and where individuals join groups for a variety of reasons, it is to be expected that political interest groups will proliferate. The important issue for the student of politics today is the extent to which the increase in group power can be balanced by a government that can serve as a stable framework for policy and for consideration of the national welfare.

Group Theorists

Early Theorists—Madison and Calhoun

Recognition of the importance of groups in the political process extends back at least as far as James Madison's discussion of the "mischief of factions" in *Federalist 10* (1787–1788). Although, he said, the numerous divi-

132 — 247

sions in American society were dangerous to a healthy republic, the expanse of the country and the institutions of government would operate to prevent any one interest from gaining dominance in the nation. Later, in his *Disquisition on Government* (1848), John C. Calhoun drew attention again to the importance of diverse interests with his description of the idea of the "concurrent majority." Attempting to protect southern interests from control by the North, Calhoun argued that proper policy decisions required more than a numerical majority. They required acknowledgement of the integrity of the interests affected. This could be accomplished through use of a "concurrent majority," a procedure whereby a majority of each interest would have to agree to a decision before it could be made.

Arthur F. Bentley

Perhaps the most thorough statement of the group explanation of the political process was made by Arthur F. Bentley in *The Process of Government* (1908). In this work, Bentley argued that everything in the political process could be explained by group behavior. Many of Bentley's concepts are still used to explain group behavior. These received more modern treatment in *The Governmental Process* (1951) by David B. Truman.

Robert Dahl

Robert Dahl's concept of pluralism, based on his study of decision making in New Haven, has been an important modification of the ideas of the group theorists. Dahl suggests that the political process can best be understood in terms of the groups that become involved in a decision.[1] Obviously, many decisions are of little or no interest to particular groups. Only those decisions which affect them will cause groups to become involved politically, and only on those decisions will the groups have some influence. Thus, from Dahl's perspective, American democracy is not a rule by numerical majority but a rule by combinations of groups. On a given issue, the important determinants of the outcome will be the groups involved in that controversy.

The New Deal Approach

Interest-group organization gained official sanction under the New Deal, which tried to attack the effects of the Great Depression by fostering organization in business and labor. The New Deal efforts to assist economic interests illustrate E. E. Schattschneider's view of government as the "socialization of conflict."[2] In this interpretation, governmental policy is seen as a response to the appeals of groups disadvantaged in their competition with other groups. The consequences may not be favorable to those groups which originally asked for government intervention, however, because appeal to government increases dramatically the number of those involved in the issue; that is, it socializes the conflict. When this happens, the issue can easily be removed from the control of the original protagonists.

Proliferation of Programs and Groups under the Johnson Administration

The New Deal approach received further impetus during Lyndon Johnson's presidency. As noted in Chapter 3, the Johnson administration greatly increased the number of grant-in-aid programs providing funds to states, localities, and the private sector. These programs invariably engendered associations to obtain and protect their share, or stake, in the funds available.

However, the Johnson administration moved beyond simply increasing domestic funding. Through regulations requiring citizen consultation and representation in the implementation of many of its programs, it deliberately sought to encourage the organization of those who had previously not been politically active. These efforts and the civil rights and antiwar movements led to a large increase in citizen groups concerned about the welfare of the disadvantaged and other social issues in addition to those newly created groups receiving direct economic benefits from the programs instituted under the Johnson administration. Because many of the groups organized during the 1960s were liberal, their activities in turn stimulated an increase in conservative groups in the 1970s.[3] This proliferation of organized political interests, combined with greater sophistication in organizational techniques and methods of media manipulation, has caused some thinkers to raise serious questions about the role of interest groups in politics generally.

Recent Critics

Theodore Lowi has been widely credited with formulating a thorough critique of the development and effects of interest-group power on democratic policy processes.[4] Lowi sees contemporary America dominated by "interest-group liberalism." In his opinion, government efforts to encourage group organization have resulted in groups controlling government policy in their areas of interest. Lowi fears that government is losing its legitimacy as an authoritative source of rule making and that interest-group power has reached a stage where it seriously impedes coherent government policy. By refusing to legislate definitive standards and clear goals for programs, Congress bears much of the blame for encouraging interest-group manipulation throughout the policy process. This policy ambiguity by Congress fosters interest-group bargaining down to the level of the "hearing examiner, the meat inspector, the community action supervisor, and the individual clients with which they deal."[5] The government stalemate engendered by such pervasive group influence may in turn threaten the stability of democracy itself.

Another commentator, Mancur Olson, has approached the question of the deleterious effects of interest-group power somewhat differently, although his conclusions are equally serious.[6] Olson argues that in a democracy, economic interests soon learn that it is easier and more profitable to utilize government for protection than to engage in competition with each other. Government eventually becomes the protector of economic interests that are unwilling to be flexible in giving up their subsidies and other advantages even though new economic developments may make them obsolete or inefficient. Olson concludes that freedom of association and access to government in a democracy must invariably lead to economic stagnation and crisis that, in turn, threaten the stability of the political system.

Group Organization — *a key step*

Because it is so dynamic and heterogeneous, American society at any given moment contains an enormous variety of interests. Many of these interests never organize and thus remain latent interest groups. It is organization that provides the threshold for group identity and effectiveness as an interest group. Some interest groups may be primarily political interest groups (for example, a local taxpayers association); others may have little interest in political activity or engage in attempts to influence government only occasionally (for example, Bonsai Clubs International). The catalysts for interest organization also vary widely. Interests may organize because they become aware of common concerns that can be enhanced through organization, as with local bird watchers or stamp collectors. Other groups may appear in reaction to perceived abuses by or threats from existing organizations. Occasionally, investigative exposures, such as Ralph Nader's *Unsafe at Any Speed*[7] or Rachel Carson's *Silent Spring*,[8] which stimulated organization of consumer groups and environmental groups, respectively, lead to greater interest organization. In the last several decades, government activity itself has encouraged group organization, as interests served or regulated by government have organized to advance their views or to protect themselves. Among groups that have been relatively stable and which have more than a handful of members, identifiable common principles that govern their internal workings tend to develop.

Leadership

Over time, a group's leadership tends to become more distant from its membership, and the leaders find it difficult to consider returning to their former occupations. Thus leaders in groups take care not to move mavericks, or those who may dissent from their views, into leadership positions. Only those group members who demonstrate the proper attitudes are encouraged to move up in the ranks. Typically, in the highest group offices there is a succession from vice president to president-elect to president or some similar sequence to ensure that no rapid change in leadership occurs. Additionally, the leadership usually closely controls the nomination and election procedures for officers, discouraging, for example, nominations from the floor of a convention. In this the leadership is aided by its control of funds and communications—often in the form of a journal or newsletter—with its members. Group leadership also can now keep in daily contact with members through the use of computer networks that provide continual updates on group activities and policy issues.

Because of the political environment within which they must operate, most groups make serious efforts to maintain a semblance of democracy in their proceedings. Internal procedures that appear democratic give legitimacy to the group's leaders and their negotiations in the policy process. An exception to this approach was the International Brotherhood of Teamsters, whose leaders simply sat around a table and selected a president. However, in 1991, after three of their last five presidents had been sentenced to prison, the Teamsters, under the watchful eyes of government overseers, for the first time held an open convention in which several candidates ran for the presidency.

Cohesion

An exceptionally important goal of a group's leadership is the maintenance of cohesion among group members on issues of importance to the group. The loss of cohesion and rise of conflict and division within a group pose a threat to the leadership and weaken the group's ability to present a united front to government officials whom it hopes to influence. Thus group leaders often will not take positions on issues that can be expected to divide the membership, or they may use the group's newsletter to give the impression that there are no contrary positions or views among the membership on an issue. Leaders also will try to incorporate as much of their members' lives as possible within the group framework, providing units for children or spouses, for example.

Closely tied to the concept of cohesion is that of intensity. A group can be fairly small in terms of number of members, but if its members are cohesive and intensely involved in an issue, the group can have far greater political influence than larger, less committed groups.

Structure

Organizational structure can be an important determinant of how a group will approach an issue. Two common forms of organizational structure are unitary and federative. The unitary approach has a central office and membership that communicates directly with that office. The federative model often parallels the federal governmental system, although it need not, as with the American Federation of Labor and Congress of Industrial Organizations (AFL-CIO), which has individual unions as its most powerful components. Under this approach, component units deal directly with the membership and report to a national office. In many ways a federative organizational structure makes maintaining cohesion more difficult because the constituent units within the group, owing to geographic or other variations, tend to institutionalize variety within the group. On the other hand, the federative approach may strengthen the group at local levels.

A more encompassing form of organization is the peak association. This kind of organization is essentially an organization of groups. The National Association of Manufacturers is an example of a peak association. Many groups combine organizational forms by allowing both organizations and individuals to become members.

Size

Size can be one of the more misleading indicators of group effectiveness. Groups with large memberships appear impressive as potential voting threats, but group leaders may be unable to mobilize their membership in particular elections. Group membership is difficult to move across party lines, and thus a group may become essentially the captive of a party. Group leaders can, however, encourage their members to sit out an election, and that can have a serious impact on a party that has enjoyed their support in the past.

An important factor weakening the influence of large groups is the inability of members in these groups to see that they make much difference or that their individual activity will gain them much. This is part of what has been aptly labeled the "free rider" problem.[9] In smaller groups it is more obvious that individual activity and support are important and that shares of benefits achieved, such as market subsidies, will be larger. Thus smaller groups tend to be more intense and active in the pursuit of group goals. But in larger groups, the rational group member pursuing his or her own self-interest may well ask why put forth much effort for the group since he or she will benefit from the

real problem for unions

group's success regardless. Groups face this problem in terms of building membership as well. Individuals may refuse to join a union and will still benefit from the higher wages and improved conditions that union activity achieves. To help to offset this problem, many groups offer members incentives other than group goals. These might include reduced rates on insurance, access to important information, or social activities. Despite these efforts to induce membership and membership activity, the free rider problem seems to be an inherent limitation on the political effectiveness of large groups and on the size of groups formed to pursue goals not directly rewarding the self-interests of their members.

Group Strategies: Access and Influence

Access

seems true but a fault of the electoral

Without question, the primary goal of any political interest group is access to policy decisions, which means, in essence, access to those who make these decisions. The rule of thumb is that the earlier access is achieved, the more effective it is. Thus, in the electoral process, those who supported a candidate before the primary in which he or she was nominated tend to have more influence with that person than those who threw in their support just prior to the general election.

In its simplest form, access can be broken down into three steps: (1) locating the point of decision, (2) establishing contact with those involved in the decision, and (3) persuading those involved in the decision.[10] Although this appears clear-cut, it may be less so in practice. For example, locating the point in an agency at which the actual decision is made on an issue can be fairly involved. Agency heads may merely ratify recommendations made by staff people below them, and the group aiming at effective influence needs to move beyond the ostensible decision maker to those actually responsible for the decision. Moreover, it is inaccurate to envision access in terms of influence that narrowly focuses on specific votes. Lobbyists agree that effective access results from long-term social and political relationships with policy people—relationships that allow group representatives to develop a climate of interaction within which decision makers are favorably inclined in general to listening to their views.

Lobbying

Effective access can be achieved through the time-honored practice of lobbying on a person-to-person basis, and this remains in many ways the best approach to decision makers. The lobbyist who has built a reputation for integrity and knowledge on issues can be an important resource for public offi-

this is the crux
subjective?

cials and often will be granted a hearing when others will not. Interest groups also may utilize a more indirect approach by trying to create a favorable image at the grass-roots level. This may involve fairly sophisticated subliminal efforts or more blatant appeals to influence voters' opinions in the hope that they will in turn communicate with their representatives. Some organizations, such as the National Rifle Association (NRA), are exceptionally well organized and do not hesitate to rate candidates at election time for their membership or to produce avalanches of constituent mail on issues of concern to the members. Others, such as the pro-Israel lobby, are more subtle in their portrayal of their cause, aiming at creating a generally sympathetic attitude toward it among the public.

Differential Access

Important to understanding interest-group influence is the idea of differential access. Some interests have an inherent advantage in influencing particular public officials or agencies. Thus, Democratic presidents will naturally be sympathetic to the concerns of organized labor. The Veterans Administration will be expected to be responsive to veterans' organizations. Other interests can have access to policy decisions in these areas, but they will be at a disadvantage if they intend to oppose the positions of those possessing the benefit of differential access.

Group Influence in the Processes of Government

Group Influence in the Electoral Process

In the electoral process, interest groups are most effective in a supportive role. They can offer a tremendous amount of assistance to a candidate in terms of financial aid and human resources. Obviously, the smaller groups do not have the numbers to equal the work force of a labor union, but they can provide funds. Organizations the size of labor unions, however, can contribute both funding and willing hands to do the phoning, door-to-door campaigning, and election-day activities that help ensure a large turnout for the candidate. Organizations can give mailing lists to candidates and publicize candidates' positions in their newsletters. Such organizations also may be able to furnish assistance with publicity, polling, and other areas that require some expertise. If their candidates win, they may further supply office staff in the home offices or in the capital.

Organizations with sufficient resources may attempt to ensure access by providing aid to candidates from both parties, although not necessarily to those candidates competing for the same position. However, interest groups dependent on voting support for their influence tend to be less flexible in their ability to straddle the two major parties. Voters do not change their party preferences easily, and thus they do not respond readily to suggestions from their group leaders that they modify their voting habits. The danger to groups in this situation is that they can easily become prisoners of the parties. Black voters, for example, have given Democratic candidates a very high level of support, and it is unlikely that many of them could be persuaded to switch their support to Republican candidates readily. Thus, in a sense, Democratic candidates can take the black vote for granted, with their major concern being to get these votes to the polls on election day.

The most important recent development in the relationship between elections and interest groups has been the appearance and proliferation of political action committees (PACs). PACs were encouraged by the Federal Election Campaign Act of 1971 and its amendments of 1974 and 1976. As a result, any interest of consequence has a PAC for providing funds to candidates, and through the use of PACs, the larger and wealthier interests have had a significant effect in campaigns. The result has been an increase in the influence of special interests in campaigns in relation to the influence formerly exercised by party organizations, which had been the primary source of funds for many candidates. The fragmentation caused by interest-group influence in the policy process may now have moved into the electoral process, and this, in turn, may lead to an increase in electoral volatility. (For additional discussion of PACs, see Chapter 6.)

Group Influence in Congress and the Executive Branch

Several of the interest-group approaches to Congress and agencies have already been discussed. The reader should remember some basic principles of this process. Person-to-person contact remains the most effective form of persuasion. Resources that can be utilized by interest groups include money, expertise, and labor. Use of these resources in a supportive fashion appears to be the more common approach to obtaining influence and the one that provides the most potential for a long-term beneficial relationship. Computer technology has improved the response time and increased the impact of grass roots appeals to Congress and agencies. Through computer networks and the use of fax machines, interest-group leadership in Washington can activate members affected by policy proposals in a very short time.

The construction of long-lasting relationships that are of mutual benefit has enabled interest groups to link congressional and agency policy through what are called iron triangles, cozy triangles, or subgovernments. (These are described in more detail in Chapter 10.)

Although they often pass unnoticed, the cozy triangles have a tremendous influence on national policy. In many different policy areas, they have formed entrenched relationships that enable their members to resist change vigorously. Supported and protected by their related interest groups and congressional committees, agencies can significantly limit a president's ability to effectively direct the federal bureaucracy. They can also exert pressure on the budget by continually advocating increased spending for their programs. Presidents may oppose an agency's request for additional funds, but interest-group activity in Congress can encourage the relevant committees to provide additional funding regardless of the chief executive's position.

Congressional committees and subcommittees tend to be supportive of the agencies they oversee because such committees are "stacked" with individuals favorable to those programs. Concerned about their reelection, members of Congress naturally try to become members of committees that will enable them to build support in their home districts. Thus, representatives or senators from rural areas will tend to see appointment to the Agriculture Committee as politically important. The stacked characteristic of congressional committees increases their sensitivity to the concerns of affected interests.

One of the most powerful and long-lived cozy triangle relationships has developed around the U.S. Army Corps of Engineers' work in water resource management. The Corps' authority to build dams, reservoirs, harbors, and canals enables it to provide members of Congress with water-resource projects for their constituents. The House and Senate Public Works Committees authorize these projects and use this power to enhance their members' political positions within Congress. Contractors and local government officials organized in such associations as the National Rivers and Harbors Congress work closely with both the Corps and members of the Public Works Committees. Everyone in this subgovernment benefits substantially, although the taxpayers at large must foot the bill for the costs involved. Aroused by what he considered the marginal value of many of these rivers and harbors projects, President Carter, early in his administration, attempted to eliminate funding for a number of them. Congress was outraged at this effort at presidential intervention, and although some projects were cut, the loss in congressional goodwill for the president undoubtedly far outweighed any benefits he gained from cost cutting in the name of the taxpayer. Effective cozy triangles operate quietly outside the attention of the institutional presidency, and attempts to interfere with these established relationships can be very costly to a president.[11]

Group Influence in the Judicial Process

The formalities of the judicial process place important constraints on the techniques that interest groups can use to influence policy in this area. Nonetheless, over the years, some groups have been very successful in their use of the courts. These groups—the American Civil Liberties Union (ACLU) is perhaps the prime example—have often used the courts as their principal area of activity. For groups advocating unpopular or minority causes, lack of support in the politically responsive branches of government may leave them with no recourse but the courts.

Interest groups can be more effective in the judicial process than individuals because they have the funding and organization to carry a case through to its conclusion. Two important devices for groups using the judicial process have been the test case and the class-action suit. The National Association for the Advancement of Colored People (NAACP) and the Jehovah's Witnesses used these with great success in the 1930s, 1940s, and 1950s. The test case is a case in which facts favorable to a group's position are so closely intertwined with a legal issue at stake that the courts will have difficulty separating them. Groups have the ability to select the case that fits these criteria and guide that case through the courts. If possible, the test case is litigated as a class-action suit, meaning that it is pursued on behalf of all individuals similarly affected. This is particularly appropriate in civil rights cases. If an interest can litigate a test case to the Supreme Court and receive a favorable decision, it has changed the law of the land in its favor, because decisions rendered by the Supreme Court are the supreme law of the land. Thus, concentration on the legal process can be an effective way of expanding rights claimed by an organized interest.

In the 1980s and 1990s, interest groups have become more heavily involved in the appointment of judges to the federal courts, especially the Supreme Court. The struggle over the nominations of Robert Bork and Clarence Thomas to that court illustrate graphically how interest groups can use the Senate and the Judiciary Committee and its staff to insist that their views on a judicial nominee be taken into consideration. The Bork nomination battle also demonstrated the effectiveness of group alliances in advocating positions at the national level. In that case, liberal organizations coordinated their efforts for maximum effect in influencing public opinion, using the media, and appearing before the Senate Judiciary Committee. At the same time, the Reagan administration, responding to other interests, was reasonably successful in placing ideologically conservative judges on the lower federal courts.

Group Legitimacy

Up to this point, the discussion of group tactics has assumed the ability of an interest group to operate within the policy process. Some interests have lacked sufficient legitimacy, however, to be able to engage in even the most rudimentary form of policy activity. Their challenge has been to achieve sufficient social and political status to have their issues considered on the policy agenda. At one time or another, blacks, homosexuals, and women have all found themselves on the outside of the policy process trying to get in.

Organization has been an essential first step in moving such groups to a point where they could begin to make policy gains.[12] Often organization has been followed by use of the courts to insist that certain inequities be corrected. In the current era, some groups also have tried to change social norms and attitudes. They have undertaken direct action activities such as marches and sit-ins to bring public attention to their positions and have tried to restructure fundamental public perceptions about them. This latter effort has focused on the use of language—for instance, use of the words "black," "gay," and "Ms."—and on revising historical accounts to give greater status to the activities and accomplishments of members of a particular group.

Types of Interest Groups

Economic Groups

Although the numbers and kinds of interest groups have increased in the past several decades, the interest-group world remains heavily dominated by economic groupings, particularly business groups. There are general business groups such as the Chamber of Commerce and the National Association of Manufacturers. Other organizations represent specific business interests from florists to truck-stop operators to the automobile industry to the coal and steel industries. No business activity seems to be without an association to represent and protect its interests in governmental policy circles.

Labor also, of course, has a variety of organizations representing its interests. Typically, these are unions, but there is tremendous diversity among unions. There are craft unions, mass production unions, clerical unions, private-sector and governmental unions, and professional sports unions. In this respect, one of labor's most effective political action forces for years has been the Committee on Political Education (COPE) of the AFL-CIO.

Along with business and labor groups, agriculture is a member of the so-called big three in organizational power. Again, there are organizations representing particular areas of agriculture, such as milk producers. But there are also more broadly based associations, such as the American Farm Bureau Federation, the National Farmers Union, and the National Grange. These organizations have given farmers political power beyond their numbers, but it would be fair to say that even effective organization is no longer sufficient to protect the farmer from continued decline in political clout.

*— business
— labor
— Ag   professional*

changing world is sometime too much

Also in the economic area are a range of professional associations. The American Bar Association and the American Medical Association are leaders in this respect, with such others as the American Association of University Professors trailing far behind in terms of political influence.

Public Interest Groups

Since the 1960s, in particular, organizations aiming at speaking for the public interest have been reasonably successful in terms of influencing public policy and managing to survive. Typically, these groups are not vital to the economic interests of their membership. Because they are not organized to promote the immediate self-interest of their members, they are sometimes labeled altruistic groups. Salient among these is Common Cause, which works hard at making government more responsive and honest. Ralph Nader's public interest groups also have exerted continual pressure on government, primarily in the interests of the American consumer. Somewhat more difficult to label are the various environmental groups—the Audubon Society, Friends of the Earth, and the Sierra Club—and the ACLU.

These advocacy groups claim to speak for a public interest in particular policy areas, although on many issues it is not clear that the public would agree with their positions. This is particularly true with regard to many of the most recent groups. Sophisticated direct mail techniques now enable a small number of people in Washington to target citizens interested in their causes and to raise sufficient funds through the mail to maintain offices in the nation's capital even though they have no appreciable grass-roots support compared to the older, better-organized interest groups.

Think Tanks

Related to the public interest groups are the research policy groups, often called think tanks, that have proliferated within the past 20 years. Some of these groups, or institutions (such as the Brookings Institution, which was founded in 1916), have existed for many years. More recent are the Heritage Foundation (1973); the American Enterprise Institute for Public Policy Research (1960); the Cato Institute (1977); and the Hoover Institution on War, Revolution, and Peace (founded as the Hoover War Library in 1919 but reinstituted as the Hoover Institution after World War II). Although some of the think tanks, such as the Brookings Institution and the Urban Institute, accept the need for government intervention as a policy technique, most appear to be conservative in orientation in that they are critical of expansive government and favor private-sector solutions to social problems. These groups see themselves as educational in orientation and spend much of their time and money hosting conferences and workshops on issues and supporting research on policy. Conservatives in particular have been active in establishing think tanks at the state level. In the early 1990s there were state-level policy study institutes in over 30 states. These provided analyses of state policies and a network for a national conservative agenda at the grass-roots level. _→ part of a comprehensive Rep'b strategy_

Governments

Governments have also become involved in the lobbying game. These efforts have taken a variety of forms. First, there are associations of governments—the National League of Cities—and of government officials—the U.S. Conference of Mayors. Second, the states have established offices in Washington to represent their interests at the national level. Third, some larger metropolitan areas—New York City, Chicago, New Orleans—have set up shop in the nation's capital to make certain that their positions within their states are accurately represented. Fourth, to protect their programs, agencies at the national level have been known to encourage mobilization of interest-group support on their behalf. Direct financing of such efforts appears to run counter to federal regulations, however, as the Department of Energy learned in 1987 after it had provided funds to bring clientele groups to Washington to lobby against congressional attempts to ban nuclear testing.

Single-Issue Groups

Single-issue interest groups have already been mentioned at several points. They are characterized by rigidity on policy, are usually noneconomic in orientation, tend to have the characteristics of movements, and are often seen as threats to coherent policy-making. Perhaps the best-known of these groups are those associated with the antiabortion movement. Another might be the National Rifle Association (NRA). These types of groups can be seen as shading over into more ideological associations, such as the Moral Majority, or into movements advocating the rights of particular groups, such as blacks or women. All these groups tend to focus heavily on noneconomic issues such as moral beliefs or individual rights and thus make compromise on issues more difficult. This, in turn, makes life very uncomfortable for politicians on whom their attention is brought to bear. _→ So frustrating_

Issue Networks and Alliances

Another way of describing the activities of group organization in the policy arena is to categorize groups according to substantive policy areas such as health, law enforcement, and education.[13] In these areas, what Hugh Heclo has termed "issue networks" may develop. These networks bring together groups from a range of backgrounds to support or oppose particular issues. These networks, or alliances, are becoming more common because of the greater complexity of the problems with which government deals.

When government proposes to act in one of these areas, a variety of influential organizations immediately become interested in a fashion that illustrates Dahl's group interpretation of the policy process, discussed earlier in this chapter. In the area of health care, for example, the American Medical Association, the American Hospital Association, the National League of Nursing, corporations (which may be required to provide more extensive health benefits), health consumer groups (such as those representing the elderly), and state governments can be expected to be vocal on many issues. Similarly, with regard to proposals aimed at dealing with poverty, labor, civil rights, welfare, and church groups might insist on becoming involved.

Issue networks can also develop around legislation and programs that at first glance appear to have little relevance to many of the groups that make up the network. The interstate highway program provides an example of this phenomenon. As James Q. Wilson has pointed out, the original legislation of 1956 simply provided funds for building an interstate highway system. But the Intermodal Surface Transportation Efficiency Act of 1991, which continues authority for the interstate highway system, adds over "20 new goals and constraints." Wilson lists some of these as "preserve historic sites, reduce erosion, encourage the use of seat belts, control outdoor advertising, hire Indians, reduce drunken driving, use recycled rubber in making asphalt."[14] What has happened here, as with other federal programs, is that numerous interests wanting a variety of goals have tied into the interstate highway construction program and now act as another layer of interests on top of the agency–construction industry–congressional committee triangular relationship that originally powered the efforts to build the interstate highway system.

The results of alliances formed to deal with specific issues can sometimes make for unconventional ad hoc coalitions, such as when the automobile manufacturers and the United Auto Workers cooperated to delay automobile emissions standards in 1976 or when Common Cause joined with conservative groups in 1987 to oppose attempts to provide for walk-in voter registration on voting day. The 1993 battle over approval of the North American Free Trade Agreement (NAFTA) was another instance in which alliances on both sides of the issue featured cooperation among interests with fundamental ideological differences. The opposition of Jesse Jackson, Ross Perot, and Patrick Buchanan to the agreement gives one indication of the extent of this ideological diversity. These kinds of group alliances differ from issue networks in that typically they form only temporarily to respond to a question of common concern; issue networks are composed of individuals and groups with longer-term interests in a program.

Regulation of Group Activity

In response to critics of the interplay of interest groups in the political process, group theorists have argued that group competition contains its own mechanisms of control. First, they assert that overlapping memberships of individuals in several groups will limit the claims and behavior of any one group. Thus, factory workers who are both union members and active in environmentalist groups will tend to moderate the positions of both interests. Second, group theorists have posited the existence of a latent interest in society that is concerned with keeping interest-group activity within the rules of the game. These rules might include ethically and legally responsible behavior. When these bounds are overstepped by groups, the theorists argue, the latent interest in fairness will actively organize to offset and regulate group behavior more closely. In some respects, the legislation that has been enacted to regulate interest groups has been a response to perceived abuses by them.

Attempts to regulate interest-group political activity have invariably encountered two formidable obstacles: the reluctance of legislators to act vigorously, and the First Amendment's guarantees of freedom of speech and the right to petition the government. Consequently, when Congress has roused itself to act to regulate lobbying activity, the Supreme Court has, in turn, limited the application of the legislation enacted.

The 1946 Regulation of Lobbying Act utilized the principle of publicity to provide some limits on interest-group activity. It provided that individuals lobbying Congress directly had to file quarterly forms providing information on whom they represented and the amounts of money expended in this effort. In 1954, the Supreme Court limited the application of this statute by interpreting it to apply only to those whose "principal purpose" was to influence Congress.[15]

As noted earlier, the Federal Election Campaign Act of 1971, as amended in 1974 and 1976, stimulated the formation of PACs. These statutes allowed unions and corporations to establish PACs and to contribute to campaigns. Limits are set on how much an individual can contribute to a PAC and, in turn, on how much a PAC can contribute to a candidate, but there are no limits on how many candidates a PAC may support. Moreover, there are no limits or reporting requirements on the amounts that a PAC may contribute to political parties as opposed to specific candidates. The courts have further limited the scope of this act by holding that PACs without a direct connection to a campaign may spend as much as they wish in support of a candidate or cause.[16] This allowed conservative PACs, separate from the Reagan campaign, to spend enormous sums in support of his two election efforts.

Finally, some attention should be given to the 1978 Ethics in Government Act, which attempts to limit the revolving door of government officials, corporate officers, and lobbyists. It prohibits former government officials from representing interests before agencies in which they have worked, and it establishes a waiting period of one year before a former high-level official may contact the agency for which he or she worked. The law is aimed at preventing conflicts of interest in which departed government employees sell their influence to interests.

Today the influence of interest groups is pervasive in the policy process, and these groups provide a powerful dynamic element in the formulation of public policy. Federal law has encouraged their financing of campaigns, and the use of sophisticated public relations techniques enables them to have influence at the grass-roots level of politics. In the policy process, they have often helped to form cozy triangles to strengthen their positions, and increasingly they have affected the making of judicial policy. The primary internal goal of group leaders is the maintenance of cohesion, and the primary external goal is effective access. The emergence of single-issue groups appears to have increased the intensity of the group struggle. The question raised by many students of American politics is whether the institutions of government are capable of producing coherent national policy in the face of intensified interest-group pressures. Certainly these pressures seem to have increased the problems of governmental fragmentation, and efforts to regulate interest-group activity through law have been quite limited.

The prevalence of interest-group activity provides strong support for the pluralist interpretation of American politics. The variety of interest groups undermines an elitist view of the policy process because of the difficulty in locating any single group of people or combination of groups that appears to control or direct that process, although it is true that the internal politics of individual groups often are elitist in character. At the same time, interest groups contribute to a modified version of democratic theory. They replace the concept of the citizen who carefully calculates his or her best interests with organizations that serve as surrogates for that citizen in the policy process. In the interest-group universe, those without the funds or knowledge to organize tend to be excluded, or at least disadvantaged. But even here, organiza-

tions have formed to speak for those who have not been able themselves to organize effectively.

Recommended Reading

Jeffrey M. Berry: *The Interest Group Society,* 2d ed., Scott, Foresman, Glenview, Ill., 1989.

Dan Clawson, Alan Neustadtl, and Denise Scott: *Money Talks,* Basic Books, New York, 1992.

Stokely Carmichael (now Kwame Ture) and Charles Hamilton: *Black Power,* Random House, New York, 1992.

Nancy McGlen and Karen O'Connor: *Women's Rights,* Greenwood Press, New York, 1983.

Mancur Olson, Jr.: *The Logic of Collective Action,* Harvard University Press, Cambridge, Mass., 1971.

Kay Schlozman and John Tierney: *Organized Interests and American Democracy,* Harper & Row, New York, 1986.

Jack L. Walker, Jr.: *Mobilizing Interest Groups in America,* University of Michigan Press, Ann Arbor, Mich., 1991.

James Q. Wilson: *Political Organizations,* Basic Books, New York, 1973.

CHAPTER 8

Congress: Institutions and Processes

Of all the policy-making bodies at the national level, Congress is the most complex. This complexity stems from its bicameral structure, its size, and its lack of any formal or informal coordinating power. The separate bodies of the House of Representatives and the Senate make Congress bicameral. The House has 435 members, who have two-year terms, and the Senate has 100 members, who have six-year terms. The House membership alone is large for a legislative chamber and combined with the Senate makes Congress an unwieldy body. This unwieldiness is worsened by the fact that Congress lacks central direction or coordination. Within each house of Congress, numerous power centers exist. The result is a tremendous amount of fragmentation in the congressional policy process. Working successfully with Congress requires negotiation and coordination among a variety of power holders, who in each instance must be satisfied that positive action is in their best interests.

The growth of the presidency in the twentieth century has overshadowed the policy position of Congress. During the late nineteenth century, Woodrow Wilson, in his classic Congressional Government, *could treat Congress as the dominant power at the national level. In more modern times, however, even with relatively weak and inept presidents, Congress has moved to a position of deferring to executive initiative. Post–World War II relations between the presidency and Congress have been complicated by the fact that*

150

primacy of president

*the presidency has often been held by a Republican while Congress has, with
rare exceptions, been under Democratic control. During the Reagan administration, the fragmentation of party control in Congress and the continued
Democratic control of the House forced the administration and the congressional leadership to circumvent the normal legislative route when major policy proposals, such as social security reform, budget control, and defense
base closures, had to be enacted. However, even Democratic presidents have
found Congress a difficult body to lead. Despite early majorities in both
houses of Congress, President Clinton frequently had difficulty holding the
Democrats together in support of his proposals. The basic problem has been
that the presidency answers to a national constituency and the members of
Congress see themselves as responsible first and foremost to their districts
or their states. Without major procedural reforms and a marked increase in
party discipline, it is difficult to envision Congress as a coequal policy partner of the president.* *so certain regions have more power*

Basic Relationships

An understanding of congressional activity must begin with recognition of the pervasive importance of three relationships or variables—the role
of party affiliation, the importance of seniority, and the function of procedure.

↳ like the other book

Party Affiliation

Although party affiliation is the basis on which leadership control is allocated in each Congress, it has not provided a strong basis for leadership
direction. The presiding officers in each house and the committee and subcommittee chairs are all members of the majority party. When Congress is organized every two years at the beginning of each new Congress, every
legislator supports his or her party. From this point, however, party discipline
fades rapidly. In the British House of Commons, if the Conservatives have a
majority, Conservative proposals are almost guaranteed passage because
every Conservative member of that body is expected to vote with the party.
Such is not the case in the U.S. Congress. Democrats and Republicans often
cross party lines on votes. Although party affiliation gives a general indication of how a member of Congress will vote, only in rare instances will all
party members vote together on an issue. The lack of party discipline increases
the importance of other forms of control and power. Two of these are seniority and the use of procedure.

↳ interesting...

Seniority

Seniority refers to the length of time a member of Congress has served in the House or the Senate. Usually, the more senior members are automatically considered for leadership positions, although in recent years some exceptions have been made. This use of seniority builds the power of the older members and eases the problem of allocating important positions. However, seniority in a less formal sense is also important because, through years of service, the older members have gained a thorough knowledge of procedures and policy issues and have built close relationships with members from both parties. When a senior member of Congress is in difficulty, he or she may be able to manipulate the rules and draw on obligations of colleagues to affect the outcome.

Procedure

The procedures of Congress are quite involved and are not neutral. They protect individual legislators, and at times the entire legislative body, from being held accountable for their actions by the public, and they operate to inhibit or prevent change. On especially controversial or sensitive issues, members of Congress may wish to avoid taking a public stand. At these times, they may resort to procedural ploys to delay or quietly kill a measure. It is not unusual in Congress for the important votes determining the fate of a bill to be on procedural questions, with the vote on the substance of the measure being essentially anticlimactic. Because of the complexity of the legislative process, new proposals must win approval at numerous stages in that process, whereas those forces opposing change have to be successful at but one or two points to defeat a measure. Congress, then, more closely resembles an obstacle course for legislation than an open conduit for legislative passage.

How Representative?

Although members of Congress pride themselves on being close to the people, Congress as a whole does not closely reflect the population characteristics of the nation.

Gerrymandering

The House of Representatives is based on population, but the Senate represents states. Each state has two senators regardless of how large or small it is. Representation in the House must be based on congressional districts that have nearly the same population within a state. However, state legislators have mastered the art of manipulating district boundaries. Usually this is done to favor incumbents, and because until 1995 the Democrats controlled the House since the 1950s, redistricting has tended to favor them. This kind of manipulation is called gerrymandering. Partly because of gerrymandering, the partisan division in the House can vary considerably from the partisan division in the popular vote for members of the House. In 1985, for example, the Democrats in the House outnumbered the Republicans 253 to 182, a 58 to 42 percent division, while the popular vote for members of the House in 1984 was 52 percent Democratic to 47 percent Republican. The figures for the 367 House seats that were contested in 1984 are even more graphic. In these congressional races, the Republicans actually had 500,000 more total votes nationwide, but district by district the Democrats won 30 more seats.[1] This trend continued through the 1990 election, in which Democratic candidates received 54 percent of the popular vote to 45 percent for Republican candidates yet won slightly over 61 percent of the House seats to slightly over 38 percent for the Republicans.

The 103rd Congress (1993–1994) reflected the effects of legally sanctioned gerrymandering. In 1982 Congress had amended the Voting Rights Act of 1965 to provide that when redistricting occurred, special efforts should be made to facilitate representation of blacks and Hispanics. In a rather unlikely political coalition, Republicans worked with black and Hispanic leaders after the 1990 census to ensure implementation of this part of the law. Republicans calculated that if Hispanic and black voters, who tend to vote heavily Democratic, were concentrated in single districts, Republican candidates would have greater chances of success in the remaining districts. These efforts resulted in some very strangely configured districts, of which the 12th Congressional District of North Carolina and the 4th District in Illinois were two of the most contorted (see Figure 8.1). As a consequence of this imaginative gerrymandering, blacks and Hispanics increased their representation in the 103rd Congress, and most of this increase came from the newly drawn districts.[2] Republicans, however, did not fare as well. Their gain was a modest 10 seats in the new House of Representatives. The constitutionality of North Carolina's 12th District has been challenged, but, whatever the courts decide on this point, the deliberate use of district boundaries to favor one group over another raises broader questions that focus on the issue of electoral equity across the population.

Nonpartisan Biases

In nonpartisan terms, the bias in Congress is markedly toward wealthy white men. Women make up a very small percentage of the House and Senate. The 54 women in the 103rd Congress constituted only 10 percent of the

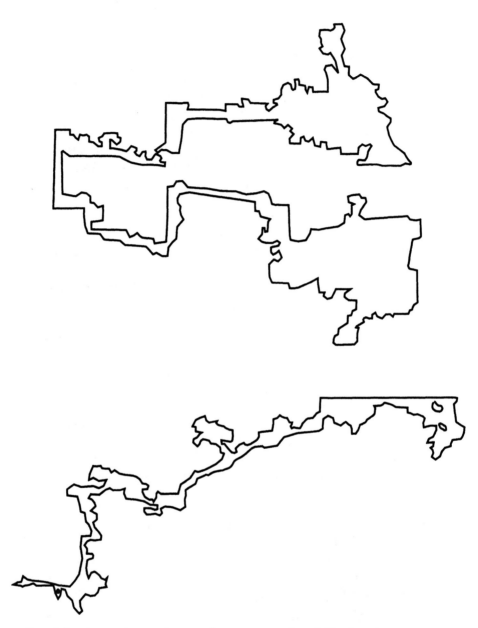

Fig. 8.1   Approximate shapes of two congressional districts drawn to
maximize minority representation. The Illinois 4th Congressional District
(top) was drawn to favor Hispanic voters. The North Carolina 12th
Congressional District (bottom) was drawn to favor black voters. The 12th
District's boundaries are currently being challenged in the federal courts.

total membership. Hispanics were also underrepresented with 17 members. In contrast to these two population groups, the 39 blacks in the 103rd Congress constituted a percentage of congressional membership that was only slightly below their percentage of the nation's population. Perhaps most significant is the lack of working-class and poor people in Congress. People in these socioeconomic groupings are simply without the knowledge and finances to mount effective campaigns. Although congressional salaries may appear high to the average person, the expenses entailed in maintaining two residences are a serious financial burden for those members of Congress dependent on their congressional income. In fact, efforts to keep congressional salaries low help ensure that only the wealthy or those with extensive financial backing will be able to serve in Congress. Occupationally, Congress remains overpopulated with attorneys (239 in the 103rd Congress). However, recent Congresses have shown some greater occupational heterogeneity.

Attitudes of the Members

An evaluation of how well Congress represents constituent interests also must consider the attitudes of the legislators themselves. One determinant of attitude is simply whether the member is serving in the House or in the Senate. Members of the House, until they have served several terms, find that they are running for office continually. They no sooner have been elected than they must begin preparing for the next election. Senators, on the other hand, serve six-year terms and represent entire states. They can be more independent than representatives in their voting behavior.

A second consideration of major importance is how a member of Congress—whether in the House or the Senate—individually views his or her role. Is that role one of a delegate, one who simply reflects the desires of constituents? Or is it one of more deliberate decision making in which the elected representative considers the desires of constituents but also uses his or her judgment as to what is appropriate? Former Representative Barber Conable (R–N.Y.), for example, acted in the latter fashion, having become interested in international finance and tax policy while in the House. Most members of Congress, however, feel that they must give a substantial amount of attention to constituency service, sometimes termed errand running. They recognize that their intervention on behalf of their constituents with administrative agencies and in other areas is a needed service for people puzzled or stymied by government. They also know that constituency service well done translates fairly directly into voting support. After several terms in office, a member of Congress who attends carefully to the requests of constituents becomes difficult to unseat. For example, in a very tough reelection campaign in 1992, Senator Alphonse D'Amato (R–N.Y.) ran as "Senator Pothole" to emphasize his dedication to the needs of his constituents, and he won a narrow victory against a strong challenger in a state that in the same election voted heavily for Bill Clinton.

Much less interested in constituency service would be someone like Robert Kennedy, who ran for the Senate from New York State in 1964 primarily to keep alive his possibilities for running for the presidency. In this respect, some senators can be seen as congressional senators, those whose primary goal is to work within the Senate. Others might be characterized as presidential senators in that they use their positions to generate a national image. Recently, former Representative Jack Kemp (R–N.Y.), who served as Secretary of the Department of Housing and Urban Development in the Bush administration, and Representative Richard Gephardt (D–Mo.) have been examples of members of the House of Representatives who have focused on building a national image.

Organization

Leadership

The leadership positions in each house of Congress are the key coordinating mechanisms for legislative action. The leaders are also important as communication links between the White House and Congress. In meetings with the president, congressional leaders will give the president a sense of how Congress feels on issues, and at the same time, they will obtain information about the plans of the chief executive. This information is an important source of power for congressional leaders in their dealings with the membership. Leadership in Congress is an uncertain matter. An individual may hold an official leadership position and yet be defeated on important issues. In a practical sense, that person is no longer seen as capable of leading members of his or her party. Congressional leaders are careful to avoid being associated with too many defeats. If an issue is headed toward probable defeat, they will distance themselves from it. On the other hand, they will hasten to attach themselves to issues that have a lot of support among the membership.

Leadership in the House

Majority Leadership.   The leader of the House of Representatives is the Speaker of the House, who is elected at the beginning of each Congress every two years, as are the majority and minority leaders of each house. In practical terms, the Speaker is selected by the majority party in the House. The Speaker's powers are extensive. This official has control over floor debate, control over which committees receive what bills, significant influence over what committee assignments members of the majority party receive, and the right to appoint the chair of the powerful Rules Committee. Aiding the Speaker in the House is the majority leader. The majority leader leads the members of the party in guiding legislative issues through the House and is particularly important in influencing the fate of legislation once it has left a committee. The majority leader is assisted in turn by the majority whip. The whip, with the aid of a number of assistants, has the task of maintaining communication with the membership on issues and trying to line up votes for measures favored by the leadership. Although the House leaders have important procedural advantages over the membership, ideological flexibility on issues remains an essential component of really effective leadership. *lots of books on this*

Minority Leadership. The minority party in the House also has a leader and a whip system. The minority leader speaks for the party on major policy issues. Because of the size of the House, procedure is fairly rigorously controlled by the majority party. This leaves the minority party and its leadership at a decided disadvantage. The minority leadership can have its greatest impact when the majority party splits on an issue and provides the minority with the opportunity to provide the winning margin. Continuous Democratic control of the House from 1954 until 1995 meant that the Republicans were perennially the minority party and had to search for opportunities to influence legislation. *very not used to being in charge now*

Leadership in the Senate

The Senate presents a different leadership picture because of its smaller size and because, constitutionally, the vice president is designated as its presiding officer. In fact, the vice president rarely presides over the Senate and votes only in the case of a tie. The vice president's appearance in the Senate usually means that a major bill under consideration may need a tie-breaking vote. Some vice presidents, such as Nelson Rockefeller, have taken an interest in presiding over the Senate, but in Rockefeller's case this caused considerable apprehension on the part of Senate Democrats because he was a Republican presiding over a Democratic-controlled body. Unlike the House, the Senate, with its smaller membership, allows considerable flexibility in procedure and is suspicious of any effort by a presiding vice president to control debate or manipulate discussion in favor of the president's position. In the absence of the vice president, the Senate's presiding officer is the president pro tempore, who is usually a senior member of the majority party selected by that party. Even this person, however, does not often actually preside. Most often the task devolves to junior members of the majority party.

Leadership power in the Senate is exercised by the majority leader. This person, in consultation with the minority leader, decides when and how issues will be brought to the Senate floor. Both the majority and minority parties also have whips, whose primary function is to line up voting support on issues.

As in the House, the most effective majority leaders appear to be those senators who have no strong ideological positions but who are adept at working with their colleagues to fashion an acceptable policy position. Senator Robert Byrd (D–W.Va), for example, made his reputation as a majority leader on this basis and on his knowledge of the parliamentary procedures of the Senate. In 1987, when many of his colleagues were concerned about having to take a position on the nomination of Robert Bork to the Supreme Court, Senator Byrd moved to assist them. He suggested that the Senate Judiciary Committee report the nomination out with no recommendation. He expected that the nomination would then be successfully stopped by a filibuster on the Senate floor, the intended result being that the Bork nomination would be killed and no senator would have had to vote on the nomination directly. This did not happen (the nomination was defeated on a direct vote), but Byrd's proposal indicates how Senate procedures can be used by an able majority leader to protect his or her colleagues.

Committees

The standing committees and their subcommittees are the core of the congressional process. Votes on the floor of the Senate or House may finally determine the success or failure of a proposal, but the important decisions that determine its ultimate fate have normally already been made in the committee that considered it.

Congressional committees derive their power from a number of contributions to the legislative process:

1. They perform a necessary division of labor for Congress, which is annually faced with a tremendous number of issues covering a wide variety of subjects. The committee system apportions these issues to committees that have developed experience in particular areas.

2. This subject-related experience has given committee members expertise in their areas. It is difficult for other members of Congress to challenge a committee's decisions on a bill because they must confront legislators thoroughly familiar with the subject matter. It is also difficult, however, because legislators themselves do not in turn wish to be challenged. Thus there is a tendency for members of Congress to defer to the decisions of their committees.

3. Some committees and subcommittees have built powerful political relationships with agencies and interest groups. They are one of the points of the cozy triangles, or subgovernments, that form important units of political power in the policy process. They are the source of authority and funding for agency programs, and they tend to be very sensitive to the views of the organized interests affected or served by the programs.

Committee Jurisdiction

Jurisdiction, or the subject matter considered by a committee, makes some committees more powerful than others. The standing committees within each house make up the largest number of committees in Congress. Standing committees continue from Congress to Congress without having to be reauthorized. The most important of these are the House Rules Committee, the House and Senate Budget Committees, the House and Senate Appropriations Committees, the House Ways and Means Committee, and the Senate Finance Committee. The Rules Committee is powerful because in the House most major legislation must receive favorable action from it, but in recent years it appears to be increasingly under the direction of the Speaker. The Budget Committees, which have existed only since 1974, can exercise considerable control over other committees through their enforcement of spending limits. The Appropriations Committees provide funding for many programs. The Ways and Means and Finance Committees consider tax or other revenue legislation. In this respect, the Ways and Means Committee has somewhat more stature than its Senate counterpart, the Finance Committee, because the Constitution requires that all revenue measures originate in the House. Similarly, the Senate Foreign Relations Committee has more status than its parallel committee in the House because of the Senate's power over treaties and presidential appointments of ambassadors. This committee also has attracted the lion's share of media coverage. Stephen Hess reported that for the period from February 1979 through June 1984, the Senate Foreign Relations Committee had more than twice as many major network television cameras present than the next most popular committee, the Senate Judiciary Committee. Not surprisingly, over the years, many senators who have served on this committee have developed presidential ambitions.[3]

Committees that consider particular subject matter areas become influential as issues in those areas move onto the agenda for consideration, but they are also important to legislators whose constituency interests or personal interests make it useful for them to serve on a particular committee. For example, a legislator elected from an agricultural area would find it advantageous to his or her reelection chances to serve on the Agriculture Committee. Legislators compete for positions on choice committees. Appointments to committees are made by party committees for each party in the two houses. These choices are subject to nominal ratification by the entire party membership, but in practice, the party leadership plays the primary role in seeing who is placed where. The most important committees are attained by those who have sufficient seniority to move onto them, but the committees dealing with particular subjects are still important to junior members of Congress. The result is that committees tend to be composed of members who are favorable to the interests that are regulated by them. The Senate Committee on Agriculture, Nutrition, and Forestry in the 103rd Congress, for example, consisted of 18 members, all of whom were from the South, Midwest, and West, with the exception of 1 member from Vermont. The Agriculture Subcommittee of the Senate Appropriations Committee exhibited the same pattern. In that instance, 1 senator was from Pennsylvania and the other 10 members were from the South, Midwest, or West.

A particularly flagrant example of leadership power in making appointments to committees is the case of Shirley Chisholm. Chisholm, a Democrat, was black and from inner-city New York. In terms of seniority, race, gender, and geography, she was at the margins of power in the House and in 1969 was given the House Agriculture Committee as her first assignment. Ms. Chisholm's reaction to this obvious attempt to put her on the back shelf politically was sufficiently vociferous to force the Democratic leadership to reconsider. She was quickly reassigned to a committee dealing with issues considerably more important to her constituents than agriculture.[4]

Committee Chairs

Committee chairpersons are the centers of power on the committees and are the bases of power within each house of Congress. The more important the committee an individual chairs, the more important that individual is in the House or Senate. Chairpersons are usually selected on the basis of being the most senior member of the committee in the majority party. However, in the House, senior Democratic committee members have occasionally been deprived of chairs because they were not considered sufficiently loyal to the party or were thought to be weak representatives of the party's positions. In 1985, for example, Les Aspin (D–Wisc.) became chairman of the House Armed Services Committee over several more senior committee members. (Later, under President Clinton, Aspin became the secretary of defense.) The House leadership and committee members apparently wanted someone who projected a knowledgeable, positive image in this important area. Chairpersons have considerable power over their committees. They control most of the staff appointments and money. They determine the flow of committee business, and they are important in floor debates and other consideration of measures from their committees. Members of a committee will not easily move to oppose a chairperson, and when a committee meets without the chairperson or attempts in other ways to oppose that person, it is a clear sign that the chair is in serious difficulty with the committee.

Although chairpersons are powerful, they are subject to sanctions if committee members wish to challenge them. The chair's image of powerfulness works to the advantage of the membership because it allows members to hide behind that person. For example, a committee member may have a bill that he or she believes is not very good but that has public support. The committee member can give public support to the measure and encourage the committee chair to avoid bringing it up in the committee. In this way the committee member can appear to be supportive of the measure but ensure that no serious action is taken on it. Committee chairs are willing to do these favors for their members, but in return they expect to have the support of their members. Most committee chairs operate fairly carefully with their committee member's backing. They are, in short, able politicians.

The number of permanent standing committees in the House and Senate is not large. In the 103rd Congress, the House had 22 such committees and the Senate had 16. Each of these committees is subdivided into subcommittees, with members from the whole committee apportioned among the subcommittees. Over the years, the number of subcommittees has multiplied, so that there are now over 100 in each house. From the legislators' point of view, there are advantages in having a large number of subcommittees: more members obtain chairs, and power is more widely distributed. However, for the congressional process and the public, the proliferation of subcommittees further fragments and complicates the congressional process, and it aggravates the work load of each legislator by increasing the number of subcommittee assignments that he or she must carry.

Other Types of Committees

In addition to the standing committees, Congress has joint committees and select committees. These committees undertake studies, hold hearings, and issue reports, but they do not have the power to propose legislation.

Select Committees.   Select committees are intended to be temporary and to deal with a particular investigation or problem. Some of these select committees, the House Select Committee on Aging, for example, have been continued from Congress to Congress. However, in the 103rd Congress, authorizations for this select committee and three others in the House were allowed to expire in response to demands that Congress make greater efforts to control its spending.

Joint Committees.   Joint committees are composed of members from each house, with the chair rotated between houses each year. Currently, the Joint Economic Committee is the best example.

Informal Organization: Party Committees

The most important area of congressional organization outside the legally established committee system and leadership positions are the committees established by the parties to further their interests. Both parties in each house have meetings of the entire party membership. In each house, the Republicans also have a committee on committees, which chooses Republican members of committees, and a policy committee, which meets to try to formulate party positions on issues. In the House, the Democrats have combined these two functions in the Steering and Policy Committee. In the Senate, the Democrats have a Policy Committee and a Steering Committee, which considers appointments to committee positions. In addition to these committees, the parties have campaign committees in each house. These committees are naturally oriented toward helping members of Congress win reelection, although the Republican House Campaign Committee sponsors a training program for challengers for House seats. Each of these committees is an important conduit for funds for congressional races.

Congress is also networked with many other informal groups, some of which have become institutionalized. The Democratic Study Group was formed in the 1950s to give greater voice to liberal Democrats in the House. The Wednesday Group gives moderate and conservative Republicans in the House an opportunity to meet to discuss common concerns. There are caucuses representing the interests of frost-belt states versus those of the sunbelt states. Other caucuses include those of minority members in Congress who have organized in an effort to give their common concerns greater voice. With President Clinton, a Democrat, in the White House and an increase in the number of black representatives, the Congressional Black Caucus became an important political force in the 103rd Congress.

Congressional Staffing

Staff Serving Members and Committees

Each senator and representative is provided with funds for a staff, and each committee and subcommittee has staff assigned to it.

The increase in subcommittees and subcommittee staff has had the effect of further fragmenting the policy process. Subcommittee staff became important points of access for the clientele groups of the agency programs that the subcommittee supervises. In an important sense, they owe their jobs to the existence of those programs. If the programs were eliminated or severely reduced, there would be no need for a subcommittee to oversee them, and the subcommittee members to whom staff members owe their allegiance and their jobs could suffer a loss of influence in a policy area. The result is that the subcommittee staff people often have a vested interest in preserving the strength of the cozy triangle relationship that has developed among their subcommittee, their agency, and that agency's clientele.

Staff Serving Congress as a Whole

Since World War II, in response to expansion of the executive bureaucracy, Congress has become increasingly concerned about the need for adequate staff assistance for itself. There has been a growing reluctance to depend on the executive branch for information and analyses. Thus, in addition to the staff directly serving the members and their committees, Congress has established agencies that answer directly to it. One of the most important of these is the General Accounting Office (GAO). Established in 1921, this agency undertakes audits of government programs and studies of how programs are being run. The GAO is headed by a comptroller general who is appointed by the president and approved by Congress for a 15-year term. The GAO reports directly to Congress.[5] The Congressional Research Service, created in 1914 as a unit of the Library of Congress, has become important as a source of data and analysis for Congress. The Office of Technology Assessment, established in 1972, undertakes studies for Congress. Of considerable recent importance is the Congressional Budget Office (CBO). Since 1974, the CBO has provided Congress with budget figures and interpretations of budget plans, separately from the executive branch. This agency also monitors congressional legislation to coordinate cost estimates of congressional decisions.

The Legislative Process

Enough has been said to indicate that the successful passage of legislation through Congress involves a great deal of political skill and persistence, knowledge of procedure, and some luck. The following discussion traces the path of a bill through Congress and notes some of the procedural pitfalls that can threaten it along the way (see Figure 8.2).

Origins of Legislation

Most legislation stems from the needs of the executive branch. Agencies have problems with their programs and ask Congress for legislation to correct them. Appropriations bills providing funds for many programs must be passed annually. Laws authorizing programs tend to expire after four or five years at

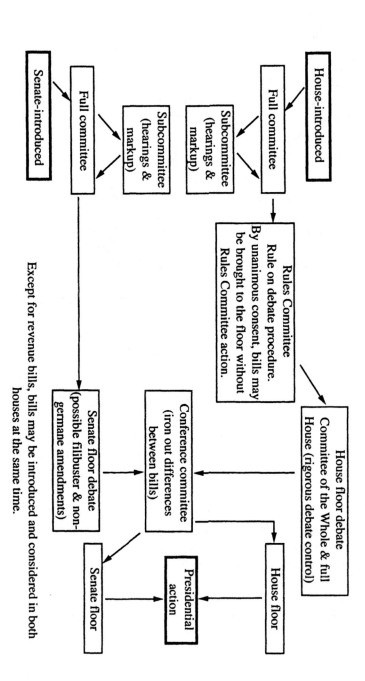

Fig. 8.2   Normal Legislative Route for Major Bills

the most, and they need to be renewed. And last but certainly not least, the White House has important initiatives that it asks Congress to consider.

Individual members of Congress, congressional committees, and interest groups also are sources of legislation. Because of the bicameral structure of Congress, these legislative proposals face a difficult hurdle—the transition from one house to the other. A legislator may have sufficient status and power in his or her house of Congress to gain approval there for a bill, but once a bill leaves the house in which it originated, its sponsor will not have comparable power in the other house. With rare exceptions, interest groups have the same problem. The wisest course for any of these sponsors is to obtain White House support for their proposals. If the president takes an interest in a bill, congressional liaison people can push for its passage in both houses. The president is the one force that can consistently bridge the gap between the two houses. However, securing presidential support is not an easy task. Presidents have an ample number of issues confronting them and normally are not eager to add to the list.

Writing of a Bill

Many bills, especially those dealing with defense and international issues, are written within agencies; others are authored in committees or in the offices of individual members of Congress. Wherever they are written, good politics and effective policy formulation dictate consultation with affected parties. In this manner potential difficulties in the language of the bill can be anticipated and perhaps avoided. Consultation also allows the parties affected by the proposed legislation some feeling of involvement in it. President Johnson, for example, was distrustful of the bureaucracy. Several of his major and most controversial proposals were formulated by task groups separate from the agencies that were to implement them. The result was that the effectiveness of these programs was limited because neither the agencies nor Congress had much attachment to their success.

Introduction of a Bill

If a bill is to be considered seriously in Congress, it must be introduced by someone with political stature. Anyone in Congress may introduce a bill, and thousands of bills are introduced every session. But most bills are referred to a committee and never seen again. Usually administration proposals are introduced by the chairperson of the committee or subcommittee that will consider them. Members of Congress who have developed recognized expertise in an area can introduce bills for themselves or an interest group and expect them to receive attention.

A bill may be introduced in either house or both houses at once, with the exception of revenue measures. By constitutional mandate, tax bills must be considered by the House of Representatives first, and this requirement is what gives added status to the House Ways and Means Committee.

Referral to Committee

After introduction, a bill is referred to committee. The Speaker in the House and the presiding officer in the Senate are empowered to make these referrals, but in practice these decisions are usually made by the parliamentarians for each house.[6] The determination as to which committee will consider a bill can be an important procedural point. Committee jurisdictions often overlap, so a number of committees might be appropriate to consider a particular bill. Some may be much more sympathetic to the bill than others, and obviously, the bill's sponsors want it referred to the committee most likely to be favorable to it. Where jurisdiction over a bill is not clear, several committees may be given the opportunity to consider it.

Committee Consideration

Most bills quietly disappear once they are sent to committee. Those which have serious support are usually referred to a subcommittee of the committee. It is here that most of the significant action on a bill occurs.

Subcommittee Hearings

Often the subcommittee holds hearings on proposed legislation. Supporters and opponents of the legislation are invited to appear before the subcommittee and testify and respond to questions from subcommittee members.

The hearings appear to serve the purpose of providing the subcommittee with information, but this appearance is misleading. Much of the testimony is repetitious, and the subcommittee has staff people who could gather the input from the witnesses more easily and economically. The real function of the hearings is to draw public attention to the issue being considered. Testimony by important public figures receives press coverage and increases public awareness about a proposal. The more important the witness, the more press coverage that will result. The status of a witness gives an indication of how important the issue is to the group that the witness represents. Thus, if the president of the AFL-CIO appears before a subcommittee, that is a clear signal that organized labor has considerable interest in the proposed legislation.

At the same time, hearings easily can be used as weapons of attack or defense. Legislators can stack the witnesses to give an unfavorable image of proposed legislation or of those supporting or opposing it. Or they can set up hearings to whitewash what could be a potentially embarrassing situation.

However they function, hearings may provide some sense of fairness to the parties on both sides of an issue. At least opponents of a measure have had a chance to appear and to place their views on the record.

Markup Session

After the hearings are concluded, the subcommittee usually holds a markup session. For most subcommittees, these sessions are public. It is here that the subcommittee decides what to do with a bill. The subcommittee staff is very important at this stage. Its members have been making notes on problems with the bill and proposed changes. These are considered at this point. The subcommittee has essentially three choices. It can kill the bill, amend it, or report it out unchanged. Procedurally, amendment at this stage can be a very effective way of crippling a measure, leaving the bill's proponents with a bill that does very little. The proponents are then faced with the dilemma of supporting a do-nothing bill or opposing a bill that they had originally sponsored. If the subcommittee kills the bill, at least its supporters have the clear-cut option of coming back with another proposal later.

Full Committee Action

After a bill leaves the subcommittee, it is considered by the full committee. Typically, the full committee defers to the judgment of its subcommittee. On particularly controversial issues, serious debate and close votes may ensue at the full committee level. Also, if the subject is of great national significance, hearings may be held by the entire committee instead of at the subcommittee level. But these situations are rare. Usually, the full committee ratifies the decision of the subcommittee. In the Senate, the bill is reported out and placed on one of the calendars for floor consideration. In both houses, the calendars are simply ways of classifying legislation and scheduling it for floor action. In the House, if the bill is major legislation, it must pass through an additional gauntlet, the Rules Committee.

The Rules Committee

The Rules Committee exists in the House primarily because of the size of that body. Over the years, it has functioned as a traffic cop that sets the procedures by which legislation will be considered on the floor of the House. The Rules Committee grants a rule for each bill that it allows to proceed to the floor of the House. The rule specifies the amount of time to be permitted for debate and whether a measure can be amended on the floor. A rule may be closed, meaning no amendments are allowed; it may be open, allowing amendments; or, as has occurred with increasing frequency in the 1980s and 1990s, it may allow some amendments and not others.

The type of rule can affect the outcome on the House floor. For example, in the early years of the Reagan administration, supporters of the Equal Rights Amendment attempted to resurrect it for a second time. After committee consideration, it went to the Rules Committee. Supporters of the amendment feared that the rule granted it would allow floor amendments on such issues as abortion and military service and that these additions would doom it to defeat on the House floor. To avoid the Rules Committee, Speaker Thomas P. O'Neill (D–Mass.) brought the proposal to the floor under suspension of the rules. This procedure allows only 40 minutes of debate and prohibits amendments. It is normally used for routine bills that are not controversial. Speaker O'Neill's parliamentary maneuver, however, backfired. Many members of the House were outraged that the leadership would try to circumvent the normal procedures on such an important measure, and 14 of the measure's original cosponsors joined the opposition to send it down to defeat by 6 votes.

The Rules Committee is more than a traffic cop. If it refuses to grant a bill a rule, that bill is for all practical purposes dead. In the late 1930s, when the conservative Democrats on the Rules Committee began to vote with the Republicans, the Rules Committee became a conservative bastion in the Democratic-controlled House and was a serious thorn in the side of activist presidents. Today, it has been made more responsive to House leadership by giving the Speaker the power to nominate its majority members and to select its chairperson. Still, if the Rules Committee does not favor legislation before it, the originating committee has the choice of modifying the proposal or watching it disappear. The latter alternative may, of course, be the preference of the committee. Despite criticisms of it, the Rules Committee will cover for members of the House by killing bills they do not want to see get to the floor but which they do not want to take personal responsibility for defeating. Increasingly, however, the House leadership has used its control of the Rules Committee to obtain "special rules" limiting amendments and other challenges to legislation that they support.

Removing a Bill from Committee

As indicated earlier, bills may reach the floor of the House without going through the Rules Committee. Routine bills can be brought to the floor by unanimous consent, which allows suspension of the rules. These bills must, however, be passed by a two-thirds majority.

The Discharge Petition

A procedure that allows the House to override the negative judgment of a committee on a bill is the discharge petition. Through this device, a bill can be discharged from a committee and brought to the floor. A discharge petition lies on the Speaker's desk until it receives 218 signatures. The House then votes to bring the bill to the floor. Committee members may watch the number of signatures, however, and report the bill out on its own if it appears that 218 will be achieved. By acting first, the committee can amend the bill; if the discharge petition is successful, the bill must be reported out unchanged. The Senate also has a discharge petition procedure, but it is considerably easier to use than that of the House.

Floor Amendments

An approach to removing a bill from a committee in the Senate that is more direct than the discharge petition is the use of floor amendments. Unlike the House, the Senate has no rule of germaneness for amendments on the floor. In other words, an amendment to a bill does not have to have any relationship to the subject matter of that bill. Thus, if senators are unhappy that a bill is not being released by a committee, they can simply propose it as an amendment to legislation on the floor. For example, the 1960 Civil Rights Act was brought to the Senate floor as an amendment to a bill allowing an officers' club building on a military base to be used as a temporary school building. From the point that it was successfully added as an amendment, it, of course, became the focus of debate and discussion.

Effectiveness of Overruling Attempts

A word of caution on discharge petitions and other attempts to overrule committee decisions should be given at this point. Members of Congress are proud of their committees and solicitous of their power. They rarely will act to trample on what they see as a committee's prerogatives. Further, committee chairpersons usually have a good sense of how much support there is for a measure regardless of the number and intensity of public statements. As a consequence, discharge petitions that are successful do not often result in legislation.

Floor Action

To this point, except for the role of the Rules Committee in the House, there is not much difference between Senate and House treatments of legislation. This is not the case once a bill reaches the floor of the House or Senate. Because of its size, the House operates with considerably less flexibility in debate. Members are given a specified amount of time to speak, and if they have not been allotted time during debate on a bill, the Speaker need not recognize them if they rise to speak. In the Senate, on the other hand, debate is technically unlimited unless extraordinary action is taken to shut it off, and senators are careful to see that everyone has an opportunity to participate.

Filibusters

Probably the procedure that gains the most attention in Senate debate is the filibuster. The Senate prides itself on being one of the last major legislative bodies that allows its members unlimited debate. The filibuster, however, is more than a form of unlimited debate. It is a means by which a minority of the Senate can kill legislation by gaining the floor and refusing to relinquish it. This tactic blocks consideration of other Senate business and, if successful, will force the leadership to drop the offending bill in order to proceed with other matters. One person can hold the floor of the Senate to dramatize a particular concern, but physically no one person can delay the Senate for more than approximately 24 hours. The real threat of the filibuster arises when several senators divide into teams and hold the floor in shifts of several hours each. Using this approach, a group of senators can filibuster for weeks.

The primary means of stopping a filibuster is the imposition of cloture. If 60 senators vote to end a filibuster, the filibustering senators, after a specified additional period, must give up the floor. This means that if 41 senators oppose a bill and mount a filibuster against it, there is no way they can be stopped unless they inadvertently give up the floor through some parliamentary miscue. The filibuster is one point in the congressional process where minority power clearly can frustrate majority desires. Not only does the technique give negative power to a minority in the Senate, but, of course, the Senate itself distorts majority views by representing states equally no matter how small or large they are.

House Debate on the Rule for a Bill

When the House begins debate on a bill, the first hour, which is in addition to the time allotted by the Rules Committee, is on the rule provided by that committee. Actually, the debate is usually on the measure itself, and the technicality allows the House an additional hour of debate time. At the end of that hour, the House votes whether to accept the rule. If it rejects the rule, the bill is in serious trouble because the Rules Committee does not look kindly on rejection of its rules.

To his discomfort, President Reagan discovered that House rejection or acceptance of the rule for a bill can be an important procedural point in consideration of legislation. In trying to get his 1986 tax reform legislation through Congress, President Reagan was faced with revolt from conservative Republicans in the House. After some arm-twisting, they pledged to vote for the legislation on the House floor. However, when the measure reached the floor of the House, they voted against the rule for the bill and defeated it. It took some explaining to the president before he realized that his procedural ploy threatened to defeat the entire bill. After considerable embarrassment to the administration, and more arm-twisting of recalcitrant Republicans, the House was persuaded to bring the bill up again. This time the rule was accepted, and debate proceeded on the tax bill itself.

Committee of the Whole

When the rule for a bill has been approved on the floor of the House, the House usually resolves itself into the Committee of the Whole. To anyone observing the House in person or watching it on C-SPAN, there is no discernible difference between this committee and the House proper except that the mace (an ornamental staff consisting of 13 rods representing the original states surmounted by a globe and eagle that symbolizes the authority of the House) is not mounted in its usual place on a table to the right of the Speaker's podium and the Speaker is not presiding. Although little is written about it, much of the business of the House is conducted as the Committee of the Whole because the rules of procedure are more flexible. A quorum, the number needed to officially conduct business, for the Committee of the Whole is only 100, whereas for the House it is 218. Measures can be killed or amended in the Committee of the Whole but cannot be finally passed there. For this to occur, the Committee of the Whole must resolve itself back into the House of Representatives proper.

Use of Procedures for Legislative Advantage

Although often characterized by long-winded speeches, floor action at its best can be fascinating. Those with knowledge of the rules and a good sense of timing can accomplish a great deal. Senator Robert Byrd has been one of the ablest operators in this respect in recent years. When the Senate was considering the nomination of Daniel Manion to a federal judgeship in 1986, Byrd called for a vote on short notice, hoping to catch the Republican majority off guard. There had been considerable criticism of Manion's credentials, and a number of Republicans had their doubts about his nomination. Nonetheless, on the first vote the Senate voted 48 to 47 to confirm Manion. Because the vote was so close, Byrd switched his vote to the majority before the vote was finally recorded. This allowed him to move for reconsideration of the vote, which he did, and then he tabled the motion. Byrd hoped to convince one senator to change his or her mind, which would be enough to defeat the nomination on a second vote. However, in the later vote to reconsider, Byrd again lost by a narrow margin, and Manion became a federal judge. In 1987, when he was in the majority party, Byrd used the same ploy in an attempt to override

President Reagan's veto of a highway spending bill. This time he persuaded Senator Terry Sanford (D–N.C.) to switch his vote. On the second vote, the Senate overrode the President's veto by one vote.

In 1988, with the Republicans now in the minority in the Senate, Senator Jesse Helms (R–N.C.) demonstrated again that knowledge of parliamentary procedure can work benefits for the minority. At issue in this instance was a bill authorizing funds for AIDS education and treatment. There was overwhelming bipartisan support for this legislation, and it was clear that Helms and his sympathizers were heavily outnumbered. The bill's proponents expected an amendment from Helms prohibiting the use of funds for organizations that "promote or encourage, directly, homosexual sexual activity," and they were prepared with language to dilute this amendment if he offered it. Helms, however, outmaneuvered his opponents by offering his language as an amendment to a pending amendment rather than as an amendment to the bill itself. Helms knew that under Senate rules an amendment to an amendment could not be further amended. In other words, the Senate had to vote directly on his exact wording. As one knowledgeable commentator described this parliamentary ploy, Helms and his allies "were able to craft their proposals so that members found it politically impossible to vote against them," and Helms's amendment passed 71 to 18.[7]

Voting Procedures

Voting in the House and Senate differs slightly. In the House, there are four forms of votes: a voice vote, a standing vote, a teller vote, and a roll-call vote.

Voice Vote

A voice vote is simply a call for the yeas and nays, and the presiding officer must make a judgment as to who has the majority. This decision can be challenged, and a more precise form of voting must then be used.

Standing Vote

The standing vote requires those for or against to stand. Again, the presiding officer makes an estimate of the outcome. Both these forms of voting are imprecise, but they have the merits from the point of view of the participants of not forcing them to go on the record and of saving time.

Teller Vote

The teller vote is more precise, but it still enables members of the House to avoid responsibility for their votes. Under this procedure, those for a bill file down the center aisle first; those opposed follow. The members are counted as they reach the end of the aisle. Since 1970 it has been possible to request a recorded teller vote, which has eliminated much of the advantage of the device. Further limiting the use of the teller vote has been the availability of electronic voting.[8]

Roll-Call Vote

On roll-call votes, each member's vote is recorded. In the House these are now electronically entered, allowing them to be taken accurately and quickly. The Senate does not have electronic voting and does not use the teller vote.

Conference Committee and Final Action

Often, after a bill has passed both houses of Congress, there are differences between the two versions. In order to resolve those differences, the leadership in the two houses usually appoints delegates to a conference committee. A conference committee is purely ad hoc, or temporary, for dealing with one particular bill. The delegates from each house are normally the senior majority and minority members of the committee and subcommittee that considered the bill. Each house has one vote in the conference committee, and the two sides must agree before an issue is resolved. Their failure to agree on a part of a bill may doom the entire bill to defeat. On difficult bills, a conference committee may have to meet a number of times before a common bill is fashioned.

The conference committee is another point in the congressional process where important parts of a bill may be eliminated or seriously weakened. This was even more of a possibility in the past when these committee meetings were secret. Ample opportunities for clever maneuvers remain, however. The fact that much legislation logjams at the end of each congressional session increases the power of conference committees. During the final two or three weeks of a session, Congress may be working day and night to complete its business. Conference committees are meeting on many different bills at this time, and it is exceptionally difficult to keep track of what these committees are doing. Some major bills are several hundred pages in length, and very few people know what is in them. The Tax Reform Act of 1986, for example, made the cost of season tickets to University of Texas and Louisiana State University football games tax deductible, a detail that gives some idea of the complexity of bills of this sort and an indication as well of the political clout of the legislators from those two states. The 1987 comprehensive appropriations measure, passed late in the first session of the 100th Congress, was 1193 pages in length and was estimated by the Senate minority leader to weigh between 10 and 12 pounds.

When the conferees have reached agreement, the bill is presented on the floor of each house for final passage. Normally, each house accepts the conference committee's version of the bill. If a part is reported out in disagreement, each house has the choice of retreating from its original position or ordering the conferees to try again. In the House of Representatives, unanimous consent is necessary for immediate consideration of the final version of a bill. Such consent is routinely given. However, if such consent is not forthcoming, the bill must go back to the Rules Committee for a rule. Once again, in the rush of business at the end of a session, the Rules Committee can kill a bill by refusing or delaying a rule. If both houses agree to the final version of a bill, it is sent to the White House for presidential action.

Legislative Oversight Function

In addition to the constituency service and legislative roles of members of Congress, oversight of executive agencies is an important legislative function. When the White House is held by a party different from that controlling Congress, the oversight function of Congress can easily be turned to political advantage. Regardless of the political motivations involved, legislative oversight of their activities is a serious matter for federal administrators, and most make every effort to remain in the good graces of those members of Congress responsible for their agencies. Where a cozy triangle relationship has been achieved, members of Congress and administrators work within a framework of understanding that makes life easier for both parties.

Committees and Subcommittees

The committee and subcommittee system is the mechanism through which most oversight occurs. Agency people have to appear before the subcommittees to receive authorization for new programs and renewal of existing ones. They also must answer to appropriations subcommittees each year to receive funding. When special problems arise, a committee or subcommittee may undertake an investigation and hold hearings. These can be very difficult experiences for an administrator who is not in favor with the legislators. The questioning can become verbal harassment of the most vicious sort. For example, David E. Rosenbaum of the *New York Times* reported that seminars were offered to prepare witnesses called to testify in investigations undertaken by Representative John D. Dingell (D–Mich.), who had a reputation as "the most feared inquisitor on Capitol Hill."[9]

The Legislative Veto

Over the years, Congress evolved a technique known as the legislative veto to give it closer control of agency policy. The legislative veto allowed Congress, one house of Congress, or a committee to veto agency decisions in an area. In *Immigration and Naturalization Service v. Chadha* (462 U.S. 919 [1983]), the Supreme Court ruled that the legislative veto was unconstitutional because it circumvented the constitutional requirement that legislation must be presented for presidential approval or disapproval. Clearly, the legislative veto made presidential direction of the bureaucracy, of which the president is chief executive, more difficult.

Use of Special Prosecutors

Another area of legislative oversight that has raised constitutional questions has been Congress's authorization of the use of independent counsels, often called special prosecutors in the media. The use of special prosecutors independent of the Justice Department to investigate scandals extends back at least to the administration of President Ulysses S. Grant, but since the Watergate scandal, their appointment has become almost commonplace. During the Nixon administration, Congress forced the president to appoint a special prosecutor to investigate the Watergate scandal. In order to protect these prosecutors from the president, Congress institutionalized the device in the Ethics in Government Act of 1978. Under this approach, the attorney general must make a finding that there is sufficient evidence to warrant an investigation. A panel of three federal judges then selects a special prosecutor to investigate the matter and to prosecute any illegalities found. The 1978 act was extended for another five years, and the term "special prosecutor" was changed to "independent counsel" in 1982. Many in the Reagan administration contended that the special prosecutor approach is unconstitutional because it involves federal constitutional courts in the prosecution of cases. They argued that Congress had imposed on the courts a nonjudicial duty that was properly exercised by the Executive Branch. In 1987, a reluctant President Reagan signed into law legislation authorizing the independent counsel system for another five years, and in 1988 the Supreme Court upheld the constitutionality of the approach.

Impeachment

A form of oversight of last resort, often characterized as judicial in nature, is impeachment. Congress has the power to impeach judges and the president and vice president. Seven lower federal court judges have been impeached and convicted. No presidents or Supreme Court justices have been convicted through impeachment. Under the impeachment procedure, the House of Representatives votes the articles, or charges, of impeachment and the Senate tries the defendant on the charges. Since 1986, the Senate has allowed a panel of 12 senators to make recommendations for impeachment and then voted on those recommendations. It takes a two-thirds Senate vote to convict and remove an individual through impeachment.

Congressional Reform

Criticisms of Congress vary, but there is little question that as an institution it is held in low esteem by the public. One of the most serious problems has been the decentralized nature of the congressional process. This is worsened by the decline in party discipline and the continued power of committees and subcommittees. From the perspective of public, the decentralized nature of Congress renders it incapable of effective, coherent responses to problems and encourages individual members to avoid responsibility to their constituents.

The Budget Process

An area where congressional fragmentation has had serious repercussions has been in the annual consideration of the budget. Basically, the difficulties that Congress has had with the budget stem from rivalries between the authorizing committees and the appropriations committees. These rivalries, which began to have serious policy effects in the 1960s, became most intense in the House because members of the House Appropriations Committee do not serve on other major committees, and in the 1960s they tended to be fiscally conservative. The essence of the problem was that an authorizing committee—for example, the Agriculture Committee or the Armed Services Committee—would approve a program for a number of years and authorize the agency to spend a specified amount of money during that period. The Appropriations Committee would then each year appropriate a portion of the total that was authorized, but this committee tended to be stingy with the public's money and often did not appropriate sufficient money fast enough to satisfy the authorizing committees.

To counter the power of the appropriation committees, authorizing committees began to devise ways of limiting their control over programs. They used annual authorizations that forced the agency to return to them every year for authorization before going to the appropriations committees. They established borrowing programs that allowed an agency to avoid the appropriations process for most of their money. They instituted entitlement programs that were open-ended as long as the recipients met the qualifications for receiving money. The result of all this was that the budget process took more time in Congress and control of spending became even more difficult.

The Budget Impoundment and Control Act

In response to presidential criticism of its inadequacies in the budgetary area, Congress passed the Budget Impoundment and Control Act of 1974. This act instituted a number of changes aimed at giving Congress more control over the budgetary process. It moved the beginning of the fiscal year to October 1 to give Congress more time to enact a budget. It established a House Budget Committee, a Senate Budget Committee, and the Congressional Budget Office. Finally, it set up a schedule by which Congress was to vote on budget totals and move budget bills through the legislative process. The act did institute a more comprehensive view of the budget that gave Congress a better idea of what it was doing. Congress still had difficulty completing the budget by the new fiscal year deadline, however, and it failed to bring spending and a ballooning deficit under control.

The Balanced Budget and Emergency Control Act

The rapidly increasing size of the federal budgetary deficit finally reached what were seen by many members of Congress as crisis proportions. In 1985, with the Balanced Budget and Emergency Control Act, popularly known as the Gramm-Rudman-Hollings Act, Congress enacted a draconian approach to cutting federal spending. Essentially, the act set up deadlines by which budget deficit reductions had to be met. If Congress and the president could not agree on budget reductions, the comptroller general of the GAO was empowered to make percentage cuts across the board, with some programs exempted. This latter provision was challenged in the courts by dissident House members, and in *Bowsher v. Synar* (478 U.S. 714 [1986]), the Supreme Court held it unconstitutional because it violated the constitutional provision that the president shall see that the laws are "faithfully executed." In the Court's view, the comptroller general, although appointed by the president, was responsible to Congress, and Congress cannot both make and execute a law. As the deficit threatened to continue to grow, Congress in 1987 fashioned an alternative approach to implementing the Gramm-Rudman-Hollings Act by modifying the deadlines and placing the authority to make mandated cuts in the director of the Office of Management and Budget, an executive agency.

The revised Gramm-Rudman-Hollings Act was not effective in holding federal spending and the deficit in check. In the fall of 1990, under the act, President Bush was faced with allowing deep cuts in spending that would have been politically harmful or revamping the budgetary rules in Congress. The president and the Democratic-controlled Congress opted for the latter course. After extensive meetings between the White House people and congressional leaders, Congress approved new budgetary rules that focused on spending limits rather than on the size of the deficit. Federal programs were apportioned into three areas—domestic, international, and defense—and separate spending caps were put on each area. Even this did not prove effective in controlling the deficit, however, and President Clinton made a comprehensive tax and spending plan one of his first priorities in an effort to slow the growth of the federal deficit.

The conclusion to be drawn from Congress's attempts to control federal spending is that not much hope exists for increased congressional responsibility in dealing with difficult problems. Attempts to provide greater coherence to the legislative consideration of the budget illustrate the difficulties posed by the competing sources of power within Congress. Legislated deadlines are meaningless when the divisive forces in Congress cannot be brought under control. The plan that Congress was finally able to provide for budgetary control implicitly acknowledged the likelihood that it would be unable to make tough budget decisions.

Congressional Ethics

Further eroding Congress's public image have been the numerous scandals involving members of Congress. The Abscam investigation (1980), in which seven members of Congress were convicted of taking bribes, was the largest recent scandal. One response of Congress to the Abscam scandal was to investigate the methods of the FBI to ensure that none of its members were entrapped by that agency's methods and perhaps also to convey a subtle warning to the federal investigators.

In the 102nd Congress (1991–1992), many members of the House of Representatives were embarrassed when information on their misuse of House banking privileges became public. Traditionally, House members had written personal checks on their accounts with the House bank, which the bank honored without interest even if the member had no funds in his or her account. In 1990 and 1991, as the result of GAO audits, it became apparent that some House members were abusing their checking privileges in this respect and were essentially giving themselves no-interest loans by writing checks for which they had no funds and repaying their overdrafts later. The House leadership initially attempted to prevent disclosure of the extent to which House members had overdrawn their checking accounts, but the public outcry finally forced a listing of all House members who had overdrawn checks that were covered by the House bank. This information indicated rather clearly that some members of the House had consistently used the House bank as a source of additional money by writing checks for amounts that they did not have in their accounts. In all, 325 current and former members had overdrafts, and 22 members were formally cited by the House Ethics Committee for abusing the privilege. In response to the unfavorable publicity, the House closed its bank as of December 31, 1991. By this time, however, the scandal had further eroded public confidence in Congress as an institution and had motivated a number of members of the House to retire rather than face the electorate in a reelection campaign.

Largely because many of its members are constantly in need of funding, a fact reflected in each of the major scandals described above, Congress has consistently failed to act forthrightly to limit the power of interests to influence its members. Its strongest measures have been requirements that members report sources of income and observe limits on outside income. Political action committees (PACs), however, have almost free rein in providing funds to members of Congress, although they are limited in how much each may contribute to individual legislators. For its elections, Congress refuses to provide federal campaign financing and limitations on campaign contributions similar to those that it has provided for presidential elections. As a result, the influence of special-interest PACs has continued to increase at the congressional level.

Related to the issue of congressional ethics are the attempts to make members of Congress more responsible for their actions by requiring that committee markup sessions and conference committees be open to the public. Instead of increasing responsible action, these changes may have inhibited it further. In the past, individual legislators were willing to act in terms of broader interests if they could do so privately. Today, however, interest representatives watch every move and vote of legislators, making it extremely difficult for legislators to act flexibly. By trying to make individual legislators more responsible to the public, the reformers may have made Congress as a whole less responsible to the public interest.

Term Limits

One concern of students of Congress has been the fact that turnover from one Congress to the next has typically been low. In 1992, it was believed that voter dissatisfaction with Congress might lead to greater losses for incumbents. It was true that there was greater turnover, but this was largely due to redistricting required by the 1990 census and a large number of retirements. Although there were 114 new faces in the House of Representatives and 14 new senators in the 103rd Congress, only 24 of the House incumbents running in the general election lost (an additional 19 incumbents had been defeated in the primaries) and only 4 of 27 Senate incumbents lost in November.

Concern about the entrenched position of incumbents has led to calls for term limits on members of Congress, and one of the biggest stories of the 1992 election was the enthusiasm with which voters supported such proposals. Term limits were approved in all 14 states in which they appeared on the ballot, and 10 of these proposals received at least 60 percent of the vote. So in 1993, with the previous approval of term limits in Colorado, there were 15 states with a total of 181 senators and representatives that limit the terms that members of Congress can serve. Typically these provided for a 6-year limit on representatives and a 12-year limit on senators. The number of members of Congress abiding by the concept of term limits is, however, greater than these figures indicate because increasingly candidates are running for office on the promise that they will voluntarily leave office after a specified number of terms.

Supporters of term limits are currently striving for a constitutional amendment that would apply to all of Congress. The constitutionality of term limits is being challenged in the courts, and those favoring term limits hope to offset the possibility of unfavorable rulings with a constitutional amendment. Additionally, a constitutional amendment would ensure that all states are equally affected in Congress.

Toward Effective Reform

It seems clear that effective change in Congress will require structural and procedural changes that will move it toward greater centralization. Some one group or individual must be able to provide direction to Congress. One answer might be more disciplined political parties that present clear programs and insist on a greater party loyalty in Congress. Such a change would be unlikely without some weakening of the influence of the PACs. Another change that has been suggested is to make the terms of members of the House of Representatives coterminous with that of the president. Making their terms four years would relieve them of having to run continually for office, and tying their elections to that of the president would perhaps make them more responsive to presidential leadership.

Suggesting approaches to reform is far easier than achieving even moderate reforms. Americans seem to prefer legislators who respond to their particular needs, and members of Congress are not eager to become more responsible to a national electorate. These attitudes reinforce and encourage continued fragmentation in the making of policy in Congress. Effective reform will require more than structural changes. Fundamentally, it requires changed attitudes about legislators and their proper role.

Epilogue: The 1994 Congressional Elections

The results of the 1994 congressional elections assured that for the first time in 40 years the Republicans would control both houses of Congress. The results in the House of Representatives were especially dramatic. There the Republicans gained more than 50 seats to wipe out what had been a 256 to 178 Democratic advantage. Most of the Republican gains in the House and the Senate were in races where incumbents were not seeking re-election. At the same time, no Republican incumbent seeking re-election in either house lost.

Despite the dramatic partisan changes occasioned by the 1994 elections, the gender and racial makeup of the 104th Congress did not differ significantly from that of its predecessor, although for the first time in history a major Senate committee had a woman as chair. In the House, the new Republican majority focused on reducing the number of standing committees and congressional staff. Nonetheless, the basic structure and procedures of Congress remained essentially intact. That body's approach to policy issues, however, promised to be considerably different from the business as usual posture that had come to characterize many of the preceding Congresses.

Although Congress is expected to represent the electorate, there are serious questions about how representative Congress is. Organizationally, the locus of power and activity in Congress is in the committees and subcommittees. Overall, Congress is characterized by fragmented organization and procedures. Party leadership and affiliation have some effect on members' actions, but neither provides sufficient discipline to coordinate the many power centers provided by committees and subcommittees or the complexities of procedure. Because of this lack of party discipline, the procedures become important devices for members of Congress to attack legislation without taking responsibility for a position on an issue. The inability of congressional leaders to coordinate and direct policy has been especially obvious in Congress's faltering attempts to deal with budgetary problems. At the same time, the growing tendency for members of Congress to rely on special interests for financial support has increased pressures toward fragmentation and encouraged illegal behavior. Reform seems tied to changing basic American atti-

tudes toward legislators and to slowing or reversing the weakening of party discipline among members of Congress.

Recommended Reading

In addition to reading the following books, which cover important aspects of Congress, the student is encouraged to watch Congress in action on the C-SPAN television network, which carries many debates and hearings live.

Joel D. Aberbach: *Keeping a Watchful Eye: The Politics of Congressional Oversight,* Brookings Institution, Washington, D.C., 1990.

John M. Barry: *The Ambition and the Power: A True Story of Washington,* Viking Penguin, New York, 1990.

Congressional Quarterly Almanac, Congressional Quarterly Press, Washington, D.C., published annually.

Congressional Quarterly Weekly Report, Congressional Quarterly Press, Washington, D.C., published weekly.

Roger H. Davidson, ed.: *The Postreform Congress,* St. Martin's, New York, 1992.

Morris Fiorina: *Congress: Keystone of the Washington Establishment,* 3d ed., Yale University Press, New Haven, 1989.

Alvin M. Josephy, Jr.: *On the Hill: A History of the American Congress,* Simon and Schuster, New York, 1979.

Paul C. Light: *Forging Legislation,* Norton, New York, 1992.

Walter J. Oleszek: *Congressional Procedures and the Policy Process,* 3d ed., Congressional Quarterly Press, Washington, D.C., 1989.

Steven S. Smith: *Call to Order: Floor Politics in the House and Senate,* Brookings Institution, Washington, D.C., 1989.

CHAPTER 9

The Presidency

Time Line

1789	The Constitution grants executive power to an independent, elected president.
1860	During the Civil War, Abraham Lincoln dramatically expands presidential power.
1921	The Budget and Accounting Act shifts responsibility for preparing the budget from Congress to the president.
1932	To combat the Great Depression, Franklin Roosevelt's New Deal programs expand the role of government in American life.
1941	Presidential foreign policy responsibilities increase during and after World War II.
1946	The Employment Act of 1946 calls on the president to promote steady economic growth, high employment, and stable prices.
1973	The Watergate scandal intensifies concerns about a too-powerful "imperial" presidency.

| 1980 | Ronald Reagan reasserts strong presidential leadership, promoting tax cuts, domestic spending cuts, and military spending increases. |
| 1988– | Difficult economic conditions and controversial social issues erode popular and congressional support for the Bush and Clinton presidencies. |

Of all American political institutions, the presidency is the most visible. This chapter identifies the powers of the president as they are spelled out in the Constitution and how these powers have expanded during the twentieth century. The role of the presidency in American politics has evolved over time, and the office provides opportunities for and imposes limitations on every newly elected president.

Presidents do have important power resources, but other important checks limit presidential power. In recent decades, some writers have argued that the presidency is too weak, unable to provide leadership or to carry out electoral mandates. Others have claimed that the presidency is too strong, threatening the liberties of free Americans and upsetting the constitutional balance of power. Complicating the discussion is the fact that the presidency is a highly personalized office. The look of the presidency at any time reflects the management style, political skills, and personality of the incumbent president. International events, economic conditions, and social issues largely beyond the president's control constrain his or her opportunity to lead.

The Presidency in the Constitution

The Founding Fathers struggled to define the proper role of the executive branch in the new system of government. On the one hand, their experience with the English monarchy gave them ample reason to fear that a strong executive might abuse the rights and liberties of free citizens. On the other hand, the Founding Fathers were meeting in Philadelphia in 1787 precisely because they were dissatisfied with the weak central government provided in the Articles of Confederation.

Alexander Hamilton argued forcefully for a strong executive. In *Federalist 70,* he wrote that only a strong president could adequately protect the nation from foreign attack and administer laws in an effective and consistent manner. The Constitution is filled with compromises balancing the concerns of those who wished to create a president strong enough to execute the laws with the concerns of those who sought to protect the liberties of free citizens from potentially abusive executive power.

Article I of the Constitution spells out the legislative powers granted to Congress in ten rather detailed sections. Article II describes the executive powers of the president in general terms and in four brief sections. Section 1 states, rather generally, "The executive power shall be vested in a President of the United States of America." Section 2 provides the basis for presidential dominance in foreign affairs, making the president "the Commander in Chief of the army and navy" and granting the president "the power, by and with the advice and consent of the Senate, to make treaties." Section 3 authorizes the president "to give to the Congress information of the state of the Union, and recommend to their consideration such measures as he shall judge necessary and expedient." This section also charges the president "to take care that the laws be faithfully executed." Section 4 provides for the impeachment, or removal from office, of a president guilty of serious crimes.

Important checks on presidential power are built into the Constitution. For example, the Senate confirms important presidential appointments and ratifies treaties before they go into effect. The House of Representatives must initiate any laws requiring citizens to pay taxes. The president may not remove federal judges after appointing them.

The Founding Fathers were satisfied that Congress, the lawmakers, would be the dominant power in our constitutional system and that the president would simply implement the laws Congress enacted. They construed the brief and ambiguous powers granted in Article II narrowly.

However, Article II allows presidents considerable discretion in defining the scope of their duties. During the Civil War, Abraham Lincoln dramatically expanded presidential power. For example, he raised an army and spent funds without seeking congressional approval. In the post–Civil War period, presidents tended to interpret their constitutional power narrowly, allowing Congress to set the national agenda. In the twentieth century, presidents have often acted boldly to advance American foreign policy interests, to defend the nation in time of war, to counter the effects of economic depression, or to deal with other pressing domestic problems. Today, the presidency is the pivotal institution in the American political system.

Contemporary Presidential Roles

Commander in Chief

In the aftermath of two world wars and America's emergence as a dominant world power, the president's role as commander in chief has assumed great importance. About 23 percent of the federal budget is devoted to military spending, and some 6 percent of America's productive resources are devoted to paying soldiers and building weapons systems. While the Constitution does authorize Congress to declare war, appropriate funds for the military, and ratify treaties, in practice Congress has allowed the president great latitude as commander in chief. President Ronald Reagan sent American troops into Lebanon and Grenada; President George Bush took military action to depose drug-dealing dictator Manuel Noriega in Panama in 1989, and 400,000 U.S. troops drove Iraq out of Kuwait after Saddam Hussein's army invaded its neighbor in 1990, and President Bill Clinton sent troops to Haiti to depose military rulers in 1994. The president has committed troops overseas on some 200 occasions; Congress has declared war only 5 times.[1]

Successful conduct of foreign affairs requires that our government continuously assess other nations' political objectives and military strength. The State Department, the Department of Defense, and the Central Intelligence Agency (CIA) collect information about other nations and conduct talks with their political leaders. These executive agencies report to the president, not to Congress; indeed, Congress depends on the president for much of its information about our foreign policy and military preparedness.

The president also has a dominant role in foreign affairs because only the president has a national constituency and can claim to speak for all the people. The president speaks with one voice and can act quickly in time of military crisis.[2] Congress, by contrast, is a deliberative body well suited to hearing many diverse voices and examining carefully all aspects of an issue from many points of view. However, these qualities are not appropriate when a diplomatic crisis requires an instant decision about using military force or when secrecy is imperative to preserve delicate diplomatic negotiations or to protect the identity of intelligence sources.

Contemporary presidents typically spend over half of their time on foreign policy and national security issues. Presidents enjoy dealing with foreign policy because they have much greater autonomy. On domestic issues, presidents must share power with Congress, interest groups, bureaucrats with their own programs and professional interests, and state and local officials. Indeed, we may think of foreign affairs and domestic affairs as two distinct presidencies.[3]

Head of State

The president is the symbol of shared national identity. The president leads national celebrations on the Fourth of July, Veterans Day, and Thanksgiving. The president leads us in mourning the highly publicized deaths of soldiers in battle, accident victims, and cultural heroes. The president celebrates the achievements of 4-H award winners, distinguished scholars and artists, and successful sports teams. The president entertains visiting heads of state. These ceremonial functions promote a sense of unity and solidarity among Americans, and they take up many hours of the president's day.

In Great Britain and many other countries, head of government and head of state are two separate offices. A prime minister is responsible for developing and carrying out policy, while a king or queen presides at ceremonies and embodies symbolic national unity. In the United States, we combine head of government and ceremonial head of state in the same person. On a typical day, a president's policy meetings with staff and cabinet members, work on a forthcoming speech, and review of a delicate Middle East issue will be mixed with meeting a group of Girl Scouts, signing a proclamation for National Stamp Collecting Week, and hosting a dinner for the president of Venezuela.

Chief Legislator

The Constitution directs the president to inform Congress about the state of the union and to recommend measures for legislative action. Every year, Congress expects and depends on the president to present a package of major legislative requests. Presidents Reagan and Bush favored sharp cuts in domestic spending and favored lower taxes than did Democratic majorities in Congress. President Bill Clinton sought to reduce the size of the federal budget deficit and to reform health care during the first year of his presidency. Enacting major policy initiatives requires full-scale mobilization of political resources, and presidents usually concentrate their resources on guiding a few major proposals through Congress.[4]

The Constitution also gives the president power to veto acts of Congress, that is, to prevent an act of Congress from becoming law. If the president vetoes a proposed law, Congress can override the action if a two-thirds majority in both House and Senate agree. Congress rarely musters the two-thirds vote needed to override a presidential veto.

The president has ten days in which to act on a bill before it becomes law without his signature. A president who receives objectionable legislation within the last ten days of an annual congressional session, however, may simply ignore it. Congress has no opportunity to override this "pocket veto."

Over the last 25 years, Republican presidents have used the veto to thwart Democratic majorities in Congress. Republicans Eisenhower, Nixon, Reagan, and Bush have used the veto twice as frequently as recent Democratic presidents.[5] Even threatening to veto objectionable bills allows presidents to influence the legislative process. Congress may take into account the president's strong legislative preferences so as to avoid a veto.

Budget Maker

Money is the lifeblood of government, and the president coordinates taxing and spending through the budget process. Originally, Congress was fully responsible for the nation's finances. It received requests for funding directly from government agencies and crafted the federal budget itself. In 1921, however, following a surge in government spending during World War I, Congress passed the Budget and Accounting Act.

This law created a Bureau of the Budget (now the Office of Management and Budget, or OMB) to assist the president in drawing up an annual budget for Congress to consider. In effect, this important act shifted primary budget responsibility from Congress to the president. The president sets the budget agenda, which Congress then modifies. The budget process determines whether the role of government in society grows or shrinks, how much we as a society spend on weapons or domestic programs, what priority we assign to loans for students or subsidies to farmers, and how we pay for what we spend. After President Reagan sponsored deep tax cuts in 1982, the federal budget deficit escalated to alarming proportions.[6] In 1993 President Clinton successfully fought for a budget that cut military spending and raised taxes on high-income households while reducing the federal budget deficit.

Manager of the Economy

Since the Great Depression, the nation has increasingly looked to the president to protect the economic fortunes of individual Americans. With Franklin Delano Roosevelt's election in 1932 and landslide reelection in 1936, the role of the government in economic and social affairs increased rapidly. Government began to regulate financial institutions. The right of workers to form unions and to bargain with their employers was protected. A social security program was enacted, and the principle that federal dollars be spent to assist the needy was established.

In the Employment Act of 1946, Congress authorized the president to assess trends in the national economy and to prepare policies fostering steady economic growth with high employment and stable prices. President Reagan favored a program of reduced taxes for the wealthy and less government regulation to stimulate the economy. President Clinton proposed to raise taxes on the wealthy and to cut the federal budget deficit in order to lower interest rates and stimulate economic growth. See Chapter 13 for further discussion of how the federal government attempts to manage the economy.

Sources of Presidential Power

Americans expect much of their president. They expect the president to set national priorities, to make legislative proposals, to draft a budget, to manage the economy, to conduct foreign affairs, to symbolize our shared identity as Americans, and to administer countless federal programs efficiently. To establish their authority, new presidents draw upon several resources.

The Electoral Mandate

After a grueling election campaign, a newly elected president enjoys the support and good wishes of a majority of the voting public. Presidents typically receive high approval rates early in their term, when voters are hopeful that the president will address perceived problems effectively. Since many senators and representatives feel indebted to the president who successfully headed their party's ticket, presidents typically introduce bold new legislative initiatives early in the term. The president's electoral mandate can be a potent political asset during the first year in office.

Access to Media

What the president says and does is news, covered in detail by newspaper and television reporters and relayed to every American home every day. Theodore Roosevelt called the presidency a "bully pulpit," meaning that he could educate and exhort his national audience with a message of his own choosing. The media give the president an opportunity to build support for the presidential agenda among members of Congress and the general public.[7] The president's press secretary and other advisors write catchy and quotable speeches, prepare the president for questions reporters are likely to ask at press conferences, and arrange "photo opportunities" to keep the president in the public eye.

Presidential Popularity

Unfortunately for presidents, their approval ratings tend to be highest early in the term and lowest at the end. The Gallup pollsters regularly ask a sample of Americans whether or not they approve of the president's handling of the job. Table 9.1 presents poll results for the last nine administrations.

The strong popularity ratings of a newly elected president are often related to reverses suffered by the preceding administration in foreign policy and the economy. Eisenhower and Nixon replaced presidents bogged down in the Korean and Vietnam wars. Carter, Reagan, and Clinton won their victo-

Table 9.1   Changes in Presidential Popularity Ratings

| | Average Approval Rating (%) | | |
Administration	First Year in Office	Last Year in Office	Change
Truman (1949–1952)	63	30	–33
Eisenhower (1953–1960)	69	61	–8
Kennedy (1961–1963)	76	61	–15
Johnson (1963–1968)	75	42	–33
Nixon (1969–1974)	61	26	–35
Ford (1974–1976)	48	48	0
Carter (1977–1980)	62	32	–30
Reagan (1981–1988)	58	51	–7
Bush (1989–1992)	64	39	–25

Sources: Public Opinion, January/February 1989, p. 40; Gallup Report, No. 322, July 1992.

ries in the context of a sluggish economy with high inflation and/or high unemployment. Voters are hopeful that a new president will bring an end to war and international crises and create a stronger economy.

Notice that five recent presidents slid at least 25 percentage points during their term in office. Truman and Johnson left office in the midst of unpopular wars in Korea and Vietnam. Nixon was forced to resign after covering up evidence of criminal wrongdoing in the Watergate scandal. Carter was defeated by the failure to secure the release of American hostages held in Iran and by poor economic conditions. A weak economy cost President Bush reelection in 1992.

Reagan's popularity plummeted during the deep economic recession in his first term, suggesting that the public is quick to reward and punish presidents for the performance of the economy. But he claimed credit for strong economic conditions late in his term, and he benefited from the tendency of Americans to rally around the flag in support of their president during confrontations with the Soviet Union and terrorist groups. Within limits, presidents can manage public opinion.[8]

Presidents are rarely able to deliver all they promised during their election campaigns. Candidates court business and labor, propose programs to aid cities and farmers, and promise lower taxes and more social spending. As the next election approaches, rival politicians underline the president's shortcomings, and those who once supported the president are disappointed and critical.[9]

Republican presidents maintain their popularity more easily than do Democrats, whose complex coalition of Catholics, unions, blacks, and Southern supporters is harder to maintain. Bill Clinton's presidential popularity rating slid from 60 to 43 percent in his first months in office, in part because he addressed concerns of traditional Democratic groups at the expense of middle-class voters who supported him in the 1992 election. For example, he pressed the military to allow homosexuals to serve in the armed forces, a policy which did not enjoy wide popular support. His deficit reduction program required unpopular tax increases and did not cut deeply into social spending.

The Power to Persuade

How powerful the presidency is at any particular moment depends in large part on who is president. The modern presidency has considerable potential power, but converting potential power to actual power requires much skill. In his classic study of the presidency, Richard Neustadt argues that the president's power is ultimately the power to persuade.[10] Members of Congress, career civil servants, cabinet members with close ties to clientele groups, and party officials alert to the opinions of party rank and file all have autonomous power bases. Therefore, the successful president must be able to persuade these significant political actors that a proposed policy initiative or decision is in their best interest.

The Capacity to Reward and Punish

Effective presidents know how to get what they want by artfully using their capacity to reward and punish. The president administers a trillion-dollar budget and has considerable influence in making individual spending decisions and setting priorities. If a legislative proposal which the president wants badly is short of majority support, the president has the resources to sway the crucial votes. The president can decide whether or not a local military base will be closed. The president can decide whether or not to support a farm subsidy program. The president can decide whether a program to curtail drug use will focus on breaking distribution networks in New York or supply lines in Florida.

A president who is not happy with a Cabinet member making statements at odds with administration policy can ignore the offender's request for new policy initiatives or enhanced budgeting support.[11] A meeting with a city mayor or state governor loudly critical of the president may result in an increased flow of federal funds to the city or state and much more cordial relations.

The White House Staff

To help them assign and manage the work load, presidents rely heavily on a few key aides. The White House staff is the president's instrument to coordinate and control the Cabinet departments and executive agencies that draw up a budget (OMB), monitor use of offensive language on daytime radio (FCC), and design rules to reduce air pollution from industrial smokestacks and automobiles (EPA). White House staffers help the president to choose policy priorities, resolve conflicts between agencies over jurisdiction, and monitor agency activities to ensure they are consistent with the president's wishes. White House staffers also write the president's speeches, draw up the president's daily schedule, lobby Congress to pass the president's policy proposals, monitor the president's standing in public opinion polls, and protect the president's political base within the party.

Presidents need to have confidence in the judgment and loyalty of their top advisers. That is why presidents typically surround themselves with close friends and longtime political associates. John F. Kennedy turned to his home state of Massachusetts for key staff; Lyndon B. Johnson's closest advisers came from among his Texas associates; Jimmy Carter drew heavily from his staff as Georgia governor; Ronald Reagan's White House staff were close personal friends and political advisers in California conservative politics; and Bill Clinton brought his political associates from Arkansas to Washington. Presidents can choose their team, and they look for advisers who are ideologically compatible and personally loyal.

Supervising a large staff with multiple responsibilities calls for considerable skill. Managing a complex organization is a highly personal art, but presidents tend to organize their key aides in one of two ways. Some prefer a highly structured, hierarchical White House staff, appointing a strong chief of staff who controls access to the president and closely supervises the work of other staff. Eisenhower's powerful chief of staff was Sherman Adams; Nixon relied upon H. R. Haldeman to run the White House; and in Reagan's second term, Donald Regan for a time had unquestioned authority to speak for the president.

Having a strong chief of staff worked for these presidents, who had no wish to be immersed in the details of administration or confronted with contradictory points of view and complex information. Nixon preferred to think and work alone in the privacy of the Oval Office. Eisenhower and Reagan were eight-hour-day presidents who depended on their chiefs of staff to see that their wishes were carried out and to keep administrators with policy questions and jurisdictional quarrels out of their offices. Bush relied heavily on the advice of trusted intimates like James Baker and Nicholas Brady to provide him with essential advice and guidance. For other administration officials, the road to President Bush passed through Chiefs of Staff John Sununu and James Baker.

Other presidents prefer a hub-and-spokes organization with the president at the center and many top administration officials having direct access to him. Presidents Kennedy, Johnson, Carter, and Clinton were eager to run their own administrations and used their chiefs of staff to coordinate White House staff activity. Kennedy enjoyed discussion with staff and expected them to present him with various policy options. Johnson jealously guarded his own power and was quite unwilling to be overly dependent on a chief of staff.

President Jimmy Carter earned a reputation for not delegating adequately. Carter immersed himself in the details of presidential administration, working 16-hour days and meeting with top Cabinet and executive agency officials about policy issues. However, he spent too much time resolving small disputes between individuals or agencies, getting involved in the details of implementing programs, and scheduling the White House tennis courts.[12]

Clinton placed himself at the center of his presidency, as he had controlled the office during his tenure as governor of Arkansas. He participated directly in key economic, foreign, and health care policy discussions; he talked to many advisers on a daily basis; and he did not rely heavily upon his chief of staff. But Clinton soon discovered that Washington was much more complicated than Little Rock, and within a year, he was attempting to strengthen his staff and to focus on fewer issues.

Variation in Presidential Effectiveness

Presidential effectiveness varies from one administration to another. The personality, character, and political style of presidents differ markedly. Global and societal circumstances, the context in which they govern, also vary.[13] In the aftermath of Watergate, Presidents Ford and Carter were unable to make particularly effective use of their office. Ford confronted huge Democratic majorities in the House and Senate. Having moved up from vice president to president, he could claim no mandate from the people, especially after his unpopular Watergate-related pardon of former President Nixon. Carter lacked the political skills to work with Congress and the Washington establishment. For some, his informality downgraded the symbolic dignity of the presidency. He was victimized by Iran's seizure of American hostages and an untimely economic recession brought about in part by sharp increases in petroleum prices.

In contrast to Ford and Carter, Reagan made effective use of the presidency's potential power. He avidly pursued his conservative political agenda of more military spending, lower taxes, less domestic spending, deregulation, and decentralization. He used his personal popularity and media skill effectively to combat the spirited opposition of members of Congress, clientele groups, and federal bureaucrats committed to existing domestic spending programs. He combined unwavering adherence to his basic political principles with a willingness to compromise with his opponents, to the frequent distress of his most conservative supporters.

George Bush presided over the dissolution of the Soviet empire and rolled back Iraq's invasion of Kuwait in 1991. In domestic policy he and a Democratic-controlled Congress were gridlocked. His own failure to stimulate a weak economy cost him reelection in 1992.

Bill Clinton wasted valuable time searching for an effective White House organization and spent scarce political resources promoting integration of homosexuals into the military. Controversial issues on his first-term agenda included reduction of the massive $300 billion annual budget deficit, health care reform, and ratification of the North American Free Trade Agreement (NAFTA).

Recent Abuses of Presidential Power

Abuses of presidential power during the Johnson and Nixon presidencies raised the specter of "imperial" presidents aggrandizing their power, subverting checks and balances, and evading democratic control.[14] Americans confronted the possibility that while activist presidents might provide leadership and break political stalemates, imperial presidents might usurp power and pursue personal agendas. Congress was sensitive to the fact that its constitutional authority was being undermined by presidential actions; and in foreign affairs, presidents routinely circumvented Congress by expressing accords with other nations through executive agreements, which do not require the approval of two-thirds of the Senate, rather than by treaty, which does require Senate approval.

Impoundment

Domestically, President Nixon used the power of impoundment in an unprecedented way to thwart the intentions of Congress. Many presidents have in the past impounded or refused to spend sums of money appropriated by Congress, but infrequently and usually for reasons Congress understood and approved. For example, if serious design flaws are detected in a military airplane or a space vehicle, the project may be put on hold while engineers determine what went wrong.

President Nixon, however, impounded large sums of money because he did not approve of Congress funding municipal water pollution control projects or farmer loan programs. Constitutionally, Congress is empowered to enact legislation and authorize spending. Members of Congress objected strongly to Nixon's encroachment on their right to legislate.[15]

The Vietnam War

Fears about a dangerous concentration of power in the White House followed the Vietnam war. The active presidency had deteriorated into an imperial presidency, wrote Arthur Schlesinger. Presidents Johnson and Nixon had abused their authority, subverting constitutional checks and balances and usurping congressional prerogatives.[16]

During the Vietnam war, presidents lied and provided misleading information to Congress and the American people about the war effort. President Johnson gave Congress inaccurate information in 1964 to gain passage of the Gulf of Tonkin resolution, which escalated the American military commitment in Vietnam. In 1969 and 1970, President Nixon authorized secret military operations in Laos and Cambodia without congressional authorization and knowledge. By 1967, America was fully committed to fighting the war in Southeast Asia, and that war was going badly. As the war vividly filled television screens every evening, Americans began to question why we were fighting there. The alarming lesson of the Vietnam war was that the president as commander in chief could deceive Congress and the American people and pursue disastrous military adventures unchecked.

The Watergate Scandal

Even more damaging to the authority of the president was the Watergate scandal. The Watergate investigations revealed that in 1973, high-ranking White House staff had paid the burglars who broke into the National Democratic Party Headquarters in search of information, used the CIA and the IRS to harass political opponents, and engaged in illegal mail surveillance and wire tapping. When journalists discovered parts of the story, President Nixon authorized a cover-up effort to obstruct congressional investigation.

When the Senate Judiciary Committee investigating the Watergate revelations requested relevant documents, tapes, and testimony, Nixon refused to cooperate, invoking executive privilege. Executive privilege claims that the constitutional separation of powers gives a president the right to withhold information from Congress. The dispute was brought before a federal district court, which ruled that the president could claim executive privilege if release of information could compromise national security but not if the information would simply embarrass the president or reveal presidential wrongdoing. The tapes provided a full account of presidential illegal behavior. Faced with certain impeachment, Nixon resigned from office.[17]

The Iran-contra Affair

President Reagan's tendency to delegate authority extensively without monitoring how subordinates used their authority hurt the Reagan administration in the Iran-contra affair. Reagan approved a plan to ship weapons secretly to moderates in Iran in exchange for efforts to secure the release of Americans held hostage by Iranian-backed groups in Lebanon. A low-ranking National Security Council staff member, Colonel Oliver North, diverted the profits to the Nicaraguan contras, despite a congressional ban on further government aid to them. North had the approval of National Security Council head John Poindexter, who chose to protect President Reagan by not telling him of the illegal diversion of funds.

When the Iran-contra scandal was exposed in November 1986, North quickly shredded many relevant documents to thwart a congressional investigation. Joint congressional hearings revealed that Secretary of State George Schultz and Secretary of Defense Caspar Weinberger had dissented from the original decision to ship arms to Iran and were not consulted on the project to divert funds to the contras, despite its obvious relevance for their missions. President Reagan's chief of staff and personal friend, Donald Regan, was forced to resign because he had not known about North's and Poindexter's actions and because he had insulated the president from competing points of view. President Reagan himself was sharply criticized for creating an atmosphere in which top subordinates would even consider making major decisions without getting explicit presidential approval.

Curbing the Imperial Presidency

The most important check on presidential power is the system of checks and balances provided in the Constitution.

Impeachment

The Constitution provides that a president can be charged with criminal actions or abuse of power and removed from office if found guilty. The House of Representatives serves as prosecutor and the Senate serves as judge. A majority of those voting in the House is needed to impeach; a two-thirds vote of Senators present is needed to convict and remove from office.

No president has ever been impeached and convicted. President Andrew Johnson was impeached in 1868, but he narrowly escaped conviction in the Senate. The House began impeachment proceedings against President Richard Nixon in 1974. As the entire story of presidential wrongdoing unfolded, President Nixon resigned to escape almost certain impeachment. He was succeeded by Gerald Ford, who subsequently issued a full pardon to block any future court action against Nixon.

Ford's pardon was controversial. Presidential pardons are normally used to correct obvious errors and miscarriages of justice, but pardons are not usually granted before an accused person is brought to trial. Critics wondered whether Ford and Nixon had made a resign-and-pardon deal which would make Ford president and protect Nixon from any judicial action. Ford firmly insisted that no deal had been struck and that he acted only to shift attention from past misdeeds to current issues.[18]

Although Watergate forced a Republican president to resign in disgrace and facilitated the election of Democrats in unprecedented numbers to Congress and state legislatures, the damage to the institution of the presidency ultimately hurt the Democratic party. The Democratic party has supported a strong, activist role for the federal government. Watergate eroded public confidence in the integrity and effectiveness of government and paved the way for the election of Ronald Reagan in 1980. He was committed to a program of deregulation, lower taxes, decentralization of responsibility to the states, and less domestic spending. This agenda reversed the emphasis of activist Democratic presidents since Roosevelt's New Deal. The only Democratic presidents elected since Watergate, Jimmy Carter (1976–1980) and Bill Clinton (1992–), ran as moderate centrists and as political outsiders uncorrupted by Washington politics.

Congressional Action

To curb potential abuse of presidential power in foreign affairs, Congress passed the War Powers Resolution (1973), enabling Congress to force the president to withdraw troops committed in combat overseas after 60 days in the absence of a formal declaration of war. Although American troops have engaged in military actions in Lebanon, Grenada, Libya, and the Persian Gulf since the War Powers Resolution was passed, Congress has never invoked it. Congress would be likely to curb the commander in chief's war-making authority only if American troops became bogged down in an unpopular, Vietnam-style war. Both the Senate and the House set up intelligence committees to supervise the CIA and the FBI more closely and to provide secure, leak-free channels for the president to keep Congress informed on sensitive intelligence matters. Congress also has refused presidential requests for funds to aid government opponents in Angola and Nicaragua.

Domestically, the Budget and Impoundment Control Act of 1974 established a Congressional Budget Office to provide Congress with its own more detailed taxing and spending information, created permanent House and Senate Budget Committees, spelled out new procedures intended to streamline the budget process, and placed limits on the president's right to impound funds.

Limits on Presidential Power

Many students of the American presidency are more struck by the limits on presidential power than by the president's potential to abuse power. The president has emerged as the pivotal figure in the American political system. After Roosevelt's election in 1932, many Americans were persuaded that the best hope of addressing various defects in American society rested with a strong, active president. Roosevelt and his successors pledged to find ways to ease the burden of economic depression, erase the post–Civil War legacy of legal racial segregation in the South, defeat fascism in World War II, and contain the expansionist Soviet Union. Influential students of the presidency, however—notably, Clinton Rossiter[19] and Richard Neustadt[20]—wondered whether the responsibilities of the president had grown more rapidly than the president's ability to carry them out. Several factors inherent in the American political system work together to limit a president's power.

Autonomy of Other Political Actors

One important limit on presidential power is the autonomy of other political actors. Particularly in domestic policy, the president shares power and responsibility with other political actors having their own interests and political resources. While the president is expected to provide leadership, other political actors can all too easily thwart the president's best efforts.

Members of Congress, for example, are insulated from presidential influence. Their power base is within their constituencies, and keeping the folks back home satisfied is crucial to their political future. They will support the president only when it is advantageous to do so.

This problem has been particularly acute in recent decades when Republican presidents have had to work with Democratic Congresses. Ideological confrontation has been the rule, and Republican presidents have had infrequent success at persuading Congress to follow their lead.[21] Yet Democrat Bill Clinton also encountered strong, effective resistance within Congress to his proposals to raise taxes, reform health care, and liberalize trade. Members of Congress found presidential influence less compelling than the preferences of important interests and voter opinion in their home constituencies.

The president is similarly constrained by our federal system, for city mayors and state governors are also independently elected. These local officials decide whether to support, tolerate, or oppose the president's policies. A president who punishes an uncooperative mayor or governor may earn the active displeasure of local interest groups, political party activists, and irate citizens.

Even getting the White House staff to pull together is a major challenge for a modern president. Part of the difficulty lies simply in the growth of the presidential establishment. In 1944, President Roosevelt had a White House staff of 48. By 1963, President Kennedy's staff had swelled to 263. And in 1980, President Carter had 417 White House staffers to coordinate and control.[22] In 1990, President Bush used the services of 623 full-time employees.

Also, since top White House staffers tend to be strong-willed, ambitious people used to having their own way, conflicts rooted in personal ambition or jurisdictional disputes are common. To some extent, conflict is desirable, since the president needs to hear competing policy proposals and suggestions for implementation. Presidents must beware of surrounding themselves with "Yes, boss" advisers who will carefully tailor their comments to suit the president's biases. Postmortems on the lost Vietnam war dwelled on Johnson's refusal to give skeptical advisers a chance to express their doubts about how the war effort was going. "Groupthink," which can impel presidential advisers to develop a collective opinion consistent with the president's own biases, is an important factor when decisions produce poor results.[23]

Size and Complexity of the Federal Government

Another limitation on presidential power is the size of the federal government. Table 9.2 compares the size of America's largest corporations and federal government departments.

Note that the Department of Defense dwarfs General Motors in both annual budget and number of employees, and even the smaller cabinet departments spend more dollars or hire more employees than do our largest corporations. The larger an organization, the more difficult is the chief executive's job of supervising and coordinating the work. The president as chief executive officer of the federal government has an enormous task.

Most of the 3 million federal government employees are protected by civil service regulations. High-level managers with supervisory and policy responsibilities cannot be dismissed easily should they disagree with the president's priorities. In fact, the president can appoint supporters to about 2000

Table 9.2   Sizes of Largest Corporations and U.S. Government Departments in 1992

Corporation	Fortune 500 Rank	Annual Sales (billions)	Number of Employees	Government Department	Annual Budget (billions)	Number of Employees
General Motors	1	$132.8	750,000	Defense	$322.3	1,034,000
Exxon	2	$103.5	95,000	Agriculture	$61.8	122,600
IBM	4	$65.1	308,000	Transportation	$33.4	67,400
PepsiCo	15	$22.1	372,000	Education	$26.5	17,731
Weyerhauser	51	$9.3	39,000	Housing and Urban Development	$24.2	13,600
Northrup	100	$5.6	33,600	Energy	$15.7	17,700
Briggs & Stratton	350	$1.0	7,800	NASA	$13.8	24,900
Block Drug	500	$0.6	3,300	EPA	$5.9	17,100

Sources: Fortune, April 19, 1993, p. 49; United States Statistical Abstract, Government Printing Office, Washington, D.C., 1992, pp. 322, 331.

top jobs. Of these 2000, some are politically necessary appointments to reward campaign supporters. Other appointments have independent credentials and bases of power. For example, the secretaries of labor, commerce, and agriculture must be acceptable to leading labor, business, and farm interests. Environmental groups push hard for a sympathetic EPA administrator. In these cases, top managers may place the priorities of their supporting clientele above the priorities of their president.[24]

Coordination problems and jurisdictional conflicts within the federal government are commonplace. A proposal to widen an urban highway typically requires the approval of federal transportation, housing, and environmental bureaucrats as well as consultation with numerous state and city officials. Conflict between the State Department's diplomatic perspective and the Department of Defense's military perspective is a staple feature of all presidencies. Washington insiders refer to these jurisdictional conflicts as "turfing."

Within the executive branch, the president can more easily cajole, persuade, and bargain than order and instruct. George Shultz, who ran the Bechtel Corporation as well as the labor, treasury, and state departments for two presidents, observed that in business, the chief executive can decide policy and expect that subordinates will make a good-faith effort to carry out decisions. In the federal government, there is not much hierarchy, and policy evolves out of discussions between the department, White House staff, other departments, and Congress. In a similar vein, Harry S Truman ruefully predicted that his successor, Dwight Eisenhower, would find running the federal government far more difficult than commanding an army. Truman mused, "He'll sit here and he'll say, 'Do this! Do that!' and nothing will happen. Poor Ike—it won't be a bit like the army. He'll find it very frustrating."[25]

Presidential Inexperience

To make their job even more difficult, presidents typically are inexperienced. They do not know the inner workings of the organization they are expected to administer. Our presidents have had political careers in the Senate (Kennedy and Johnson), the House of Representatives (Ford), the military (Eisenhower), and state government (Nixon, Carter, Reagan, and Clinton). They are brought in from outside to administer a huge, complex organization; by contrast, the chief executive officer of a typical corporation has risen through the ranks, having served a long apprenticeship before being asked to run the organization.

Length of Term

Presidential authority is also weakened because the president is elected to a four-year term and may be reelected only once. Dissenters in Congress and within the bureaucracy know that patience and delay will inevitably defeat the president. The president's authority problems are particularly acute in the last two years if indications are the president will not run again. The president's top advisors leave their Cabinet and White House staff posts to pursue more lucrative opportunities. They write books, deliver lectures, or use their contacts and knowledge of the administration on behalf of clients. Others leave the government because the excitement and challenge are over. No new policy initiatives will be undertaken. The balance of power within the bureaucracy inevitably shifts from the president's enthusiastic supporters to the president's opponents. And the president cannot get high-powered replacements to come to Washington for one year of caretaking.

When it is clear that the president will not run again, attention shifts to the next presidential race. The quest for the party presidential nominations begins at least 18 months before the presidential election, and political attention tends to shift from what the president says and thinks to the views of the possible next president.

Some reformers propose giving the president a single six-year term. Free from the pressures of special-interest and party politics, our chief executives could then exercise greater independence of judgment and pursue policies they judge to be best for the nation rather than policies which are politically expedient. Presidents Johnson and Carter supported the idea of a single six-year term.

However, our democratic system is built on the idea that the president should be closely attentive to the moods of the electorate. Limiting the president to a single six-year term also would hamstring the president's ability to build support for policies. Why should members of Congress follow the lead of a president who will not be around to head their party's ticket in the next election? Will bureaucrats be more likely to resist a president whose six-year term will end at a known date or a president who might be around for eight years? A six-year term might well aggravate the difficulties of a "lame duck" president seeking to persuade other political actors to support presidential initiatives.[26]

Our distant presidents, especially George Washington, Thomas Jefferson, Abraham Lincoln, and Franklin Roosevelt, are now heroic figures, and contemporary presidents seem to compare unfavorably to them. The mythic reputations of our past presidential heroes, however, ignore the political controversies, such as states' rights and the proper role of the federal government, that surrounded their presidencies. They would not have fared so well in the court of contemporary public opinion, either. Thomas Cronin has concluded, "Perhaps the ultimate paradox of the modern presidency is that it is always too powerful because it is contrary to our ideals of a government by the people . . . yet always inadequate because it seldom achieves our highest hopes for it."[27]

Controversy inevitably surrounds the presidency. Advocates of democratic, pluralist, and elitist perspectives differ sharply about how to interpret the president's role in the American system of government.

From a democratic perspective, a president strong enough to provide leadership is a president strong enough to abuse power. How to make the president responsive to the people is an enduring question in American politics, asked by the Founding Fathers and in recent years by critics of the imperial presidency.

From a pluralist perspective, presidents are weakened because they must share power with Congress and local officials. Presidential power is the power to persuade. The reality of domestic politics is that a president will find it difficult to pursue policies which are good for the nation as a whole but unfavorable to special interests such as farmers, retired persons, or the inner-city poor.

From an elitist perspective, the president is a powerful part of a small economic, political, and social elite that establishes economic and social prior-

ities. Citizens live their lives in a context shaped by this elite, and the importance of elections in American politics is much overstated. Elitists say that the notion that the people influence important presidential policy decisions is largely a myth.

Recommended Reading

Thomas E. Cronin: *The State of the Presidency,* Little, Brown, Boston, 1980.

George C. Edwards III: *At the Margins: Presidential Leadership of Congress,* Yale University Press, New Haven, 1989.

Stephen Hess: *Organizing the Presidency,* Brookings Institution, Washington, D.C. 1976.

Barbara Kellerman: *The Political Presidency,* Oxford University Press, New York, 1984.

Samuel Kernell: *Going Public: New Strategies of Presidential Leadership,* 2d ed., Congressional Quarterly Press, Washington, 1992.

Richard Neustadt: *Presidential Power,* Wiley, New York, 1980.

Benjamin I. Page and Mark P. Petracca: *The American Presidency,* McGraw-Hill, New York, 1983.

Richard Waterman: *Presidential Influence and the Administrative State,* University of Tennessee Press, Knoxville, 1989.

CHAPTER 10

The Bureaucracy

Some 3 million civilian employees implement policies devised by the president and authorized by Congress. These employees, called bureaucrats, have considerable discretion in implementing generally broad policy directives, and therefore, they have considerable power to shape our lives. Yet we citizens have little direct control over what these bureaucrats do.

This chapter begins with a discussion of the basic principles of bureaucratic organization. The focus then narrows to the public sector bureaucracy, paying special attention to the growth of government responsibilities in the twentieth century, how the federal bureaucracy is organized, and the evolution of the civil service system for hiring bureaucrats.

Finally, the chapter specifies some sources of bureaucratic power and autonomy and examines some criticisms of bureaucratic performance. Our assessment of how well the bureaucrats serve us and how responsive they are to our demands is important to our sense of the quality of American political life.

Complex Organizations in American Life

When the American republic was founded in 1789, most Americans lived on small farms and provided for many of their own needs. A farmer was, for better or worse, his own carpenter, furniture maker, weather forecaster, veterinarian, soil analyst, and leather repairer. A farm woman was candlemaker, food preserver, tailor, pharmacist, and nurse. Whatever services they needed or could afford were available in the local town—a general store, the community church, a one-room schoolhouse, a blacksmith's shop.

Two hundred years later, most Americans live in metropolitan areas, work at specialized jobs, and depend heavily on others to provide for life's needs. People work as carpenters or tailors and pay others for shoe repair and veterinary services. Goods and services are often provided by large, complex organizations—industrial firms, television stations, hospitals, supermarkets, department stores, schools, and government.

Large, complex organizations are known as bureaucracies, and the people working within them are called bureaucrats. Bureaucracies flourish because they are a superior form of social organization. Max Weber, writing in the early twentieth century,[1] noted that goods and services are provided more efficiently when people work together in complex organizations than if each person works alone or with very few others, as they did in frontier America.

Today, the labor force consists of about 125 million workers. Most are employed in the private sector; only 15 percent work for government. Five out of six government employees work at the state and local levels. They are schoolteachers, police officers, health care providers, and public works employees.

As we saw in Chapter 3, state and local governments administer many programs for which the federal government pays the bills. This is why the federal government generates about 23 percent of our annual gross national product while employing less than 3 percent of the labor force. About 200,000 federal bureaucrats, 1 in every 14, work in Washington, D.C.

The Expanding Role of Government in the Twentieth Century

Before World War I, the philosophy of laissez-faire was firmly in place, and government's role in society was quite modest. But the role of government has expanded over the course of the twentieth century, and Americans today expect much more of their government than did their grandparents.

Providing Collective Benefits

Government provides some services which a private company could not. Most important, government provides military security. Since the outbreak of World War II, our stake in a stable world has forced us to increase military spending dramatically. Military security is a collective benefit in the sense that whatever level of security is achieved benefits everyone, and all should pay their fair share. Only governments can collect taxes from everyone to pay for military spending.

Similarly, highways and schools benefit everyone, and everyone should pay for them through taxes. If these services were provided by private entrepreneurs, only direct users would pay for them and fees would be prohibitively expensive. Roads would not be built, and too few children would be educated. A private police force offering protection to a community would have no legal way to require all to contribute, even though all would benefit from lower crime rates. Some households would neglect to pay their fair share. This behavior is known as the free rider problem; some people "ride free" on the efforts of their responsible neighbors. Since government can require all to pay for needed community services through taxes, government builds the roads, operates the schools, and provides police and fire services.[2]

Regulating Abuses of Private Power

Sometimes the private marketplace fails to work efficiently. The first regulatory commission, the Interstate Commerce Commission (ICC), was established in 1887 to protect rural communities from the predatory pricing practices of railroads. (Often small communities were served by only one railroad, which could use its monopoly position to charge very high rates and make very high profits.) For the same reason, rates charged by "public utilities," those private companies that provide telephone service, electricity, and natural gas to our homes, are regulated by state public utility commissions.

Protecting Health and Safety

Much government regulation is intended to protect the health and safety of the public. The Food and Drug Administration (FDA) protects the buying public from unwholesome food and dangerous drugs. The FDA exists because consumers cannot know what the manufacturer put into a container of food or whether a drug might have dangerous side effects. The Occupational Safety and Health Administration (OSHA) establishes rules for the workplace in an effort to reduce accident and illness rates among American workers. The Department of Transportation requires automobile manufacturers to install turn signals, safety belts, and impact-resistant bumpers to reduce automobile accident and injury rates. The Environmental Protection Agency (EPA) prevents industries from dumping pollutants into the air and water, protecting the health and quality of life of communities downwind and down-stream.[3]

Implementation

Bureaucrats are so important because after Congress enacts a law or the president issues a policy directive, most of the implementation work remains. Once a food stamp program is authorized, for example, bureaucrats must determine eligibility standards, set up a distribution system, and ensure that local governments and recipients are complying with program regulations. Congress enacts, and the president signs, a law requiring that strip-mined land be restored to its original contours and replanted, leaving to bureaucrats the task of devising regulations consistent with the law's intent and responsive to very different terrains, soil types, and climatic conditions.[4]

How Government is Organized

Looking at the federal bureaucracy from the top down, we see that the work is divided among some 70 units which report to the president.

Cabinet Departments

Cabinet-level departments are headed by a secretary who is assisted by a network of undersecretaries, deputy secretaries, and assistant secretaries. The 14 Cabinet departments employ about 60 percent of our federal civil servants. The biggest employer is the Department of Defense, which purchases weapons, recruits troops, and designs military strategy. The unit with the fewest employees is the Department of Education, which sponsors educational research and administers scholarship and loan programs. Some Cabinet departments are formed around specialized functions such as foreign affairs, finance, and transportation. Others (e.g., Labor, Commerce, Veterans Affairs) are devoted to promoting the interests of particular social groups.

Executive Agencies

Executive agencies, like the Cabinet departments, are fully responsible to the president. Some units, like the EPA and the CIA, have policy-making responsibilities and close access to the president and the White House staff. Other units implement less visible programs and receive little presidential attention. For example, the National Science Foundation funds scientific research; the General Services Administration buys, cleans, and repairs the thousands of buildings and automobiles owned by the federal government.

Independent Regulatory Agencies

Most independent regulatory agencies were established to protect consumers from monopoly pricing and dishonest business practices. Among important regulatory agencies are the Federal Communications Commission, which regulates the broadcast industry; the Federal Elections Commission, which monitors candidate compliance with federal election laws; the Securities and Exchange Commission, which regulates trading in stocks and bonds; and the Federal Trade Commission, which prohibits deceptive advertising.

Independent regulatory agencies are governed by commissioners appointed by the president for four- to seven-year terms. They have legislative, administrative, and judicial responsibilities and operate independently of the president, who cannot set policy or remove the commissioners from office. These agencies were insulated from close political control in order to encourage objective, nonpartisan, technically competent regulatory practice.[5]

Government Corporations

Government corporations charge customers for services and operate much like a private business. Two familiar examples of government corporations are the United States Postal Service, which delivers the mail, and Amtrak, which provides rail passenger service. The Tennessee Valley Authority has built a network of dams on the Tennessee River to provide electricity, flood control, and recreational opportunities in the Tennessee Valley.

Principles of Bureaucratic Organization

The Department of the Interior, a city government, a college or university, an automobile manufacturer, and a fast-food franchise are all complex organizations designed according to bureaucratic principles. Max Weber noted that several characteristics of bureaucracies make them more efficient than less cooperative, more individualistic patterns of organization.

Hierarchy

At each level of the organization, higher-level superiors direct and coordinate the activities of numerous subordinate employees. The constellation of units, often called offices, divisions, or bureaus, resembles a pyramid or triangle. Several units report to the next level up the hierarchy, where activities are monitored and efforts are coordinated. The principle of hierarchy makes it possible for an organization to harness the efforts of thousands of employees toward a common purpose.

Figure 10.1 presents a portion of the organization chart for the Department of the Interior. A ranger maintaining trails and monitoring campsites in Yellowstone National Park is one of 78,000 employees of the Department of the Interior, of whom about 85 percent work outside Washington, D.C. Within the National Park Division (at the bottom of Figure 10.1), supervisors decide how many rangers should be allocated to each of the national parks and whether they will emphasize information and education activities or trail monitoring and maintenance. At the top of the Department of the Interior, a dozen offices and bureaus report to the secretary (three are shown in Figure 10.1).

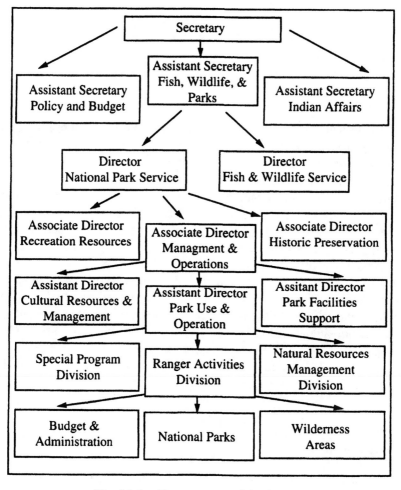

Fig. 10.1 Department of the Interior

The secretary decides policy, coordinates efforts, and represents department interests to the president and to other departments (such as the EPA) whose activities affect the parks.

The full organizational chart forms a pyramid with a very broad base. Most employees work within the national parks or in bureaus consisting of experts with specialized training and skills.

Specialization

Complex organizations are efficient because each employee specializes in rather narrowly defined activities. The Department of the Interior employs experts in Native American languages and culture, accountants, wildlife biologists, librarians, and media specialists for national park visitor centers. After learning a certain kind of work and gaining experience, employees tend to make a career of that kind of work. Today's 30-year-old secretary, accountant, or forestry officer will often be working at the same type of job at age 50.

Formal Rules

Formal rules govern the hiring of employees to ensure that every position is filled by a person qualified in terms of aptitude, training, and experience. While knowing someone in the Park Service may help an individual to land a ranger job, that person must meet the basic qualifications.

Organizations also spell out how employees are expected to carry out their work. The job of ranger or receptionist is defined, and whoever fills that job is expected to do the job in about the same way, regardless of personality or personal preference. Employees are expected to follow standard operating procedures or established routines.

Bureaucrats apply organization rules impersonally to their clients. The Department of Agriculture bureaucrat asks the same questions of every person who requests food stamps to determine whether or not the applicant is eligible. The bureaucrat at Housing and Urban Development allocates funds for housing project construction among communities according to a clearly defined set of criteria. In a modern complex organization, the personal inclinations of the bureaucrat are not a major factor in applying the rules.

Hiring the Federal Work Force

The Spoils System

For a century after the founding of the republic, the president and his appointed department heads hired and fired federal employees very much as they pleased. In the hiring process, political connections sometimes outranked training and experience. Indeed, the hiring process became known as the "spoils system" in the 1820s during Andrew Jackson's presidency. A newly elected president would fire many of the incumbent bureaucrats and appoint his political supporters to replace them. "To the victor belong the spoils" became a well-established principle of nineteenth-century American politics.[6]

The spoils system worked well enough when most jobs were easily learned and did not require much training or experience, but by 1880 the federal bureaucracy had expanded in size and jobs were more complex and detailed. Critics of the spoils system demanded reform. Jobs should be filled by workers with experience and training, not political hacks, thought reformers. The cause of the reformers was aided when President Garfield was assassinated in 1881 by a disappointed office-seeker. Two years later, the Pendleton Act (1883) established a civil service system to develop and administer a personnel system in which employees would be hired, fired, and promoted on the basis of their job performance.

The Civil Service Commission

The Civil Service Commission (now the Office of Personnel Management) established many procedures to foster a technically competent, politically neutral federal work force. Important civil service practices include the following:

1. Defining appropriate experience, education, and testing requirements for each federal job. An accountant must be familiar with accepted accounting practices, and a bricklayer must know how to lay bricks. A person is not put on the federal payroll because of his or her personal or political connections.

2. Rank-ordering all civil service jobs according to level of difficulty. The general schedule (GS) grades all jobs from GS-1 (unskilled jobs paying an annual salary of $10,600) to GS-18 (upper-level management positions paying $90,000 per year). At lower and middle grades, federal salaries and benefits are comparable to private sector salaries; at higher grades, federal salaries are lower than those usually paid in the private sector.

3. Developing procedures for dismissal of federal employees. Originally intended to protect civil servants from dismissal for political reasons, these procedures make it very difficult to dismiss incompetent employees. Workers have an interest in doing minimally acceptable work, and managers seek to avoid the costs of training replacements. Thus, dismissal rates tend to be low.

4. Setting up performance evaluation programs, which assist supervisors in making promotion decisions and motivate employees to improve the quality of their work.

Discrimination

The civil service system upgraded the quality of government, building a core of well-trained, experienced bureaucrats better able to implement public programs. But these bureaucrats were largely white males; the system tended to exclude women and minorities. Managers assumed that women and blacks would not fit in, would make clients or other workers uncomfortable, were not capable of doing many kinds of work, and did not need well-paying jobs.

Equal Opportunity and Affirmative Action

The federal Civil Rights Act of 1964 declared that "it shall be the policy of the United States to ensure equal employment opportunities for all employees." The principle of equal opportunity for all, regardless of race, religion, or gender, was widely accepted. More controversial were affirmative action programs, which encouraged government agencies to seek out well-qualified minority applicants to fill positions. Under affirmative action plans, when a minority or female and a male candidate were equally qualified, the minority or female candidate would receive preference. The objective was to increase the share of minority and female employees in the work force quickly.

Affirmative action programs have improved the job opportunities of women and, to a lesser extent, minorities. The proportion of women among holders of federal jobs rose from 33 percent in 1970 to 48 percent in 1989. Representation of women in middle management jobs (GS 13–15) rose sharply, from 3 percent in 1970 to 17 percent in 1989.[7]

Affirmative action has generated much controversy. White males have claimed that affirmative action policies deny them the equal protection of the law under the Fourteenth Amendment, and recently federal courts have placed limits on the extent to which employers can use affirmative action programs.

Civil Service Reform Act

The civil service system was overhauled in 1978 with passage of the Civil Service Reform Act (CSRA). This law replaced the Civil Service Commission with an Office of Personal Management; upgraded performance appraisal methods to facilitate dismissal of incompetent employees and promotion of effective employees; established a Senior Executive Service (SES), a core of top-level managers at the GS-16 to GS-18 levels who would receive bonus payments of up to 20 percent of base salary for exceptional performance; and set up a Merit System Protection Board to protect worker rights.

The CSRA was enacted to upgrade the quality of the federal bureaucracy. Existing practices were well established, however, and modest changes, not major reform, characterize the CSRA's first decade. It remains difficult for supervisors to dismiss incompetent employees. Supervisors often find it easier to make the life of an unwanted employee miserable by giving the employee nothing to do or assigning jobs that the employee dislikes than to document the employee's deficiencies adequately.[8] It also has been difficult to tie the bonus payments of SES personnel to their job performance.

What Motivates Bureaucrats?

Bureaucrats are at the center of a complex network of political activity. The president sets broad priorities, Congress monitors agency programs and intervenes on behalf of constituents, and interest groups affected by agency decisions take the agency to court and speak out at public hearings. How do bureaucrats go about their business of setting goals and making decisions when so many outsiders are interested in their activities?

Observers of bureaucracy have approached this question in three ways. The public interest approach assumes that bureaucrats seek to allocate resources for the well-being of society. The self-interest approach emphasizes that individual bureaucrats and agencies are motivated primarily by the desire for personal and organizational success. The political response approach describes bureaucratic decisions as reaction to the political pressures of clientele groups, the general public, and elected politicians.

Public Interest

Writing in 1887, Woodrow Wilson described an important difference between politics and administration. Politics, thought Wilson, involves making basic policy choices. Administration implements these policy decisions. Bureaucrats are expected to closely follow the policy directives of elected officials and to use their specialized skills and experience to implement the policies in an efficient, businesslike way. While politicians should be responsive to the people, bureaucrats should be politically neutral experts.[9]

The idea that government employees should pursue the public interest is well established among government workers and within society. The ethically responsible bureaucrat serves the people and must subordinate self-interest to the public good. Indeed, we commonly call a government worker a public servant. Some bureaucrats see themselves as protecting the public from special-interest-oriented elected officials; they perceive that politicians seek to maximize their reelection chances, while bureaucrats are more inclined to pursue the public interest.[10]

Limits on the Rights of Bureaucrats

To encourage the view that bureaucrats serve all of the people, society restricts the right of federal employees to participate in political party activity. The Hatch Act (1939) allowed a federal employee to run for office in nonpartisan elections, make campaign contributions, and vote in primary contests. It prohibited any political activity in the workplace, campaigning in local partisan elections, or running for office as a Republican or as a Democrat. In 1993, a new law extended the freedom of federal employees to engage in political activities away from the workplace.[11]

The right of public employees to join unions and to strike against society is also limited. In 1962, President John F. Kennedy issued an executive order which gave federal employees the right to join unions and engage in collective bargaining with the federal government. However, compensation is not subject to collective bargaining, and federal workers do not have the right to strike. Postal workers illegally walked out in 1970. When air traffic controllers walked off the job in 1981, they were summarily dismissed and replaced.

The Cost-Benefit Factor

Bureaucrats serve the public interest by "making a profit" for society, providing goods and services whose value to society is greater than the cost of the resources needed to provide them. If OSHA issues a workplace regulation, the value to society of reduced injuries and workers' peace of mind should be greater than the cost of complying with the regulation. The Department of Transportation should allow states to set speed limits on rural interstates at 65 miles per hour only if the value of faster travel exceeds the cost of higher accident rates and increased fuel consumption. An agency should not provide its own staff training program if it can contract with another agency to provide the same program at lower cost.

Recent administrations have required government agencies to make more use of cost-benefit analysis, which asks bureaucrats to calculate the costs and benefits of proposed programs and to undertake only those programs whose benefits are greater than their costs. Traditionally, cost-benefit calculations have not been widely employed because measuring benefits in the public sector is rather difficult. Private corporations sell their product for a price, and the bottom line, profit, is a ready comparison of costs and benefits. For a government agency, however, how does one tell what benefits are generated by a billion-dollar highway program? What contribution does a $20 billion weapons system make to national security? How do we establish the aesthetic value to society of a river that does not smell?

While useful techniques for measuring benefits are available, they have been used infrequently because Washington has tended to be dominated by lawyers rather than economists. Economists think naturally in cost-benefit terms and have developed techniques for measuring benefits in the public sector.[12] Lawyers often respond to political pressure, writing a regulation on behalf of their agency and then enforcing compliance with that regulation. Economists are trained to compare costs and benefits; lawyers are trained to make the strongest possible case on their client's behalf, not to judge the merit of their client's case.

Self-Interest

Personal Concerns

The self-interest approach to bureaucratic motivation assumes that government bureaucrats maximize their individual self-interest, not the interests of the taxpaying public.[13] In this view, individual bureaucrats pursue income, status, and power within their agency. Family concerns and leisure preferences may also affect work performance. Bureaucrats engage in a perpetual process of weighing benefits and costs in making daily decisions about whether to make an exception to agency rules, whether to stay home with a sick child, whether to implement a new policy directive in good faith.

Organizational Goals

Bureaucrats may also pursue organizational goals, expanding the agency's mission or budget and protecting turf in bureaucratic struggle with other agencies. William Niskanen argues that government grows because bureaucrats are continuously seeking to expand the size of agency budgets. Bureaucrats seek to maximize some combination of salary, reputation, power, and service output, all of which are enhanced when agency budgets are expanding. In the 1970s and 1980s, bureaucrats proposed many ways to spend money and expand agency services. In the 1990s, bureaucrats struggle to avoid layoffs and cutbacks as legislators cut spending to shrink the budget deficit and avoid hefty tax increases.[14]

Bureaucrats want their agencies to be successful. The scientific researcher studying air pollution at the EPA believes that cleaner air is an important social goal. The weapons purchasing specialist at the Department of Defense is convinced that military preparedness is an essential national objective. The lawyer who works in the Department of Justice's antitrust section wants to protect the public from high prices and poor service, a possible result of a proposed merger between two competing corporations.

Political Response

According to this view of motivation, bureaucrats work within the context of a political system in which power is scattered among various elected politicians, interest groups, and other bureaucrats. As they do their work, bureaucrats engage in a continuous process of negotiation. They negotiate with legislators about how to implement imprecise laws stating broad goals and with special interests who are affected by bureaucratic decisions.[15]

Regulators are sometimes puppets manipulated by a dominant interest. Sometimes they are impartial umpires weighing the evidence and arguments presented by competing interest groups. And often regulators are spirited participants whose strong preferences may be tempered in the course of bargaining and negotiations with the regulated interests. Thousands of regulatory dramas unfold each year, with different scripts and actors playing different parts.

Policy Triangles

Agencies typically devote much care to building and maintaining the policy triangles formed by the agencies, their clientele groups, and congressional committees. For example, the Department of Agriculture is attentive to the needs of farmers and consults closely with farm interest groups such as the Grange and the Dairy Farmers Association. The Veterans of Foreign Wars and the American Legion are strong supporters of the Veterans Administration, which provides medical and educational benefits to veterans.

Agencies also cultivate good relations with the congressional committees which authorize spending and appropriate funds. The policy triangles formed by these political relationships are described as iron triangles, which emphasizes their durability, or cozy triangles, which indicates that like-minded bureaucrats, legislators, and interest groups work comfortably together. Policy triangles are common in routine, day-to-day government.

Agency Capture

While policy triangles are pervasive, the links between government agencies and those affected by agency activities are varied, especially when the agency must satisfy several constituencies. One pattern is that an agency established to regulate an industry for the benefit of the public ultimately works closely with the regulated industry. The Interstate Commerce Commission (ICC), established in 1887 to protect farmers from high rates set by monopolistic railroads, eventually came to regulate competition, setting rates at high enough levels that all railroads could make a profit and discouraging competition.[16]

This pattern, called agency capture, was characteristic of the airline and trucking industries before deregulation in the late 1970s.[17] The Civil Aeronautics Board set fares and assigned routes to passenger airlines, discouraging innovation and guaranteeing profits. The ICC limited the number of carriers and set rates that truckers could charge. In both cases, customers paid lower rates and enjoyed better service after deregulation. Agencies tend to be captured because members of the general public, who initially demand action to correct industry abuses, subsequently lose interest in agency decision making. However, the regulated industry continues to have a keen interest in agency decisions and works hard to shape those decisions.

Issue Nets

On controversial policy matters, bureaucrats must take into account sharply different viewpoints. For example, the automobile industry and environmental groups pressure the EPA to issue favorable rules on urban air pollution. The pharmaceutical industry and consumer groups attempt to influence the FDA on how much testing for a new drug is adequate to protect consumer health and safety. These issue nets involve small numbers of people with expertise and interest in a particular policy area, competing points of view, and valuable expertise. Unlike policy triangles, issue nets involve conflict between competing interests which the bureaucrats who make and implement policy must reconcile.[18]

In the intense political conflict generated in issue net politics, bureaucrats must engage in a process of negotiation with competing groups in search of a set of rules minimally acceptable to each.[19] Government regulators sometimes have to choose between well-organized competing groups. In these circumstances, the regulatory agency acts as a more or less impartial umpire, drawing on the information and arguments presented by competing groups to reach a decision fair to the competing groups and the general public. The Nuclear Regulatory Commission must make rules promoting safe operation of nuclear power plants, balancing the opposing preferences of industry groups and environmental interest groups. The industry wants to limit construction and operating costs, while antinuclear groups seek to minimize the risk of a nuclear accident at any cost. FDA regulators expect the pharmaceutical industry to test new drugs thoroughly before marketing them, while the industry complains that years of testing in search of unexpected side effects make drugs prohibitively expensive and deny sick people access to them.

Both issue nets and policy triangles imply that policy is made by elites with expertise far beyond that of the ordinary citizen. From a pluralist point of view, issue networks are an improvement over policy triangles because a wide range of competing interests is represented.

Criticisms of Bureaucracy

Our high standard of living and centralized, interdependent culture are possible because of bureaucracy. Large, complex organizations are efficient and highly productive because they embody the principles of hierarchy, specialization, formal rules, and impersonality which Max Weber first described. However, if you ask people what bureaucracy means to them, they are likely to mention inefficiency, red tape, and delay. Consumers of private sector goods and services want what they are buying; taxpayers often cannot see an equally direct connection between publicly provided goods and services and the taxes they pay.

Inefficiency and Low Productivity

Bureaucracies (whether public or private) may be inefficient because bureaucrats may attempt to ride free on the efforts of their fellow workers, anticipating that the organization's work will get done without their making a fair contribution.[20] Free riding is common because no one can judge precisely the value of an individual worker's contribution to an organization. That is why all employees who do similar work are paid at the same rate. Most federal jobs are classified into 18 categories according to training required, level of difficulty, and level of responsibility. A mechanic, a nurse, and a librarian with the same job rating are paid at the same rate regardless of how well they work. In effect, the employee is paid the average salary for employees in that work classification.[21]

A shirking worker who does the job poorly, reads the newspaper at work, and goes home early hurts the organization's productivity, and these losses are borne by everyone. Meanwhile, the shirker gains 100 percent of the value of a more relaxed approach to the job. Why should an office worker sacrifice a longer coffee break in order to process more applications?

Organizations seek to minimize shirking by monitoring how employees are spending their time and by establishing and enforcing rules. They can require employees to punch a time clock to record their arrival and departure times and can instruct them to limit their coffee breaks to 10 minutes. They can set out detailed rules and regulations that describe how employees are to do their jobs. And they can institute work load measures that keep track of how many letters an office worker types, how many factories an inspector visits, and how many licenses a clerk issues.

One problem is that monitoring is itself costly. An agency head who spends time and energy monitoring workers has less time for making policy decisions, and for coordinating the work effort, and for communicating with legislators, the department head, and related agencies. A supervisor may well conclude that close monitoring takes too much time and energy or has too little effect on employee behavior.[22]

An additional problem is that supervisors themselves have an incentive to shirk their monitoring responsibilities. The supervisor who is paid a salary of $45,000 regardless of how well the organization works has little incentive to spend time in the thankless task of monitoring workers closely.

Close monitoring is not feasible in complex, nonroutine situations where subordinates need to be flexible and use their judgment. In enforcing workplace safety regulations, for example, the individual enforcement officer must decide whether a marginal improvement of workplace safety justifies imposing a costly regulation on a workplace.

Fortunately, many bureaucrats do not shirk even if they are not closely monitored. In those organizations which establish an ethic of hard work, bureaucrats will work diligently without close supervision. When individuals see that others are working hard, they will be more inclined to work hard too.[23]

Many workers also have a sense of professional pride in doing their job well. Many occupational fields now require higher education, foster adherence to standards of work and behavior, and create a sense of identity among practitioners. These professionals may draw their behavioral cues from their professional organizations. Accountants, teachers, and nurses are more likely than sanitation workers and file clerks to have a sense of professional responsibility. Over time, the federal work force is becoming more professionalized. The Bureau of Labor Statistics estimates that the professions grew from 4 percent of the work force in the 1920s to 15 percent in the 1970s.[24]

Red Tape

As bureaucracies grow larger and more complex, coordination becomes more necessary and more difficult. More rules are written and procedures specified to ensure that similar situations are handled in similar ways. On the one hand, these rules and procedures protect against arbitrary, inconsistent case-by-case decisions; on the other, the rules can seem like foolish red tape.

Consider the case of Arlo Van Veldhuizen, an aging Iowa dairy farmer. He agreed to sell his dairy cattle for slaughter under the Department of Agri-

is more complexity
inevitable?

culture's Dairy Termination Program, a plan to shrink milk production. An assistant secretary decided that participating dairy producers had to sell all their cattle to discourage cheating and to minimize the need for case-by-case dickering (which would open the door to the appearance of favoritism). When Van Veldhuizen asked if he could keep "Old Mama," who no longer gave milk, as a pet, Department of Agriculture bureaucrats said no. The policy rule was no pets, because exceptions would require thousands of difficult case-by-case decisions. ("Yes, my pet cow does give some milk but not much." "Can I keep pets for each of my children?").

From the Department of Agriculture's point of view, the "no pet" policy made sense. Hiring more bureaucrats to authorize exceptions and monitor compliance would cost taxpayers more money. However, from the farmer's point of view, he and Old Mama were innocent victims of Department of Agriculture red tape. The farmer's congressman agreed, and the department was successfully pressured to grant the exception.[25]

Turfing

As the government addresses complex issues, problems of coordination mount. When the Department of Transportation proposes to build a highway, it must work closely with for example, HUD, whose buildings may be knocked down; the EPA, for air pollution levels may be affected; and the Department of the Interior, whose historical landmarks may be in the way. Endless meetings and memos delay the process until each affected agency is satisfied and "signs off" on the project. This lengthy coordination process is necessary because frequently what one agency proposes affects the work of another agency.

Occasionally, agencies compete for jurisdiction in what is a competitive, not a cooperative, process. In Washington, bureaucratic struggles over jurisdiction are known as turfing. One recurring example is the conflict between the CIA, the Department of Defense, and the State Department, all of which gather and interpret information. Turfing also occurs along the Texas-Mexico border, where agents of the Immigration and Naturalization Service have clashed with agents of the Drug Enforcement Agency while pursuing their respective missions of preventing illegal border crossing and drug smuggling.

Inconsistent Policies

Bureaucrats are expected to provide services efficiently and to respond to political pressures, two objectives which are not always compatible. The Army Corps of Engineers may decide to build a dam project in a key congressional district for political reasons, not because potential flood damage is great or because irrigation is needed at that site. HUD may take into account a phone call from the White House suggesting that the application of a powerful mayor's city for an urban development grant receive favorable consideration. HUD bureaucrats may believe that the money can be best used in city A, yet award the grant to city B because of the political pressure. Moreover, citizens may shake their heads to learn that government agencies are following con-ʼ tradictory policies, for example, providing subsidies to tobacco growers while the surgeon general is waging a campaign to discourage smoking.

Bureaucratic Jargon

Bureaucrats are also criticized for their impenetrable prose. Their graceless, jargon-filled sentences alternately irritate or amuse citizens who wish to communicate with bureaucrats. How is one to interpret the following sentence from a New York State Department of Environmental Conservation memo? "The department has the responsibility under the state environmental quality review act and under its regulations to ensure that its determinations on applications for permits, for which environmental impact statements are prepared, to construct and operate solid-waste management facilities will minimize to the greatest extent practicable adverse environmental impacts relating to those facilities."[26] Few readers would have the patience or interest to decipher such a sentence, which translated into ordinary English means "The department will grant permits to construct and operate solid-waste management facilities that minimize adverse environmental impact."

Bureaucrats frequently use passive verbs and place the subject at the end of long sentences, habits which frustrate all but the most patient of readers. For example, the thought "The department should study the situation" can be bureaucratized by writing "It is felt that the situation should be subjected to further study by the department." Another common practice in writing bureaucratic jargon is to convert words that are nouns into verbs. Thus a bureaucrat might write, "I tasked the committee to prioritize projects and undertake those which will impact on the problem." Unflattering caricatures of how bureaucrats speak and write are commonplace.[27]

The 3 million federal bureaucrats convert general policy statements of the president and Congress into specific rules and regulations binding upon each of us. Bureaucrats shape the programs and provide the services which we pay for through taxes and borrowing.

A large, powerful bureaucracy poses serious questions for democratic theory. For nearly 100 years, bureaucrats have been selected according to the civil service principle of technical competence and political neutrality. Bureaucrats, accordingly, are partially insulated from close control by our democratically elected president. Bureaucratic decisions are binding upon us and affect our lives, but we citizens have little direct control over them. We do, however, have considerable indirect leverage through our elected members of Congress, who watch over agency activities, appropriate funds annually, and attend to the complaints of their constituents. Citizens also have indirect control through the interest groups they support.

Pluralists assign great importance to these checks on bureaucratic performance to ensure that the ruled have a substantial measure of control over their rulers. Elitists tend to focus on broad policy issues, not the details of policy implementation. For elitists the activities of bureaucrats are of less interest than the policy priorities of their masters.

Recommended Reading

Anthony Downs: *Inside Bureaucracy,* Little, Brown, Boston, 1967.

Judith Gruber: *Controlling Bureaucracy: Dilemmas of Democratic Governance,* University of California Press, Berkeley, 1987.

Kenneth Meier: *Regulation: Politics, Bureaucracy and Economics,* St. Martin's, New York, 1985.

Gary J. Miller: *Managerial Dilemmas: The Political Economy of Hierarchy,* Cambridge University Press, New York, 1992.

William Niskanen: *Bureaucracy and Representative Government,* Aldine-Atherton, Chicago, 1971.

Francis E. Rourke: *Bureaucracy, Politics and Public Policy,* Little, Brown, Boston, 1984.

Irene Rubin: *The Politics of Public Budgeting,* Chatham House, Chatham, N.J., 1993.

James Q. Wilson: *Bureaucracy: What Government Agencies Do and Why They Do It,* Basic Books, New York, 1989.

CHAPTER 11

The Federal Judiciary

Eras of Judicial Interpretation

1789–1800	The early Supreme Court period
1800–1835	Marshall Court protects private property and furthers national power
1836–1864	Taney Court supports state police power and is deeply divided by slavery issue
1864–1875	Civil War and Reconstruction lead to decline in the position of the Court
1875–1937	Court increases in status and becomes protective of corporate property against national and state regulation
1937–1953	Court removes itself from determining economic and social policy and begins to expand individual rights
1953–1969	Warren Court expands rights in the areas of speech and association, religion, voting, race, and the criminal process
1969–present	Burger and Rehnquist Courts slow the expansion of individual rights and give greater deference to state power

Of the three branches of government at the national level, the judiciary remains the most insulated from political influence. It is, however, an important part of the policy-making process. Throughout the nation's history, the courts have used the Constitution to protect various interests against the effects of majority power. The authority of courts to interpret the Constitution and statutes often enables them to give the final definition to a policy position.

This chapter describes the structure and operations of the federal courts. It begins with a general explanation of the legal basis for the federal courts and the basic principles of law and legal process within which they operate. Then it examines the structure and operations of the courts themselves. Finally, it discusses the role of the Supreme Court in shaping American public policy.

Legal Framework

Article III

Article III of the Constitution provides the basis for the federal court system. By specifying the kinds of cases that can be heard by these courts, it defines both judicial jurisdiction and the requirements of standing.

Jurisdiction

Jurisdiction refers to the range of cases that a court may hear. If a case does not fall within a court's jurisdiction, it must be pursued in another court. The most basic forms of jurisdiction are original and appellate. A court that has original jurisdiction hears cases for the first time and makes determinations of guilt or innocence. A court that has appellate jurisdiction hears cases on appeal from lower courts and rarely makes determinations of guilt or innocence. Appellate courts normally confine their decisions to questions of proper procedure or interpretation of the law and refer cases that they overrule back to the original court for further proceedings.

Standing

Standing, on the other hand, refers to the criteria that a party to a suit must meet to be able to use a particular court. Article III states that the federal judicial power extends to cases and controversies involving specified subjects or parties. These criteria define both the jurisdiction of the federal courts and the basis on which a party may claim standing to use these courts.

Because Article III was the result of a compromise between those Founding Fathers who wanted strong national power and those who favored state power, it specifies only that a Supreme Court shall be established. The establishment of lower federal courts is left to Congress. Even more limiting to the Supreme Court is the fact that Article III gives it the power to hear cases in the first instance (original jurisdiction) in only two areas: those cases in which a state is a party and those involving "ambassadors, other public ministers and consuls." Without the establishment of lower courts, these would be the only cases that the Supreme Court could consider. Many of the cases that receive wide publicity today, such as those questioning the constitutionality of statutes, would not be within the jurisdiction of the Supreme Court.

Article VI (Supremacy Clause)

The supremacy clause of Article VI, Section 2, is one of the most important parts of the Constitution because it gives that document preeminent legal status by declaring that the Constitution, all laws "made in pursuance thereof," and all treaties made "under the authority of the United States" are the "supreme law of the land." It further provides, however, that the judges in every state will be "bound thereby." Clearly, in the absence of federal courts other than the constitutionally specified Supreme Court, the Founding Fathers intended that the state courts would be the final interpreters of the Constitution, federal law, and federal treaties, except where the Supreme Court could exercise its original jurisdiction. This would, of course, have left the Supreme Court in a very weak position.

interesting

Judiciary Act of 1789

Fortunately for the emergence of uniform interpretation of national law, the first Congress chose to act quickly and comprehensively through the Judiciary Act of 1789 to establish the framework for a powerful national judiciary. First, the act established lower federal courts that could hear the whole range of cases defined as within federal judicial jurisdiction in Article III. These cases could then be heard on appeal by the Supreme Court, if necessary. Second, in Section 25, the act provided that state court decisions involving a "federal question"—a claim under the Constitution, federal law, or federal treaty—then could be appealed to the Supreme Court. By these two actions, the first Congress tremendously increased the power of the federal courts and of the Supreme Court. Not only did cases heard in the lower federal courts become reviewable by the Supreme Court, but state court decisions involving federal power also were made subject to final approval by the Supreme Court.

This last power is particularly important because it establishes the national government as the final determinant of the extent of its powers. Standing alone, the Constitution would have encouraged a situation where courts in Montana could have interpreted federal law differently from those in Mississippi. Section 25 of the Judiciary Act eliminates this possibility by giving the Supreme Court the power to overrule state court decisions involving the Constitution, federal laws, or federal treaties to provide uniform national interpretation. Furthermore, these state court decisions need not be those of the highest court in the state. If a case involving a federal question cannot proceed beyond a local or intermediate state court because the next-highest court refuses to hear it, that case may be appealed directly to the U.S. Supreme Court. Section 25 of the Judiciary Act has been aptly called the linchpin that holds together the federal system. Without it, the interpretation and application of federal law would at best be a patchwork affair.

Marbury v. Madison—Judicial Review

Ironically, the most important power exercised by the Supreme Court—that of judicial review—has little support in the wording of the Constitution. *Marbury v. Madison* (1 Cranch 137 [1803])[1] is generally conceded to be the basis for the Supreme Court's power of judicial review. Judicial review occurs when a court rules a statute or executive action unconstitutional. It derives from the belief that the courts are specially qualified to interpret the Constitution. This perspective has been a characteristic of American political culture. Other countries have not been willing to grant their judges such powerful status, although a few now grant a limited power of judicial review to specific courts. It remains an anomaly of American politics that nonelected judges with life tenure are allowed to overturn decisions made by a majority of duly elected representatives.

In the *Marbury* case, Chief Justice John Marshall was faced with a dilemma. William Marbury had been denied a judicial appointment to which it appeared he was legally entitled. At the same time, the Court confronted a hostile and powerful President Jefferson and a Congress controlled by him. It was likely that if the Court ordered the president to deliver Marbury's judicial commission, it would be ignored. Such a result would have been exceptionally damaging to the status and authority of the Court as an institution.

Marshall resolved the dilemma by holding unconstitutional the law under which Marbury appealed to the Court. Thus, Marshall avoided a direct confrontation with President Jefferson and at the same time gained status for the Supreme Court by ruling null and void a portion of a congressional statute. A reading of Marshall's opinion will reveal that his reasoning is based largely on the logic derived from the belief that judges are uniquely qualified to interpret the law. It has little basis in the Constitution or in legal precedent. However, the Jeffersonians appear to have accepted the Court's right to declare a congressional statute void, and the Court has retained that power ever since.

The American Legal System

Forms of Law

The American legal system is bound by the Constitution. As Article VI states, the Constitution is the "supreme law of the land." This means that state constitutions and state laws, as well as federal statutes, must conform to the Constitution. Because the Supreme Court is the final interpreter of the Constitution, its decisions regarding the Constitution also become the supreme law of the land. The only formal recourse from Supreme Court decisions in these instances is a constitutional amendment. Because it is so difficult to change a Supreme Court decision based on the Constitution, the Court tries to decide cases on other bases if possible. If the Court simply interprets the meaning of a law without reaching a constitutional issue, Congress is free to pass another law overruling the Court's interpretation.

Common Law

The Constitution, congressional statutes, and agency regulations all are examples of written law. An older form of law that has served as the basis for Anglo-American law for centuries is the common law. Common law differs from statute law in that it is created by judicial decisions. Judicial reasoning from one decision to another forms the core of the common law. As indicated by the term "stare decisis" (Latin for "let the decision stand"), judges are guided by precedents—previous judicial decisions in similar cases—and cases are argued by attorneys in terms of which precedents are most appropriate in a particular case. This form of law must inherently remain uncertain because the rule of law in a case is never definite until the judge makes the decision. The authority of judges to determine the substance of the common law has been an important factor in elevating the status of the judiciary in common-law countries.

It is an interesting twist of judicial history that, despite its long tradition, common law has only limited relevance at the national level. Early in the nineteenth century, the Supreme Court held that there was no federal criminal common law. For an act to be a crime at the federal level, it must be specified in a statute. Thus, when Lee Harvey Oswald was accused of assassinating President Kennedy, he was arrested and held by Texas authorities because there was no federal statute making murder of a president a crime, although that shortcoming has since been remedied. When noncriminal cases are before the Supreme Court, elements of a common-law approach may appear if a case involves a controversy between two states or citizens of two states, but the Court remains very reluctant to move far beyond the written law. The meaning of important parts of the Constitution has evolved through judicial precedent over the years, but technically, the Court's interpretations remain rooted in the document itself. Common law finds its widest use at the state level, where it remains important in many areas of noncriminal law. However, at any level of government, the basic rule is that where there is a conflict, statute law overrides common law.

Equity Law

A form of law that developed in reaction to the rigidity of the early common law was equity law. Equity law focuses on preventing wrongs that cannot be adequately compensated once they have been committed. It provides judges with considerable discretionary power. An injunction is a common form of equity law. Courts may be asked to enjoin behavior before it occurs to prevent irremedial damage. Thus, unions may be enjoined from striking, or a group may be enjoined from a march or demonstration on the fear that such action would lead to a riot. In recent years, the federal courts have gained fairly extensive equity powers, and these have been broadly used in the area of racial discrimination and on behalf of other disadvantaged segments of society. Federal judges have successfully ordered states, localities, and school boards to comply with their orders in these areas. Judge W. Arthur Garrity in Boston went so far as to act as the school board and essentially ran the Boston schools for a time.[2]

Statute Law

Although the Supreme Court's exercise of judicial review tends to receive more public attention, most of the Court's work involves interpreting the meaning of statute law, which is law enacted by a legislative body. This can be difficult and controversial because Congress has developed the practice of passing laws that are ambiguous. The problem of assembling majorities to pass legislation has discouraged the use in statutes of specific, precise language that may antagonize particular interests. The consequences of this ambiguity are that final policy decisions are deferred to agencies and finally to the courts. Federal statutes are, of course, the supreme law of the land subordinate only to the Constitution, and state laws and constitutions must conform to them. The Supreme Court's interpretation of the compatibility of state laws and constitutions with federal law has been a source of controversy throughout its history.

Regulations promulgated by federal agencies also have legal standing. Because they draw their authority from either the Constitution or congressional statute, they are superior to state action. Agency regulations can be a problem for the Supreme Court because it must determine not only their meaning and application but also whether they accurately reflect the often ambiguous intent of Congress. B. Guy Peters, for example, points out that phrases such as "maximum feasible participation," "equality of educational opportunity," "special needs of educationally deprived students," and "full employment" are elements of program guidelines established by Congress that are "subject to a number of different interpretations" which could vary considerably from the original intentions of their legislative creators.[3]

Criminal and Civil Law

Although the distinction is not clear, the major difference between criminal law and civil law is that criminal law involves prosecution by the state that could result in a jail sentence, fine, or other form of punishment. While civil law can involve suits by the government, it predominately involves litigation by private parties. Usually these suits ask for monetary damages of some sort, although they may be attempts to force a party to act in a certain manner. Thus, an individual who has entered into a business contract with another individual might be forced to sue for damages suffered if the contract is not fulfilled. In other instances, professional football clubs have sued players under contract to them to prevent them from playing for other clubs.

Constitutional legal protections come into play primarily in the area of criminal law. Thus, even though a civil lawsuit can cause a defendant serious losses, the courts do not afford that individual the same level of protection that an individual has against state prosecution in a criminal case. Following this same line of reasoning, the standards of proof are less rigorous in civil cases than in criminal cases. In a civil case, one does not have to be found guilty beyond a reasonable doubt to lose, and usually, a unanimous jury verdict is not required.

Legal Processes

The Adversary Process

The American judicial system operates through the adversary process. In its purest form, this means that issues are determined by combat in the courtroom. The theory behind the adversary process is that through the confrontation of the two parties to a suit, the facts of a controversy will be most effectively obtained. The American judicial system gives broad latitude to the two contending parties in a lawsuit and limits the powers of a judge to guide the proceedings. Such is not the case in England or on the Continent, where judges have far more power to insist that the parties to a trial remain focused on the issues involved.

The adversary process makes an American trial an expensive and uncertain undertaking. In some respects, its most important function may be to encourage the disputing parties to settle their differences without going to court. In fact, in both criminal and noncriminal litigation, most cases are settled before going to trial. This allows certainty in outcome for the litigants, saves them considerable expense, and relieves the case burden on the courts.

The parties to a case are the plaintiff and the defendant. The plaintiff is the party who initiates the action; in a criminal case, the plaintiff is the prosecution, or the government.

Appellate Procedure

The grounds for appeal are laid during the trial. At this time, one of the attorneys may object to an action of the court or of the opposing attorney. If this objection is overruled by the judge, his or her decision on this point may be used as the basis for an appeal. In an appeal, the losing party in a case also may claim other procedural irregularities. These are presented to the appellate court in a written brief that is usually answered by the winning side. The two sides then are normally given the opportunity to summarize their positions in oral arguments before the appellate court. After oral arguments, the appellate court issues a written opinion that may sustain the lower court decision or may overrule it. If the lower court is overruled, the case normally is sent back to that court for correction of the errors found.

It is particularly important to understand that in a criminal case, the prosecution may not appeal an acquittal. A defendant may appeal a conviction, but in doing so, he or she waives the right not to be retried if the conviction is overturned in the appeal. Also, the appellate stage of the judicial process focuses on interpretations of law and procedures. Except for highly unusual circumstances, it does not involve the introduction of new evidence or the interrogation of witnesses.

Court Structure

Constitutional Courts

The backbone of the federal judicial system is the constitutional courts. These courts are established under Article III of the Constitution. Their judges have judicial independence and life tenure. In many respects, the structure of these courts serves as a model of efficiency in comparison with the complicated court systems often found at the state level. The constitutional courts are organized in a three-tiered structure: district courts, courts of appeal, and the Supreme Court.

District Courts

The district courts are the courts of original jurisdiction in the federal judicial system. They hear both civil and criminal cases and hold both jury and nonjury trials. At this level each case is heard by one judge. Each state has at least one judicial district; most contain several districts, and each district may have a number of district court judges. At any one time in these districts, several district court cases may be in progress. Including the states and territories, there are 94 judicial districts.

The federal judicial districts also contain other federal legal staff. The most important of these are the U.S. magistrates, marshals, and district attorneys. The U.S. magistrates are appointed by the district court judges. They perform important pretrial functions for the judges and hear civil cases and nonfelony criminal cases with the permission of the two parties to a case. The district attorney for a district is the federal government's prosecutor and can become quite well known. (Rudolph W. Giuliani, for example, gained a national reputation for his vigorous prosecution of corruption in the New York City area.) U.S. marshals provide some of the basic law enforcement functions for the federal government in the judicial districts. They make arrests, are responsible for prisoners, and serve judicial orders and writs. Both the U.S. attorneys and marshals are appointed by the president with the consent of the Senate.

Courts of Appeal

The U.S. courts of appeal are the first line of appeal from the district courts, and most cases end at this level. The nation is divided into eleven circuits, or appellate districts, that encompass several states each, and the Court of Appeals for the District of Columbia. This latter court is particularly important because it handles much of administrative law involving federal agencies. In 1982, Congress established an additional court of appeals, the Court of Appeals for the Federal Circuit, whose jurisdiction is defined solely by subject matter. The courts of appeal are multijudge courts. Most cases are heard by three-judge panels, but for important litigation, more judges may sit on the case. In addition to appeals from the district courts, the courts of appeal hear cases from federal regulatory agencies.

A hybrid of the district courts and the courts of appeal is the three-judge district court. A three-judge district court is a temporary court with original jurisdiction appointed to handle particular kinds of cases. Congress may specify that challenges to a law's constitutionality be heard by such a court. Applications for injunctions against legislative reapportionment proposals also must be heard by three-judge district courts. The three-judge district court is normally composed of a court of appeals judge and two district court judges. Its primary advantage is that its decisions can be appealed directly to the Supreme Court. By skipping the intermediate appellate stage, the litigants to a case can receive a final decision much faster.

Supreme Court

Of all the federal courts, the Supreme Court receives the most attention and is the most powerful. Today, the Court consists of nine members, although its size is subject to change by Congress. It originally began as six justices, and at one time during the Civil War period it was expanded to ten. After the Civil War, Congress lowered its size to seven and finally settled on nine members. It has remained at nine since that time.

Routes to the Supreme Court

Writ of Certiorari.   Cases come to the Supreme Court primarily through the writ of certiorari. If the Court grants a petition for a writ of certiorari, it has agreed to hear the case being appealed. The advantage of the writ of certiorari is that it allows the Court to control its work load and to select those cases which it deems of national significance. In deciding on whether to grant a petition for a writ of certiorari, the Court operates under the "rule of four," by which only four of the nine justices have to vote affirmatively for a case to be heard. If the Court refuses to hear a case, the lower court decision stands, but the justices have consistently maintained that their refusal does not necessarily mean that they agree with the lower court's decision. Other reasons may lead the Court to refuse to grant a petition for the writ. The justices may think that the facts of the case unnecessarily complicate the issue. Or they may conclude that the issue involved simply does not present a substantial federal question or that the Court is too divided on an issue to render a useful decision.

Right of Appeal.   Cases also may be brought to the Court by the right of appeal. In 1988, under its authority to control the appellate jurisdiction of the Supreme Court, Congress severely restricted this route to the Court. Today, those appeals that the Court must hear are limited to decisions of three-judge district courts. Even in these instances, the Court may deal with the case briefly and overturn or affirm the lower court's decision with a short statement.

In Forma Pauperis Petition.   Many applications to the Supreme Court are in forma pauperis petitions. These petitions proceed on the basis of a federal statute that permits anyone who completes a pauper's oath declaring indigency to enter a case in a federal court. These petitions need not be in any particular form, and many sent to the Court are simply written up by the petitioners themselves. These are almost always prisoners in state or federal institutions. The Court considers these petitions and may occasionally grant a hearing or otherwise act positively on them. The vast majority of them are frivolous, however, and their number has caused some justices, notably former Chief Justice Warren Burger, to argue that they should be dealt with in some other manner.

Supreme Court Procedure

Once an application for a hearing by the Supreme Court has been granted, the parties to a case file written briefs with the Court. These briefs argue the issues on appeal, urging the justices to either affirm or reverse the lower court. The case is then set for oral arguments, and attorneys for the litigants appear before the Court to state their positions. Today, these oral presentations have strict time limits. Furthermore, an attorney may have carefully prepared his or her presentation only to discover that the justices have questions from the bench that they want answered or considered. This can lead to lively interchanges between the bench and the attorney, who may never get beyond the first few lines of prepared material. The oral argument period presents the justices with an opportunity to raise questions about points in the written briefs, and their questions reflect their interest in the positions suggested there.

Supreme Court Opinions

The term of the Supreme Court is from October through June. During this time the Court is hearing oral arguments and the justices are holding conferences among themselves to decide the cases that have been argued. These conferences are held on Wednesday afternoons and Fridays in the Supreme Court conference room. No one is allowed into the room while the justices are in conference, and throughout history, the justices have been very circumspect about what has happened in that room. One can only speculate that discussion in conference has at times been heated and emotional. What is known is that the chief justice speaks to the case first and that the discussion then proceeds from the most senior justice to the most junior.[4] If the chief justice is in the majority, the chief justice assigns the justice who will write the opinion; if not, the senior justice in the majority makes the assignment.

The writing of an opinion takes time. Drafts of opinions are circulated among the justices, who make suggestions as to revisions. Occasionally, dissenting justices may be drawn onto the majority side with a few changes in wording, and less frequently, a dissenting opinion may be so persuasive that it gains sufficient support to become the majority opinion. When the Court is finally satisfied with the form of an opinion, it is announced from the bench, usually in a summary fashion. Often the most difficult and controversial opinions are not announced until the last week or two of the Court's session, perhaps because it has taken that long for the justices to reach a satisfactory statement.

On the contemporary Court, unanimous opinions have been less frequent than divided ones. Typically, there is an opinion for the Court, which is the majority opinion, but often there are also concurring opinions and dissenting opinions. A concurring opinion is one in which the justice agrees with the outcome of the decision, but he or she would use a different approach in reaching that outcome. A dissenting opinion is just that; it disagrees with the majority's position and may at times be vehement in tone. A per curiam opinion differs from the preceding forms in that it is a short, unsigned statement by the Court acting on an appeal. Normally, it simply cites a previous ruling that settles the issue as far as the justices are concerned. Per curiam opinions may be accompanied by dissents that are signed.

Other Federal Courts

In addition to the constitutional courts, Congress has established other courts. These courts have begun as legislative courts—courts to help Congress implement its legislative powers under Article I of the Constitution. Today, these appear to fit into two categories: those courts which remain essentially legislative in origin and character and those which began from the legislative source but have evolved into constitutional courts.

Legislative Courts

Legislative courts are courts that have been assigned legislative and administrative functions by Congress that the independence of constitutional courts does not allow. Their judges serve for specified terms.

The more clearly legislative courts are the Tax Court, the Court of Military Appeals, the Court of Veterans Appeals, and the territorial courts. The Tax Court hears claims against the Internal Revenue Service. The Court of Military Appeals hears appeals from military tribunals. The Court of Veterans Appeals reviews decisions regarding veterans' benefits made by the Department of Veterans Affairs. The territorial courts are part of Congress's responsibility for administering the nation's territories. They have broad jurisdiction in these territories.

Legislative/Constitutional Courts

The more difficult courts to categorize are those which still have legislative characteristics reflecting their origins but have been given some constitutional status. These are the United States Claims Court, the Court of International Trade (formerly the Customs Court), and a newly created Court of Appeals for the Federal Circuit. The Claims Court hears claims against the national government, which through its establishment has consented to be sued in certain kinds of matters. The Court of International Trade hears cases involving customs disputes, such as the proper classification of imports and questions about the duties levied on imports. The Court of Appeals for the Federal Circuit was created by Congress in 1982 and technically constitutes a thirteenth court of appeals. However, its jurisdiction is defined by subject matter, not by geography. Its functions include those of the previous Court of Customs and Patent Appeals. It hears appeals on customs, appeals from the Patent Office, and personnel issues from the Merit System Protection Board.

Judicial Selection and Removal

The processes of judicial selection and removal have become much more important as the federal courts have become more heavily involved in the policy process. The political activism of the courts has made the political issues involved in the selection of federal judges more salient. These considerations become even more important in light of the recognized difficulty of removing federal judges, whose tenure is protected by Article III of the Constitution.

The Supreme Court

Supreme Court justices are nominated by the president and approved by the Senate. During the nineteenth century, it was not unusual for presidential nominations to the Supreme Court to become heavily involved in congressional politics. Such was not the case during much of the twentieth century. Until the Nixon presidency, only one presidential nomination had, in this century, been rejected by the Senate.

Senate Opposition

The Nixon difficulties were presaged by the failure of Lyndon Johnson's effort to move Justice Abe Fortas from the position of associate justice to the chief justiceship. Technically, this nomination was not rejected by the Senate. It failed because the Johnson forces were not able to break an opposition filibuster against the nomination. Justice Fortas then withdrew as a nominee and resigned from the Supreme Court. Faced with vacancies in the positions of chief justice and associate justice, President Nixon first filled the chief justice position with Warren Burger. However, his nomination of Clement Haynsworth for the remaining vacancy was defeated by the Senate, as was his next nominee, G. Harrold Carswell. Finally, Nixon nominated Harry Blackmun, who was approved by the Senate. The opposition of the Senate in these instances reflected a more aggressive stance toward presidential Supreme Court nominations.

This willingness to confront a president on his Supreme Court nominations was confirmed by the Senate's treatment of President Reagan's nomination of Robert Bork to the Supreme Court. After Senate Judiciary Committee hearings that were unprecedented in this century in length and bitterness, the Senate rejected the Bork nomination. President Reagan's next nominee, Douglas Ginsburg, withdrew before the Senate could act on his nomination. The president's third nominee, Anthony Kennedy, was quickly and rather easily confirmed by the Senate. The Bork nomination battle was the most obvious instance of the Senate directly disagreeing with the ideological stance of a nominee, but ideological opposition also had formed the basis for much of the Senate opposition to the unsuccessful nominees of Johnson and Nixon. The Bork nomination was further complicated by the perception that the next justice on the Court could very easily prove to be the swing vote on important social issues, including the constitutional status of abortion.

A nominee's stance on abortion continued to be a concern during consideration of the next three appointments to the Court, although in the cases of David Souter and Ruth Bader Ginsburg, opposition on this point was somewhat muted because Souter's stance was carefully ambivalent and by the time of the Ginsburg nomination, a new Court majority supporting abortion had appeared. The close battle over Clarence Thomas's nomination to the Court undoubtedly involved the belief that his conservatism encompassed opposition to abortion, but the immediate and most obvious basis for attacking his nomination was the charge by a former employee, Anita Hill, that as her supervisor ten years previously he had used sexually inappropriate language in discussions with her. After airing these accusations in several days of sensational hearings before the Senate Judiciary Committee that gripped the attention of the nation, the full Senate rather quickly confirmed Thomas's nomination by a vote of 52 to 48, making him the second black justice in the nation's history.

Nomination Considerations

Ideological Compatibility with the President's Views.   This is probably the foremost consideration that enters into a nomination to the Court. Presidents naturally want people on the Supreme Court who will be sympathetic to their policies. Since the Eisenhower presidency, Republican presidents have usually nominated lower court judges to the Supreme Court. Eisenhower argued that a person should not sit on the Supreme Court without previous judicial experience, although during his presidency the appointment of Earl Warren was a conspicuous exception to this rule. The primary attraction of this approach, however, appears to be the predictability that it provides. Presidents can examine a nominee's previous record as a judge and have a pretty good idea of how that individual will act as a Supreme Court justice. On the present Court, Sandra Day O'Connor and David H. Souter were former state court judges (Souter was also a federal judge for approximately six months), and Antonin Scalia, John Paul Stevens, Anthony Kennedy, Clarence Thomas, Ruth Bader Ginsburg, and Stephen G. Breyer all were previously lower federal court judges. Moreover, six of the eight were appointed by Republican presidents.

Geography.   Geography also enters into consideration in Supreme Court nominations, but often this is more a reflection of the influence of political interests than it is any conscious attempt to provide geographic dispersion on the Court. Thus, over time the Court tends to represent the shifts in political power in the nation. For a long period, for example, New York State was expected to have at least two seats on the Court, but until the appointment of Justice Ginsburg in 1993, the Court had gone 21 years without a justice from that state. On the other hand, two of the justices—Sandra Day O'Connor and William Rehnquist—are from Arizona, and the western and midwestern states are well represented.

Other Factors.   At one time it was thought that one of the seats on the Court should be held by a person of the Jewish faith. That string of justices— Louis D. Brandeis, Felix Frankfurter, Arthur Goldberg, Abe Fortas—was broken by Nixon's appointments to the Court and resumed with the appointment of Ruth Bader Ginsburg. President Clinton's second nominee to the Court— Stephen G. Breyer—was also Jewish. Today, the presence of Clarence Thomas, a black, and two women, Sandra Day O'Connor and Ruth Bader Ginsburg, raises the question of whether gender and race will continue to be important factors in appointments to the Court. In a similar vein, Justice Scalia's easy passage through the nomination process was widely credited to the fact that he was the first Italian-American nominated to the Court.

Lower Federal Courts

Selection of lower federal court judges usually does not receive the public attention given Supreme Court nominations, but these choices can have a tremendous impact on the legal system and public policy. Because they have original jurisdiction over cases, the district courts in particular have considerable latitude in framing the facts and legal issues in a dispute. Used skillfully, this power can influence heavily the subsequent decisions of appellate courts. District courts have in recent decades also gained a great deal of power over the implementation of judicial decisions. Especially in the area of racial discrimination, they have assumed the authority to order or to prohibit actions by agencies at the national, state, and local levels.

Senatorial Courtesy

Presidential discretion in the appointment of district court judges is severely limited by the practice of senatorial courtesy. In brief, this practice requires that the president appoint someone acceptable to the senators from the same party as the president to any district court vacancies in their state. If the president ignores these senators in making the nomination to a district court in that state, one of them will simply note this fact when the Senate is considering the appointment. The Senate will then reject the nomination in support of their colleague.

Senatorial courtesy is one ramification of the fragmented nature of American political parties. In many states, the political parties have various factions, some of which support the state's senator, others of which may be more supportive of the president. No senator wants a president to intervene in his or her state's politics with patronage appointments to district court positions. Thus senators will maintain a united front on this issue to protect themselves. If, on the other hand, there are no senators from the president's party from a state, the president has considerably more leeway in making a district court appointment, although the party leaders in the state may be consulted as a courtesy. Appointments to the courts of appeal allow the president more flexibility in selection because one or two senators do not have a veto power.

Evaluation of the Candidates

All these judicial nominations are considered first by the Senate Judiciary Committee, which may make a recommendation to the Senate as a whole. At this point as well, the American Bar Association will provide a recommendation as to whether, in their view, the candidate is exceptionally well qualified, well qualified, qualified, or not qualified. (Nominees to the Supreme Court receive one of the last three ratings.) Nominees also must undergo investigation by the FBI.

The Reagan administration, to a greater degree than any previous administration, made a concerted effort to select conservative judges. Nominations of individuals were preceded by extensive interviews and investigations. With the Senate in Republican control, all but one of the president's nominees were approved. When the Democrats gained a Senate majority in 1986, action on Reagan nominees slowed perceptibly. Nonetheless, President Reagan placed over 300 judges on federal courts, more than any previous president had appointed, and their influence over judicial policy is expected to extend into the twenty-first century.

Read book an Obama era

Judicial Removal

One of the concerns that enters into the selection and approval of federal judges is the fact that they have tenure during good behavior, meaning in essence that they are appointed for life.

Impeachment

The primary method for removing a federal judge remains the exceedingly cumbersome impeachment process. No Supreme Court justice has ever been removed through impeachment, and as of 1992 only seven lower court judges had been so removed.

Some of the recent impeachment convictions have had rather bizarre aspects. One of these involved District Court Judge Harry E. Claiborne of Nevada, who, even though he had been convicted of a crime and was serving a prison term, refused to resign from the bench. Under these circumstances, in October 1986, an outraged Senate made short work of his impeachment trial, convicted him, and removed him from the federal bench. In 1989, Alcee L. Hastings was removed from the federal bench through impeachment and conviction, although he had been acquitted of the criminal charges against him; and in 1992, he returned to public office as a duly elected member of Congress from Florida. In 1993, the Supreme Court upheld the constitutionality of the Senate's use of a 12-member committee to hear evidence regarding impeachment charges and then make a recommendation to the full Senate. This streamlined approach, which avoids tying up the entire Senate in an impeachment proceeding, was first used against Judge Claiborne.

In other instances of judicial misconduct, the judicial councils of courts of appeal have removed cases from judges, allowing them to remain as judges but depriving them of any opportunity to act judicially. Congress appears to have supported such actions by passing legislation enabling judicial councils to discipline judges in their circuits.

Retirement

Another approach to providing some movement on the federal bench has been to encourage retirement. Chief Justice Warren left the Court because he believed that judges should not remain active after age 75, although he was 78 when he finally left the Court. The same sort of thinking may have influenced his successor, Chief Justice Warren Burger, who also retired at age 78. Others have not been of the same view, as demonstrated by Justices William Brennan and Thurgood Marshall, who retired at ages 84 and 83 respectively.

In the past, the Court itself has acted to encourage retirements. Thus, as a junior justice in the middle of the nineteenth century, Justice Stephen J. Field was called on to suggest to Justice Robert Grier that it was time to retire. Justice Grier, who would occasionally break into song while attorneys were arguing before the Court, accepted Field's suggestion and retired. Later, in his nineties, Justice Field refused a similar suggestion from his brethren and remained on the Court with varying degrees of lucidity until his death.[5] Modern medical technology has complicated the problem, and Justice William O. Douglas, determined to establish the record for Court tenure, remained on the Court in a greatly reduced capacity with the aid of such technology. His tenure of 36 years did set a record for Court service, although it seems a bit unfair to justices such as John Marshall, who served almost as long without the benefit of antibiotics and life-support systems. Ha!

The Supreme Court in History

Students of the Supreme Court have generally agreed that the Court has evolved through a number of fairly definable eras, or phases, of interpretation. These eras have reflected the political climate of the nation. This is to be expected, since the Court has responded to appointments by presidents, who, in turn, have been popularly elected. Moreover, as an institution, the Court has found it wise to remain somewhat sensitive to community feelings. When the justices have lagged too far behind changes in public sentiment or have moved too far in advance, the Court has been subjected to severe attacks.

The Marshall Court

Although the early Supreme Court rendered a few decisions of importance, it lacked both a sense of institutional identity and a national status. This changed dramatically under the chief justiceship of John Marshall from 1801 to 1835. During this period, Marshall had a tremendous influence on the Court and on the nation. Discarding the tradition of having each justice issue an opinion in a case, Marshall instituted the practice of giving one opinion for the Court, and for the first decade of his tenure, that opinion was usually written by him. Furthermore, Marshall was adept at obtaining agreement among the justices and discouraging dissenting opinions. Thus, the Court was able to present a more cohesive image to the public in its decisions.

Under Marshall's tenure as chief justice, the Supreme Court had the opportunity to interpret for the first time many provisions of the Constitution. This allowed Marshall to build the constitutional basis for a powerful national government. Marshall's first concern was the protection of private property. He was convinced that the most certain route to such protection was a strong national government that could withstand and limit the threats posed to people of property by the state legislatures. Most of Marshall's major decisions can be explained within this simple framework: the protection of private property through support for strong national government.

The Taney Court

Roger Brooke Taney (pronounced "Tawney") headed the Supreme Court from 1836 to 1864 and reflected the growing concern for state power during this period. The Taney Court was largely responsible for building the constitutional basis for state police power, which is the inherent power of a state to act for the health, welfare, morals, and safety of its citizens. Concern for state power also grew out of attempts to deal with the slavery issue. The Taney Court was never able to resolve the slavery controversy, and its attempts to do so were one of the reasons why it was less cohesive than the Marshall Court. The low point of the Taney era was the infamous Dred Scott decision, in which Taney held that a Negro could never become a citizen of the United States (*Dred Scott v. Sandford,* 19 Howard 393 [1857]). This decision caused Justice Benjamin Curtis to resign from the Court in protest.   *Good!*

Civil War and Reconstruction

During the Civil War and Reconstruction period, the Supreme Court was overshadowed by the war and the ensuing control of Congress by the Radical Republicans. The Republican control of Congress enabled them to ignore much of what President Johnson attempted to do and to manipulate the Supreme Court. When it appeared that the Court might declare unconstitutional the Reconstruction statutes governing the occupied southern states, Congress simply repealed the appellate jurisdiction for the case and thereby removed it from the Court's jurisdiction. To prevent President Johnson from having the opportunity to nominate anyone to the Supreme Court, Congress reduced the size of the Court to seven, and then with President Grant in office, it increased the size of the Court to nine.

The Era of Corporate Power

From about 1890 until 1937, the Supreme Court's approach to constitutional interpretation was sympathetic to the growth of corporate power in the

United States. The Court tended to view the Constitution as a limit on reform attempts to regulate corporations. Its decisions limited both the national government and the states. This was a period in which the nation underwent vast industrialization and growth, but it also was a period when the working classes and minorities, especially blacks, found little support in the law of the land as interpreted by the Supreme Court.

The onset of the Great Depression and the election of Franklin D. Roosevelt to the presidency were to bring a historic confrontation between the Court and the presidency. Through his New Deal program, Roosevelt initiated extensive governmental measures to alleviate the effects of the depression. The Court, however, was not receptive to the dramatic move toward greater government activity. During the first term of the New Deal, it ruled unconstitutional numerous New Deal statutes. When Roosevelt was reelected in 1936 by a huge majority, he resolved to move against the Court, the one remaining obstacle to his New Deal program. He proposed to Congress that the Court be enlarged to 15 members. This would allow him to appoint sufficient new justices to give him a Court favorable toward the New Deal. Even though Roosevelt had just won a popular mandate and had large majorities in both houses of Congress, there was considerable public discomfort with his proposal. It was viewed as an effort to "pack" the Court in his favor.

As events worked out, the Court itself acted to undermine support for the president's proposal. While Congress was considering the plan, the Court began to uphold the constitutionality of state and national laws regulating economic activity. With the major reason for enlarging the Court removed, Congress defeated the attempt to increase its size to 15. Thus, while President Roosevelt was defeated on his specific proposal, he achieved the more important goal of making the Court supportive of his programs.

The essential point for the student of American politics is that the confrontation in 1937 was a major turning point in constitutional history. Since that time, the Supreme Court has consistently refused to rule against economic or social legislation (unless it involves threats to civil rights or liberties).[6] Its position has been that these issues are properly determined through the political process.

The Warren Court

The next major recognizable era of Supreme Court interpretation occurred under the leadership of Chief Justice Earl Warren (1953–1969). During these years, the Court was dominated by a liberal majority that did not hesitate to interpret the Constitution in favor of the disadvantaged. The most important decision of this period was *Brown v. Board of Education* (349 U.S. 294

[1954]), which invalidated racial segregation in public education. The Court also acted vigorously in the areas of free expression, voting discrimination, criminal protections, and separation of church and state. The Warren Court stimulated a major restructuring of American society and, from the perspective of many, moved further and faster than was desirable. Running for the presidency in 1968, Richard Nixon articulated these feelings with his call for a "strict constructionist" Court, by which he appeared to mean a Court that was less willing to effect social change through its decisions. The era following the Warren Court has been one of greater conservatism on the part of the Court, but none of the principal Warren Court decisions have been directly overruled.

The Burger and Rehnquist Courts

Under Chief Justices Warren E. Burger (1969–1986) and William H. Rehnquist (1986–) the Supreme Court has counterbalanced the activist, nationalistic tendencies of the Warren Court. During the Burger and Rehnquist years, the Court has expanded some individual rights, particularly in the areas of abortion and gender issues. Moreover, it has strongly supported First Amendment free expression rights. Primarily, however, during the 1970s and 1980s, the Court fairly consistently deferred to state courts and policy processes, encouraging a variety of approaches toward fundamental legal rights in contrast to the national standards promulgated by the Warren Court. Thus, in cases involving capital punishment, obscenity, criminal procedure, and homosexual rights, the Court has given the states much greater leeway in determining individual rights. And, while it has not overturned major Warren Court precedents, in areas such as obscenity, abortion, and criminal procedure it has trimmed them by allowing the states flexibility in their interpretation and application.

Also under the Burger and Rehnquist Courts there has been increasing concern for maintaining the formal constitutional boundaries of the three branches of government. Much of the Court's activity in this area has been directed at Congress. Thus, it has ruled that the legislative veto (the negation of agency decisions without passing a statute) and the use of the General Accounting Office (GAO) to enforce budget cuts were unconstitutional attempts by Congress to circumvent the allocation of powers in the Constitution. On the other hand, it has upheld Congress's use of the independent counsel and the Senate's approach toward the impeachment of federal judges. With regard to the president, the Court confirmed that the exercise of executive privilege (the confidentiality of conversations with the president) has a constitutional basis at the same time that it insisted that in a criminal judicial proceeding the president must release taped conversations relevant to that proceeding. The Court has also declared that presidents are immune from civil liability for any actions taken while they are in office acting as presidents. These decisions are important for the substantive law that they have articulated, but, taken in total, they also indicate a greater willingness on the part of the Court to assert its power to define the constitutional limits of the authority of the president and of Congress.

Major Early Decisions

As previously noted, the Marshall Court rendered a number of original interpretations of constitutional clauses. These provided early support for national power and are still seen as having legal significance.

McCulloch v. Maryland

While that Court's *Marbury v. Madison* decision established judicial review limiting congressional power in favor of the Court, its decision in *McCulloch v. Maryland* (4 Wheaton 316 [1819]) provided a broad base for congressional power. At issue was the power of the national government to charter a national bank under the "necessary and proper" clause of the Constitution. The Constitution specifically limits Congress to those powers "herein granted," but at the end of its listing of powers it provides that Congress shall have the power "to make all laws which shall be necessary and proper for carrying into execution the foregoing powers." In the *McCulloch* case, Marshall decided that the "necessary and proper" clause should be interpreted expansively and as an additional grant of power to Congress, not as a limit on congressional power. If Congress can establish that a program is related to carrying into effect one of its specifically delegated powers, then that activity can be justified by the "necessary and proper" clause. The Supreme Court's continued support of Marshall's broad definition of that clause has allowed Congress to undertake programs such as the vast hydroelectric complex of the Tennessee Valley Authority and the interstate highway system on the grounds that they bear some relationship to providing for the national defense and other delegated powers.

Gibbons v. Ogden

In *Gibbons v. Ogden* (9 Wheaton 1 [1824]), the Supreme Court rendered the first interpretation of the scope of the clause giving Congress power to regulate commerce "among the several states," which is usually termed the interstate commerce clause. In this decision, Marshall ruled that Congress's power over interstate commerce was clearly superior to state power in this area. Furthermore, commerce did not have to cross state boundaries to become subject to national regulation; it needed only to "concern more states than one." Although succeeding Courts' interpretations of Congress's commerce power restricted and expanded its scope, Marshall's early expansive approach has survived as the basis for extensive exercise of national power. Today, there are few areas of economic activity that Congress could not regulate under its commerce power if it chose to do so.

The Courts and Public Policy

Throughout its history, the Supreme Court has functioned as a policy-making institution. Because its interpretations of the Constitution have been accepted as definitive, it has inevitably become another part of the policy process involving the president and Congress. Although it has assumed a powerful policy position, this position has always been more tenuous than those of the president and Congress. Unlike the president and Congress, the Court cannot claim the legitimacy of electoral support, nor does it have the means to implement its decisions. The Court must remain dependent on general public support to be effective, and when it is under sustained attack, its status as an institution is endangered.

Judicial Activism/Judicial Restraint

An issue that has received attention throughout the twentieth century is the extent to which the Court should actively engage in the making of public policy. This has often been cast in terms of judicial activism versus judicial restraint. The judicial activist uses his or her power as a judge to overrule legislative judgments. The disciple of judicial restraint, on the other hand, tends to defer to the decisions of elected bodies. In this respect, Justice Oliver Wendell Holmes, Jr., might be taken as one model of judicial restraint. Holmes personally did not favor active government reform or intervention in the economy, but he was unwilling in most instances to interpose his personal judgment in place of that of elected officials.[7] Although Holmes left the Court in 1932, the Court's withdrawal from economic and social policy in 1937 was compatible with his views. Up to that time, the Court had been active in substituting its views of the value of limited government for those of Congress and the president. Later, the Warren Court demonstrated another form of activism by advancing individual protections, often in the absence of legislative or executive support.

Two Approaches toward Constitutional Interpretation

In the 1980s, the judicial activist/judicial restraint debate took a somewhat different twist. In this debate, Attorney General Edwin Meese and Justice William Brennan were two of the major protagonists. Meese argued that the Supreme Court should interpret the Constitution based on its specific words and as far as possible on the intentions of those who wrote those words. In his view, the Warren Court engaged in judicial legislation that moved beyond constitutional authority, and nonelected judges have no right to impose their particular views on the nation. Justice Brennan, an important member of the Warren Court majority, argued, in opposition to the Meese view, that the Constitution must be treated as a flexible document that allows judges to make decisions relevant to contemporary circumstances. Further, Justice Brennan saw the Court as the primary protection for minority interests in society.

The reader will have to decide which position seems to be more sensible. An important question to be considered, however, has to be what constitutes the basis for effective democracy. Can a democratic majority be trusted to govern effectively and fairly, or are there fundamental rights that require judicial protection from majority control if a democracy is to realize its full potential? How one stands on this question will have a direct bearing on how one views the proper role of the judiciary in the American political system.

Article III of the Constitution provides for the Supreme Court and specifies its original jurisdiction. Other courts and appellate jurisdiction are left to the discretion of Congress. In the Judiciary Act of 1789, Congress established the basic framework of the federal judicial system, and it retains control over the structure, size, and jurisdiction of the federal courts. In the twentieth century, these courts have used the power of judicial review to play an important role in the formulation of national policy. This position and the difficulty of removing federal judges have made the selection of judges an increasingly important and ideologically sensitive process. Throughout the nation's history, the Supreme Court's views of national power and of the extent of its own powers have gone through recognizable phases. Today, observers of the Court are again engaged in debate over the proper role of the judiciary in a democracy.

Recommended Reading

Henry J. Abraham: *The Judicial Process,* 6th ed., Oxford University Press, New York, 1993.

Lawrence Baum: *American Courts,* 2d ed., Houghton Mifflin, Boston, 1990.

Craig R. Ducat and Harold W. Chase: *Constitutional Interpretation,* 5th ed., West, St. Paul, Minn., 1992.

Jerome Frank: *Courts on Trial,* Atheneum, New York, 1963.

John A. Garraty: *Quarrels That Have Shaped the Constitution,* Harper & Row, New York, 1987.

Alfred H. Kelly, Winfred A. Harbison, and Herman Belz: *The American Constitution,* 7th ed., Norton, New York, 1990.

William H. Rehnquist: *The Supreme Court,* Morrow, New York, 1987.

Stephen L. Wasby: *The Supreme Court in the Federal Judicial System,* 3d ed., Nelson-Hall, Chicago, 1988.

Bob Woodward and Scott Armstrong: *The Brethren,* Simon and Schuster, New York, 1979.

CHAPTER 12

The Public Policy Process

Making public policy is, very simply, the business of government. The policy process, however, is not a simple one, although it involves a series of easily identifiable stages. The first stage is problem recognition, just being aware that there is a problem. If there is agreement that a problem exists, the next step is agenda setting, deciding whether anything should be done about it. To be placed on the agenda signifies that the problem is deemed important enough for government to consider taking action. In short, public leaders decide what to decide about, which is the focus of the next stage, decision making. In a complex process, decision makers enact a policy to meet the problem originally defined in agenda setting.

After a decision is made, it must, of course, be implemented. The law that is printed on paper must now be made real, with services actually getting delivered. There is a last stage, program evaluation, which takes place after service delivery has begun. Here, government examines the program to see how well it is meeting its goals. If the program is functioning smoothly, nothing at all may be done; if it is not, it can be terminated or refined to make it work better.

These, then, are the basic stages in the policy process. The pages to follow consider for each stage the actors who are involved and the nature of the policy process at that stage. This discussion serves to pull together points made in previous chapters and to provide a context for the next three chap-

ters on specific policy areas. Earlier chapters have focused on key policy-making institutions—Congress, the president, the courts, and bureaucracy—and on the basic processes or forces that influence government—political parties, public opinion, the media, and interest groups. The latter serve to provide input to governmental institutions. Each is a source of pressure on government, as discussed in individual chapters. In making and carrying out decisions, the institutions of government in one way or another take into account such input as well as each other's views. Politics is about policy—who gets what, when, and how. Each of the elements explored in preceding chapters has some role to play.

What Is Public Policy?

In the most common definition, public policy is what government does. When government takes actions or makes decisions, it creates policy. The policy process has been described as "public problems and how they are acted on in government."[1] Others point out that policy should be taken to include what government intentionally decides not to do. For instance, when the Gary, Indiana, city government refused to press U.S. Steel to work toward reducing air pollution for fear of seeing the giant corporation pull out of Gary, the city's government might be considered to have carried out a policy of inaction in order to keep U.S. Steel happy.[2] Public policies, however the term is defined, run the gamut from "big" issues (national health care policy or deficit reduction) to "little" ones (a flood-control project on Ellicott Creek in Buffalo, New York).

Tradeoffs

Most policy involves what are called tradeoffs. Tradeoffs can be thought of by recalling the phrase "There ain't no such thing as a free lunch" (referred to as "TANSTAAFL" in Robert Heinlein's science fiction novel *The Moon Is a Harsh Mistress*). More technically, a government decision carries with it costs of one kind or another, just as it confers some benefit.

To get anything from government costs something. This is tradeoff: what one gets versus what one gives up. For instance, to increase U.S. energy supplies, government might encourage exploration for oil in Alaskan wilderness parks. This creates potential benefits—a likely increase in oil supplies and, hence, less dependence on other countries' oil. Nonetheless, there is a cost (remember, TANSTAAFL); the environment may well suffer some significant damage. Thus, one trades off more environmental damage to obtain more oil. Another example would be the goal of deregulating industry to make production more efficient and enhance profits; the tradeoff here is likely to be more pollution and more injuries in the workplace as regulations on health and the environment are deemphasized.

Unintended Consequences

When government makes policy, the results may not be as expected. These unintended consequences are important to consider. For instance, in the 1960s and 1970s, federal courts ordered busing of schoolchildren to achieve racial integration in a number of school districts. Ironically, an unintended consequence of this policy choice was *increased* racial segregation in some districts. Why? Many white parents pulled their children out of public school systems in which there was busing. The end result was fewer white children going to the public schools and a continuation of dominantly black schools.[3]

Types of Policy

Perhaps different types of policy lead to very distinct political dynamics and outcomes. That is, the particular species of policy shapes the politics surrounding it. One view posits three substantive types of policy—developmental, redistributive, and allocational.[4] Each of these carries with it a unique set of political implications.

Developmental Policy

Developmental policy aims to enhance a government's economic position. Such policies are designed to strengthen the economy and enlarge the tax base. Central in defining a policy as developmental is a cost-benefit calculation: does the cost-benefit ratio lean in the direction of the average and above-average taxpayer? Governments like to devise policies that benefit taxpayers, thereby providing those who provide revenues to government with an incentive to be supportive. At the state and local level, such policies induce the average and above-average taxpayer to stay in that locale rather than move elsewhere to receive a more attractive set of services for relatively lower taxes. Examples of developmental policies are industrial parks and wildlife preserves.

Redistributive Policy

Here, money is taken from the better off and shifted to the hands of the less well-off. Welfare programs such as Aid to Families with Dependent Children (AFDC), for instance, redistribute money from those who can pay taxes to those who pay little or no taxes. Politicians are often leery of this type of policy since it may arouse the ire of those who can afford to pay taxes; taxpayers often see those on welfare as undeserving, and they believe they are being penalized for the "shiftlessness" of others. State and local governments especially dislike such policy, since average to above-average taxpayers may decide that the cost-benefit ratio of staying and paying is not worth it and move to another area where taxes going to welfare recipients are lower.

Allocational Policy

Allocational policies, which involve basic services, tend to affect all taxpayers—but many citizens benefit as well. In a sense, taxpayers break even. Everyone gains alike. Many basic services can be deemed allocational, such as police and fire protection and garbage pickup at the local level; national defense would be a similar example at the national level.

Political Implications of Policy Type

Political implications differ for each of these. Allocational policies tend to be least controversial, since these involve many basic services that are deemed to serve all citizens well. Because city and state governments do not want to see their tax base evaporate, they have a major incentive to minimize redistributive policies and maximize developmental policies. One implication is that, everything equal, the federal government would have to pick up the tab for redistributive policies. And there is often resistance from the voters for this type of action. Thus, political unpopularity of redistributive policies leads to a contentious and controversial political dynamic.

On the other hand, citizens tend to support developmental activities, at the state, local, and national levels. People define such policies as investments. Indeed, it was no coincidence that President Clinton referred to the economic stimulus proposal and his deficit reduction package as an investment in America's future. The President tried to tap into the positive connotations of developmental policy (with mixed success).

The "Messiness" of the Policy Process

One characteristic of the policy-making process is its "messiness." Many actors at all levels of government, of varying ideological and party persuasions compete to affect outcomes, as Table 12.1 illustrates.[5]

Table 12.1   Messiness in the Policy-making Process:

A Tale of Three Institutions
Separation of Powers

Levels of Government	Executive		Legislative		Judicial	
National	R	D	R	D	R	D
State	R	D	R	D	R	D
Local	R	D	R	D		

R = Republican control
D = Democratic control

Separation of powers divides power among three coequal branches of government. Add to this the possibility of divided party control between the branches, and the process can become tangled in the combination. Consider also the situation after the election of Democrat Bill Clinton in which the Supreme Court is dominated by Republican justices appointed by Republican presidents; even with unity between a Democratic president and a Democratic Congress, conflict can still develop between the branches. And, given the Republicans taking control of Congress in 1994, the degree of messiness increases further.

In addition, the intergovernmental relations system divides power across the three levels of government: national, state, and local. If the federal government is moving in one direction, such as limiting the effects of environmental regulation as it did under President Reagan, and the states increase their vigilance with respect to environmental degradation, the policy thrust of the national government is blunted. And, of course, divided government control can occur at the state and local level as well as at the national level.

Put in such terms, it seems amazing that anything gets accomplished. However, the system has worked historically and messiness has not prevented government from taking action. The Founding Fathers wanted such a system, as pointed out in Chapter 2. They produced something that is perhaps even more complex than they had desired.

Stages in the Policy Process

Problem Recognition

Before government acts, it must perceive that there is some problem. Jones defines problems as "Human needs . . . for which relief is sought."[6] If many Americans are hungry but no one recognizes that hunger is so widespread, then hunger is not a problem politically. Only if significant political actors (from the general public to the president to interest groups) recognize that nutritional needs are not being met will hunger become defined—politically—as a problem.

How Problems are Identified

Social Indicators. Social indicators are measures of society's functioning, such as the number of people living in poverty, the gross domestic product, the annual crime rate. These indicators can signal the existence of problems. For example, if the number of individuals who are unemployed goes up sharply, a problem is developing. This may produce pressure for government officials to place more emphasis on dealing with lack of jobs.

Events.   Sometimes events focus attention on a problem. For instance, if builders have been using shoddy materials for public housing projects and structures thus built collapse in an earthquake, this disaster may lead to recognition of a problem.

Feedback.   A third route to problem recognition is feedback, the process by which public officials hear about how well or how poorly existing programs are working. John Kingdon notes one example: "Transportation officials monitor the performance of Amtrak and of urban mass transit systems by regularly following such indicators as ridership, load factors, on-time performance, inflation in construction costs, and operating deficits."[7] Simply, officials check out how programs are performing.

The Issue-Attention Cycle

The desire to solve problems can fade away, too. Some claim that even though problems may continue to be as acute as ever, if people lose interest or get bored with the issue, then there will be no impetus for action and the problem will increasingly be ignored. Anthony Downs has spoken of an issue-attention cycle, in which some problem soars into public consciousness and political leaders become energized to "do something."[8] After the initial burst, interest begins to decline as people come to recognize the costs involved and the difficulties with properly addressing the problem. As these difficulties are accepted, people turn their attention elsewhere. For instance, when Ethiopia's famine first became widely known to the public through vivid photos and news videos, there was an outpouring of contributions by concerned American citizens. After the original burst of enthusiasm, interest declined, as if by having contributed to the cause by purchasing the record single "We Are the World" or by pledging money to Live Aid, people had done all that was required.

Actors in Problem Recognition

A number of actors play a role in problem recognition.

Bureaucrats.   By monitoring social indicators, experts in the bureaucracy can detect problems as they develop. By publishing reports of increased homelessness, for instance, bureaucrats can spur recognition.

The Public.   When the general public becomes convinced that a problem exists, public officials take notice. As the public came to see crime as a serious problem in the early 1990s, government responded with anticrime legislation that in part went against the interests of the powerful National Rifle Association, usually very difficult to defeat on matters in which it takes an active part.

Interest Groups.   Interest groups are surely important actors, too. For example, the NAACP worked to make the public and political leaders aware of the problems engendered by racial discrimination.

Elected Officials.   Elected officials also may be involved in this stage of the policy process. Members of Congress—especially the House of Representatives—in carrying out errand-running activities for their constituents may come to see a pattern in the problems that they are dealing with, a pattern that may suggest the existence of an underlying problem. For example, if more and more constituents are complaining about not receiving social security payments on time, a problem is signaled in service delivery that must be dealt with.

Policy entrepreneurs.   Sometimes, a single person can spotlight a problem and bring it to the attention of the larger political system. Individuals who devote themselves to getting a problem highlighted in this manner are called policy entrepreneurs. By writing a book on automobile safety many years ago, Ralph Nader alerted Americans to a number of safety problems; more recently, astronomer Carl Sagan and others spoke of the danger of nuclear winter, trying to get the public to recognize an as yet undiscussed problem associated with nuclear warfare.

Agenda Setting

Problem recognition is one prerequisite for an issue to be placed on the agenda. However, even if some people believe that a problem exists, the problem may not make the agenda. John Kingdon observes that at least two other conditions must be met: political circumstances must be right, and significant political actors must back agenda placement.

Political Circumstances

Political conditions must be ripe for items to be placed on the agenda. As Kingdon observes:

Political events flow along according to their own dynamics and their own rules. Participants perceive swings in national mood, elections bring new administrations to power and new partisan or ideological distributions to Congress, and interest groups of various descriptions press (or fail to press) their demands on government.[9]

A kind of consensus among key actors may emerge that certain conditions call for government consideration. This consensus is often a product of bargaining, negotiation, and compromise among the multitudes of participants.

Actors in Agenda Setting

In agenda setting, visible political actors are most important, such as the president, Congress, key high-level appointees in the administration, top administrators, the media, parties, and interest groups. However, sometimes a single person (a policy entrepreneur) can make a difference. Among entrepreneurs trying to get particular issues on the agenda have been Phyllis Schlafly as an opponent of the Equal Rights Amendment, Jack Kemp as an apostle of supply-side economics, and C. Everett Koop as a proponent of AIDS education. In each case, an individual doggedly pursued his or her position and lobbied and worked to gather support. Therefore, an individual *can* have some impact. Nonetheless, issues normally do not make the policy agenda because of the activity of policy entrepreneurs.

Hidden or less visible participants have a role. Academics, "think tank" specialists, career bureaucrats, policy analysts, and congressional staffers tend not to have great overt impact on getting an issue placed on the agenda. They may be critical, however, in developing alternative proposals that "bubble up" through various policy communities, groups of people who focus on specific problems and push specific policies, and become adopted by the visible political actors.

Biases

Another element in the agenda-setting process is the effect of biases built into the system. E. E. Schattschneider has noted that "all forms of political organization have a bias in favor of the exploitation of some kind of conflict and the suppression of others because *organization is the mobilization of bias. Some issues are organized into politics, while others are organized out.*"[10] In other words, a political system's basic values narrow the range of issues considered appropriate for agenda placement. As noted in previous chapters, the dominant American value system is Lockean liberalism, with its emphasis on materialism, a free market, individualism, and equality. For instance, efforts to place on the agenda government ownership of private sector businesses would be conceived as illegitimate and unworthy of serious discussion; such a policy would not fit the American mobilization of bias. Built-in biases such as this radically reduce the scope of debate in the agenda-setting process and prevent certain policy alternatives from ever being examined—irrespective of their objective merits.

Decision Making

Models

In the social sciences, models, simplified perspectives on how things work, are often used. Four models of decision making are discussed below. These models provide different understandings of how decisions get made. The totality of what happens in the decision-making stage is complex, so models help to make sense of what is going on.

Rational-Comprehensive. This model assumes that rationality best describes how decisions are (or should be) made. Ideally, as Figure 12.1 shows, officials first carefully define a problem facing the nation. Then specific goals are formulated to correct that problem. The problem could be a housing shortage; the goal might be provision of enough housing units to meet the needs of those who do not have access to adequate housing. The third step in the sequence is enumeration of alternative policies—such as public housing projects, tax breaks, rent supplements, vouchers, and so on. Then, fourth, the single best alternative (or combination of alternatives) among this set is selected. Normally, the proposal with the greatest benefits for the cost of the program, that is, the most cost-effective program, is the one chosen. The fifth step is implementation.

Some time after the program has been put into effect, it is evaluated to determine how well it is working. Evaluation research may provide suggestions on how to modify the program to make it work better, may show that the program is proceeding smoothly and needs no alterations, or may indicate that the program is a failure and should be terminated. (The process of using research findings to alter a policy is often called feedback.) In the public housing example, research might indicate that the projects become "high-rise ghettos" and do not, in fact, lead to provision of adequate housing. At this point, the process would begin anew, with decision makers examining what policies might do better.

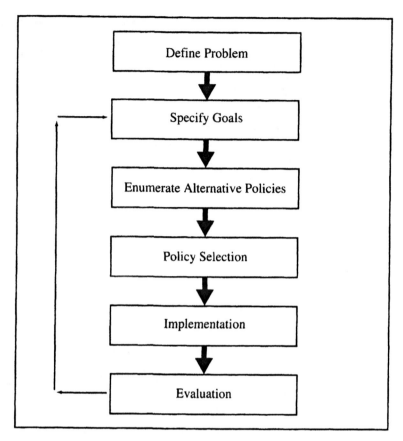

Fig 12.1   The Rational-Comprehensive Process

Incrementalism. This model assumes that a policy continues what has been done before, with some modest tinkering. In an important article, Charles Lindblom contends that decision makers cannot each year comprehensively review every decision made prior to that time to see whether or not changes are called for.[11] Practically, decisions are made with the expectation that previous decisions will stand, that policymakers will suggest minor modifications to improve the functioning of programs. This makes sense, too, for the following reasons.

First, decision makers have neither the time nor the information to closely examine every program and all alternatives and to select the best alternative. Rational-comprehensive decision making is not practical. Second, it is politically easier to accept continuing existing programs. Efforts to effect great change will yield political controversy as groups who benefit from existing policies try to defend them. Politicians would not want to engage in such battles routinely. Finally, it seems unnatural for humans, including political leaders, to think along rational-comprehensive lines.[12] People tend to look for a decision that will be satisfactory (that will work)—not optimal (the single best one). People stop searching for alternatives when they find one that looks like it will work.

The rational comprehensive and incremental models focus on the process of policy-making, *how* decisions get made. The next two models concentrate on who makes decisions.

Elitism. This model is defined in detail in Chapter 1. Simply stated, elitism assumes the following:

1. Society is divided into the few with power and the many without;

2. The few who have power are not typical of the many who do not possess it;

3. The elite share basic values that work to support the system that, in turn, maintains their power; and

4. Policy does not reflect the wishes of the mass of people but, instead, is made by the elite to advance their own interests.

An elite theorist would easily explain the Reagan income tax cuts (25 percent over a three-year period) and the tax simplification scheme enacted several years later (including lowered income tax rates for the richest Americans) by saying that the rich and powerful used government to give themselves a real, concrete monetary benefit. Or, an elitist might suggest that American involvement in the Middle East during the Persian Gulf war was intended to defend the interests of "big oil" and others dependent upon oil, such as the plastics and automobile industries.

Pluralism. Pluralism, also considered in depth in Chapter 1, is one of the major models for explaining the decision-making process. This framework begins with the assumption that society is composed of many different groups and that the interaction of some of these groups in the political process shapes government decisions.

Government responds to demands made by groups. Often, however, groups will be in competition with one another. This necessitates negotiation and bargaining among groups in order to build a coalition strong enough to win in the group struggle. Thus, a number of groups working together will all benefit. For example, when the Clean Air Act was originally proposed, broad coalitions supporting *and* opposing it formed. One provision of the act was reduction in the amount of pollutants emitted by automobiles. Environmental and health groups were in favor of tougher standards and a short time period for automobile companies to come into compliance. The automobile industry and labor unions (who feared losing jobs if the tougher standards were adopted) were arrayed on the other side. In the end, compromise took place. Stringent standards were set as goals, the amount of time granted to attain these was stretched out, and an "escape valve" was created allowing an extension to the automobile industry if it could not meet the timetable.

Actors in Decision Making

Who are the key actors in the decision-making stage of the policy process? Different models suggest different answers to this question.

In the Rational-Comprehensive Model. The demands of this model point to bureaucrats and experts as the important players. In the bureaucracy, in think tanks, and in congressional committees are experts on a subject who can fully deal with the alternatives and, using cost-benefit analysis and other techniques, select the best one.

Incrementalism. Incrementalism identifies a number of distinct actors as central. Interest groups defend programs that serve their needs, making it politically unrewarding to suggest dramatic changes in those programs. Political officials—the president and Congress—faced with myriad decisions tend to tinker with the status quo rather than engage in rational-comprehensive tactics.

Bureaucracies, interested in defending their turf, maintaining control of the programs assigned to them, and holding onto their budgets, resist major tampering. The combination of such dynamics produces incrementalism.

In Elitism. Here, the major actor is the elite, however defined. Elected officials are "tools" of the elite. Public opinion is manipulated by the elite through their control of media and other institutions. Thus, the focus must be on the elite to understand why decisions are made as they are.

In Pluralism. In this model, interest groups are obviously critical. But so too are government decision makers. Political officials must choose which course of action to take amid the clamor from competing groups. And public opinion is important. Members of the public vote elected officials into office, and these decision makers, then, must be aware of the voters' views. Interest groups try to swing public opinion to their side as part of their strategy to get government to carry out their desires.

Policy Alternatives

What about selection of the specific alternative to be adopted by decision makers? Kingdon argues that this process involves a great deal of randomness. He claims that generating policy alternatives is analogous to biological natural selection:

> In what we have called the policy primeval soup, many ideas float around, bumping into one another, encountering new ideas, and forming combinations and recombinations. . . . Through the imposition of criteria by which some ideas are selected out for survival while others are discarded, order is developed from chaos, pattern from randomness. These criteria include technical feasibility, congruence with the values of community members, and the anticipation of future constraints, including a budget constraint, public acceptability, and politicians' receptivity.[13]

The process is dependent to some extent on chance events, on political currents, and on the desires of visible political actors. Various policy communities—groups of people from government, think tanks and higher education who are interested in a particular issue—think that specific proposals would work if implemented by government. For example, the environmental policy community might advocate increasing the size of national parks, tightening the government's leasing of public lands to energy developers, and speeding the pace of cleaning up the air and water in the United States.

These ideas are publicized by the policy community. They may be ignored or taken seriously, depending on decision makers' priorities, public opinion, and events taking place at the time. At some point, however, policy proposals floating around in the "primeval soup" and pushed by policy communities may be coupled with the pressure to "do something" about a problem that has made the agenda. This increases the odds that a specific proposal will be enacted into law.

Will the policy be incremental? Or will the policy innovation be a more dramatic departure from the status quo, as suggested by the rational comprehensive model? Either is possible, depending upon the political currents and chance events. Kingdon's analysis seems to fit comfortably within the pluralist perspective, since it emphasizes the role of many actors interacting with one another.

Implementation

At this stage, decisions actually arrived at by policymakers are put into action. Paper decisions must become real. President Reagan made a decision to introduce U.S. Marines into Beirut, Lebanon, as a peacekeeping force and to add some stability to the area. That decision did not automatically get implemented. The Marines had to be outfitted and transported to Beirut, and orders had to be cut detailing the mission and the rules under which it would be carried out. Finally, the Marines had to deploy upon their arrival. The presidential decision was just the first step. The concrete steps that had to be taken afterward were the implementation activities.

Actors in Implementation

The central figures in this often invisible stage are administrators in agencies charged with putting a policy into operation. However, officials in the executive or legislative branch can have an effect by serving as "fixers," prodding if necessary the bureaucracies in charge of implementation.[14] Other actors can get involved as well. Interest groups with a stake in the specific program may, if they are part of a subgovernment or a cozy triangle, have real influence; judges, through judicial review of agency regulations, also can be key players.

Implementation Problems

What happens at this stage is affected by many other elements. Some analysts claim to be surprised that any program is successfully implemented.

Vague Wording. Laws enacted by Congress and signed by the president are often vaguely worded as a result of the bargaining and negotiation needed to get a majority to support the bill. Such a document provides unclear implementation guidelines to the bureaucracy. The same may happen in court decisions. For instance, what does the phrase "with all deliberate speed" mean in the Supreme Court's *Brown v. Board of Education* implementation decision? How are lower courts to interpret this statement? Vaguely worded laws or decisions may end up moving in a different direction than anticipated by decision makers.

Poorly Reasoned Policies. When, as sometimes happens, a program enacted by decision makers is poorly reasoned or poorly thought out, proper implementation is difficult. For example, the Economic Development Administration (EDA) tried to attack unemployment in Oakland, California, in the mid-1960s. The strategy the agency adopted was to ask several employers to draw up plans indicating how they would use EDA funds in projects (such as construction of an airline hangar) to increase jobs for hard-core unemployed minorities. In fact, although the government spent tens of millions of dollars on several projects, there was no significant job creation. The logic was flawed. Those receiving federal funds were required only to promise to hire minority unemployed; there was no provision for paying the employers only upon performance, that is, when they actually hired the jobless. And, as is clear in retrospect, the promises were not kept.[15]

Inadequate Resources.   Resources are often inadequate for programs. Programs created by Congress may, in subsequent action, be budgeted at an insufficient level for proper implementation.

Turf Conflicts.   Often, several agencies will be given a role in implementing a single program. This can lead to a problem in properly implementing the policy as the different agencies engage in turf conflict. A classic example occurred during the Cuban missile crisis of 1962. To ascertain whether or not Soviet offensive missiles were being placed in Cuba, a U-2 reconnaissance flight over suspected construction sites was necessary. President Kennedy ordered the flight; however, implementation of this seemingly simple decision was delayed a matter of days. Why? The Air Force and the CIA were locked in turf conflict over whose pilot would fly the plane. The result was a delay in implementing what seems like a very simple decision.[16]

Hostile Agencies.   It also happens that a hostile agency is charged with implementing a policy. Given the frequently vaguely worded policy mandate, this can end up producing botched implementation as the agency undermines the original intent.

New Policies.   Some policies are more likely to present implementation problems than others.[17] New policies can prove difficult to implement properly. When a new program begins, it is often given just enough resources to get off the ground, not necessarily enough to function properly. For instance, Congress designed the Education for All Handicapped Children Act to assist handicapped students in leading as normal a life as possible in the schools. However, Congress allocated less money for the program than was deemed appropriate by educational experts and the congressional committee which reported out the bill. The result was a much heavier burden on state and local governments to pay for making school buildings accessible to the handicapped (such as providing elevators and ramps) and more resistance to carrying out the program.[18] Another problem is that new programs may not fit easily with an agency's preexisting procedures and priorities, and the agency may be resistant, as a consequence, to implementing the program as designed.

Controversial Policies.   Controversial policies pose challenges to successful implementation. First, controversial decisions often lead to laws couched in vague language; implementors cannot be completely sure what

Congress really meant when it passed the law. Furthermore, controversial laws may find resistance in the bureaucracy. It is likely that if a law was controversial, there was much opposition to enacting it. And if the agency assigned to implement the law was one actor opposed to it, that agency may subvert the program in its implementation.

Program Evaluation

In rational-comprehensive decision making, evaluation is a key component. Here, one sees how well a program is working and the extent to which it is meeting its goals. Theoretically, if the program is not working and is not expected to ever perform as advertised, it will be terminated. Inherently, then, program evaluation can be threatening to the backers of any program—whether those implementing the program, its clients, or its supporters in government and in the public at large, such as interest groups.[19] Evaluation, then, is not simply an objective effort at discerning program impacts, although it might well be undertaken in such a manner; it is political from the start.

Whether or not evaluation is taken seriously is, to some extent, the result of how popular a program is. When early evaluations of Head Start were disappointing, there was no hue and cry to terminate the program. People liked the program and it had considerable political support.

Democratic theorists see the people's policy desires as important influences on government decisions. Public opinion, manifest through interest groups and political parties, is viewed as shaping what government does. Democratic theorists point to the evidence that the public's priorities are associated with actual government policy (recall the discussion of the effects of public opinion and political participation on policy in Chapter 4).

Elitists contend, to the contrary, that popular control is an illusion. They argue that top government officials and leaders in the private sector clearly outweigh the people as forces influencing public policy. Further, through the elites' alleged control of the media, the masses can be duped into supporting the elites' priorities.

Pluralists emphasize the centrality of groups. In fact, as stated earlier in this chapter, pluralism is one of the basic models that many use in order to explain the policy process.

The next three chapters examine particular decision areas—economic policy, civil liberties, and foreign policy. For each of these policy areas, the reader should apply the framework laid out in this chapter. First, who are the key actors in each area? Second, what happens at the different stages in the policy process for each? Third, what view of "who has power" seems to work best in understanding the decisions actually reached?

Recommended Reading

James Anderson: *Public Policymaking: An Introduction,* 2d ed., Houghton Mifflin, New York, 1993.

John W. Kingdon: *Agendas, Alternatives, and Public Policies,* Little, Brown, Boston, 1984.

Janet M. Martin: *Lessons from the Hill,* St. Martin's, New York, 1994.

B. Guy Peters: *American Public Policy,* 3d ed., Chatham House, Chatham, N.J., 1993.

Paul E. Peterson: *City Limits,* University of Chicago Press, Chicago, 1981.

Randall B. Ripley and Grace A. Franklin: *Policy Implementation and Bureaucracy,* 2d ed., Dorsey, Chicago, 1986.

CHAPTER 13

Economic Policy

Time Line

1776	In *The Wealth of Nations,* Adam Smith argues that governments should not interfere with the natural workings of the economy
1890s	Abuses of corporate power lead to calls for some government regulation
1936	In *The General Theory of Employment, Interest and Money,* John Maynard Keynes explains how governments can use fiscal and monetary policy to prevent depression or inflationary price increases
1973–1980	Rising petroleum prices trigger a period of high unemployment and high inflation
1983–1994	Large budget and trade deficits, low levels of saving and investment, intensified global competition, and emergence of a twin-tier economy of high- and low-wage jobs pose difficult economic challenges

A major responsibility of government today is to promote steady economic growth, low unemployment, and stable prices. How can we attain these laudable goals? This chapter describes four policy perspectives (laissez-faire, fiscal, monetary, and supply-side) which recommend how government can best pursue these economic goals. It also assesses recent economic performance, describes key institutions which make economic policy, and discusses budgetary issues in an era of $200 billion deficits. Since government taxing and spending account for one-fourth of our gross national product, the budgetary process inevitably shapes our economy.

The Politics of Economic Policy

Americans produce and exchange a multitude of goods and services, and government is part of this economic activity. Government builds highways, educates our children, and disposes of our waste products. Government regulates economic activity, preventing monopoly pricing, insider stock trading, careless dumping of solid waste, and packaging of unwholesome food. Government enacts food stamp and medical care programs, builds military weapons, and taxes tobacco and gasoline. These spending and taxing decisions affect where people work and what they produce. Government manipulates the strength of our currency, which affects how much grain American farmers can export and how many Japanese and South Korean textiles we import. Government uses its taxing, spending, and money-printing powers to counter soaring unemployment or rising prices.

The fortunes of every American citizen are profoundly affected by governmental economic policy-making. Every time government makes a decision, some people win and others lose. The resulting conflicts are the very stuff of politics. Consider the following examples:

1. Government must manage the economy, and policy decisions affect rates of unemployment and inflation. In the early 1980s, the Reagan administration chose to control inflation at the cost of higher unemployment. This decision helped retirees on fixed incomes and workers in no danger of being laid off, while hourly workers lost.

2. Government regulatory decisions improve living conditions for some while raising costs for others. Environmental regulations improve the quality of our air and water at the expense of polluting factories and their customers. Regulation of workplace conditions and consumer product safety imposes costs on producers for the benefit of workers and consumers.

3. Some people pay more in taxes than do others. The 1981 tax reform law cut taxes for corporations and wealthy individuals, while higher social security taxes came out of worker paychecks. The Deficit Reduction Act of 1993 cut the federal deficit by $500 billion over 5 years by raising taxes on incomes of wealthy individuals and on gasoline and tobacco sales.

4. Citizens benefit heavily from particular government spending programs and support these programs. Farmers receive crop subsidies, veterans are entitled to education and health care benefits, and students enjoy low-interest loans. The interest groups which represent farmers, veterans, and students and universities fight to retain these programs because group members alone benefit while all taxpayers share in the cost. Representatives and senators fight to keep military bases in their districts or states, get urban development grants for their cities, and win government contracts for local factories. Government spending creeps upward over time because voters, interest groups, and elected politicians fight hard to keep programs beneficial to their parochial interests. And other taxpayers pick up the tab.[1]

5. Government policies affect the broad distribution of income. Indexing social security payments to changes in the cost of living in the late 1970s helped today's retirees at the expense of tomorrow's workers. President Reagan's budget cuts in 1981 and 1982 hit particularly hard at food stamp, housing subsidy, and other programs that supplement the incomes of poor people. Legislation to protect jobs in textile, shoe, and automobile manufacturing from foreign competition help particular industries at the expense of consumers denied low-cost, high-quality imports.

Managing the Economy: Four Perspectives

Over the 200-year history of our republic, people have tended to move from farm to city, and the average standard of living has risen. However, if economic growth has made material prosperity possible, change in a dynamic economy also imposes great hardship. Events such as the devastating Great Depression of the 1930s, high rates of unemployment and inflation in the 1970s, massive budget deficits in the 1980s, and the swelling tide of imports manufactured in Japan, South Korea, China and Brazil have forced economic policymakers to continually rethink what government policy actions will best help the American economy.

There are four main perspectives on how government can best promote a growing economy with stable prices, low unemployment, and rising standards of living:

Laissez-faire policy. The government should keep its hands off the economy, allowing price changes to determine what the economy produces and where people work.

Keynesian fiscal policy. The government should make taxing and spending decisions to promote full employment.

Monetary policy. The government should increase or decrease the supply of money to promote stable prices.

Supply-side policy. The government should lower tax rates to encourage more savings and investment in high productivity.[2]

Laissez-Faire Policy

We saw in Chapter 1 that advocates of laissez-faire dominated eighteenth- and nineteenth-century economic policy. Liberals believed that the interests of society would be best served if individuals were allowed to pursue their own self-interest. Price changes in markets would signal changes in relative supply and demand of labor, capital, and raw materials. Free market exchanges between buyers and sellers would allocate scarce resources efficiently, contributing to the prosperity of society as a whole. So Adam Smith argued in *The Wealth of Nations,* an influential book published in 1776. Advocates of laissez-faire were reacting against the economic policies of kings, who sold exclusive economic rights to court favorites and used economic activity to foster state power rather than to provide for the people's material needs.

Support for laissez-faire as economic policy began to fade in the late nineteenth century when critics charged that great concentrations of wealth and power under laissez-faire industrial capitalism did not serve the people well. For example, factory owners could hire women and children to work long hours in poor conditions for little pay. And capitalism was vulnerable to periodic depressions. Major depressions in 1893 and 1929 threw people out of work, disrupted lives, and eroded support for a political system seemingly unable to stabilize the economy.

Laissez-faire is still relevant today. In the 1980s, President Reagan charged that big government stifled the economy. In his view, the clumsy efforts of the government in Washington to solve problems for people had failed miserably and expensively. The federal government should tax and spend less, reduce government regulation of industry, and cease redistributing wealth through government programs. Republicans pledged to promote these ideas after they won control of the House of Representatives and the Senate in the November 1994 elections.

The process of transferring responsibility for providing services to private firms is called privatization. Privatization is a contemporary example of laissez-faire economic policy at work.[3] It assumes that private firms can provide some services better and at less cost than government. For example, Conrail, the once federally owned railroad, has been sold to private buyers. Reformers suggest that parents should be allowed to choose between paying tax dollars to support their public schools and paying tuition at private schools.

Advocates of laissez-faire policy prefer that citizens purchase goods and services from privately owned firms rather than pay government to provide services with tax dollars. However, Table 13.1, which compares the role of government in advanced industrial democracies, shows that Americans do not rely heavily on government to provide goods and services. In Western Europe, social welfare programs such as subsidized medical care and unemployment benefits are funded at more generous levels than in the United States. Governments in European democracies are more committed to providing day care for the children of working parents, free schooling, free health care, unemployment insurance, a retirement income, and other social welfare benefits. Their citizens have demanded that government provide strong social welfare and income security programs.

Keynesian Fiscal Policy

The idea that government can stimulate or dampen the level of economic activity by adjusting its taxing and spending policies developed in response to capitalism's periodic depressions. John Maynard Keynes published *The General Theory of Employment, Interest and Money* in 1936, in the depth of the Great Depression, when one-fourth of the labor force was out of work and the production of goods and services had fallen sharply. Keynes and his followers addressed the problem of reversing the slide into deeper and deeper

Table 13.1   Tax Burdens in Ten Industrial Countries

Country	Tax Revenues as a Percentage of Gross Domestic Product
Sweden	57%
Norway	48%
Netherlands	48%
France	45%
Ireland	40%
United Kingdom	38%
Italy	36%
Canada	34%
Japan	30%
United States	30%

Source: Statistical Abstract of the United States 1990, p. 845.

depression. When the demand for goods and services slipped, workers were laid off, causing a further reduction in demand for goods and services and leading to even more unemployment. Once the economy started down the slope of economic decline, modest recession accelerated to deep depression.

Keynes proposed that government adjust its taxing and spending practices in light of economic conditions. When private-sector demand declined, government could stimulate demand for goods and services by spending more than it collected in taxes. That is, government would deliberately run a deficit, with the amount of the deficit being a net addition to the demand for goods and services in the economy. Government would be hiring more people, buying more paper clips, building more tanks, and making larger social security payments.

What happens when the economy rights itself? Then factories are busy, unemployment is low, and industries are able to raise their prices. Inflation, a general increase in the price of goods and services, is now the problem. Government could cool the fires of inflation by running a budget surplus, taking in more taxes than it spent on government programs.

Keynesian fiscal policy prescribes balancing the budget when levels of inflation and unemployment are normal, running a budget deficit to stimulate demand when unemployment and recession loom, and accumulating a budget surplus when prices begin to rise in a fully employed economy. Over the full economic cycle, the budget is balanced, but in any given year, government runs either a deficit or a surplus to counter recession or inflationary trends in the private economy.

For 50 years, fiscal policy has been a well-established tool for managing the economy to prevent depression. In the late 1930s, large government deficits incurred for rearmament ended the Great Depression. In 1963, the Kennedy-Johnson tax cut successfully headed off recession and made possible another five years of economic expansion with stable prices. In the mid-1980s, a series of $200 billion budget deficits pulled the economy out of recession.

However, fiscal policy is less useful for managing the economy in the 1990s. Projected annual deficits of $300 billion in the 1990s impose a growing debt burden on the economy, drive up interest rates, and slow long-term economic growth. That is why President Bill Clinton made deficit reduction his first order of business in 1993. But many experts feared that taking money out of the weak economy (as deficit reduction would do) invited renewed recession.

Keynesian fiscal policy has not been used to combat inflation. To do so, the government would have to tax more than it spent, running a budget surplus and weakening demand. Since 1960, the budget has been balanced only once, and no one expects a balanced budget any time in the 1990s. The reason is political. Both spending cuts and tax hikes are required for government to generate a budget surplus which would dampen economic activity. The president, Congress, and the people who elect them are reluctant to cut valued spending programs or raise taxes.[4]

Monetary Policy

The intellectual father of the idea that monetary policy can combat inflation effectively is Nobel prizewinning economist Milton Friedman.[5] Monetary policy regulates interest rates, which are the cost of borrowing money, by increasing or decreasing the supply of money. The Federal Reserve Board, known as the Fed, determines how much money will be available for lending. If the Fed increases the supply of money, interest rates tend to fall. If the Fed decreases the supply of money, interest rates tend to rise. Why? Because banks charge as much as possible on their loans. If the money supply is low, only those borrowers willing to pay a high interest rate will receive loans. If banks have a great deal of money available, they lower their rates to attract additional borrowers.

How can government use monetary policy to regulate the economy? If interest rates go up, the level of economic activity tends to decline. Consumers willing to borrow money to buy a new car at an interest rate of 8 percent are likely to keep their old car on the road for one more year if the rate rises to 12 percent. A young couple who can afford to buy a home if the money to be borrowed costs 8 percent might not be able to afford the monthly mortgage payment if the loan rate rises to 12 percent. In that case, the couple will remain in their small apartment. The factory owner may build a more modern building or invest in more productive equipment at a 6 percent interest rate, but not at 10 percent. Therefore, if the government wishes to combat rapid economic growth and rising prices, it raises the interest rate to discourage borrowing.

In the 1970s, large budget deficits and escalating energy prices caused inflationary price increases. The Reagan administration used monetary policy to combat inflation by keeping interest rates high, at a cost of slower economic growth and higher unemployment.[6] The architect of inflation-fighting monetary policy was Paul Volcker, powerful chairman of the Fed from 1979 to 1987. High interest rates attracted a flood of Japanese and European investment. The dollar strengthened relative to other currencies, making Japanese cars, South Korean steel, and Brazilian shoes cheaper in the United States and making American exports more costly to foreign buyers.

To illustrate, let's say that it costs Toyota 1.4 million yen to produce a small car and transport it to America. At an exchange rate of 100 yen to the dollar, the cost of that car in America is $14,000 (1,400,000 yen divided by 100 yen to the dollar). As the dollar strengthens to 140 yen, because Japanese buy dollars to invest in high-interest-yielding American bonds, that car now costs the American buyer $10,000. The price has fallen by $4,000 just because of the exchange rate. The inflation rate plummets because American consumers buy Japanese automobiles, South Korean textiles, and Brazilian shoes at lower prices.

What happens to American producers? As the dollar strengthens, American exports fall. Let's say it costs the American farmer $4 to sell a bushel of grain in Japan. At 140 yen to the dollar, the cost to the Japanese consumer rises from 400 to 560 yen. Farmers in Australia or Canada can now undersell the American farmer. Similarly, a strong dollar means that John Deere cannot sell farm machinery and Proctor & Gamble cannot sell soap overseas. Inflation declines because Americans can buy foreign-made products cheaply. But unemployment rises in automobile, textile, and other industries because Americans buy foreign-made products and American firms cannot compete overseas.

America's growing trade imbalance in the early 1980s was in large part due to the strong dollar, and the dollar was strong due to our monetary policy, which kept interest rates high. Asian and European investors were eager to invest their funds in high-yield American corporate stocks and government bonds.

The strong dollar was not the only reason for America's large trade deficit in the early 1980s. Labor costs were lower in Brazil and South Korea, although not in Japan. Moreover, our Asian competitors used the most modern equipment and sophisticated management techniques, which enabled them to make high-quality products at low cost. But two-thirds of the deterioration in the balance of trade was due to the federal government's high-interest-rate policy during the early 1980s, which strengthened the dollar in international trading.[7]

In the late 1980s, the trade deficit remained large despite a stronger dollar and lower labor costs in manufacturing. Continued weakness in the economies of our major trading partners reduced their demand for American exports.[8]

In the early 1990s, Volcker's successor as chairman of the Fed, Alan Greenspan, continued to restrain inflation by limiting the supply of money. This policy did bring down the rate of inflation to a historic low of 3 percent, but at the cost of a sluggish 2 percent economic growth and a high 7.5 percent unemployment rate. As economic growth fell to zero in 1991–1992 and the 1992 presidential election approached, the Fed lowered interest rates to stimulate the lagging economy. But unemployment peaked in early 1992, and continued economic weakness cost President Bush his job in the November 1992 election.

Supply-Side Policy

Supply-side policy promotes lower tax rates to encourage citizens to save more and to invest their savings in high productivity. In relying heavily on private initiative to generate strong economic growth, supply-side policy is a close relative of laissez-faire policy. Supply-side policy gained a following during the 1980s when it became apparent that America had lost much of its competitive edge in global manufacturing and trade. Consumption was rising faster than productivity, causing inflationary price increases. Individual Americans saved a paltry 4 percent of their income, while the savings rate of our Japanese and South Korean competitors approached 25 percent.[9]

Supply-side advocates within the Reagan administration argued that high tax rates were stifling the incentive of our most highly paid and potentially most productive workers. If we lowered tax rates, people would save and invest more and work harder. The economy's rate of growth would accelerate, and the additional tax revenues would more than offset the cost of the initial tax reduction. The benefits of an expanding economy would "trickle down" to low-income earners in the form of more jobs and higher wages.[10]

President Reagan's Economic Recovery Tax Act of 1981 was inspired by supply-side thinking within his administration. Most of the cuts benefited higher-income taxpayers, who tend to save more than do low-wage taxpayers. Also in the supply-side spirit, President Bush championed an investment tax credit to encourage capital formation. But Democrats in Congress dismissed his proposal as another Republican tax giveaway to the rich.

By the early 1990s, most economists doubted that the 1981 supply-side tax cut had had much positive impact on productivity. Six years of modest, recession-free economic growth lasting through 1988 were followed by four years of economic stagnation. America's low national savings rate remained low.

Economic Policy-Making Institutions

After the bitter experience of the Great Depression, most Americans became convinced that the federal government should manage the economy to promote steady economic growth, low unemployment, and stable prices. Several institutions share economic policy-making responsibilities.

Council of Economic Advisers

The Employment Act of 1946 specifically charged the president to pursue its economic goals. To help the president, Congress created the Council of Economic Advisers (CEA). CEA members are appointed by the president.

They prepare an annual report on the state of the economy and advise the president on economic policies. CEA members are professional economists whose first loyalty is often to their profession, not to the president who appointed them. While economic policymakers read CEA analyses and recommendations with great interest, the chairperson of the CEA is often not a part of the inner circle of people who meet with the president to decide economic policy. The CEA is an advisory, not a policy-making, institution.

Office of Management and Budget

The Office of Management and Budget (OMB) is crucial to the president's efforts to manage the economy through spending policy. With a staff of 600, the OMB is one of the most powerful agencies in government. Each spring, the OMB's director meets with the president to discuss the economic situation and spending priorities. The OMB then sends guidelines to every government department, assembles preliminary budget requests, and drafts the official budget which the president presents to Congress in February. Agencies tend to request the dollars they need to do their jobs well, which is usually more dollars than are available. The OMB decides how much money each agency will receive in the budget, placing the OMB at the center of intense political activity.[11]

The director of the OMB is powerful because he or she meets regularly with the president to set budget priorities and to evaluate whether individual agency requests are consistent with those priorities. Recent Republican presidents have also used the OMB to prevent government agencies from imposing costly regulations on business.

The Treasury Department

The Treasury Department employs tax experts and bankers who advise the president on taxation and monetary policy. The secretary of the treasury is usually a close confidant of the president, appointed by the president and sensitive to the president's political needs. During the Bush administration, Secretary of the Treasury Nicholas Brady and OMB director Richard Darman had bitter disagreements over control of economic policy-making. Their conflict prevented the administration from responding in timely fashion to slow economic growth in 1990–1991.[12]

The Federal Reserve Board

The Federal Reserve Board, known as the Fed, is America's central bank. The Fed controls the money supply through three kinds of activities.

1. The Fed establishes reserve requirements, the amount of money banks must keep on deposit in the central bank. The higher the reserve requirements, the less money the local bank can loan to potential customers.

2. The Fed also sets a discount rate, which is the interest rate banks must pay to borrow money from the federal reserve system. The higher the discount rate, the higher the interest rate banks must charge their borrowers.

3. The Fed buys and sells government securities. When it sells government securities, the money received from the buyer is removed from the economy. Because the supply of money is reduced, interest rates tend to rise. When the Fed buys government securities, money is put into the economy and interest rates tend to fall.

The Fed's seven members are appointed by the president for 14-year terms, while the chairperson serves a 4-year term that overlaps the president's. This appointment pattern gives the Fed considerable autonomy and provides a check on a president who might pursue unsound policies for short-term political advantage. The current president never appoints a majority of the Fed's seven members, and even a president who disapproves of the Fed's monetary policy cannot fire its members.

Presidents sometimes do disapprove of Fed policy. The Fed is an institution of bankers who are more sensitive to the dangers of inflation than to problems of slow economic growth and falling incomes.[13] Presidents are more responsive to the concerns of voters who cannot pay their bills when a shortened work week shrinks their paychecks. In recent years, Presidents Reagan, Bush, and Clinton have attempted to persuade the Fed to lower interest rates. Since the mid-1980s, Fed chairmen Paul Volcker and Alan Greenspan have tended to follow a tight money policy to further reduce the rate of inflation.

Recent Economic Performance: An Evaluation

How well have these institutions promoted steady economic growth with low inflation and low unemployment? Table 13.2 summarizes some important measures of economic performance since 1977.

Under President Reagan

During the 1980 presidential campaign, candidate Ronald Reagan effectively exploited the poor economic performance of President Carter's last two years. Escalating energy prices and high food prices after crop failures in the Soviet Union caused inflationary price increases. High unemployment re-

Table13.2   Economic Performance, 1977–1992

Year	Real Economic Growth Rate (%)	Unemployment Rate (%)	Inflation Rate (%)
1977	5.1	7.1	6.5
1978	4.8	6.1	7.6
1979	2.0	5.8	11.3
1980	−1.6	7.1	13.5
1981	2.0	7.6	10.3
1982	−1.4	9.7	6.2
1983	5.2	9.6	3.2
1984	7.8	7.5	4.3
1985	3.6	7.2	3.6
1986	3.0	7.0	1.9
1987	2.7	6.2	3.6
1988	3.0	5.5	4.1
1989	1.8	5.3	4.8
1990	0.4	5.5	5.4
1991	−1.8	6.7	4.2
1992	2.6	7.4	3.0
1993	2.9	6.8	2.6

Source: Economic Report to the President January 1994, pp. 351, 390, 415. Washington, D.C., US Government Printing Office, 1994.

flected expansion of the labor force. More women were entering the labor force in the 1970s, and the baby boom generation born during the 1950s was reaching adulthood in the late 1970s. By 1980, young adults competed fiercely for jobs in a depressed economy. November 1980 was a bad time to be running for reelection, and the American people turned away from Jimmy Carter, handing Ronald Reagan a landslide victory.

President Reagan's economic policy sought to defeat unemployment by creating a combination of supply-side policy (cutting income tax rates in the hope of stimulating investment in high productivity) and fiscal policy (running an economy-stimulating deficit in the federal budget). Reagan and the Fed tackled inflation by driving up interest rates, which discouraged consumer spending on such big-ticket items as cars and houses, discouraged business from investing in new plant and equipment, and strengthened the dollar (which lowered the price of imported goods).

These policies were not particularly consistent. They did squeeze the inflation out of the American economy, with help from falling oil prices (which declined from $34 per barrel in 1980 to $14 in 1984) and a flood of high-quality, low-priced foreign imports. However, the cost of defeating inflation was recession and high unemployment. The jobless rate rose in 1982–1983 to the highest levels since the Great Depression; the collapse of oil prices shattered the economies of Texas, Oklahoma, and other oil-producing states; the loss of export markets because of the strong dollar depressed farm state economies; and many industrial states lost jobs to heavy imports of cars, steel, textiles, and shoes. By 1983, inflation and unemployment levels were showing improvement, although at the cost of large budget deficits and a stubborn trade deficit.

Reagan was reelected in 1984 by a huge majority, in part because economic performance, weak in the first two years, was strong in the second half of his term. In politics, timing is everything. Voters tend to think that recent experience is the best guide to the future. One study demonstrates that each 1 percent increase in disposable personal income yields a 2.5 percent net increase in the two-party vote received by the incumbent party's candidate.[14]

Under President Bush

A strong economy contributed heavily to George Bush's victory in 1988. President Bush supported the Fed's effort to tighten monetary policy, hoping to slow the rate of inflation without slowing the economy. As Table 13.2 shows, the effort was not successful. Unemployment rose to 7.4 percent in 1992 and the economy grew at an anemic 2.6 percent rate. Should the federal government have pursued a more expansionary fiscal or monetary policy to stimulate the economy during 1990 and 1991? President Bush's own CEA, with the benefit of hindsight, thought a more expansionary policy would have stimulated economic growth without setting the fires of inflation ablaze.[15] As the 1992 election approached, the Fed eased interest rates to stimulate the lagging economy. But poor economic performance cost George Bush his job.

Several factors contributed to the economic weakness which plagued George Bush's presidency. First, European and Asian states were hit by recession, meaning that our largest trading partners were buying fewer goods. Second, cuts in military spending hurt communities where bases were closed or military suppliers lost orders. Third, construction was slow because of the glut of commercial real estate built during the 1980s. Fourth, low birth rates in the late 1960s meant that fewer young families were forming households, building homes, and buying appliances.[16]

Under President Clinton

When Bill Clinton took office, ever higher budget deficits were projected. Slow economic growth hurt revenues. And most spending occurred in relatively uncontrollable categories such as social security, Medicare and Medicaid, and interest payments on the national debt. Clinton sponsored his Deficit Reduction Act of 1993 in one more attempt to bring the federal deficit under control. Clinton's deficit reduction plan raised taxes more than it cut spending. The tax increases targeted small businesses and wealthy individuals. The plan was painful, as indicated by single-vote margins of victory in the House and the Senate in August 1993.

The danger in Clinton's plan was that removing $100 billion per year from the economy might slow economic recovery. Also, higher taxes on job-creating small business might inhibit economic recovery. But Clinton's gamble was that deficit reduction would keep interest rates low, stimulating factory owners to invest in new plants and encouraging consumers to build houses and buy automobiles.

Can Government Manage the Economy?

Can policymakers manage the economy? They can in the sense that we now know how to use fiscal and monetary policy to cool off an inflationary economy or to stimulate a sluggish, high-unemployment economy. The stock market crash of 1929 deepened into the Great Depression of the 1930s largely because the United States and Western European governments followed precisely the wrong fiscal and monetary policies. Had governments stimulated demand by spending more than they collected in taxes and lowering interest rates, economies would have righted themselves much more quickly. These principles are now well understood, and a deep depression triggered by inadequate demand is not likely.

The sheer size of government spending also serves to stabilize the economy. The federal government spends about 23 percent of the gross national product. Nearly half that spending consists of the government writing checks to individuals (social security, Medicare and Medicaid, income maintenance, veterans benefits); most of this money goes to immediate purchase of goods and services.

However, our ability to use fiscal and monetary policy to stabilize the economy is limited. First, institutional fragmentation restricts coordination of policy. The president's chief economic advisers have different backgrounds and different organizational perspectives, and they may disagree on priorities. Should government policy emphasize high employment or stable prices? Once priorities are set, the president's advisers may disagree on how best to achieve them.

Second, we live in an economically interdependent world. American, Japanese, and German governments cannot easily coordinate fiscal and monetary policies because each government is inclined to put the interests of its own people first. The United States argued, for example, that Germany and Japan should stimulate their economies so that Germans and Japanese would buy more American goods and reduce the American trade deficit. The long-term health of the world economy requires that the American trade deficit shrink, but our trading partners are reluctant to risk higher rates of inflation by stimulating their economies and to risk higher unemployment by importing more goods and exporting less.[17]

The oil supply disruptions of the 1970s also remind us that confrontations in the Middle East (and other regional hot spots) may have economic consequences that are beyond the control of economic policymakers. In 1973, the price of oil climbed from $3 to $18 per barrel as members of the Organization of Oil Exporting Countries (OPEC) curtailed the supply to gasoline-hungry Americans. After several years of price relief, oil supplies were curtailed again following the outbreak of the Iran-Iraq war in 1979. Prices climbed again, this time to $34 per barrel. Higher energy prices led to inflationary price increases in everything that Americans buy. Inflation contributed heavily to Jimmy Carter's election defeat in 1980.

Finally, efforts to manage the economy must take political priorities into account. Do we wish to hold down inflationary price increases or the unemployment rate? Do we wish to protect jobs in industries hard hit by foreign competition or allow consumers to benefit from low-priced, high-quality imports? These questions are political, and political questions must be answered before we know what fiscal and monetary policies are appropriate. As we saw in Chapter 8, members of Congress tend to be responsive to the parochial interests of their constituents back home. Elected officials may try to stimulate the economy immediately before elections to reduce unemployment and curry favor with voters.[18] But fine-tuning a complex economy is difficult.

The Budgetary Process

Taxing, Spending, and Income Distribution

The budgetary process is an important political battlefield where participants clash over the distribution of wealth and income. Some argue that government should use taxing and spending policy to temper extremes of wealth and poverty, while others are disinclined to tamper with the natural result of differences in talent. To what extent do taxation and social spending serve to narrow the gap between the rich and poor?

The federal income tax code, developed since the enactment of the Sixteenth Amendment in 1913, is mildly progressive, which means that high-income earners are taxed at a higher rate than are low-income earners. Households earning $20,000 may pay 5 percent of their income in federal income tax, whereas households earning $60,000 may pay 15 percent. With social security, state sales taxes, and alcohol and tobacco taxes, however, it's the other way around; low-income households pay a higher percentage of their income on these regressive taxes than do upper-income households. When all taxes are taken into account, most Americans pay about 25 percent of their income in taxes, with poor families paying a few percentage points less.[19]

Government also redistributes income to poor people through transfer payments, which are checks written to individuals for social security, food stamps, housing subsidies, unemployment insurance, and medical payments. In 1966, President Lyndon B. Johnson's Great Society programs increased transfer payments to the poor, and typically about 40 percent of federal social welfare spending goes to poor people. Table 13.3 shows the distribution of family incomes after the mildly progressive effects of taxation and social service transfer payments are taken into account.

The poorest 20 percent of Americans receive about 5 percent of total family income, whereas the richest 20 percent receive 44 percent of total income. Since 1982, income growth after taxes has been concentrated in the wealthiest 20 percent of American households; the income of the poorest 20 percent has actually declined.[20]

The Politics of the Budgetary Process

The budgetary process generates intense political conflict because it asks questions about our priorities. At what levels should the government tax and spend? How should dollars be divided among various spending categories?[21]

Table 13.3   Distribution of Family Income, After Taxes and Transfers, 1966 and 1989

	Year	Year
Income Percentile	1966	1989
Lowest 20%	4.3%	5.0%
Second 20%	10.3%	10.9%
Third 20%	16.4%	16.5%
Fourth 20%	23.3%	23.4%
Highest 20%	45.7%	44.1%

Source: Joseph A. Pechman, Who Paid the Taxes, 1966–1985?, Brookings Institution, Washington, D.C., 1989; Bureau of the Census, "Measuring the Effect of Benefits and Taxes on Income and Poverty," Current Population Reports, September 1990.

Every government program has its articulate defenders among the agencies which spend the money and the people who benefit from the programs. Bureaucrats in the Department of Agriculture know that the services they provide for the nation's farmers are valuable, and the department has much support among farm groups and the general public in farm states. The employees of the Consumer Product Safety Commission are committed to protecting consumers from the hazard of poorly designed or badly manufactured products, and their activities are supported by organized consumer groups.

Agencies and their supporters commonly seek to maintain or increase their share of the governmental pie. Their political maneuvering is complex because budgetary responsibility is divided between the president and Congress. The president, through the OMB, proposes a budget, but Congress has the power to authorize spending programs, appropriate funds, and set tax rates.

Table 13.4 compares patterns of federal spending in selected years since 1970.

Military Spending

In the early 1970s, the U.S. government cut back on military spending. Relations with the Soviet Union were improving, and the Vietnam war ended. By the late 1970s, it was clear that the Soviet Union was increasing its military spending and that America's historic military superiority diminished. President Carter increased military spending in 1979 and 1980, and President Reagan resolved that even more dramatic military spending increases were needed if America was to protect the world from the expansionist aims of the "evil empire," as he referred to the Soviet Union.

Following the collapse of the Soviet Union in 1991 (see Chapter 15), military spending was cut sharply. Military strategy in 1994 assumes that the United States must have the capacity to respond quickly and decisively to two regional crises at the same time. So long as the United States wishes to be able to respond militarily to simultaneous challenges, few additional cuts in military spending are possible.

Entitlement Payments to Individuals

Payments to individuals have grown steadily, a trend which is likely to continue. Individuals legally entitled to social security, Medicare and Medicaid, and military and federal employee retirement benefits must be paid. We can see from Table 13.4 that nearly half of federal spending goes to individuals eligible to receive payment under various entitlement programs. Retirees receive social security payments, students get low-interest loans, the unemployed draw unemployment insurance, and veterans are eligible for medical care.

Table 13.4   Federal Spending, 1970–1992 ($ billion)

Category	Year									
	1970		1980		1985		1988		1992	
	$	%	$	%	$	%	$	%	$	%
Military	264	44	187	23	261	26	283	28	259	21
Payments to individuals	184	31	395	47	459	46	480	47	593	49
Interest payments	42	7	74	9	137	14	147	14	165	14
Other	108	18	176	21	144	14	117	11	176	15
Total	598	100	832	100	1001	100	1027	100	1215	99

Source: Statistical Abstract of the United States, 1992, p. 320.

Social security is the largest and fastest-growing entitlement program because Americans are living longer and payments are adjusted annually to reflect increases in the cost of living. Declining birth rates pose difficult moral and political questions for our future social security system. The large cohort of people born during the baby boom of the 1950s will reach age 65 and begin receiving social security payments after the year 2020. They will be supported by the much smaller cohort of workers born in the late 1960s and the 1970s, whose parents chose to have one or two children, not three or four as their parents did in the 1950s. The moral and political question which must be addressed in the 1990s is how much present workers should pay for the support of retired workers.[22]

Interest Payments

Recent federal budget deficits amounting to hundreds of billions of dollars reflect our reluctance to tax ourselves to pay for desired spending programs. We send the bill to future generations. We have not had a balanced budget since 1960 and are not likely to balance the budget any time in the near future.

Does it matter? Probably not, if the economy grows faster than the debt. Between 1960 and 1982, the economy grew faster than our public debt, which means that the percentage of national income devoted to making interest payments on the national debt did not increase. After 1982, slow economic growth and $200 billion annual budget deficits combined to increase the burden of the national debt on taxpayers. Present and future taxpayers are devoting a growing percentage of their tax dollars, 14 percent in 1993, to pay for past consumption.[23]

The "Other" category in Table 13.4 contains most federal programs, including law and justice; international affairs; environment and natural resources; transportation; housing; and energy. This category consumes only 15 percent of the budget. Many of these programs were cut sharply in the 1980s. Since much of this spending provides essential government services which enjoy strong political support, further cuts are hard to justify.

Deficit Reduction

President Reagan's program of military spending increases and income tax cuts during the early 1980s drove the federal budget deficit to unprecedented heights. The House of Representatives, with a large Democratic majority, insisted that constituents back home did not want large cuts in domestic spending or large increases in military spending. In addition, Democrats were certainly not going to propose politically unpopular tax hikes unless President Reagan agreed to go along with the idea publicly. The inevitable result of this continuing political stalemate was a series of distressingly large budget deficits.

The Gramm-Rudman-Hollings Act

On the spending side, Congress reluctantly went along with many of President Reagan's proposed deep domestic spending cuts in 1981 and 1982 but resisted thereafter. Congress increased military spending, but at a much slower pace than President Reagan desired. On the taxing side, the 1981 tax cut reduced the government's income by about $250 billion per year, but this was partially offset by increases in social security taxes. Large budget deficits persisted because President Reagan refused to consider raising taxes and Congress could not agree on a plan to cut spending.

As an alternative, Congress enacted a mandatory deficit reduction law in 1985. Known as the Gramm-Rudman-Hollings Act for its Senate sponsors, the law required that the budget deficit be reduced by about $35 billion each year until 1991, when the budget would at last be in balance. If Congress and the president could not agree on a $35 billion spending-cut package, Gramm-Rudman-Hollings provided that most government programs would be cut automatically until the deficit reduction target was achieved. Half the cuts would come from domestic spending, and half would come from military spending programs. A few programs including social security, the strategic defense initiative, and interest payments on the national debt, were specifically exempt.[24]

Gramm-Rudman-Hollings was a flawed approach to deficit reduction. Across-the-board cuts weaken all programs, slashing into the muscle rather than trimming the fat. Upon implementing this law, Congress abandoned its responsibility to decide which programs serve the people well and which ones are expendable. But Congress could agree on no other approach.

Ultimately, Gramm-Rudman-Hollings failed to reduce the deficit. Its revenue and spending projections were based on rosy economic forecasts and accounting gimmickry; by 1990, the annual deficit had reached $220 billion, not zero as the agreement had projected. And $300 billion deficits were forecast for the early 1990s .

In this context, President Bush and Congress agreed in 1990 to a package of spending cuts and tax increases. President Bush abandoned his famous "Read my lips—no new taxes" pledge made during the 1988 presidential campaign. But the weak economy cut into federal revenues, and projected deficits climbed to over $300 billion per year in the mid-1990s in spite of the 1990 budget agreement.[25] Americans grew increasingly frustrated with the failure of Washington to make progress toward controlling the deficit; this mood contributed to Ross Perot's winning 19 percent of the popular vote in the 1992 presidential election.

The 1993 Deficit Reduction Act

Newly elected President Clinton proposed a plan that would reduce the deficit by $100 billion per year over five years beginning in 1993. The controversial act raised taxes on gasoline and on high-income taxpayers and accelerated military spending cuts. Further progress in reducing the federal budget deficit will have to come at the expense of social security and other entitlement programs, which account for nearly half the federal budget.

Today's economic policy challenges are complex, and easy solutions are hard to find. We expect government to foster a steadily growing economy with stable prices and low unemployment—but there is no consensus on what mix of fiscal and monetary policy will best achieve these ends. We need to cut large budget deficits, but prospects for doing so are uncertain because narrowing the deficit will require unpopular tax increases or painful cuts in popular spending programs. We must narrow the persistent balance of trade deficit, preferably by saving more and investing in new factories and advanced technology. But the owners of factories, their workers, and their communities are working together to protect the automobile or textile industries from overseas competition.

Economic policy issues provide much fuel for arguments over the distribution of political power. From a democratic perspective, technical economic issues inhibit effective participation. How many Americans have the time and interest to understand the effect of large budget deficits on interest rates and the strength of the dollar? Yet Americans do seem to prefer budget deficits to spending cuts or tax increases, and the political system records this preference.

From a pluralist perspective, high levels of spending reflect the intense support of special interests who benefit from particular programs. They are better organized and more effective than opponents whose pleas for responsible tax increases and smaller deficits have no natural political constituency.

From an elitist perspective, continuing economic crises since the first enormous increases in oil prices in 1973 have shifted power and income from the poor to the rich. The supply-side tax cuts of 1981 favored upper-income taxpayers. The costs of economic transformation have largely been borne by the poor, primarily through the inflation-busting recession of 1981 and 1982 as well as cuts in social welfare spending during the early 1980s.

Recommended Reading

James E. Alt and Alec Crystal: *Political Economics,* University of California Press, Berkeley, 1983.

James E. Buchanan and Richard E. Wagner: *Democracy in Deficit: The Political Legacy of Lord Keynes,* Academic Press, New York, 1977.

Donald F. Kettl: *Deficit Politics,* Macmillan, New York, 1992.

Joseph A. Pechman: *Tax Reform: The Rich and the Poor,* 2d ed., Brookings Institution, Washington, D.C., 1989.

Paul Peretz, ed.: *The Politics of American Economic Policy Making,* Sharpe, Armonk, N.Y., 1987.

Lester C. Thurow: *Head to Head: The Coming Economic Battle Among Japan, Europe and America,* Morrow, New York, 1992.

Edward Tufte: *Political Control of the Economy,* Princeton University Press, Princeton, N.J., 1978.

CHAPTER 14

Civil Liberties and Civil Rights

Time Line

1868	Ratification of Fourteenth Amendment containing "due process" and "equal protection" clauses
1870	Ratification of Fifteenth Amendment outlawing discrimination in voting
1883	*Civil Rights Cases* decision establishing "state action" doctrine
1896	*Plessy v. Ferguson* decision establishing "separate but equal" doctrine
1925	First Amendment free expression protections applied against the states (*Gitlow v. New York,* 268 U.S. 652)
1941	Fifteenth Amendment held to apply national law to primary elections
1949–1954	Period of concern about internal subversion, often labeled the McCarthy era after the activities of Senator Joseph McCarthy from 1950–1954

1954	*Brown v. Board of Education* decision overturns "separate but equal" doctrine as applied to education
1961–1966	Warren Court dramatically expands individual rights in the criminal process
1963	March on Washington by those supporting black civil rights, led by Martin Luther King, Jr.
1964	Passage of the Civil Rights Act utilizing the "equal protection" clause and Congress's commerce power to attack discrimination
1965	Passage of the Voting Rights Act providing for effective registration of blacks in the southern states
1971	First application of equal protection clause to protect women from discrimination (*Reed v. Reed,* 404 U.S. 71)
1971	Supreme Court supports busing as means of racial integration in school districts (*Swann v. Charlotte-Mecklenberg,* 402 U.S. 1)
1973	Women's right to abortion established (*Roe v. Wade,* 410 U.S. 113)
1978	In *Regents v. Bakke,* Supreme Court begins to consider use of quotas as means of affirmative action
1986	State laws prohibiting adult homosexual activity upheld (*Bowers v. Hardwick,* 478 U.S. 186)
1992	Supreme Court narrows "fighting words" exception to First Amendment protection (*R.A.V. v. City of St. Paul, Minnesota,* 120 L. Ed. 2d 305)
1992	Three former critics of *Roe v. Wade* join to form a new majority reaffirming women's fundamental right to abortion (*Planned Parenthood of Southeastern Pennsylvania v. Casey,* 120 L. Ed. 2d 674)
1993	President Clinton orders modification of the military's policy of excluding gays and lesbians from service

---

The basic rights of the individual within the state are divided into civil liberties, which are individual rights to act and to be protected in the criminal process, and civil rights, which are protections against discrimination be-

cause one is a member of a particular class. There are both constitutional and statutory bases for these rights. Generally speaking, in the twentieth century the courts have played a key role in increasing the scope of civil liberties and rights. Legislatures have followed expansive judicial interpretations of constitutional rights with statutory support.

The courts have been primary actors in the development and protection of civil liberties and civil rights because of Americans' fundamental belief in the concept of the rule of law. Although there have been notable deficiencies in its application, the idea that all citizens are equal before the law has been a consistent theme of American political history and has been one of the key factors behind the expansion of individual rights. This belief elevates the status of judges, and it places limits on the powers of majorities. Americans believe that democracy is more than majority rule. For them, it also must include protections of basic liberties and rights that stand above the wills of executives or legislatures. These rights are to be found in the national and state constitutions, and the courts are their ultimate guardians.

Rights Within the Constitution

At the national level of government, all rights are derived from the Constitution. Statutes may elaborate rights in particular areas, but they must ultimately draw on rights found in the Constitution.

Although most of the protections for American citizens are found in the Bill of Rights and following amendments, several rights are contained in the main text of the Constitution itself. These are in large part reactions against excesses that occurred in England during the seventeenth century and that the Founding Fathers wanted to avoid in the new republic. During the turmoil of that century, Parliament and monarchs acted viciously in their treatment of political opponents. Four protections in the body of the Constitution—the definition of treason, the prohibition of bills of attainder and ex post facto laws, and the provision for the writ of habeas corpus—are attempts to guarantee that such acts will not recur in the United States.

Definition of Treason

The Founding Fathers were very careful in their definition of treason. The definition of treason in the Constitution (Article III, Section 3) as levying war against the United States or "adhering to their enemies, giving them aid and comfort" effectively limits treason, without constitutional amendment, to those acts. Further, the courts have limited what constitutes treason by declaring that one must adhere to the country's enemies *and* give them aid and comfort. However, the Founding Fathers were not satisfied with mere definition. They also specified the procedures by which a person can be convicted of treason. In the United States, a person can be convicted of treason only on his or her confession in open court or on the testimony of two witnesses to the same act. The courts, in turn, have followed the spirit of the authors of the Constitution and have interpreted its treason provisions strictly in favor of defendants.

Prohibition of Bills of Attainder and Ex Post Facto Laws

The Constitution (Article I, Section 9) prohibits both states and the national government from enacting bills of attainder and ex post facto laws, two legislative excesses that historically have often been related. Bills of attainder are essentially legislative findings of guilt. In this country, legislatures may not find an individual guilty of a crime and punish him or her. This can be done only within the judicial system. Ex post facto laws are laws that make an act a crime after it has been committed, increase the penalties for a crime after it has been committed, or make it easier to convict someone of a crime after it has been committed. Key elements of the rule of law are that the law be known and that it be impartially applied. The prohibition of bills of attainder and ex post facto laws is an important element in protecting the rule of law in this country.

Writ of Habeas Corpus

The writ of habeas corpus is another fundamental individual right protected in the Constitution (also Article I, Section 9). Application for a writ of habeas corpus from a court, in its most basic form, means that an individual who is being held prisoner is asking to either be charged with a crime or be released. Unless the writ is suspended as provided for in the Constitution in times of rebellion or invasion, a person cannot be held prisoner without the right to judicial determination of the legality of his or her imprisonment. The courts have held that only Congress has the power to suspend the writ, but Presidents Abraham Lincoln and Franklin Roosevelt, during wartime, both issued executive orders imposing military jurisdiction over areas of the nation that had the effect of suspending the writ.

The Bill of Rights

The Bill of Rights is the first ten amendments to the Constitution and contains the core of individual rights against government. Of these amendments, really only the First, Fourth, Fifth, Sixth, and Eighth have had continuing importance.

Fourteenth Amendment Expansion—Due Process

In 1833, in a decision that technically remains good law, the Supreme Court held that the Bill of Rights applies only against the national government (*Barron v. Baltimore,* 32 U.S. 243 [1833]). The effects of that decision changed, however, with the enactment of the Fourteenth Amendment in 1868. This amendment contains a clause—the due process clause—that prohibits the states from denying any person "life, liberty, or property, without due process of law." In the twentieth century, the Supreme Court began to incorporate rights from the Bill of Rights into the term "liberty" in the Fourteenth Amendment's due process clause. Thus, "liberty" became an expandable term through which most of the protections in the Bill of Rights have been applied against state governments. Today, citizens are protected by the entire Bill of Rights in relation to the national government and by most of the important protections in that group of amendments from state action as well.

The Gradual Incorporation Doctrine

The doctrine by which protections in the Bill of Rights have been applied against the states has been termed the gradual, or selective, incorporation doctrine, meaning that these protections have been applied over the years on a case-by-case basis. Some Supreme Court justices have argued that the entire Bill of Rights should be applied against the states in what is known as the total incorporation doctrine. Others have urged that the entire Bill of Rights plus other rights not listed there should be incorporated into the due process clause of the Fourteenth Amendment. Most recently, some justices have suggested that the Bill of Rights standard for incorporating rights through the Fourteenth Amendment should be abandoned and the standard instead should simply be due process. None of these latter positions have carried a Supreme Court majority, however, and the gradual incorporation approach remains the law of the land.

First Amendment Liberties

The liberties guaranteed by the First Amendment have all been applied against the states and are seen by many as the vital core of a free, democratic system. The most important of these liberties are those involving religion and free expression of ideas.

Religion

The religious protections in the First Amendment are contained in two clauses, the "establishment" clause and the "free exercise" clause. The first prohibits Congress from passing laws "respecting an establishment of religion." The second prohibits Congress from abridging the free exercise of religion.

The "Establishment" Clause

The establishment clause has been the focus of most contemporary controversy. Clearly, it means that Congress should not provide direct aid to religion. Its application against the states, however, is less clear, since at the time it was adopted Massachusetts and Connecticut both had state-sponsored and state-supported religions. In the decision that has set the framework for modern constitutional treatment of the establishment clause, Justice Hugo Black upheld the use of state tax monies to transport students to public and parochial schools (*Everson v. Board of Education,* 330 U.S. 1 [1947]). In his opinion, Black argued that the Constitution required that a "wall of separation" should be maintained between church and state. The current standard for determining the permissible relationship between church and state is the three-prong test suggested by Chief Justice Burger in *Lemon v. Kurtzman* (403 U.S. 602 [1971]). Under this test a statute must have a secular purpose; its primary effect must neither advance nor inhibit religion; and it must not lead to "excessive government entanglement with religion." A law that fails any one of these three tests is unconstitutional under the establishment clause.

Since the *Everson* decision, the Supreme Court has dealt extensively with the relation of religion and education. It has consistently disapproved use of public school facilities for religious exercises and prohibited prayer in these schools. It has, however, supported a "moment of silence" that has no religious content or context. The area of funding for parochial schools has been more complex. Here the Court has tended to follow the "child benefit" doctrine, holding that if the aid benefits the child and not religion, it is constitutional. Thus aid to parochial schools for secular texts and ancillary services has been upheld. The case of *Mueller v. Allen* (463 U.S. 388 [1983]) suggests that the Court is also willing to sustain programs of tuition assistance that treat secular and nonsecular, private- and public-school students equally.

The "Free Exercise" Clause

Cases involving the free exercise clause have come less frequently before the Supreme Court. In the case of *Bob Jones University v. U.S.* (461 U.S. 574

[1983]), Bob Jones University claimed that its right to free exercise of religion was abridged when the Internal Revenue Service removed its tax-exempt status, thus making contributions to it no longer tax deductible. From the government's perspective, Bob Jones's refusal to allow interracial dating constituted racial discrimination in violation of national policy. The Court held that the university's religious beliefs about racial relationships were contrary to national policy and precluded the university from continued support through beneficial tax exemption. *Wisconsin v. Yoder* (406 U.S. 205 [1972]) presented another conflict between state policy and religious belief and practice. In that instance, the Amish refused to send their children to school beyond the eighth grade despite the fact that Wisconsin law required school attendance until age 16. The Supreme Court held for the Amish, however, noting that their religious practices had been maintained for three centuries and that they were entitled to state deference.

Recently, claims of religious freedom have been made against state laws punishing the sacramental rituals of particular religions. In 1990, the Supreme Court upheld an Oregon statute that prohibited the use of the hallucinogenic drug peyote for religious purposes (*Oregon v. Smith*, 494 U.S. 872). But in 1993, the Court found a Hialeah, Florida, ordinance outlawing the sacrificial killing of animals to be an unconstitutional infringement of the ritual practices of Santeria, an Afro-Cuban religion that uses animal sacrifice as an important part of its ceremonies (*Church of the Lukumi Babalu Aye v. City of Hialeah*, 124 L. Ed. 2d 472 [1993]).

Freedom of Expression

Freedom of speech and press merge under the idea of freedom of expression. Both are vital to the free and robust exchange of opinion in a democratic system. The Supreme Court has wrestled throughout the twentieth century with the proper balance between government power and the right to free expression but has not discovered a way to draw definitive lines between the two. Free expression has extensive constitutional protection, but its limits have varied depending on the historical context.

Judicial Standards

The Court has tried to provide some predictability to its free speech position by fashioning tests by which speech could be measured. In *Schenck v. U.S.* (249 U.S. 47 [1919]), Justice Oliver Wendell Holmes offered the famous "clear and present danger" test, arguing that circumstances could be such as to render normally permissible speech a clear and present danger to national security. Thus, Holmes asserted, one may not yell "Fire" falsely in a crowded theater. Later, in a famous footnote in the Carolene Products case (*U.S. v. Carolene Products Co.,* 304 U.S. 144 [1938]), Justice Harlan F. Stone suggested a "preferred freedoms" standard for the First Amendment. Under this test, the Court would recognize that the freedoms in the First Amendment are more important than other freedoms in the Constitution and thus hold a preferred status. Any attempt by government to infringe these freedoms would receive rigorous scrutiny by the Court.

Justice Black soon followed with his "absolute standard" for free speech. His position was that the First Amendment's prohibition against infringing speech is absolute: it says Congress shall make *no* law abridging freedom of speech or press. Black concluded that pure speech and the printed word simply cannot be punished by the state. In a democracy, the channels of communication must be kept open. The minority must always have the opportunity to try to persuade the majority.

Other tests have also been proposed. One, Justice Felix Frankfurter's "balancing test," might be seen as the diametric opposite of Black's absolute test in that it remains highly subjective. Frankfurter would balance the value of speech against the danger that it poses to society, leaving the issue of whether it is allowable to a particular court on a particular day.

In many respects, Justice Black's position appears to have merit. Simply following the words of the Constitution would seem to make dealing with expression easier and more predictable. However, shortly after ratification of the First Amendment, Congress passed the Alien and Sedition Acts, which allowed for punishment of expression, thereby indicating that some types of expression were not protected by the First Amendment.

While the issue of punishing expression after it has occurred remains subject to whichever test the Supreme Court wishes to apply, the Court has consistently found prior restraint, suppression of expression before it becomes public, to be unconstitutional. Thus, one is free to express an opinion, but the possibility of ensuing punishment remains. However, recent courts have taken a very broad view of permissible expression where political and social issues are involved. Today, the *Brandenberg* doctrine, which holds that speech is allowable unless it threatens "imminent lawless action and is likely to incite or produce such action," seems to be the prevailing position of the Court (*Brandenberg v. Ohio,* 395 U.S. 444 [1969]).

While Justice Black was very tolerant of pure expression, he drew the line at what has been termed symbolic speech, actions (sometimes called expressive conduct) that are intended to express opinions. Members of the Court have divided over how far the First Amendment protects acts that claim to be expressions of political or social ideas. The wearing of black armbands to public school to protest the Vietnam war or the inscription "F_____ the Draft" on a jacket worn in public have been found permissible. The Court has upheld prosecution of other actions, such as burning one's draft card, that claimed symbolic speech protection, but in doing so it has refused to define the issues as involving free speech.

Previous to 1989, the Court had also taken this route with regard to cases involving desecration of the flag. But in that year in *Texas v. Johnson* (491 U.S. 397), a case that involved a state statute, and in 1990 in *U.S. v. Eichman* (496 U.S. 310), a case that involved a national statute, the Court held that laws making it a crime to desecrate the flag abridged the First Amendment's protection of free expression. The area of symbolic speech under the First Amendment must by its very nature remain one that will be determined on a case-by-case basis, although the justices will surely attempt to construct tests to make their decisions easier.

In 1992, in a case involving a so-called hate ordinance passed by the city of St. Paul, Minnesota, the Supreme Court in an opinion by Justice Antonin Scalia drew a careful distinction between action and words (*R.A.V. v. City of St. Paul,* 120 L. Ed. 2d 305 [1992]). At issue was the scope of the "fighting words" doctrine, under which for many years the Court had held that certain types of antagonistic speech directed personally at individuals did not have First Amendment protection from prosecution by government. In its hate bias statute, St. Paul incorporated this doctrine by making speech aimed at arousing "anger, alarm or resentment in others on the basis of race, color, creed, religion or gender" punishable. Justice Scalia, however, saw the statute as an attempt by the city to use its authority to restrict the free flow of opinion and debate in favor of particular groups and to leave others—the disabled, gays, and lesbians, for example—subject to verbal attack. The "fighting words" doctrine may still enable prosecution of vicious personal verbal attacks, but it is clear from this case that government cannot specify which groups it wishes to protect and which it does not. The Court has held, however, that a state may increase the penalties for crimes that are motivated by racial or other kinds of hatred (*Wisconsin v. Mitchell,* 124 L. Ed. 2d 436 [1993]).

Obscenity

Obscenity has raised questions under the First Amendment, but the Supreme Court has treated them as being different from those involved in political and social debate. Maintaining his absolutist position, Justice Black contended that the First Amendment protects speech and the printed word from being judged obscene. The Supreme Court, however, has been fairly consistent in discouraging obscene expression. Only under the Warren Court and the early

Burger Court was pornographic expression given broad license. This tolerance grew out of the standards established by the Warren Court in the famous "Fanny Hill" case (*Memoirs of a Woman of Pleasure v. Attorney General of Massachusetts*, 383 U.S. 413 [1966]), in which the Court held as part of its test for obscenity that the material must be "utterly without redeeming social value." This made it exceptionally difficult to find any material obscene, and the cloak of First Amendment protection was thrown over a wide range of pornographic expression.

In *Miller v. California* (413 U.S. 15 [1973]), the Burger Court discarded the "utterly without redeeming social value" test and substituted more restrictive standards for obscenity. One standard uses the criterion of the average person, who, utilizing community standards, would find that the dominant theme of a work taken as a whole appeals to his or her prurient interest. Another requires statutory description in detail of the kinds of behavior that may not be depicted. Finally, the Court believes that a work should have serious social, political, scientific, or educational value for it to be acceptable. Furthermore, the Court has held that a state may prohibit the sale of material not obscene by adult standards to youths under age 16. Communities may allow the sale of pornographic materials, but if a state wishes to circumscribe such activity, it is now much easier to do so than under the previous standards of the Warren Court.

National Security Issues

A primary concern about unfettered freedom of expression and association has been the danger that it might pose to governmental stability. This fear heightened with the success of the Bolshevik Revolution in the Soviet Union and its proclaimed goal of worldwide revolution. Democratic processes in the United States have been based on the value of allowing people to associate freely and to express their opinions, but revolutionary movements pose the possibility that their adherents may use these freedoms to gain power and then suppress rights of others.

The most recent sustained concern about threats to national security from internal subversion occurred during the late 1940s and early 1950s in what has become known as the McCarthy era, after Senator Joseph McCarthy of Wisconsin. McCarthy gained notoriety launching attacks against government officials and others whom he believed to be communists or communist sympathizers. For a time, all three branches of government worked to ferret out subversives.

Congress, in 1940, passed the Smith Act, which prohibits a wide variety of activities aimed at the violent overthrow of the government. In the late 1940s this law was used to successfully prosecute leading members of the

American Communist party. In 1950, Congress added the Internal Security Act to its arsenal of antisubversion weaponry. This act allowed the president to declare a state of internal security emergency that invoked substantial limits on the rights of individuals who were suspected of being subversives. The act also provided that organizations found to be "communist-action, communist-front, or communist-infiltrated" by the attorney general had to register with that office. Registration then subjected the organization to various disabilities. In 1954, Congress in the Communist Control Act of that year outlawed the Communist party.

These efforts to legislate against subversion have been diluted over the years. The Smith Act remains on the books, but it has been limited by court interpretation. The internal security emergency portion of the Internal Security Act has been repealed, and its registration provisions have been declared unconstitutional. The Communist Control Act has never been enforced because it appears to violate the First Amendment's protection of freedom of association.

Legislative efforts to control subversion were supplemented by an executive loyalty security program to investigate possible subversives in the national government. Loyalty oaths proliferated at the national and state levels. Negative loyalty oaths—oaths in which one swears to have never been a subversive or belonged to a subversive organization—have generally been ruled unconstitutional because they chill freedom of expression and association. Affirmative oaths—oaths in which one swears to support the government— however, carefully drawn, remain constitutional. State efforts to institute comprehensive loyalty security programs were limited by the Supreme Court's decision that the area of subversion control was preempted by congressional action. The McCarthy era drew to a close with the Senate's censure of Senator McCarthy in 1954.

Individual Rights in Criminal Procedure

The criminal process begins with the commission of a crime. The police then gather evidence and arrest a suspect. The suspect is arraigned before a judge and is released or held pending resolution of the case. Assuming that a plea bargain arrangement is not reached, the defendant may be indicted and then stand trial. After the trial, upon conviction, the defendant is subject to a variety of penalties.

At each point in this process, rights from the Bill of Rights apply to the individual. These rights are intended to preserve the accusatorial nature of the criminal process. In other words, a defendant does not have to participate in his or her prosecution. The state must convict the defendant on the basis of objective evidence. This, of course, does not often occur, since plea bargains resolve most cases or defendants confess. If a defendant insists on his or her constitutional rights, the state may gather objective evidence, such as fingerprints or hair samples, but it may not force the individual to provide information of a nonphysical, or subjective nature.

Search and Seizure (Fourth Amendment)

The Fourth Amendment's prohibition against unreasonable search and seizure protects the individual in his or her privacy. Essentially, the primary requisite of a reasonable search is a judicially issued warrant authorizing the search. On some occasions, however, police officers are justified in searching without a warrant. Upon arresting a defendant, police officers have the right to search that person simply to protect themselves. They also have the right to search the immediate vicinity for the "fruits of the crime." Obviously, what constitutes the immediate vicinity of the arrest has been and continues to be the subject of litigation.

Another area of justified warrantless search occurs when the police officer has "reasonable cause" to believe that an individual has committed or is committing a crime. An officer may then "stop and frisk" an individual or pull over a car and search the occupants and the interior. Even without cause, police officers may conduct automobile stops at highway checkpoints as long as they have a pattern to their stops. Such stops are often used at the state level to check for drunken driving.

Courts enforce the protection against unreasonable search and seizure through the exclusionary rule. Under this approach, the courts will exclude from a trial any evidence that has been gathered in violation of the Fourth Amendment and any evidence that has been gathered because of evidence so obtained (the "fruit of the poisonous tree" doctrine). The problem with this approach is that it often allows individuals who are clearly guilty to go free because the major evidence against them has to be excluded. For this reason, former Chief Justice Warren Burger and others have suggested that constitutionally tainted evidence be allowed into trial and that the defendant be given other remedies, such as legal judgment for damages against the offending police officers. The Supreme Court appears unwilling to abandon the exclusionary rule, although the Court has given the police increased leeway where minor infractions of the Constitution have occurred.

An important part of the search and seizure area today is the use of electronic devices to record conversations. The increased sophistication of these devices makes their control almost impossible. However, the courts have taken a strong position that the Constitution requires a warrant before evidence obtained electronically can be admissible in a trial. The primary exception to this requirement is in national security cases involving surveillance of foreign agents.

Pretrial Rights

Miranda Rights

An individual's pretrial rights commence as soon as he or she is the primary suspect in a crime. At that point and certainly upon arrest the suspect must be informed of his or her Miranda rights. These rights stem from the famous case of *Miranda v. Arizona* (384 U.S. 436 [1966]), in which the Supreme Court applied the right to counsel and protection against self-incrimination at the point at which a suspect is apprehended. These rights had been previously applied to the states at the trial stage, but the Court recognized the importance of ensuring that the defendant is protected during the sensitive period prior to trial.

The rights which must be communicated to a suspect are as follows:

1. You have a right to remain silent.

2. Anything that you say can and will be used against you in a court of law.

3. You have the right to an attorney at this point and at any point throughout these proceedings.

4. If you cannot afford an attorney, one will be provided for you.

5. You have the right to stop making statements or answering questions at any time during these proceedings.

These rights have withstood numerous challenges, and the Supreme Court has applied the exclusionary rule where they have been clearly violated. On the other hand, the Court has allowed into evidence spontaneous statements and those statements made after minor errors in the communicating of the Miranda rights.

Right Against Excessive Bail (Eighth Amendment)

Also of importance to pretrial conditions is the right against excessive bail provided in the Eighth Amendment. The purpose of bail is simply to ensure that the accused will appear before the court when ordered to do so. In cases involving drug dealers or others with considerable financial resources and great mobility, bail may be set very high. For those without funds, however, bail in any amount is beyond reach, and these people may have to remain in custody until trial, which may be a considerable period. To provide greater fairness for the poor and working classes, many jurisdictions have developed release on recognizance programs that allow those with stable roots in the community to be released on their promise to return. These programs have worked very well, allowing defendants to maintain their jobs and family lives with minimal interruption.

The Supreme Court has ruled, however, that the Eighth Amendment does not guarantee the right to bail. In *U.S. v. Salerno* (481 U.S. 739 [1987]), the Court considered the Bail Reform Act of 1984, which allows a judge to refuse bail to a defendant if that person appears likely to commit further crimes while awaiting trial. The statute was aimed at the problem posed by defendants who have been released pending trial and continue their criminal ways during this period, which can stretch out for months or even years with a series of delays. Chief Justice Rehnquist, speaking for the Court, upheld the constitutionality of the statute.

Use of the Grand Jury (Fifth Amendment)

A final stage before trial in a criminal matter is the determination as to whether there is sufficient evidence to hold a person for trial. This decision can be made through indictment. If a person is indicted, it does not mean that he or she is guilty of the crime; it means only that the grand jury, a body of individuals, believes that there is enough evidence to justify ordering the defendant to be held for trial. Typically, at the indictment stage, the prosecutor has a great deal of influence. However, if the prosecutor's case does not satisfy a grand jury, the defendant must be freed. The Fifth Amendment requires the use of the grand jury for indictment at the federal level. This right has not been applied to the states, and they may use other, less cumbersome approaches to bring individuals to trial.

The Trial Stage

Most criminal cases never go to trial. The bulk of criminal cases (estimates are 90 to 95 percent) are resolved through negotiations between the prosecutor and the defense counsel. This process, known as plea bargaining, significantly relieves the tremendous workload on the criminal courts. Although plea bargaining has often been criticized as being too lenient toward defendants, it has the advantage for both sides of avoiding the uncertainty, time, and expense of a trial. Most of the rights pertaining to criminal trials are provided by the Sixth Amendment.

Right to Counsel (Sixth Amendment)

The American legal process is an adversary process. This means that the two sides enter into legal combat under the assumption that through this contest the truth will become apparent. Key to the adversary process in the criminal area is the belief that the defendant should have a fair chance against the tremendous resources that the state can bring to bear. Basic to protecting the defendant is the Sixth Amendment right to counsel. Since 1972, the Supreme Court has insisted that a defendant may not be sentenced to jail without having access to an attorney. Previous to 1963, however, defendants in noncapital cases—cases that did not involve the death penalty—at the state level had no right to have an attorney appointed if they could not afford one.

Subpoena Power and Right to Cross-Examine (Sixth Amendment)

Other protections in the Sixth Amendment relating directly to the adversary nature of the criminal trial are the right to compel witnesses to appear (subpoena power) and the right to cross-examine, or confront, unfavorable witnesses. The latter right is particularly important; it prevents the prosecution from simply introducing written statements. With but a few exceptions, the defendant has a right to question his or her accusers directly. Recognizing the overbearing resources of the state in criminal prosecutions, the Supreme Court has also insisted that the state must provide the defendant with any information that is favorable to him or her.

Rights to a Speedy Trial and to an Impartial Jury (Sixth Amendment)

Perhaps less directly related to the adversary nature of the trial, but still of great importance, are the rights to a speedy trial and to an impartial jury. Most jurisdictions now have statutory limits on how long a defendant must wait for a trial before he or she can move to have the case dismissed. Often, however, because of agreements between the prosecutor and defense attorney, these limits are exceeded without penalty to either side.

Obtaining an impartial jury continues to be a constitutional problem, and two areas—racial discrimination and opposition to capital punishment—are of particular concern. In choosing a jury, attorneys may object to potential jurors *for cause*. These objections are unlimited in number and are usually based on some conflict of interest or prejudice regarding the case. Attorneys also have a limited number of peremptory challenges, objections for which they need give no reason. The Supreme Court has held that individuals conscientiously opposed to the death penalty may be excluded for cause from juries in capital punishment cases. Within the past two decades, the Court has turned its attention to the use of peremptory challenges and has held that neither the prosecution nor the defense may use these challenges systematically to exclude blacks from a jury. In 1994 the Court extended this reasoning to disallow the use of peremptory challenges by a state to exclude jurors based on their gender. Whether the Court will expand these decisions to include other groups in the population remains to be seen.

Protection Against Self-Incrimination (Fifth Amendment)

Also important to the trial process is the protection against self-in-crimination provided in the Fifth Amendment. Not only does this protection permit a defendant to refuse to testify in a trial; it has also been taken to mean that a prosecutor cannot comment during the trial on the defendant's refusal to testify. The courts have held that an individual may invoke the self-incrimination protection whenever he or she is in danger of providing information that could be used for criminal prosecution—for example, when testifying before a congressional committee or a grand jury. In an effort to strike more effectively against organized crime figures, Congress has provided that a federal prosecutor can give a witness immunity from prosecution, thus forcing testimony under threat of a contempt of court conviction. Obviously, for organized crime figures such a grant of immunity, which they may not refuse, can create a serious dilemma. It places them in the position of having to chose between facing a jail sentence for continuing to refuse to testify or of facing their colleagues in organized crime after they have testified.

Posttrial Rights

Double Jeopardy (Fifth Amendment)

Under the Fifth Amendment's protection against double jeopardy, once an individual has been acquitted after trial, that person cannot be retried for the same crime. Again, this protection is intended to give greater balance to the adversary process. The state may not use its power to bring repeated charges against an individual for the same crime in the hope that eventually a conviction will be obtained. This means that, normally, the prosecution cannot appeal an acquittal. On the other hand, if a defendant appeals his or her conviction, that person waives the right not to be retried. In other words, if an appeals court overturns the original conviction, the state may then again enter charges and prosecute for the same crime. Also, it is possible that an act may be a crime in both federal and state jurisdictions. Thus an individual may be acquitted at the state level and then be prosecuted by federal authorities, or vice versa.

Capital Punishment

In terms of punishment after conviction of a crime, the most controversial area is capital punishment. Although some have contended that the death sentence per se constitutes cruel and unusual punishment and as such is prohibited by the Eighth Amendment, the Supreme Court has continued to uphold its constitutionality. The Court has, however, been concerned that it be applied in only the most serious crimes and that it be applied as fairly as possible.

Opponents of the death penalty won a temporary victory in the case of *Furman v. Georgia* (408 U.S. 238 [1972]). In that case, a badly divided Court held unconstitutional most of the death penalty statutes then in existence. The decision itself was in the form of a brief per curiam opinion. The accompanying dissents and concurrences indicated, however, that three of the five justices in the majority believed that juries had been granted too much discretion in applying the death penalty and that this discretion had led to discrimination against minorities.

State legislatures responded to the *Furman* decision by revising their death penalty procedures, and four years later in the case of *Gregg v. Georgia* (428 U.S. 153 [1976]), the Court upheld the two-stage approach that Georgia took toward applying the death penalty. Under this approach, the jury first decides the question of guilt or innocence. If the defendant is found guilty, then separate argument is held on the issue of the appropriate penalty. If the defendant is sentenced to death, the jury must specify in writing which of the aggravating circumstances detailed in the law as justifying the death sentence were met in the particular case. The jury also must consider mitigating circumstances provided by Georgia law. The Supreme Court believed that these procedures, which have been copied by other states, limit the discretion of the jury and help to ensure fair application of the death penalty.

Since the *Gregg* decision, the Court has defined more precisely which crimes may justify the death sentence. In *Coker v. Georgia* (433 U.S. 584 [1977]), the Court's holding that the death sentence for rape of an adult woman was disproportionate to the crime seemed to suggest that only murder could justify the death sentence. Furthermore, subsequent Court decisions have indicated that only murders of a certain type are punishable by death. The Court has been unwilling to permit the death sentence for crimes of passion, for example, marital disputes that result in murder. Murders that are premeditated or committed in the process of other crimes, however, still clearly fall within the ambit of the death penalty.

Racial Discrimination

Attempts to eliminate racial discrimination have been an important part of the advance of civil rights in the twentieth century. Despite their passage shortly after the Civil War, the Thirteenth, Fourteenth, and Fifteenth Amendments provided little protection for blacks during the nineteenth century. In this century, the Thirteenth Amendment has not been heavily used, but the other two amendments have been exceedingly important in protecting against racial discrimination.

Prior to the twentieth century, however, these amendments were ineffective protections against racial discrimination owing primarily to the unwillingness of the Supreme Court to impose national power on the states. The "equal protection" clause of the Fourteenth Amendment, which was clearly designed to protect blacks against state discrimination, was gutted by two early Court decisions. In the *Civil Rights Cases* (109 U.S. 3 [1883]) the Court held that the federal government could not prohibit discrimination by private individuals or businesses because the equal protection clause referred only to state denial of equal protection of the laws. This became known as the "state action" doctrine. In *Plessy v. Ferguson* (163 U.S. 537 [1896]), the Court in turn allowed state discrimination by declaring that state laws could segregate, or separate, the white and black races as long as the facilities were separate but equal. Thus was born the "separate but equal" doctrine. Between these two Court doctrines, blacks had almost no protection from racial discrimination under the equal protection clause by the turn of the century.

Voting Rights

Prior to the 1940s, the Supreme Court was also unsympathetic to effective application of the Fifteenth Amendment's prohibition of racial discrimination in voting. Numerous legal "tests" and standards devised by the southern states barred most blacks from voting. An exception to the Supreme Court's support for these ploys occurred in 1911, when the Supreme Court invalidated laws with "grandfather clauses" that exempted those whose ancestors could vote before 1865 from having to pass a literacy test before being able to vote. Nonetheless, literacy tests themselves were upheld by the Court and remained an effective means of preventing blacks from voting.

During most of the first half of the twentieth century, the southern states also used the "white primary" as a means of disenfranchising blacks. The white primary was successful because the Democratic party was the only effective party in the South during this time. The Democratic primary decided who was to hold office because whoever won that election would face only token opposition in the general election. Claiming that the primary was a private party function immune from the sanctions of the Fifteenth Amendment, southern Democrats limited primary elections to whites only. Finally, in a pair of cases in the 1940s, the Supreme Court declared that primary elections were subject to the Fifteenth Amendment and proceeded to outlaw the white primary (*U.S. v. Classic*, 313 U.S. 299 [1941]; *Smith v. Allwright*, 321 U.S. 649 [1944]).

The 1960s saw the next significant attack on racial discrimination in voting. The Twenty-fourth Amendment, ratified in 1964, outlawed the poll tax, which was seen by many as discriminating against both poor blacks and whites in the South. The 1964 Civil Rights Act also contained provisions aimed at limiting the discriminatory use of literacy tests, but it was the 1965 Voting Rights Act that provided the first really effective voting rights for blacks.

The 1965 Voting Rights Act used a voter registration formula to attack discrimination. It declared any test or requirement prerequisite to voting automatically discriminatory and void in any county where 1964 registration fell below 50 percent of eligible voters. Furthermore, the attorney general was authorized to send federal agents to those counties that failed to meet the 50 percent standard and to ensure that everyone could register and could vote. Because the Democratic party had dominated the South for so long, voting turnout had become very low in that area, and entire states fell under the attorney general's power to send federal voting registrars into the counties. The result was a dramatic increase in the number of black voters and the election of black officials at the local, state, and national levels. The Voting Rights Act continues in effect, and some states remain subject to Justice Department review of any changes made in their election laws or voting districts.

Equal Education

One of the most serious sources of racial discrimination in America was in public education, where the "separate but equal" doctrine of *Plessy v. Ferguson* had been applied to establish separate schools for whites and blacks. In the famous 1954 case of *Brown v. Board of Education of Topeka* (347 U.S. 483 [1954]), the Supreme Court overturned the separate but equal doctrine as applied to public education, declaring that separate educational facilities based on race were inherently unequal. The implementation of this decision was slow and arduous because resistance in the South was bitter and sustained. Governors in Alabama, Mississippi, and Arkansas made political careers for themselves by opposing attempts to integrate schools in their states. In the climate of opposition created by such political leaders, locally elected school boards, for reasons of both personal conviction and political expedience, refused to act to implement the *Brown* decision.

The burden of taking the initiative for racial integration thus fell squarely on the shoulders of the federal district court judges, who, of course, were themselves white southerners. Nonetheless, the Supreme Court continued to rely on these courts to enforce the supreme law of the land, and here and there, courageous southern judges emboldened by firm higher court support began to make some headway. They also were assisted in this respect by attorney generals under the Johnson and Nixon administrations, who vigorously pursued integration cases in the courts.

In the process of giving the U.S. district courts the authority to enforce racial integration, the Supreme Court increased their influence greatly. In the 1970s these courts were given the power to require busing of students in order to achieve greater racial integration. In some cities, federal district court judges actually took over the schools and acted in place of school boards and administrators. Today the problem is not de jure segregation (segregation by law) but de facto segregation (segregation due to other causes). For example, housing patterns may have developed in such a way as to concentrate the races in particular areas. Thus schools in these areas would tend to be heavily of one race.

Private Discrimination

For years the primary tool for combating racism in American society was the equal protection clause of the Fourteenth Amendment. Beginning with the *Brown* decision, legally sanctioned racial segregation throughout society was invalidated. The more difficult issue was to be private discrimination, which in 1883 had been upheld by the Supreme Court under the state action doctrine (see p. 303). The approach taken by the Court was to attack the problem of private discrimination by expanding the scope of what constituted state action. Thus in 1964 the Court held that a private amusement park could not have blacks who had entered the premises arrested for trespass because the arrest invoked state action in the aid of racial discrimination. Justice Black's dissent in this case indicated, however, that the definition of what constituted state action could not be expanded much further.

At this point, Congress, through the 1964 Civil Rights Act, intervened to strengthen efforts to limit private discrimination. The Civil Rights Act was based not only on the equal protection clause but also on the interstate commerce clause. The latter clause gave Congress extensive power over commercial activity, and Congress invoked this power to prohibit racial discrimination in public accommodations in interstate commerce and in employment. Under this act, the courts have interpreted Congress's power very broadly, and few business establishments are beyond its scope. Thus, expanding the state action doctrine has become less important as a means for attacking racial discrimination.

Affirmative Action and Equal Employment

Interpretation of the Civil Rights Act soon became involved in the question of how far agencies and employers could go in applying affirmative action efforts to remedy past discrimination. Some general principles have emerged from the numerous cases in this area. The basic principle that the Supreme Court appears to follow is that an affirmative action plan should not punish individuals who have not participated in discrimination.

Thus the racially defined quotas set for admission to the medical school of the University of California at Davis were ruled unconstitutional because they prevented Alan Bakke, who was better qualified than many of those admitted under a quota, from being admitted (*Regents of the University of California v. Bakke*, 438 U.S. 265 [1978]). The *Bakke* case was decided by the swing vote of Justice Powell, who wrote the opinion of the Court. Powell voted with four of the justices to declare quotas based on race unconstitutional, but he also voted with the other four justices to suggest that schools could take race, socioeconomic background, and other factors into consideration when they made admissions decisions.

In subsequent decisions involving employment, the Court has examined the use of quotas in more detail. It has ruled that whites with more seniority than minorities just hired may not be laid off before those minorities simply to maintain a proper racial balance in the work force. On the other hand, quotas used on a temporary basis to ensure the hiring of more minorities or to facilitate their advancement in the workplace have been upheld. These have been seen as necessary measures to overcome the effects of past discrimination in a particular area. Permanent quotas based on race, however, would probably not pass constitutional muster.

Also important in the area of equality of opportunity has been the Equal Employment Opportunity Commission (EEOC) established under the 1964 Civil Rights Act. This body has the authority to investigate claims of discrimination based on gender, age, and race and to sue in the federal courts for redress if a settlement cannot be negotiated by other means. Of less importance, the Civil Rights Commission, which was established in 1957 civil rights legislation, has been the source of much controversy because of the ideological divisions among its members. Its functions are limited to making studies and recommendations.

Housing Discrimination

In 1968, Congress also passed an open housing act, which prohibited discrimination in the rental and sale of most housing. In 1974, this was extended to include gender discrimination. Enforcement of this act has been hampered by limited funding.

Gender Discrimination

Like the struggle against racial discrimination, the effort to eliminate discrimination based on gender has made extensive use of the equal protection clause and the 1964 Civil Rights Act. The Supreme Court has not been willing to apply the equal protection clause as rigorously to gender distinctions as it has to racial distinctions. Racial distinctions automatically fall into what the Court has described as a "suspect classification," meaning that any such distinction is really almost impossible to justify under the equal protection clause. The Court has, however, never placed gender distinctions in the same category. It has held that such distinctions may be permissible if they bear a rational relationship to a legitimate state goal. Thus Congress may exempt women from the military draft system. States may exclude women as guards in maximum security male prisons, and they may make age distinctions based on gender for the crime of statutory rape.

Employment

The Supreme Court began to apply the equal protection clause to gender discrimination in 1971, and since then, a large number of decisions have helped to define women's rights. Congress has aided these developments with supporting legislation. One of the most active areas for legal action has been employment. Much of this activity has been under Title VII of the 1964 Civil Rights Act, but other Congressional statutes also protect women's rights in the workplace. The EEOC has been particularly active in prosecuting gender discrimination and has obtained substantial monetary awards from major industries. The Supreme Court has also approved the promotion of women over marginally more qualified men into jobs where there has clearly been a history of gender discrimination.

An issue of particular controversy has been that of *comparable worth* in the treatment of jobs. Americans generally agree that individuals, regardless of gender, should be paid equally for doing the same jobs. The advocates of comparable worth, however, carry this position further, arguing that some jobs held largely by women, such as nursing, should be paid at the same level as men are paid in comparable jobs. This is obviously a complex issue, and the Supreme Court has not dealt with it directly, although there are lower court decisions supporting the concept.

Abortion

Another highly controversial issue related to the subject of women's rights is that of abortion. The Supreme Court entered this thorny thicket in 1973 in the case of *Roe v. Wade* (410 U.S. 113 [1973]), in which it held that a woman had a constitutional right to an abortion through the second trimester of pregnancy. During the third trimester the state could intervene and prohibit abortion. The justices based this decision on the right of privacy that they discerned in the due process clause of the Fourteenth Amendment.

Despite repeated attempts to have the *Roe* decision overturned, the Court steadfastly continued to affirm it. A majority of the justices have held, however, that neither the national government nor the states are required to provide funding for abortions for those who cannot afford the medical expenses. Also, as Justice Sandra Day O'Connor pointed out in her dissent in *Akron v. Akron Center for Reproductive Health, Inc.* (462 U.S. 416 [1983]), medical technology began to undermine the trimester approach used in the *Roe* decision. That decision assumed that viability of the fetus outside the womb before the end of the second trimester of pregnancy was unlikely. Today, however, such viability is possible earlier, thus making abortion before the end of the second trimester of the *Roe* standard more questionable on both legal and ethical grounds.

Finally, in *Planned Parenthood of Southeastern Pennsylvania v. Casey* (120 L. Ed. 2d 674 [1992]), the Supreme Court seems to have brought much of the abortion debate in the national courts to at least a temporary halt. What was especially striking about the *Casey* decision was that three justices—Sandra Day O'Connor, David Souter, and Anthony Kennedy—who had been critical of much of *Roe v. Wade* joined with two other justices to create a new majority supporting that earlier decision's declaration of a woman's right to an abortion. Despite her personal reservations about the wisdom of the *Roe* decision, Justice O'Connor declared that "liberty finds no refuge in a jurisprudence of doubt" and concluded that "the very concept of the rule of law underlying our own Constitution requires such continuity over time that a respect for precedent is, by definition, indispensable." The fact that the membership of the Court had changed substantially since the *Roe* decision was not a sufficient reason for overturning that precedent. In Justice O'Connor's view, to act on that basis would undermine respect for the rule of law and the Court itself.

At the same time that it affirmed the basic principle of the *Roe* decision, the Court modified it substantially in *Casey*. Justice O'Connor took this opportunity to discard the trimester system and to hold that the state may prohibit abortions after the point of viability but not before that point. Waiting periods before the performance of the abortion were also approved, as was the provision of certain forms of counseling to the woman. The state could also require that unmarried minors have parental consent for an abortion.

At this point certain fairly clear minimum standards for abortion have emerged from the Court's decisions. First, the state may not prohibit abortion before the point of viability. Second, the state may not prohibit abortion at all in cases of incest or rape, or where the health of the mother is threatened. Third, the state may not require the father's notification or consent for an abortion. There will continue to be cases challenging state and national efforts to regulate abortion, but it is unlikely that the Court will in the foreseeable future uphold any state regulations that do not incorporate these basic principles.

Recent Issues in Civil Rights and Liberties

Continual technological change and activity by organized interests have combined to raise difficult civil liberties questions under a constitution whose authors could not possibly have foreseen the issues involved.

Privacy

The question of the extent to which a right to privacy is provided in the Constitution remains exceptionally difficult for the Supreme Court. The Fourth Amendment's protection against unreasonable search and seizure provides some privacy protection in the criminal process. But the courts have moved toward providing substantive privacy protections as well. The problems in doing this were illustrated in the *Griswold v. Connecticut* (381 U.S. 479 [1965]) decision, in which the Supreme Court invalidated a Connecticut statute that prohibited the sale and use of contraceptives. The Court was bothered by the enforcement of the prohibition against the use of contraceptives, arguing that the marital relationship was entitled to privacy protection. Nonetheless, the Court could not find a specific protection of this sort in the Constitution and relied on a "penumbra" around the Bill of Rights. Later, this right to privacy was also important in the abortion decisions. Its future, however, may be in some doubt, as the Court's willingness to find rights not specifically provided in the Constitution has led to charges of judicial legislating and caused considerable criticism of the Court.

Sexual Orientation

Tied fairly closely to the privacy question have been the efforts of gay and lesbian rights groups to gain constitutional protections for homosexuals and homosexual activity. The Supreme Court has not been sympathetic to these endeavors. It has consistently upheld the power of prison authorities to punish such behavior, and in *Bowers v. Hardwick* (478 U.S. 186 [1986]) it specifically rejected the claim that the Constitution provided a fundamental right for consenting adults to engage in private homosexual activity. States, of course, remain free to legislate on behalf of homosexuals, and some state legislatures, executives, and courts have been supportive of gay and lesbian rights. The outbreak of acquired immune deficiency syndrome (AIDS) has focused increased attention on homosexual behavior, or alternative life-styles, primarily in the area of male homosexuality. The national government has provided funds for combating the disease. Moreover, the Supreme Court's application of Section 504 of the Rehabilitation Act of 1973 to contagious diseases has opened the possibility that this legislation also protects AIDS victims from employment discrimination by institutions covered by it.

Gay and lesbian groups contributed heavily to President Clinton's campaign and found sympathy for their claims within his administration. This support was demonstrated by President Clinton's effort to remove the ban on homosexuals in the military. After considerable opposition from the military and Congress to complete removal of the ban, in the summer of 1993 a compromise was reached under which inductees into the military were no longer asked about their sexual orientation and aggressive investigations into the sexual life-styles of military personnel were discouraged. However, open advocacy of homosexuality or engaging in homosexual activity while a member of the military remained grounds for discharge from service. While the military and most members of Congress appeared satisfied with the compromise, President Clinton himself thought that it did not go far enough toward integrating gays and lesbians into the military, and court challenges to the policy from gays and lesbians seemed probable.

The Mentally Impaired

The rights of the mentally incapacitated also have received Supreme Court attention. The Court has held that if an individual is no danger to society and can function outside a mental institution, that person cannot be institutionalized against his or her will. On the other hand, the Court has found no constitutional right to extensive treatment for the institutionalized mentally retarded, holding that such individuals are entitled only to that training that will contribute to their safety and freedom from undue restraint. In this area the Court has clearly deferred to the judgment of professionals in the mental health field.

Prisoners

The federal courts also have found themselves dealing with an increasing number of claims from prisoners. The Supreme Court has granted these individuals the rudimentary due process rights to be informed of charges against them and to have an opportunity to answer the charges before they are punished. Additionally, access to legal resources is a basic right of all prisoners.

Life Extension Issues

An area into which the Supreme Court has not yet ventured in any definitive way, although the lower federal courts and state courts have begun to act, is the legal definition of what constitutes life within the protections of the Constitution. Two aspects of this issue that pose exceedingly difficult questions are those revolving around the extension, and definition, of life both at birth and in old age. Modern technology has reached the point where it is now possible to keep human beings alive indefinitely even though they are incapable of a volitional functional existence. In most respects decisions in these areas are probably best dealt with outside the judicial arena, but if the American political tradition is any indication, the courts will inevitably be drawn into deciding fundamental ethical and cultural questions stemming from these controversies.

The Elderly

With the enactment of the Age Discrimination in Employment Act of 1967, Congress indicated its intention to protect workers and job applicants who are over 40 from discrimination solely because of their age. In 1986 the act was amended to prevent employers, with some exceptions, from mandating that their employees must retire at a specified age.

The Disabled

In 1990 Congress passed the Americans with Disabilities Act, which encompassed a wide range of disabilities. This act prohibited employment discrimination against the disabled and required access to facilities for them. Judicial suits requiring the interpretation of this and previous statutes dealing with the disabled will undoubtedly increase, and these can be expected to produce a substantial body of case law defining the rights of the disabled.

This chapter began with examination of individual rights protected by the Constitution. These include rights in the body of the document and those in the Bill of Rights and Thirteenth, Fourteenth, and Fifteenth amendments. Protections in the Bill of Rights have been applied to the states through the due process clause of the Fourteenth Amendment. Freedom of expression is given wide latitude today by the courts. The key concepts behind criminal protections have been the adversary process and the need to preserve an accusatorial criminal system.

Attempts to eliminate racial discrimination have given primary impetus to the expansion of protection of civil rights. In this area the equal protection clause has been the most important constitutional basis for action. Since the 1960s, Congress has enacted legislation to give further protection against discrimination. Both constitutional and legislative protections have been expanded to include gender discrimination. Today, major issues remain as to which groups are entitled to similar protections and to what extent governments and private organizations may take affirmative action to compensate for past discrimination.

The courts have been the major force in protecting and advancing civil liberties and civil rights in America. In this effort they have often had to stand as barriers to policies supported by the majority. Their position has been that democracy requires the maintenance of fundamental rights free from majority interference. Minority interests must be allowed the opportunity to exercise free belief and to change the opinions of the majority. Similarly, the minority interests encouraged by pluralism have increasingly turned to the courts for protection. The result has been that the judiciary, one of the most elitist institutions in American government, has been vital in protecting both basic democratic rights and the forces of pluralism.

Recommended Reading

Henry J. Abraham: *Freedom and the Court.* 5th ed., Oxford University Press, New York, 1988.

Peter Irons: *The Courage of Their Convictions: Sixteen Americans Who Fought Their Way to the Supreme Court,* Penguin Books, New York, 1990.

Yale Kamisar, Wayne R. LaFave, and Jerold H. Israel: *Criminal Procedure,* 7th ed., West, St. Paul, Minn., 1989.

Richard Kluger: *Simple Justice,* Knopf, New York, 1976.

Anthony Lewis: *Gideon's Trumpet,* Vintage Books, New York, 1966.

Susan Gluck Mezey: *In Pursuit of Equality: Women, Public Policy and the Federal Courts,* St. Martin's, New York, 1992.

Nancy McGlen and Karen O'Connor: *Women's Rights,* Praeger, New York, 1983.

CHAPTER 15

Foreign Policy

Time Line

1823	The Monroe Doctrine broadens the isolationist foreign policy first articulated by President George Washington
1941	Following the bombing of Pearl Harbor, the United States enters World War II
1945	The United States drops two atomic bombs on Japan, ending World War II and beginning cold war competition with the Soviet Union
1973	America becomes more dependent on oil imports and the balance-of-trade deficit widens sharply
1990	Collapse of the Soviet Union brings the cold war to an end

This chapter divides American foreign policy into three historical periods. From 1789 to 1941 isolationism prevailed, as the United States remained distant from European balance-of-power politics. During the cold war pe-

riod from 1945 to 1990, the United States sought to contain the Soviet Union within its post–World War II borders, and the two powers aimed their massive nuclear arsenals at each other. After 1990, the collapse of the Soviet Union and the economic ascendancy of Asian and European nations marks the beginning of a post–cold war era. The United States can no longer isolate itself from the rest of the world, nor can it dominate the world. Many nations are now in a position to affect American foreign policy interests.

Opinions differ on appropriate principles for conducting foreign policy in the 1990s. Some analysts point to the renewed relevance of isolationism when events are largely beyond American control. Isolationist principles may be appropriate, for example, in refraining from military intervention in remote regional conflicts, erecting barriers to immigration, and inhibiting imports of products manufactured overseas. Other analysts believe that multilateral competition is essential in an era where America no longer has the economic and political strength to dominate the world. For example, the United Nations may play a peacekeeping role in international crises, and international agreements are needed to curb drug trafficking and to slow production of ozone-depleting chemicals.

The foreign policy-making process may be pictured as a series of concentric circles with the president at the center. The president's important advisers have differences in perspective rooted in personal experience and institutional position. Legislators, interest groups, and politically active citizens with a strong interest in foreign policy issues also participate in the foreign policy-making process. In crisis situations, the circle of participants narrows; in routine trade, foreign aid, and weapons development discussions, the circle of participants widens.

Isolationism 1789–1941

A fledgling United States in 1789 had neither population nor resources to compete effectively with the great powers of Europe. During George Washington's presidency, the United States did not even maintain armed forces. In his farewell address, Washington warned his successors to avoid "entangling alliances" which might drag the United States into European wars and bring those wars to this continent. Future presidents heeded Washington's advice, and the United States avoided any alliance commitments for more than 150 years. Wide oceans insulated the United States from Europe and made isolationism possible.

The Monroe Doctrine

Washington's advice found direct expression in the Monroe Doctrine in 1823. The Monroe Doctrine stated that the United States would stay out of European wars and that European powers should not attempt to extend their influence into the western hemisphere. When World War I broke out in 1914, the United States could no longer maintain its isolationist posture toward Europe. The United States was now an important economic power, and American merchant shipping supplied Britain's munitions, food, and other vital materials during the war.[1]

The League of Nations

In the aftermath of World War I, the League of Nations was created to prevent major wars through collective security. Member nations agreed not to use force to settle their disputes. They also agreed to unite against any nation that attacked its neighbors. Although President Woodrow Wilson lobbied hard to build support for American participation in the League, Congress refused to ratify the treaty. The United States retreated into its traditional posture of isolationism. Isolationism ended once and for all when Japan bombed Pearl Harbor in December 1941 and the United States joined the war effort against Germany and Japan.

The Cold War, 1945–1990

After World War II, the Soviet Union acted quickly to occupy and establish political control in Eastern Europe. The Soviets had the military capacity to invade Western Europe as well. Only the United States, with its economy intact and holding a virtual monopoly on atomic weapons, could protect Western Europe from possible Soviet invasion.

Nuclear Weapons and Military Policy

Deterrence

American military policy in the cold war era was based on the premise that direct conflict between the United States and the Soviet Union would be avoided through deterrence. Overwhelming superiority in armed forces, coupled with a demonstrated willingness to use them, would convince adversaries that attack must fail.[2]

Massive Retaliation

The bombing of Hiroshima and Nagasaki in 1945 demonstrated the destructive power of nuclear weapons and U.S. willingness to use them. Deterrence in the 1950s was based on the doctrine of massive retaliation. American policy pledged that the United States would respond to serious acts of provocation by the Soviet Union with an all-out nuclear retaliatory attack.

By the late 1950s, the Soviet Union had developed a substantial arsenal of its own. The United States could no longer apply massive retaliation without being bombed itself. The threat of massive retaliation was therefore less credible, and theorists began to consider alternatives. President Kennedy in 1961 developed a new strategic weapons policy known as flexible response.

Flexible Response

Flexible response called for the buildup of conventional and tactical nuclear weapons to provide the president with military alternatives to all-out nuclear war. Thus, the level and form of response could be geared to the nature and scope of the attack. During a crisis, flexible response would make retaliation more believable yet provide time for leaders to work out a truce before full-scale nuclear exchanges took place.

The value of flexibility for nuclear peace was underscored by the Cuban missile crisis, in which the superpowers came closer to the brink of nuclear war than at any other time since World War II. American intelligence confirmed in October 1962 that the Soviet Union was constructing sites in Cuba for launching medium-range missiles capable of hitting major U.S. targets.[3] President Kennedy considered this activity an unacceptable threat to the United States. He and his advisors considered a set of alternative responses that included (1) a full-scale bombardment of the missile sites by the Air Force, (2) a naval blockade to force the Soviet Union to remove the missiles, and (3) taking merely diplomatic actions.

Kennedy selected the blockade; it represented a firm U.S. response while not requiring the Soviets to accept a humiliating military defeat or running the risk of nuclear war. The Soviet Union backed down in this crisis, partly because the United States had superiority in nuclear weapons. The Soviet Union then resolved to close the nuclear weapons gap.

Mutual Assured Destruction

Following the expansion of Soviet nuclear capability, American theorists refined the concept of nuclear deterrence. The doctrine of mutual assured destruction—or MAD, as it came to be called—was based on the premise that some weapons would survive a first-strike nuclear attack by an opponent.[4] If enough weapons could survive a first strike to allow a devastating retaliatory strike, those surviving second-strike weapons would be sufficient to deter the opponent from launching a first strike. If each side maintained enough second-strike weapons, then first use of nuclear weapons would be suicidal. Therefore, both the United States and the Soviet Union built large nuclear arsenals. After 1963, the use of strategic nuclear weapons implied mutual assured destruction.

Arms Control

As the Soviets approached parity with the United States in the 1960s, arms control became an attractive alternative to the costs and risks of an uncontrolled nuclear arms race. Shortly after the Cuban missile crisis in 1963, a "hot line" agreement was signed with the Soviets to allow direct communication between leaders during crises, as well as a Partial Test Ban Treaty to limit environmental effects of atmospheric nuclear testing, slow the development of new weapons, and reduce superpower tensions.

Strategic Arms Limitation Treaty (SALT) talks between the United States and the Soviet Union led to the Anti-Ballistic Missile (ABM) Treaty in 1972, limiting defensive weapons, and a treaty, SALT I, freezing the number of offensive nuclear weapons held by both sides. In 1979, a SALT II treaty placed additional constraints on the arms race. The United States agreed to reduce its superiority in warheads while the Soviet Union destroyed some of its missile launchers. Although neither nation formally ratified SALT II, both nations agreed to respect its terms.

In December 1987, Soviet President Mikhail Gorbachev and President Reagan signed a treaty virtually banning intermediate-range nuclear forces (INFs) and began negotiations on reducing long-range strategic forces. In the United States, an expensive military buildup contributed to an unacceptably high national budget deficit. In the Soviet Union, Gorbachev was even more interested in relief from the burden of the arms race, as he attempted to reform and revitalize the Soviet economy. Where SALT had involved agreements limiting the pace of the arms race, the Reagan-Gorbachev negotiations achieved some actual nuclear disarmament. The Start II treaty, signed by President Bush and Russian President Boris Yeltsin in July 1991, ended the American-Soviet nuclear arms race.

Many observers were relieved that the world was escaping the security dilemma fostered by the nuclear arms race. A security dilemma is created when one nation acquires arms for defensive purposes but a rival nation perceives that arms buildup as threatening. An arms race follows, and political conflict is more likely to lead to war.[5]

Containment as Political Strategy

The military strategy which evolved during the cold war was supported by a political strategy of containment. For more than four decades after World

War II, containment aimed at preventing the expansion of Soviet power into new areas of the world without provoking direct military confrontation.

Containment in Europe

At the end of World War II, the United States recognized Soviet power and international communism as a primarily European threat to American national interests. The West feared that the Soviets, having installed communist governments in power in Eastern Europe, would seek political control throughout Europe by encouraging and supporting the efforts of European communist parties to seize power. Communists had played important roles as resistance fighters opposing the German occupation during World War II, and they enjoyed much popular support afterward.[6]

The Truman Doctrine

In response to a communist threat in Greece and Turkey in 1947, President Truman announced that the United States would "support free peoples who are resisting attempted subjugation by armed minorities or by outside pressures." This pledge became known as the Truman Doctrine. President Truman's commitment to support "free peoples" everywhere helped lay the foundations for competition between the capitalist and communist worlds for the allegiance of less developed countries (LDCs) in Asia, Africa, and Latin America.

The Korean War

An important test of containment policy occurred in Korea in 1950, when the North Korean army attacked South Korea. President Truman assumed that North Korean aggression was sponsored by the Soviet Union and that containment of communism in Europe required containment of communism throughout the noncommunist world. Truman's earlier commitment to free peoples was now given a truly global meaning.

The United States intervened forcefully in nationalist conflicts throughout the 1950s and 1960s under its policy of global containment, overtly in Lebanon (1958), the Dominican Republic (1965), and Vietnam (1965) and covertly in Iran (1953), Guatemala (1954), and Cuba (1961). Vietnam was the most significant effort at containment.

The Vietnam War

In 1954, France had suffered a major defeat at the hands of Ho Chi Minh's nationalist movement and granted independence to the new government of North Vietnam. Provisions for internationally supervised elections to reunify North and South Vietnam peacefully were rejected by the U.S.-supported government in South Vietnam in 1956. Nationalist forces in South

Vietnam—the National Liberation Front (NLF)—began military action to overthrow the South Vietnamese government, with the support of communist North Vietnam.

Insurgency spread for several years, and the increasingly repressive and unpopular Diem government was removed in a coup in 1963. Already deeply involved in supporting the South Vietnamese government through military and economic aid, President Johnson committed the United States to direct, large-scale combat involvement in 1965 to prevent a military victory by the communists. Despite increasing U.S. bombardment and eventual commitments of over 500,000 troops, in 1968 the communist forces mounted the Tet Offensive, a large-scale attack throughout South Vietnam. Faced with a war that appeared both unsuccessful in Vietnam and politically unacceptable at home, President Johnson agreed to begin peace talks with the North Vietnamese. By 1973, American troops were withdrawn and Vietnam was reunified under North Vietnamese rule.[7]

The Korean and Vietnam wars were fought to implement the policy of global containment. If unopposed, it was argued, international communism would spread from country to country, toppling noncommunist governments like a row of dominoes.

Peaceful Coexistence

In the 1970s, both the United States and the Soviet Union acknowledged the inherent dangers of direct confrontation in an atomic age and the realistic need to pursue their global power competition through political, diplomatic, and economic means, not military conflicts. Soviet Premier Nikita Khrushchev instituted the doctrine of peaceful coexistence between East and West as official Soviet policy. In the United States, detente was the concept used to describe the relaxation in tensions between East and West during the 1970s.[8]

Detente replaced the concept of cold war because of the Soviet Union's growing power and the desire by President Nixon and Henry Kissinger to promote friendly relations with China as a counterpoint to the Soviet Union. Arms control, trade, tourism, and scientific cooperation were among the features of detente between the United States and the Soviet Union. Discussions between the superpowers provided a means for managing their conflicts at a low level of tension. Military force would be used in pursuit of national objectives, but not directly between Soviet and American armed forces.

A developing pattern of Soviet aggressiveness in Central America, Africa, and Afghanistan from the mid-1970s led to growing criticism in the United States of the concept of detente. In effect, the Soviets took advantage of the preoccupation with Watergate and the weariness of the American public with the Vietnam war. The late 1970s may be characterized as a period of waning detente, and by 1980, the Carter administration was adopting a much tougher posture toward the Soviet Union.

The Reagan administration took over the reins of government in 1981 determined to restore the commitment to containment in American foreign policy. Thus began the largest peacetime military buildup in history. Through primarily covert means, the United States also supported insurgencies against Soviet-supported regimes in Afghanistan in Asia, Angola in Africa, and Nicaragua in Central America.

Economic Affairs in the Cold War Era

We now turn to economic affairs in the cold war period. In 1945, Western Europe lay in ruins. The United States assumed the role of world economic leader and assisted the European states to rebuild their shattered economies. The Marshall Plan, named after Secretary of State George Marshall, provided over $12 billion to the Western European nations. The goal was to ease the conditions of human suffering in war-devastated nations and to promote strong capitalist economies as a bulwark against the spread of international communism and Soviet power.

The Bretton Woods conference of the world's major trading states established a system for the multilateral management of the world's money supplies, including such institutions as the International Monetary Fund (IMF) and the World Bank. The system was designed to stabilize the value of international currencies, regulate currency reserves and imbalances, and facilitate world trade.

The dollar became the principal international currency, with its value fixed by gold—the dollar was "convertible" at the rate of $35 per ounce. To revive war-ravaged economies in Western Europe and Japan, the United States deliberately ran a balance-of-trade deficit by importing more from these countries than it exported to them.[9] In the post–cold war period, foreign policymakers would devote much more time and attention to global economic issues, as we shall see below.

The Post–Cold War Period

Collapse of the Soviet Union

The collapse of the Soviet Union in 1991 ended the intense nuclear confrontation that defined military strategy in the cold war period. The arms race had been a heavy burden to the Soviet Union. To compete with the United

States militarily, the Soviet Union spent a larger share of its much smaller economy to pay soldiers and buy weapons. Fewer resources were available for production of housing and consumer goods. Furthermore, the centrally planned Soviet economy did not allocate resources efficiently. Shortages of essential consumer goods, poor quality, and long waiting lines were part of the Soviet way of life.

In this setting, the forces for change in the Soviet political system gathered strength in the 1980s. President Mikhail Gorbachev initiated a broad program for reform. He was convinced that the Soviet Union could not reform its domestic political economy without reducing military spending and abandoning its costly imperial foreign policy initiatives. Under Gorbachev's leadership, the Soviet Union agreed to deep cuts in Soviet nuclear weapons, unilaterally withdrew Soviet troops from Eastern Europe, encouraged political self-determination in Eastern Europe, and tore down the Berlin Wall.[10]

Domestically, Gorbachev introduced *glasnost*, which meant broadening participation in political life, including free elections for the first time in Soviet history. He also pledged *perestroika*, or structural reform that meant that the centrally planned economy would be dismantled and free market principles introduced. Gorbachev sought to move slowly, to minimize the inevitable dislocation associated with a free market economy. Still, factories closed, people were thrown out of work, inflation soared, and uncertainty prevailed about how quickly market institutions would be introduced. The republics of Estonia, Lithuania, and Latvia, which had been forcibly incorporated into the Soviet Union after World War II, demanded full independence. Other republics, such as the Ukraine and Azerbaijan, which had been forcibly incorporated into the Soviet Union after the Bolshevik Revolution, successfully sought a degree of autonomy.

In August 1991, Communist hard-liners detained Gorbachev in a coup attempt, hoping to roll back political and economic reforms. Boris Yeltsin, President of Russia, the largest republic within the Soviet Union, successfully led popular resistance to the coup attempt. By December 1991, Yeltsin had forced Gorbachev from office, dissolved the Soviet Union, and demanded faster economic reform. In the early 1990s, the struggle continues between conservatives—who do not want to entirely dismantle the shabby social equality, central economic planning, and political authoritarianism of the communist state—and the reformers who want to speed the pace of economic and political reform.

The Transformation of Military Strategy

After the Soviet collapse, the primary foreign policy concern of the United States, providing for the common defense against potential enemies, has changed. A major issue is to what extent military spending can be cut without compromising the military's ability to protect essential American interests abroad. The general consensus among foreign policymakers is that levels of nuclear weapons should be reduced, although not eliminated. During the 1990s, the number of troops in uniform will be reduced, development of new weapons systems slowed, and military spending cut by approximately 30 percent from its 1988 cold war high.[11]

Arms Sales to Less Developed Countries

The process of cutting back on military spending is politically difficult. Unneeded military bases must be closed, and the communities which lose their bases lose thousands of jobs. A decision to forgo a new weapons system is economically devastating to arms-producing communities; about 1 million workers in the American arms industry are expected to lose their jobs by 1997.[12]

To cushion the blow, policymakers authorize sale of sophisticated airplanes, ships, and tanks to less developed countries (LDCs). The United States is the world's largest seller of weapons to other nations. While arms sales do keep American armaments workers employed, other consequences are unfortunate. The arms are purchased by governments in conflict with their neighbors; if they fight, better weapons are more destructive. The poorest nations are most heavily burdened by military expenditures. Resources spent on guns cannot be spent on schools and fertilizer to improve the lives of their people.[13]

Nuclear Proliferation

Nuclear proliferation means the spread of nuclear weapons capability to new states. In 1990, nuclear powers included the United States, the Soviet Union, Great Britain, France, China, and India. Some 30 other states have the economic and technological resources to build nuclear weapons. A great concern for the 1990s is that aggressive states (for example, Iraq, Iran, North Korea, and Libya) might develop nuclear weapons and threaten to use them. The Nuclear Nonproliferation Treaty requires signatories to allow international inspection to ensure that nuclear materials are not diverted to weapons production. But these controls are not foolproof.[14] In 1993 Saddam Hussein thwarted efforts by international inspectors to inspect Iraqi nuclear materials. In 1994, President Kim Il Sung of North Korea embarked upon a program to develop nuclear warheads, in clear violation of the Nuclear Nonproliferation Treaty.

Contemporary Economic Issues

Although the U.S. economy is still the world's largest, other nations are challenging America's economic primacy. Members of the European Economic Community have made substantial progress toward a single common market in Western Europe by reducing tariff barriers, moving toward a common currency, and coordinating economic policy. Japan, Taiwan, South Korea, and other Pacific Rim nations take advantage of low labor costs and high rates of investment to produce high-quality and low-cost automobiles, textiles, and electronics for export to the United States.

Meanwhile, the American economy has lost its competitive edge. Since 1945, the United States had borne the burden of paying for the military requirements of Europe and Asia, and its investment in civilian research and development lagged behind that of the countries it was protecting.[15] Many manufacturing firms closed their doors and moved production to Europe, Asia, and Latin America. Americans imported more than they exported, creating large trade imbalances and putting pressure on the value of the dollar. An abysmally low rate of savings and investment eroded American technological leadership.

With the end of the nuclear confrontation between the United States and the Soviet Union, economic issues have become relatively more important in foreign policy debate.

Trade

One set of economic issues involves trade. Should the United States aggressively promote free trade, or should it take action to protect American jobs from overseas competitors? For example, the North American Free Trade Agreement (NAFTA) enacted in 1993 reduces trade barriers between Canada, the United States, and Mexico. NAFTA was condemned by those who feared that American factories would close and production would shift to Mexico to take advantage of low-cost labor. Most experts agreed that more jobs would be created than lost and that the economic effects of NAFTA would be small. But the opponents were strong because the jobs that were lost belonged to specific voters in specific congressional districts, and they fought hard for NAFTA's defeat.

Another trade issue is whether some nations, especially Japan and France, engage in unfair trade practices by maintaining tariff barriers on agricultural products, banning imports which fail to meet unreasonably exacting standards, selling products in America below production cost, and subsidizing industries so they can sell products in the United States at low prices.

A related trade issue is how major trading nations can best stimulate global economic growth. Japan and Germany argue that the United States must reduce its $300 billion annual budget deficit, which will increase funds available for research and investment and stimulate economic growth. The United

States argues that the central banks in Japan and Germany should stimulate their economies by reducing interest rates, even if some small increase in inflation might result. These negotiations are difficult, because all nations seek to protect their own national interest in trade and economic policy discussions.[16]

Immigration

Another economic issue is immigration. An American tradition is to welcome hard-working immigrants who want to build a better life for their families. The 1990 census reveals that 20 million American residents, 8 percent of the population, are foreign-born. About 2 million legal immigrants arrive in America annually, mostly from Latin America. Some are escaping political persecution, but most seek economic opportunity. Immigration is now a political issue because large numbers of immigrants are arriving at a time when unskilled jobs are dwindling. Trade unions and unskilled workers are concerned that immigrants will work for less, and middle-class taxpayers worry that they will have to pay for schools and other social services used by a swelling immigrant population.

Foreign Policy Principles in the Post–Cold War Era

Several principles are appropriate for making and analyzing foreign policy decisions in the post–cold war era.

1. *Define national interests narrowly.* The objective of statecraft is to preserve the nation-state in a potentially hostile environment. As long as the United States is dependent upon oil imports, foreign policymakers must guarantee the flow of oil from the Middle East to the industrial countries. They must protect the security interests of America's major trading partners in Asia and Latin America. Ultimately, the United States must be prepared to defend its essential interests with military power.[17]

The military policy issue in the post–cold war era is how to enable the military to respond flexibly and quickly to regional conflicts using conventional weapons. For example, the military was asked to drive Iraq out of Kuwait in 1991 and to quell civil war in Somalia in 1992. The military plans to keep enough aircraft carriers, aircraft wings, and troops to respond to two international crises at the same time.

During the cold war era, the United States supported anti-Soviet or anti-communist governments regardless of their authoritarian nature and sometimes brutal record of repression and human rights abuses. It also undermined governments that were Soviet-influenced and opposed nationalist revolutionary movements that contained potential communist elements. In the early post–cold war years, many nations are experimenting with democratic political reform. The United States is inclined to support these efforts.

However, whether promoting democracy is an essential American interest is doubtful. United States policymakers need stable governments with which they can work predictably, even if those governments are not democratic. When political conflicts grow too intense, some current democracies are likely to succumb to authoritarian challenges.[18] And in a few states, it is possible that Islamic fundamentalist majorities may run roughshod over the rights of Western-oriented minorities.

2. *Refrain from interfering in distant conflicts when prospects for success are uncertain.*[19] The America intervention in Somalia in 1992 to prevent mass starvation demonstrates that it is sometimes easy to alleviate a crisis situation but hard to solve the underlying political problems. American influence in the Middle East is limited by the rise of anti-Western Islamic fundamentalism. The U.S. government chose not to depose Iraq's Saddam Hussein after the 1991 Persian Gulf war because the United States could not ensure that Iraq would then have a stable government able to counter Iran in the Middle East. The United States can encourage the Israeli-Palestinian peace initiative begun in September 1993, but success ultimately depends upon the participants.

The United States has been reluctant to intervene in Bosnia despite the horrors of "ethnic cleansing" because American weapons cannot easily alter the deep ethnic antagonisms that underlie the conflict. Similarly, ethnic animosities in Sri Lanka, South Africa, Rwanda, and India cannot easily be calmed.

3. *Deploy military force only if clearly specified goals are likely to be achieved quickly and at minimal cost.* Local conflicts rooted in personality, ethnicity, and religious differences are too complex to be resolved through military intervention. The Vietnam war taught us the limits of military power. Ethnic tensions in Eastern Europe, in the republics of the former Soviet Union, in South Asia, and in the Middle East are certain to erupt in warfare occasionally. As arms sales increase, those conflicts will be ever more destructive. That will raise the costs should the United States decide to intervene to defend vital national interests.

Ronald Reagan's invasion of Grenada in 1983 and George Bush's Operation Desert Storm against Iraq in 1991 achieved their objectives quickly. Similarly, American troops could be sent to Somalia to pacify warlords who had prevented distribution of food to several hundred thousand starving Somalis. But they could not be sent to Bosnia to end Serbian "ethnic cleansing" against Croats and Muslims. American public opinion turns against foreign military adventures when American troops return home in body bags. As American troops died in Somalia in 1993, foreign policymakers concluded that creating a stable government there was too uncertain and that troops should be withdrawn quickly.

4. *Pursue national objectives through multilateral actions.* Sovereign nations object to great powers using their military might to pursue their own national objectives. American soldiers were liberating heroes in Europe during World War II, but today they are regarded as imperialist aggressors in LDCs which experienced European colonial rule or American economic domination. Sentiments of anticolonial nationalism are strong in LDCs.

That is why the United States has supported United Nations decisions to send troops to several global trouble spots. For example, the United Nations condemned the Iraqi invasion of Kuwait in 1991 and authorized military action against Iraq. The United States provided most of the troops, weapons, and leadership, but many countries contributed some troops or paid part of the costs. United Nations peacekeeping forces have sought to prevent local fighting in Bosnia, Somalia, Lebanon, and Cambodia. These actions are authorized by a consensus of United Nations Security Council members; no single nation-state can be accused of pursuing its own foreign policy interests by intervening in a troubled area unilaterally.

The United States can no longer maintain a global police force. Other regional powers in Asia, the Middle East, and Europe will work out regional security arrangements and take the initiative in dealing with regional issues. For example, the United States is likely to defer to Western Europe in dealing with conflicts in Eastern Europe. Now that the United States has lost its lease on its military bases in the Philippines, Japan and China can be expected to take a larger role in Asian military affairs.

Many American foreign policy interests can be pursued effectively only through close cooperation with other nation-states. We cannot interdict the flow of illegal drugs into the United States without the cooperation of governments where farmers grow poppies and coca and dealers organize drug distribution. Recently, 70 percent of the federal drug budget has been spent on supply-interrupting activities. The success of these operations ultimately depends upon the willingness of governments in Mexico and Colombia to persuade local farmers to plant less profitable crops and to clamp down on processing laboratories.

Rapid population growth in LDCs and economic growth in the large more developed countries (MDCs) increase pollution and deplete productive resources. In general, the relatively affluent MDCs are more concerned with environmental issues than are the LDCs, which prefer to exploit resources to raise the standard of living of their impoverished populations. For example,

LDCs prefer to exploit their rain forests now rather than worry about global warming.[20] Having access to low-cost refrigerants today is more important to China than is the prospect of reducing the incidence of skin cancer in years to come. These environmental policy differences can be resolved only through negotiation and cooperation.

Foreign Policymakers

The structure of foreign policy-making resembles three concentric circles. The innermost circle consists of the president and trusted chief advisors. The middle circle includes other important executive branch personnel and congressional foreign policy leaders. The outermost circle is composed of interest-group representatives and the attentive public, who speak their minds and are heard but who do not participate directly in the decision-making process.

The President

The president is the chief foreign policymaker. As commander in chief of the armed forces, the president makes the ultimate decisions about committing American armed forces abroad. With input from a team of advisors, President Kennedy decided how the United States would respond in the 1963 Cuban missile crisis. President Bush sent an army to drive Iraq's Saddam Hussein out of Kuwait in 1991.

The president also appoints all key personnel in the foreign policy establishment: secretaries of the state and defense departments; leaders of semiautonomous agencies, including the Arms Control and Disarmament Agency, the U.S. Information Agency (USIA), the Agency for International Development (AID), and the Central Intelligence Agency (CIA); and all U.S. ambassadors. Presidents tend to appoint individuals to these roles who share their image of foreign policy problems and priorities.

These considerable powers guarantee that presidents play a strong role in shaping U.S. foreign policy, as the framers of the Constitution intended.

The National Security Council

The National Security Council (NSC), established in 1947, provides a personal staff of foreign policy advisors to the president. Its membership includes the president, the vice president, the secretaries of state and defense, and normally the director of the CIA and the chair of the Joint Chiefs of Staff. Its director is the president's national security advisor.

In its early years, the NSC was primarily a coordinating rather than a policy-making body. Since President Kennedy, the national security advisor has largely eclipsed the secretary of state as the principal architect of foreign policy. The NSC studies problems, coordinates policy with other agencies, conducts policy analyses, and provides information to the president. The NSC is supreme because many government agencies need to be consulted on foreign policy issues, and the NSC is a convenient forum.[21]

Presidents must take into account that the Department of State, Department of Defense, and CIA are bureaucratic organizations with their own agency objectives and standard operating procedures. Their leaders tend to interpret the national interest in terms of their organizational goals and personal ambitions.[22] Henry Kissinger, President Nixon's foreign policy adviser, observed that foreign policy advisers do not present disinterested analysis in policy discussions. "Each of the contending factions has a maximum incentive to state its case in its most extreme form because the ultimate outcome depends, to a considerable extent, on a bargaining process. The premium placed on advocacy turns decision making into a series of adjustments among special interests," wrote Kissinger.[23]

Central Intelligence Agency

The Central Intelligence Agency (CIA) also was established in 1947, taking over the functions performed by the Office of Strategic Services during World War II. The CIA reports to the NSC, and its director is an important advisor to the president on foreign affairs.

CIA activities fall into two broad categories: intelligence and operations. The intelligence function includes acquiring, analyzing, and interpreting information from diverse sources on subjects ranging from agricultural production abroad to estimates of military spending by foreign governments. The operations function includes involvement in the domestic politics of other countries. CIA plots to overthrow unfriendly governments and to assassinate foreign political leaders have aroused controversy. An important issue has been balancing the CIA's desire for secrecy with the responsibility of Congress to oversee and monitor intelligence activities.[24]

Department of State

The Department of State is responsible for the conduct of American diplomacy and the development and implementation of nonmilitary dimensions of U.S. foreign policy. Internally, the department is organized in terms of functions, such as political and economic affairs; issue areas, such as terrorism, drugs, and human rights; and geographic areas, such as oceans, Africa, and inter-American affairs. The department operates a network of some 300 embassies, missions, and consulates around the world and represents the United States in 50 international organizations. It is the official link between the government of the United States and the governments of other nations.

Department of Defense

The Pentagon is the symbol and headquarters of the Department of Defense. Its annual budget exceeds a quarter of a trillion dollars, and it employs 3 million civilian and armed forces personnel. This department spends over $100 billion per year on weapons, research, and construction. Therefore, military spending has a major impact on the American economy. In the 1990s, decisions on whether to continue funding weapons systems are made on the basis of both military considerations and the economic impact on local communities.

The United States has maintained a tradition of civilian control of the military. The secretary of defense is a civilian, and civilian secretaries are appointed to direct each branch of the armed forces. The senior officers or chiefs of staff for each branch of the services advise their civilian counterparts and, with the commander of the Marine Corps, constitute an advisory group called the Joint Chiefs of Staff. The chairman of the Joint Chiefs is appointed by the president and confirmed by the Senate. This body, drawing on substantial staff and other resources, advises the president and Congress on armaments, military aid to other countries, and other security issues.

Congress

The principal congressional check on the executive branch in foreign policy is the power of the purse. Decisions on new weapons systems, aid to foreign governments, and all other policies involving public expenditure require that Congress appropriate funds. The Senate also has the constitutional right to approve treaties, but most international agreements are negotiated by the president and do not require Senate approval.

Congress also passes acts and resolutions to curb the president's foreign policy-making independence. The War Powers Resolution, passed in 1973 over President Nixon's veto, requires the president to seek congressional authorization after committing U.S. armed forces in combat roles abroad. Under this resolution presidents may commit forces on their own authority if the lives of American citizens are in danger or if U.S. armed forces have been attacked, but protracted involvement requires congressional approval. Presidents have regarded this resolution as a violation of the power of the commander in chief.

The Iran-contra affair in 1986 renewed congressional interest in strengthening its oversight of the intelligence community. In congressional hearings, Reagan administration officials admitted deliberately misleading members of Congress to avoid reporting on covert operations that violated congressional restrictions on aid to the contras. Members of Congress worried that a hidden body within the NSC, unaccountable within the executive branch or to Congress, had assumed the authority to conduct foreign policy. In defense, administration officials argued that secrecy was necessary to the success of their activities and that congressional intelligence oversight committees could not be trusted.[25]

One underlying issue illustrated in this case is the tradeoff between maintaining a democratic process of foreign policymaking and preserving secrecy and dispatch in foreign action. In time of military crisis and when fundamental national interest is involved, bipartisan support in Congress for presidential initiatives is likely. But in the post–cold war world, we must anticipate lack of consensus on foreign policy issues. Should the United States intervene in regional conflicts, lower trade barriers, cut down on immigration, and cooperate with other nations on global environmental issues? These issues are likely to be controversial. We can expect Congress to play an active role in the foreign policy decision-making process.

Bipartisanship

In crisis situations when the nation is confronted by a foreign enemy, politics tends to stop at the water's edge, and elites at the center of the foreign policy-making process tend to dominate. Elites in Washington also have a free hand to make policy decisions on foreign policy issues which do not affect strong domestic political constituencies.

During much of the post–World War II period, Congress accepted a diminished role in foreign policy, partly because presidents and Congress were in fundamental agreement on major foreign policy questions. Democrats and Republicans in Congress viewed the Soviet Union as the preeminent threat to U.S. national security and agreed that a policy of containment was the appropriate U.S. response. Presidents from Truman through Johnson could count on congressional support for their national security policies.

This bipartisan consensus culminated in the Tonkin Gulf Resolution in 1964. The Joint Chiefs had recommended increasing the U.S. involvement in Vietnam early in 1964. Based on what later appeared to be very questionable evidence that North Vietnamese forces had fired on U.S. ships, the Senate, by a near-unanimous vote, passed this resolution authorizing President Johnson's subsequent actions to widen the war.[25] Opposition to the Vietnam war broke the bipartisan consensus on U.S. foreign policy, setting the stage for Congress to assert greater influence.[27]

With the end of the cold war, the president must expect less bipartisan support in making controversial foreign policy decisions. Should American troops be sent in harm's way on humanitarian grounds when essential foreign policy interests are not involved? Should we forgo production of a new weapons system if doing so will force layoffs at a major military contractor? Should we lower trade barriers if doing so will help American farmers but hurt automobile workers? In the 1990s, these foreign policy issues are subject to the same partisan and ideological disputes as domestic issues.

When domestic political considerations are important, the influence of the outer circle expands.[28] For example, the earnings of farmers, automobile workers, and steel and textile producers are affected by foreign policy actions, and these groups take an active role in the policy-making process. Farmers supported a $13 billion foreign aid package to the former Soviet Union, some of which would purchase grain. Ethnic groups with roots in old Russia also supported the aid bill. In deference to American Jews, American policymakers have consistently supported Israel in Middle Eastern political issues. The United States continues an economic embargo of Cuba in 1994 only because of the strong feelings of anti-Castro Cuban exiles in Florida.

Isolationism, or avoiding entanglement in European political disputes, was the first principle of American foreign policy from 1787 until 1945. After World War II, Europe lay in ruins and America emerged as a military and economic superpower. During the cold war era from 1945 until 1990, the United States was the only nation with the military and economic power to contain possible Soviet aggression.

The post–cold war era, which began in 1991 with the collapse of communism in the former Soviet Union, poses a new set of foreign policy challenges. Policymakers are likely to define national interests more narrowly, to refrain from interfering in distant conflict when prospects for success are uncertain, and to cooperate with other nations in pursuit of shared objectives.

The president is preeminent in foreign policy. However, presidents depend on their advisers to identify problems, propose alternative solutions, and recommend courses of action. Representing different bureaucratic agencies and departments, these advisers bring different views and interests to bear. Presidents also clearly depend on public and congressional support for success in foreign policy. Foreign policy-making involves interactions among the president and various agencies and departments within the administration, relations between these actors and Congress, and involvement of special-interest groups. Bipartisanship often prevailed during the bipolar cold war confrontation with the Soviet Union. In the 1990s, partisan conflict on foreign policy issues is much more evident.

Recommended Reading

Graham Allison: *Essence of Decision: Explaining the Cuban Missile Crisis,* Little, Brown, Boston, 1971.

Roger J. Art and Seyom Brown: *U.S. Foreign Policy: The Search for a New Role,* Macmillan, New York, 1993.

Roger Hilsman: *The Politics of Policy Making in Defense and Foreign Affairs: Conceptual Models and Bureaucratic Politics,* Prentice-Hall, Englewood Cliffs, N.J., 1987.

Charles W. Kegley, Jr., and Eugene R. Wittkopf, eds.: *The Domestic Sources of American Foreign Policy: Insights and Evidence,* St. Martin's, New York, 1988.

George F. Kennan: *Realities of American Foreign Policy,* Norton, New York, 1966.

Hans Morgenthau: *Politics Among Nations: The Struggle for Power and Peace,* Knopf, New York, 1973.

Jerel A. Rosati: *The Politics of United States Foreign Policy,* Harcourt Brace Jovanovich, Fort Worth, 1993.

APPENDIX 1

The Declaration of
Independence

*The original spelling, capitalization, and punctuation
have been retained in this version.*

*In Congress, July 4, 1776, the unanimous Declaration of the thirteen
United States of America.*

When, in the Course of human events, it becomes necessary for one people to dissolve the political bands which have connected them with another,
and to assume, among the Powers of the earth, the separate and equal station
to which the Laws of Nature and of Nature's God entitle them, a decent respect to the opinions of mankind requires that they should declare the causes
which impel them to the separation.

We hold these truths to be self-evident, that all men are created equal, that
they are endowed by their Creator with certain unalienable Rights, that among
these, are Life, Liberty, and the pursuit of Happiness. That, to secure these
rights, Governments are instituted among Men, deriving their just Powers
from the consent of the governed. That, whenever any form of Government
becomes destructive of these ends, it is the Right of the People to alter or to
abolish it, and to institute new Government, laying its foundation on such Principles, and organizing its Powers in such form, as to them shall seem most
likely to effect their Safety and Happiness. Prudence, indeed, will dictate that

Governments long established should not be changed for light and transient causes; and, accordingly, all experience hath shewn, that mankind are more disposed to suffer, while evils are sufferable, than to right themselves by abolishing the forms to which they are accustomed. But, when a long train of abuses and usurpations, pursuing invariably the same Object, evinces a design to reduce them under absolute Despotism, it is their right, it is their duty, to throw off such Government, and to provide new Guards for their future Security. Such has been the patient sufferance of these Colonies; and such is now the necessity which constrains them to alter their former Systems of Government. The history of the present King of Great Britain is a history of repeated injuries and usurpations, all having in direct object the establishment of an absolute Tyranny over these States. To prove this, let Facts be submitted to a candid world.

He has refused his Assent to Laws, the most wholesome and necessary for the public good.

He has forbidden his Governors to pass Laws of immediate and pressing importance, unless suspended in their operation till his Assent should be obtained; and when so suspended, he has utterly neglected to attend to them.

He has refused to pass other Laws for the accommodation of large districts of People, unless those people would relinquish the right of Representation in the legislature; a right inestimable to them and formidable to tyrants only.

He has called together legislative bodies at places unusual, uncomfortable, and distant from the depository of their Public Records, for the sole Purpose of fatiguing them into compliance with his measures.

He has dissolved Representative Houses repeatedly, for opposing, with manly firmness, his invasions on the rights of the People.

He has refused for a long time, after such dissolutions, to cause others to be elected; whereby the Legislative Powers, incapable of Annihilation, have returned to the People at large for their exercise; the State remaining in the mean time exposed to all dangers of invasion from without, and convulsions within.

He has endeavoured to prevent the Population of these States; for that purpose obstructing the Laws for Naturalization of Foreigners; refusing to pass others to encourage their migrations hither, and raising the conditions of new Appropriations of Lands.

He has obstructed the Administration of Justice, by refusing his Assent to Laws for establishing judiciary Powers.

He has made Judges dependent on his Will alone, for the tenure of their offices, and the amount and payment of their salaries.

He has erected a multitude of New Offices, and sent hither swarms of Officers to harrass our People, and eat out their substance.

He has kept among us, in times of Peace, Standing Armies, without the Consent of our legislatures.

He has affected to render the Military independent of and superior to the Civil Power.

He has combined with others to subject us to a jurisdiction foreign to our constitution, and unacknowledged by our laws; giving his Assent to their Acts of pretended Legislation;

For quartering large bodies of armed troops among us:

For protecting them, by a mock Trial, from Punishment for any Murders which they should commit on the Inhabitants of these States:

For cutting off our Trade with all parts of the world:

For imposing Taxes on us without our Consent:

For depriving us, in many cases, of the benefits of Trial by Jury:

For transporting us beyond Seas to be tried for pretended offences:

For abolishing the free System of English Laws in a neighbouring province, establishing therein an Arbitrary government, and enlarging its Boundaries, so as to render it at once an example and fit instrument for introducing the same absolute rule into these Colonies:

For taking away our Charters, abolishing our most valuable Laws, and altering fundamentally the Forms of our Governments:

For suspending our own Legislatures, and declaring themselves invested with Power to legislate for us in all cases whatsoever.

He has abdicated Government here, by declaring us out of his protection, and waging War against us.

He plundered our seas, ravaged our Coasts, burnt our towns, and destroyed the Lives of our People.

He is at this time transporting large Armies of foreign Mercenaries to compleat the works of death, desolation and tyranny, already begun with circumstances of Cruelty and perfidy scarcely paralleled in the most barbarous ages, and totally unworthy the Head of a civilized nation.

He has constrained our fellow Citizens, taken Captive on the high Seas, to bear Arms against their Country, to become the executioners of their friends and Brethren, or to fall themselves by their Hands.

He has excited domestic insurrections amongst us, and has endeavoured to bring on the inhabitants of our frontiers, the merciless Indian Savages, whose known rule of warfare, is an undistinguished destruction of all ages, sexes, and conditions.

In every stage of these Oppressions, We have Petitioned for Redress, in the most humble terms: Our repeated Petitions have been answered only by repeated injury. A Prince whose character is thus marked by every act which may define a Tyrant, is unfit to be the ruler of a free People.

Nor have We been wanting in attentions to our British brethren. We have warned them from time to time of attempts by their legislature to extend an unwarrantable jurisdiction over us. We have reminded them of the circumstances of our emigration and settlement here. We have appealed to their native justice and magnanimity, and we have conjured them, by the ties of our common kindred, to disavow these usurpations, which, would inevitably interrupt our connexions and correspondence. They too have been deaf to the voice of justice and consanguinity. We must, therefore, acquiesce in the necessity, which denounces our Separation, and hold them, as we hold the rest of mankind, Enemies in War, in Peace Friends.

WE, THEREFORE, the Representatives of the UNITED STATES OF AMERICA, in GENERAL CONGRESS assembled, appealing to the Supreme Judge of the World for the rectitude of our intentions, DO, in the Name, and by Authority of the good People of these Colonies, solemnly PUBLISH and DECLARE, That these United Colonies are, and of Right ought to be FREE AND INDEPENDENT STATES; that they are Absolved from all Allegiance to the British Crown, and that all political connection between them and the State of Great Britain, is and ought to be totally dissolved; and that, as FREE and INDEPENDENT STATES, they have full Power to levy War, conclude Peace, contract Alliances, establish Commerce, and to do all other Acts and Things which INDEPENDENT STATES may of right do. AND for the support of this Declaration, with a firm reliance on the protection of divine Providence, we mutually pledge to each other our Lives, our Fortunes, and our sacred Honour.

APPENDIX 2

The Constitution of the United States of America

*The original spelling, capitalization, and punctuation
have been retained in this version.*

We the People of the United States, in Order to form a more perfect Union, establish Justice, insure domestic Tranquility, provide for the common defence, promote the general Welfare, and secure the Blessings of Liberty to ourselves and our Posterity, do ordain and establish this CONSTITUTION for the United States of America.

Article I

Section 1. All legislative Powers herein granted shall be vested in a Congress of the United States, which shall consist of a Senate and House of Representatives.

Section 2. The House of Representatives shall be composed of Members chosen every second Year by the People of the several States, and the Electors in each State shall have the Qualifications requisite for Electors of the most numerous Branch of the State Legislature.

No Person shall be a Representative who shall not have attained to the Age of twenty-five Years, and been seven Years a Citizen of the United States, and who shall not, when elected, be an Inhabitant of that state in which he shall be chosen.

Representatives and direct Taxes shall be apportioned among the several States which may be included within this Union, according to their respective Numbers, which shall be determined by adding to the whole Number of free Persons, including those bound to Service for a Term of Years, and excluding Indians not taxed, three fifths of all other Persons. The actual Enumeration shall be made within three Years after the first Meeting of the Congress of the United States, and within every subsequent Term of ten Years, in such Manner as they shall by Law direct. The Number of Representatives shall not exceed one for every thirty Thousand, but each State shall have at Least one Representative; and until such enumeration shall be made, the State of New Hampshire shall be entitled to chuse three, Massachusetts eight, Rhode-Island and Providence Plantations one, Connecticut five, New York six, New Jersey four, Pennsylvania eight, Delaware one, Maryland six, Virginia ten, North Carolina five, South Carolina five, and Georgia three.

When vacancies happen in the Representation from any State, the Executive Authority thereof shall issue Writs of Election to fill such Vacancies.

The House of Representatives shall chuse their Speaker and other Officers; and shall have the sole Power of Impeachment.

Section 3. The Senate of the United States shall be composed of two Senators from each State, chosen by the Legislature thereof, for six Years; and each Senator shall have one Vote.

Immediately after they shall be assembled in Consequence of the first Election, they shall be divided as equally as may be into three Classes. The Seats of the Senators of the first Class shall be vacated at the Expiration of the second Year, of the second Class at the Expiration of the fourth Year, and of the third Class at the Expiration of the sixth Year, so that one-third may be chosen every second Year; and if Vacancies happen by Resignation, or otherwise, during the Recess of the Legislature of any State, the Executive thereof may make temporary Appointments until the next Meeting of the Legislature, which shall then fill such Vacancies.

No Person shall be a Senator who shall not have attained to the Age of thirty Years, and been nine Years a Citizen of the United States, and who shall not, when elected, be an Inhabitant of that State for which he shall be chosen.

The Vice President of the United States shall be President of the Senate, but shall have no vote, unless they be equally divided.

The Senate shall chuse their other Officers, and also a President pro tempore, in the absence of the Vice President, or when he shall exercise the Office of the President of the United States.

The Senate shall have the sole Power to try all Impeachments. When sitting for that purpose they shall be on Oath or Affirmation. When the President of the United States is tried, the Chief Justice shall preside: And no person shall be convicted without the Concurrence of two thirds of the Members present.

Judgment in Cases of Impeachment shall not extend further than to removal from Office, and disqualification to hold and enjoy any Office of honor, Trust, or Profit under the United States: but the Party convicted shall nevertheless be liable and subject to Indictment, Trial, Judgment, and Punishment, according to Law.

Section 4. The Times, Places and Manner of holding Elections for Senators and Representatives, shall be prescribed in each State by the Legislature thereof; but the Congress may at any time by Law make or alter such Regulations, except as to the Places of Chusing Senators.

The Congress shall assemble at least once in every Year, and such Meeting shall be on the first Monday in December, unless they shall by Law appoint a different Day.

Section 5. Each House shall be the Judge of the Elections, Returns and Qualifications of its own Members, and a Majority of each shall constitute a Quorum to do Business; but a smaller number may adjourn from day to day, and may be authorized to compel the Attendance of absent Members, in such Manner, and under such Penalties, as each House may provide.

Each House may determine the Rules of its Proceedings, punish its Members for disorderly Behaviour, and, with the Concurrence of two thirds, expel a Member.

Each House shall keep a Journal of its Proceedings, and from time to time publish the same, excepting such Parts as may in their Judgment require Secrecy; and the Yeas and Nays of the Members of either House on any question shall, at the Desire of one fifth of those Present, be entered on the Journal.

Neither House, during the Session of Congress, shall, without the Consent of the other, adjourn for more than three days, nor to any other Place than that in which the two Houses shall be sitting.

Section 6. The Senators and Representatives shall receive a Compensation for their Services, to be ascertained by Law, and paid out of the Treasury of the United States. They shall in all Cases, except Treason, Felony, and Breach of the Peace, be privileged from Arrest during their Attendance at the Session of their respective Houses, and in going to and returning from the same; and for any Speech or Debate in either House, they shall not be questioned in any other Place.

No Senator or Representative shall, during the Time for which he was elected, be appointed to any civil Office under the Authority of the United States, which shall have been created, or the Emoluments whereof shall have been increased, during such time; and no Person holding any Office under the United States shall be a Member of either House during his continuance in Office.

Section 7. All Bills for raising Revenue shall originate in the House of Representatives; but the Senate may propose or concur with Amendments as on other bills.

Every Bill which shall have passed the House of Representatives and the Senate, shall, before it become a Law, be presented to the President of the United States; If he approve he shall sign it, but if not he shall return it, with his Objections, to that House in which it shall have originated, who shall enter the objections at large on their Journal, and proceed to reconsider it. If after such Reconsideration two thirds of that House shall agree to pass the bill, it shall be sent, together with the Objections, to the other House, by which it shall likewise be reconsidered, and if approved by two thirds of that House, it shall become a Law. But in all such Cases the Votes of both Houses shall be determined by Yeas and Nays, and the Names of the Persons voting for and against the Bill shall be entered on the Journal of each House respectively. If any Bill shall not be returned by the President within ten Days (Sundays excepted) after it shall have been presented to him, the Same shall be a Law, in like Manner as if he had signed it, unless the Congress by their Adjournment prevent its Return, in which Case it shall not be a Law.

Every Order, Resolution, or Vote to which the Concurrence of the Senate and House of Representatives may be necessary (except on a question of Adjournment) shall be presented to the President of the United States; and before the Same shall take Effect, shall be approved by him, or being disapproved by him, shall be repassed by two thirds of the Senate and House of Representatives, according to the Rules and Limitations prescribed in the Case of a Bill.

Section 8. The Congress shall have Power To lay and collect Taxes, Duties, Imposts and Excises, to pay the Debts and provide for the common Defence and general Welfare of the United States; but all Duties, and Excises shall be uniform throughout the United States;

To borrow money on the credit of the United States;

To regulate Commerce with foreign Nations, and among the several States, and with the Indian Tribes;

To establish an uniform rule of Naturalization, and uniform Laws on the subject of Bankruptcies throughout the United States;

To coin Money, regulate the Value thereof, and of foreign Coin, and fix the Standard of Weights and measures;

To provide for the Punishment of counterfeiting the Securities and current Coin of the United States;

To establish Post Offices and post Roads;

To promote the Progress of Science and useful Arts, by securing for limited Times to Authors and Inventors the exclusive Right to their respective Writings and Discoveries;

To constitute Tribunals inferior to the Supreme Court;

To define and punish Piracies and Felonies committed on the high Seas, and Offenses against the Law of Nations;

To declare War, grant Letters of Marque and Reprisal, and make Rules concerning Captures on Land and Water;

To raise and support Armies, but no Appropriation of Money to that Use shall be for a longer Term than two Years;

To provide and maintain a Navy;

To make Rules for the Government and Regulation of the land and naval forces;

To provide for calling forth the Militia to execute the Laws of the Union, suppress insurrections and repel Invasions;

To provide for organizing, arming, and disciplining the Militia, and for governing such Part of them as may be employed in Service of the United States, reserving to the States respectively, the Appointment of the Officers, and the Authority of training the Militia according to the discipline prescribed by Congress;

To exercise exclusive Legislation in all Cases whatsoever, over such District (not exceeding ten Miles square) as may, by Cession of particular States, and the acceptance of Congress, become the Seat of the Government of the United States, and to exercise like Authority over all Places purchased by the Consent of the Legislature of the State in which the Same shall be, for the Erection of Forts, Magazines, Arsenals, Dock-yards, and other needful Building;—And

To make all Laws which shall be necessary and proper for carrying into Execution the foregoing Powers, and all other Powers vested by this Constitution in the Government of the United States, or in any Department or Officer thereof.

Section 9. The Migration or Importation of such Persons as any of the States now existing shall think proper to admit, shall not be prohibited by the Congress prior to the Year one thousand eight hundred and eight, but a tax or duty may be imposed on such Importation, not exceeding ten dollars for each Person.

The privilege of the Writ of Habeas Corpus shall not be suspended, unless when in Cases of Rebellion or Invasion the public Safety may require it.

No bill of Attainder or ex post facto Law shall be passed.

No capitation, or other direct, Tax shall be laid unless in Proportion to the Census or Enumeration herein before directed to be taken.

No Tax or Duty shall be laid on Articles exported from any State.

No Preference shall be given by any Regulation of Commerce or Revenue to the Ports of one State over those of another: nor shall Vessels bound to, or from, one State, be obliged to enter, clear, or pay Duties in another.

No Money shall be drawn from the Treasury, but in Consequence of Appropriations made by Law; and a regular Statement and Account of the Receipts and Expenditures of all public Money shall be published from time to time.

No Title of Nobility shall be granted by the United States: And no Person holding any Office of Profit or Trust under them, shall, without the Consent of the Congress, accept of any present, Emolument, Office, or Title, of any kind whatever, from any King, Prince, or foreign State.

Section 10. No State shall enter into any Treaty, Alliance, or Confederation; grant Letters of Marque and Reprisal; coin Money; emit Bills of Credit; make any Thing but gold and silver Coin a Tender in Payment of Debts; pass any Bill Attainder, ex post facto Law, or Law impairing the Obligation of Contracts, or grant any title of Nobility.

No State shall, without the Consent of the Congress, lay any Imposts or Duties on Imports or Exports, except what may be absolutely necessary for executing its inspection Laws; and the net Produce of all Duties and Imposts, laid by any State on Imports or Exports, shall be for the use of the Treasury of the United States; and all such Laws shall be subject to the Revision and Control of the Congress.

No state shall, without the Consent of Congress, lay any duty of Tonnage, keep Troops, or Ships of War in time of Peace, enter into any Agreement or Compact with another State, or with a foreign Power, or engage in War, unless actually invaded, or in such imminent Danger as will not admit of delay.

Article II

Section 1. The executive Power shall be vested in a President of the United States of America. He shall hold his Office during the Term of four years, and, together with the Vice president, chosen for the same Term, be elected, as follows:

Each State shall appoint, such Manner as the legislature thereof may direct, a Number of Electors, equal to the whole Number of Senators and Representatives to which the State may be entitled in the Congress: but no Senator or Representative, or Person holding an Office of Trust or Profit under the United States, shall be appointed an Elector.

[The Electors shall meet in their respective States, and vote by Ballot for two persons, of whom one at least shall not be an Inhabitant of the same State with themselves. And they shall make a List of all the Persons voted for, and of the Number of Votes for each; which List they shall sign and certify, and transmit sealed to the Seat of the Government of the United States, directed to the President of the Senate. The President of the Senate shall, in the Presence of the Senate and House of Representatives, open all the Certificates, and the Votes shall then be counted. The Person having the greatest Number of Votes shall be the President, if such Number be a Majority of the whole Number of Electors appointed; and if there be more than one who have such Majority, and have an equal Number of Votes, then the House of Representatives shall immediately chuse by Ballot one of them for President; and if no Person have a majority, then from the five highest on the List the said House shall in like Manner chuse the President. But in chusing the President, the Votes shall be taken by States, the Representation from each State having one Vote; a quorum for this Purpose shall consist of a Member or Members from two-thirds of the States, and a Majority of all the states shall be necessary to a Choice. In every Case, after the Choice of the President, the Person having the greatest Number of Votes of the Electors shall be the Vice President. But if there should remain two or more who have equal votes, the Senate shall chuse from them by Ballot the Vice President.]

The Congress may determine the Time of chusing the Electors, and the Day on which they shall give their Votes; which Day shall be the same throughout the United States.

No person except a natural-born Citizen, or a Citizen of the United States, at the time of the Adoption of this Constitution, shall be eligible to the Office of President; neither shall any Person be eligible to that Office who shall not have attained to the Age of thirty-five Years, and been fourteen Years a Resident within the United States.

In Case of the Removal of the President from Office, or of his Death, Resignation, or Inability to discharge the Powers and Duties of the said Office, the same shall devolve on the Vice President, and the Congress may by Law provide for the Case of Removal, Death, Resignation, or Inability, both of the President and Vice President, declaring what Officer shall then act as President, and such Officer shall act accordingly, until the disability be removed or a President shall be elected.

The President shall, at stated Times, receive for his Services a Compensation, which shall neither be increased nor diminished during the Period for which he shall have been elected, and he shall not receive within that Period any other Emolument from the United States, or any of them.

Before he enter on the execution of his Office, he shall take the following Oath or Affirmation—"I do solemnly swear (or affirm) that I will faithfully execute the Office of President of the United States, and will, to the best of my Ability, preserve, protect, and defend the Constitution of the United States."

Section 2. The President shall be Commander in Chief of the Army and Navy of the United States, and of the Militia of the several States, when called into the actual Service of the United States; he may require the Opinion, in writing, of the principal Officer in each of the executive Departments, upon any subject relating to the Duties of their respective Offices, and he shall have power to Grant Reprieves and Pardons for Offenses against the United States, except in Cases of Impeachment.

He shall have Power, by and with Advice and Consent of the Senate, to make Treaties, provided two thirds of the Senators present concur; and he shall nominate, and by and with the Advice and Consent of the Senate, shall appoint Ambassadors, other public Ministers and Consuls, Judges of the supreme Court, and all other Officers of the United States, whose Appointments are not herein otherwise provided for, and which shall be established by Law: but the Congress may by Law vest the Appointment of such inferior Officers, as they think proper, in the President alone, in the Courts of Law, or in the Heads of Departments.

The President shall have Power to fill up all Vacancies that may happen during the Recess of the Senate, by granting Commissions which shall expire at the End of their next Session.

Section 3. He shall from time to time give to the Congress Information of the State of the Union, and recommend to their Consideration such Measures as he shall judge necessary and expedient; he may, on extraordinary occasions, convene both Houses, or either of them, and in Case of Disagreement between them, with respect to the Time of Adjournment, he may adjourn them to such Time as he shall think proper; he shall receive Ambassadors and other public Ministers; he shall take care that the Laws be faithfully executed, and shall Commission all the Officers of the United States.

Section 4. The President, Vice President and all civil Officers of the United States, shall be removed from Office on Impeachment for, and Conviction of, Treason, Bribery, or other high Crimes and Misdemeanors.

Article III

Section 1. The judicial Power of the United States, shall be vested in one supreme Court, and in such inferior Courts as the Congress may from time to time ordain and establish. The Judges, both of the supreme and inferior Courts, shall hold their Offices during good Behaviour, and shall, at stated Times, receive for their Services, a Compensation, which shall not be diminished during their Continuance in Office.

Section 2. The judicial Power shall extend to all Cases, in Law and Equity, arising under this Constitution, the Laws of the United States, and Treaties made, or which shall be made, under their Authority;—to all Cases affecting Ambassadors, other public Ministers and Consuls;—to all cases of admiralty and maritime Jurisdiction;—to Controversies to which the United States shall be a Party;—to Controversies between two or more States;—between a State and Citizens of another State;—between Citizens of different States:—between Citizens of the same State claiming Land's under Grants of different States, and between a State, or the Citizens thereof, and foreign States, Citizens or Subjects.

In all Cases affecting Ambassadors, other public Ministers and Consuls, and those in which a State shall be Party, the supreme Court shall have original Jurisdiction. In all the other Cases before mentioned, the supreme Court shall have appellate Jurisdiction, both as to Law and Fact, with such Exceptions, and under such Regulations as the Congress shall make.

The trial of all Crimes, except in Cases of Impeachment, shall be by Jury; and such Trial shall be held in the State where the said Crimes shall have been committed; but when not committed within any State, the Trial shall be at such Place or Places as the Congress may by Law have directed.

Section 3. Treason against the United States, shall consist only in levying War against them, or in adhering to their Enemies, giving them Aid and Comfort. No Person shall be convicted of Treason unless on the Testimony of two Witnesses to the same overt Act, or on Confession in open Court.

The Congress shall have Power to declare the Punishment of Treason, but no Attainder of Treason shall work Corruption of Blood, or Forfeiture except during the Life of the Person attained.

Article IV

Section 1. Full Faith and Credit shall be given in each State to the public Acts, Records, and judicial Proceedings of every other State. And the Congress may by general Laws prescribe the Manner in which such Acts, Records and Proceedings shall be proved, and the Effect thereof.

Section 2. The Citizens of each State shall be entitled to all Privileges and Immunities of Citizens in the several States.

A Person charged in any State with Treason, Felony, or other Crime, who shall flee from Justice, and be found in another State, shall on demand of the executive Authority of the State from which he fled, be delivered up, to be removed to the State having Jurisdiction of the Crime.

No Person held to Service or Labour in one State, under the Laws thereof, escaping into another, shall, in Consequence of any Law or Regulation therein, be discharged from such Service or Labour, but shall be delivered up on Claim of the Party to whom such Service or Labour may be due.

Section 3. New States may be admitted by the Congress unto this Union; but no new State shall be formed or erected within the Jurisdiction of any other State; nor any State be formed by the Junction of two or more States, or parts of States, without the Consent of the Legislatures of the States concerned as well as of the Congress.

The Congress shall have Power to dispose of and make all needful Rules and Regulations respecting the Territory or other Property belonging to the United States; and nothing in this Constitution shall be so construed as to Prejudice any Claims of the United States or of any particular State.

Section 4. The United States shall guarantee to every State in this union a Republican Form of Government, and shall protect each of them against Invasion; and on Application of the Legislature, or of the Executive (when the Legislature cannot be convened) against domestic Violence.

Article V

The Congress, whenever two-thirds of both Houses shall deem it necessary, shall propose Amendments to this Constitution, or, on the Application of the Legislatures of two-thirds of the several States, shall call a Convention for proposing Amendments, which, in either Case, shall be valid to all Intents and Purposes, as part of this Constitution, when ratified by the Legislatures of three-fourths of the several States, or by Conventions in three-fourths thereof, as the one or the other Mode of Ratification may be proposed by the Congress; Provided that no Amendment which may be made prior to the Year One thousand eight hundred and eight shall in any Manner affect the first and fourth Clauses in the Ninth Section of the first Article; and that no State, without its Consent, shall be deprived of its equal Suffrage in the Senate.

Article VI

All Debts contracted and Engagements entered into, before the Adoption of this Constitution, shall be as valid against the United States under this Constitution, as under the Confederation.

This Constitution, and the Laws of the United States which shall be made in Pursuance thereof; and all Treaties made, or which shall be made, under the

Authority of the United States, shall be the supreme Law of the Land; and the Judges in every State shall be bound thereby, any Thing in the Constitution or Laws of any State to the Contrary notwithstanding.

The Senators and Representatives before mentioned, and the Members of the several State Legislatures, and all executive and judicial Officers, both of the United States and of the several States, shall be bound by Oath or Affirmation to support this Constitution; but no religious Test shall ever be required as a qualification to any Office or public Trust under the United States.

Article VII

The Ratification of the Conventions of nine States shall be sufficient for the Establishment of this Constitution between the States so ratifying the same.

Done in Convention by the Unanimous Consent of the States present the Seventeenth Day of September in the Year of our Lord one thousand seven hundred and Eighty seven, and of the Independence of the United States of America the Twelfth. In Witness whereof We have hereunto subscribed our Names.

Articles in Addition to, and Amendment of, the Constitution of the United States of America, Proposed by Congress, and Ratified by the Legislatures of the Several States, Pursuant to the Fifth Article of the Original Constitution.

[The first ten amendments went into effect in 1791.]

Amendment I

Congress shall make no law respecting an establishment of religion, or prohibiting the free exercise thereof; or abridging the freedom of speech, or of the press; or the right of the people peaceably to assemble, and to petition the Government for a redress of grievances.

Amendment II

A well regulated Militia, being necessary to the security of a free State, the right of the people to keep and bear Arms shall not be infringed.

Amendment III

No Soldier shall, in time of peace, be quartered in any house, without the consent of the Owner, nor in time of War, but in a manner to be prescribed by law.

Amendment IV

The right of the people to be secure in their persons, houses, papers, and effects, against unreasonable searches and seizures, shall not be violated, and no Warrants shall issue, but upon probable cause, supported by Oath or affirmation, and particularly describing the place to be searched, and the persons or things to be seized.

Amendment V

No person shall be held to answer for a capital or otherwise infamous crime, unless on a presentment or indictment of a Grand Jury, except in cases arising in the land or naval forces, or in the Militia, when in actual service in time of War or public danger; nor shall any person be subject for the same offence to be twice put in jeopardy of life or limb; nor shall be compelled in any criminal case to be a witness against himself, nor be deprived of life, liberty, or property, without due process of law; nor shall private property be taken for public use, without just compensation.

Amendment VI

In all criminal prosecutions, the accused shall enjoy the right to a speedy and public trial, by an impartial jury of the State and district wherein the crime shall have been committed, which district shall have been previously ascertained by law, and to be informed of the nature and cause of the accusation; to be confronted with the witnesses against him; to have compulsory process for obtaining witnesses in his favour, and to have the Assistance of Counsel for defence.

Amendment VII

In suits at common law where the value in controversy shall exceed twenty dollars, the right of trial by jury, shall be preserved, and no fact tried by a jury shall be otherwise reexamined in any Court of the United States, than according to the rules of the common law.

Amendment VIII

Excessive bail shall not be required, nor excessive fines imposed, nor cruel and unusual punishments inflicted.

Amendment IX

The enumeration in the Constitution, of certain rights, shall not be construed to deny or disparage others retained by the people.

Amendment X

The powers not delegated to the United States by the Constitution, nor prohibited by it to the States, are reserved to the States respectively, or to the people.

Amendment XI (1798)

The Judicial power of the United States shall not be construed to extend to any suit in law or equity, commenced or prosecuted against one of the

United States by Citizens of another State, or by Citizens or Subjects of any Foreign State.

Amendment XII (1804)

The Electors shall meet in their respective States and vote by ballot for President and Vice-President, one of whom, at least, shall not be an inhabitant of the same State with themselves; they shall name in their ballots the person voted for as President, and in distinct ballots the person voted for as Vice-President, and they shall make distinct lists of all persons voted for as President, and of all persons voted for as Vice-President, and of the number of votes for each, which lists they shall sign and certify, and transmit sealed to the seat of the government of the United States, directed to the President of the Senate;— The President of the Senate shall, in the presence of the Senate and House of Representatives, open all the certificates and the votes shall then be counted;— The person having the greatest number of votes for President, shall be the President, if such number be a majority of the whole number of Electors appointed; and if no person have such majority, then from the persons having the highest numbers not exceeding three on the list of those voted for as President, the House of Representatives shall choose immediately, by ballot, the President. But in choosing the President, the votes shall be taken by states, the representation from each state having one vote; a quorum for this purpose shall consist of a member or members from two-thirds of the states, and a majority of all the states shall be necessary to a choice. And if the House of Representatives shall not choose a President whenever the right of choice shall devolve upon them, before the fourth day of March next following, then the Vice-President shall act as President, as in the case of the death or other constitutional disability of the President.—The person having the greatest number of votes as Vice-President, shall be the Vice-President, if such number be a majority of the whole number of Electors appointed, and if no person have a majority, then from the two highest numbers on the list, the Senate shall choose the Vice-President; a quorum for the purpose shall consist of two-thirds of the whole number of Senators, and a majority of the whole number shall be necessary to a choice. But no person constitutionally ineligible to the office of President shall be eligible to that of Vice-President of the United States.

Amendment XIII (1865)

Section 1. Neither slavery nor involuntary servitude, except as a punishment for crime whereof the party shall have been duly convicted, shall exist within the United States, or any place subject to their jurisdiction.

Section 2. Congress shall have power to enforce this article by appropriate legislation.

Amendment XIV (1868)

Section 1. All persons born or naturalized in the United States, and subject to the jurisdiction thereof, are citizens of the United States and of the State wherein they reside. No State shall make or enforce any law which shall abridge the privileges or immunities of citizens of the United States; nor shall any State deprive any person of life, liberty, or property, without due process of law; nor deny to any person within its jurisdiction the equal protection of the laws.

Section 2. Representatives shall be apportioned among the several States according to their respective numbers, counting the whole number of persons in each State, excluding Indians not taxed. But when the right to vote at any election for the choice of electors for President and Vice-President of the United States, Representatives in Congress, the Executive and Judicial officers of a State, or the members of the Legislature thereof, is denied to any of the male inhabitants of such State, being twenty-one years of age, and citizens of the United States, or in any way abridged, except for participation in rebellion, or other crime, the basis of representation therein shall be reduced in the proportion which the number of such male citizens shall bear to the whole number of male citizens twenty-one years of age in such State.

Section 3. No person shall be a Senator or Representative in Congress, or elector of President and Vice-President, or hold any office, civil or military, under the United States, or under any State, who, having previously taken an oath, as a member of Congress, or as an officer of the United States, or as member of any State legislature, or as an executive or judicial officer of any State, to support the Constitution of the United States, shall have engaged in insurrection or rebellion against the same, or given aid or comfort to the enemies thereof. But Congress may by a vote of two-thirds of each House, remove such disability.

Section 4. The validity of the public debt of the United States, authorized by law, including debts incurred for payment of pensions and bounties for services in suppressing insurrection or rebellion, shall not be questioned. But neither the United States nor any State shall assume or pay any debt or obligation incurred in aid of insurrection or rebellion against the United States, or any claim for the loss or emancipation of any slave; but all such debts, obligations, and claims shall be held illegal and void.

Section 5. The Congress shall have the power to enforce, by appropriate legislation, the provisions of this article.

Amendment XV (1870)

Section 1. The right of citizens of the United States to vote shall not be denied or abridged by the United States or by any State on account of race, color, or previous condition of servitude—

Section 2. The Congress shall have power to enforce this article by appropriate legislation.

Amendment XVI *(1913)*

The Congress shall have power to lay and collect taxes on incomes, from whatever source derived, without apportionment among the several States, and without regard to any census or enumeration.

Amendment XVII *(1913)*

The Senate of the United States shall be composed of two Senators from each State, elected by the people thereof, for six years; and each Senator shall have one vote. The electors in each State shall have the qualifications requisite for electors of the most numerous branch of the State legislatures.

When vacancies happen in the representation of any State in the Senate, the executive authority of such State shall issue writs of election to fill such vacancies: *Provided,* That legislature of any State may empower the executive thereof to make temporary appointments until the people fill the vacancies by election as the legislature may direct.

This amendment shall not be so construed as to affect the election or term of any Senator chosen before it becomes valid as part of the Constitution.

Amendment XVIII *(1919)*

Section 1. After one year from the ratification of this article the manufacture, sale, or transportation of intoxicating liquors within, the importation thereof into, or the exportation thereof from the United States and all territory subject to the jurisdiction thereof for beverage purposes is hereby prohibited.

Section 2. The Congress and the several States shall have concurrent power to enforce this article by appropriate legislation.

Section 3. This article shall be inoperative unless it shall have been ratified as an amendment to the Constitution by the legislatures of the several States as provided in the Constitution, within seven years from the date of the submission hereof to the States by the Congress.

Amendment XIX *(1920)*

The right of citizens of the United States to vote shall not be denied or abridged by the United States or by any State on account of sex.

Congress shall have power to enforce this article by appropriate legislation.

Amendment XX *(1933)*

Section 1. The terms of the President and Vice-President shall end at noon on the 20th day of January, and the terms of Senators and Representatives at noon on the 3d day of January, of the years in which such terms would have ended if this article had not been ratified; and the terms of their successors shall then begin.

Section 2. The Congress shall assemble at least once in every year, and such meeting shall begin at noon on the 3d day of January, unless they shall by law appoint a different day.

Section 3. If, at the time fixed for the beginning of the term of the President, the President elect shall have died, the Vice-President elect shall become President. If a President shall not have been chosen before the time fixed for the beginning of his term, or if the President elect shall have failed to qualify, then the Vice-President elect shall act as President until a President shall have qualified; and the Congress may by law provide for the case wherein neither a President elect nor a Vice-President elect shall have qualified, declaring who shall then act as President, or the manner in which one who is to act shall be selected, and such person shall act accordingly until a President or Vice-President shall have qualified.

Section 4. The Congress may by law provide for the case of the death of any of the persons from whom the House of Representatives may choose a President whenever the right of choice shall have devolved upon them, and for the case of the death of any of the persons from whom the Senate may choose a Vice-President whenever the right of choice shall have devolved upon them.

Section 5. Sections 1 and 2 shall take effect on the 15th day of October following the ratification of this article.

Section 6. This article shall be inoperative unless it shall have been ratified as an amendment to the Constitution by the legislatures of three-fourths of the several States within seven years from the date of its submission.

Amendment XXI (1933)

Section 1. The eighteenth article of amendment to the Constitution of the United States is hereby repealed.

Section 2. The transportation or importation into any State, Territory, or possession of the United States for delivery or use therein of intoxicating liquors, in violation of the laws thereof, is hereby prohibited.

Section 3. This article shall be inoperative unless it shall have been ratified as an amendment to the Constitution by conventions in the several States, as provided in the Constitution within seven years from the date of the submission hereof to the States by the Congress.

Amendment XXII (1951)

No person shall be elected to the office of the President more than twice, and no person who has held the office of President, or acted as President, for more than two years of a term to which some other person was elected President shall be elected to the office of the President more than once.

But this Article shall not apply to any person holding the office of President when this Article was proposed by the Congress, and shall not prevent any person who may be holding the office of President, or acting as President, during the term within which this article becomes operative from holding the office of President or acting as President during the remainder of such term.

This article shall be inoperative unless it shall have been ratified as an amendment to the Constitution by the legislatures of three-fourths of the several states within seven years from the date of its submission to the states by the Congress.

Amendment XXIII (1961)

Section 1. The District constituting the seat of Government of the United States shall appoint in such manner as the Congress may direct:

A number of electors of President and Vice-President equal to the whole number of Senators and Representatives in Congress to which the District would be entitled if it were a State, but in no event more than the least populous State; they shall be in addition to those appointed by the States, but they shall be considered, for the purposes of the election of President and Vice-President, to be electors appointed by a State; and they shall meet in the District and perform such duties as provided by the twelfth article of amendment.

Section 2. The Congress shall have power to enforce this article by appropriate legislation.

Amendment XXIV (1964)

Section 1. The right of citizens of the United States to vote in any primary or other election for President or Vice President, for electors for President or Vice President, or for Senator or Representative in Congress, shall not be denied or abridged by the United States or any other State by reason of failure to pay any poll tax or other tax.

Section 2. The Congress shall have the power to enforce this article by appropriate legislation.

Amendment XXV (1967)

Section 1. In case of the removal of the President from office or of his death or resignation, the Vice President shall become President.

Section 2. Whenever there is a vacancy in the office of the Vice-President, the President shall nominate a Vice President who shall take office upon confirmation by a majority vote of both Houses of Congress.

Section 3. Whenever the President transmits to the President pro tempore of the Senate and the Speaker of the House of Representatives his written declaration that he is unable to discharge the powers and duties of his office, and until he transmits to them a written declaration to the contrary, such powers and duties shall be discharged by the Vice President as Acting President.

Section 4. Whenever the Vice-President and a majority of either the principal officers of the executive departments or of such other body as Congress may by law provide, transmit to the President pro tempore of the Senate and the Speaker of the House of Representatives their written declaration that the President is unable to discharge the powers and duties of his office, the Vice President shall immediately assume the powers and duties of the office as Acting President.

Thereafter, when the President transmits to the President pro tempore of the Senate and the Speaker of the House of Representatives his written declaration that no inability exists, he shall resume the powers and duties of his office unless the Vice President and a majority of either the principal officers of the executive departments or of such other body as Congress may by law provide, transmit within four days to the President pro tempore of the Senate and the Speaker of the House of Representatives their written declaration that the President is unable to discharge the powers and duties of his office. Thereupon Congress shall decide the issue, assembling within forty-eight hours for that purpose if not in session. If the Congress, within twenty-one days after receipt of the latter written declaration, or, if Congress is not in session, within twenty-one days after Congress is required to assemble, determines by two-thirds vote of both Houses that the President is unable to discharge the powers and duties of his office, the Vice President shall continue to discharge the same as Acting President; otherwise, the President shall resume the powers and duties of his office.

Amendment XXVI (1971)

Section 1. The right of citizens of the United States, who are eighteen years of age or older, to vote shall not be denied or abridged by the United States or by any State on account of age.

Section 2. The Congress shall have the power to enforce this article by appropriate legislation.

Amendment XXVII (1992)

No law varying the compensation for the services of the Senators and Representatives shall take effect, until an election of Representatives shall have intervened.

APPENDIX 3

Presidents of
The United States

		Party	Term
1.	George Washington		1789–1797
2.	John Adams	Federalist	1797–1801
3.	Thomas Jefferson	Democratic-Republican	1801–1809
4.	James Madison	Democratic-Republican	1809–1817
5.	James Monroe	Democratic-Republican	1817–1825
6.	John Quincy Adams	Democratic-Republican	1825–1829
7.	Andrew Jackson	Democratic	1829–1837
8.	Martin Van Buren	Democratic	1837–1841
9.	William Henry Harrison*	Whig	1841
10.	John Tyler	Whig	1841–1845
11.	James K. Polk	Democratic	1845–1849
12.	Zachary Taylor*	Whig	1849–1850
13.	Millard Fillmore	Whig	1850–1853
14.	Franklin Pierce	Democratic	1853–1857
15.	James Buchanan	Democratic	1857–1861
16.	Abraham Lincoln*	Republican	1861–1865
17.	Andrew Johnson	Union	1865–1869
18.	Ulysses S. Grant	Republican	1869–1877
19.	Rutherford B. Hayes	Republican	1877–1881

20.	James A. Garfield*	Republican	1881
21.	Chester A. Arthur	Republican	1881–1885
22.	Grover Cleveland	Democratic	1885–1889
23.	Benjamin Harrison	Republican	1889–1893
24.	Grover Cleveland	Democratic	1893–1897
25.	William McKinley*	Republican	1897–1901
26.	Theodore Roosevelt	Republican	1901–1909
27.	William Howard Taft	Republican	1909–1913
28.	Woodrow Wilson	Democratic	1913–1921
29.	Warren G. Harding*	Republican	1921–1923
30.	Calvin Coolidge	Republican	1923–1929
31.	Herbert Hoover	Republican	1929–1933
32.	Franklin Delano Roosevelt*	Democratic	1933–1945
33.	Harry S. Truman	Democratic	1945–1953
34.	Dwight D. Eisenhower	Republican	1953–1961
35.	John F. Kennedy*	Democratic	1961–1963
36.	Lyndon B. Johnson	Democratic	1963–1969
37.	Richard M. Nixon†	Republican	1969–1974
38.	Gerald R. Ford	Republican	1974–1977
39.	Jimmy Carter	Democratic	1977–1981
40.	Ronald Reagan	Republican	1981–1989
41.	George Bush	Republican	1989–1993
42.	Bill Clinton	Democratic	1993–

* *Died in office.*
† *Resigned.*

NOTES

Chapter 1

1. John D. Nagle, *Comparative Politics: Political System Performance in Three Worlds*, Nelson-Hall, Chicago, 1985.

2. Christopher Hill, *Reformation to Industrial Revolution*, Pantheon, New York, 1967.

3. Richard Hofstadter, *The Age of Reform: From Bryan to FDR*, Knopf, New York, 1972.

4. Upton Sinclair, *The Jungle*, New American Library, New York, 1980.

5. Albert U. Romasco, *The Politics of Recovery: Roosevelt's New Deal*, Oxford University Press, New York, 1983.

6. *Statistical Abstract of the United States 1992*, Government Printing Office, Washington, D.C., 1993, p. 460.

7. John Kenneth White, *The New Politics of Old Values*, University Press of New England, Hanover, N.H., 1988.

8. Carol Pateman, *Participation and Democratic Theory*, Cambridge University Press, Cambridge, England, 1970; Benjamin R. Barber, *Strong Democracy: Participatory Politics for a New Age*, University of California Press, Berkeley, 1984.

9. Joseph Schumpeter, *Capitalism, Socialism, and Democracy*, Allen and Unwin, London, 1976; Robert A. Dahl, *Polyarchy: Participation and Opposition*, Yale University Press, New Haven, 1971.

10. Frank Freidel, *Franklin D. Roosevelt: A Rendezvous with Destiny*, Little, Brown, Boston, 1990.

11. Giovanni Sartori, *The Theory of Democracy Revisited*, Chatham House, Chatham, N.J., 1987; Georg Sorenson, *Democracy and Democratization*, Westview, Boulder, Colo., 1993.

12.   Arend Lijphart, *Democracy in Plural Societies: A Comparative Exploration*, Yale University Press, New Haven, 1977; G. Bingham Powell, *Contemporary Democracies*, Harvard University Press, Cambridge, Mass., 1982.

13.   Thomas R. Dye, *Who's Running America? The Conservative Years*, Prentice-Hall, Englewood Cliffs, N.J., 1986.

14.   E. E. Schattschneider, *The Semisovereign People*, The Dryden Press, Hinsdale, Ill., 1975.

15.   Allen W. Imershein, Philip C. Rond, and Mary P. Mathis, "Restructuring Patterns of Elite Dominance and the Formation of State Policy in Health Care," *American Journal of Sociology*, 97:4, January 1992.

16.   Gabriel Kolko, *The Triumph of Conservatism*, New York: Free Press, 1963.

17.   Robert Tucker, ed., *The Marx Engels Reader*, Norton, New York, 1978.

18.   C. Wright Mills, *The Power Elite*, Oxford University Press, New York, 1956.

19.   See, for example, Herbert McCloskey and Alida Brill, *Dimensions of Tolerance: What Americans Think About Civil Liberties*, Russell Sage, New York, 1983.

20.   Robert A. Dahl, *Pluralist Democracy in the United States*, Rand McNally, Chicago, 1967.

21.   Robert A. Dahl, *A Preface To Democratic Theory*, University of Chicago Press, Chicago, 1956.

22.   Theodore Lowi, *The End of Liberalism*, Norton, New York, 1979.

23.   Mancur Olson, *The Rise and Decline of Nations: Economic Growth, Stagflation, and Social Rigidities*, Yale University Press, New Haven, 1983.

Chapter 2

1.   Although it may be too simplistic to claim that the United States is a consistently liberal, egalitarian society, one can make the case that there are also illiberal, inegalitarian strands in American ideology. See Rogers M. Smith, "Beyond Tocqueville, Myrdal, and Hartz: The Multiple Traditions in America," *American Political Science Review*, 87:549–566, 1993.

2.   Bernard Bailyn, *The Origins of American Politics*, Vintage Books, New York, 1968.

3.   Donald S. Lutz, "The Relative Influence of European Writers on Late Eighteenth-Century American Political Thought," *American Political Science Review*, 78:189–197, 1984.

4.   Jackson Turner Main, *The Social Structure of Revolutionary America*, Princeton University Press, Princeton, N.J., 1965.

5.   *Ibid.*, p. 287.

6.   James Wilson quoted in Alpheus T. Mason and Richard H. Leach, *In Quest of Freedom*, Prentice-Hall, Englewood Cliffs, N.J., 1959, p. 56.

7. For instance, compare Carl Becker, *The Declaration of Independence*, Vintage Press, New York, 1942; Garry Wills, *Inventing America*, Vintage Books, New York, 1978.

8. Quoted in Calvin Jillson and Rick K. Wilson, "The Continental Congress and the Origins of the U.S. House of Representatives," paper presented at the American Political Science Association meeting, Chicago, 1987, p. 24.

9. Rick K. Wilson and Calvin Jillson, "Leadership Patterns in the Continental and Confederation Congresses: 1774–1789," paper presented at the American Political Science Association meeting, Washington, D.C., 1988.

10. Jackson Turner Main, *The Sovereign States*, New Viewpoints, New York, 1973.

11. Calvin C. Jillson and Cecil L. Eubanks, "The Political Structure of Constitution Making," *American Journal of Political Science*, 28:444, 1984.

12. For basic information on the Convention, see Max Farrand, *The Framing of the Constitution of the United States*, Macmillan, New York, 1935.

13. Jillson and Eubanks, *op. cit.*, 447.

14. Charles Beard, *An Economic Theory of the Constitution of the United States*, Macmillan, New York, 1935 ed.

15. Forrest McDonald, *We the People*, University of Chicago Press, Chicago, 1958.

16. Robert Brown, *Charles Beard and the Constitution*, Princeton University Press, Princeton, N.J., 1956.

17. *Ibid.*, p. 40.

18. John Roche, "The Founding Fathers: A Reform Caucus in Action," *American Political Science Review*, 4:799–816, 1961.

19. Jackson Turner Main, *The Antifederalists*, University of North Carolina Press, Chapel Hill, 1961.

20. *Ibid.*; Roche, *op. cit.*

21. Luther Martin, "Letters on the Federal Convention of 1787," in Jonathan Elliott, ed., *Debates on the Adoption of the Federal Constitution*, vol. 1, Burt Franklin, New York, reprint of 1888 edition, pp. 360–361.

22. Cecilia Kenyon, "Men of Little Faith," in John Roche, ed., *Origins of American Political Thought*, Harper & Row, New York, 1967.

Chapter 3

1. Edward C. Banfield and James Q. Wilson, *City Politics*, Vintage Books, New York, 1963, pp. 64–65.

2. 9 Wheaton 1. (See note in Chapter 11.)

3. 4 Wheaton 316.

4. See *Hammer v. Dagenhart*, 247 U.S. 251 (1918), and *Bailey v. Drexel Furniture Co.*, 259 U.S. 20 (1922).

5. William B. Lockhart, *et al., The American Constitution,* 6th ed., West, St. Paul, Minn., 1986, p. 264.

6. See *National League of Cities v. Usery,* 426 U.S. 833 (1976), overruled by *Garcia v. San Antonio Metropolitan Transit Authority,* 469 U.S. 528 (1985).

7. 120 L. Ed. 2d 120.

8. Morton Grodzins, *The American System,* Rand McNally, Chicago, 1966, pp. 42–43.

9. 262 U.S. 447 (1923).

10. 392 U.S. 83.

11. See Robert Jay Digler, ed., *American Intergovernmental Relations Today,* Prentice-Hall, Englewood Cliffs, N.J., 1986, p. 18.

12. Kenneth T. Palmer, "The Evolution of Grant Policies," in Lawrence C. Brown, James W. Fossett, and Kenneth T. Palmer, eds., *The Changing Politics of Federal Grants,* Brookings Institution, Washington, D.C., 1984, p. 6.

13. An evaluation of the Great Society efforts from an elitist perspective that recognizes the Johnson administration's efforts to mobilize the poor is provided by Frances Fox Piven and Richard A. Cloward, *Regulating the Poor,* Vintage Books, New York, 1971, pp. 222–281.

14. Grodzins, *op. cit.,* pp. 8–9.

15. Deil S. Wright, *Understanding Intergovernmental Relations,* 3d ed., Brooks/Cole, Pacific Grove, Calif., 1988, p. 83.

16. Grace A. Franklin and Randall B. Ripley, *CETA: Politics and Policy, 1973–1982,* University of Tennessee, Knoxville, 1984, pp. 202–203.

17. See Arnold M. Howitt, *Managing Federalism,* C Q Press, Washington, D.C., 1984, pp. 39–70.

18. Quoted in William Stevens, "Governors Are Emerging as a New Political Elite," *New York Times,* March 22, 1988, p. A16.

19. See Howitt, op. cit., pp. 303–321.

20. See Brenda Avoletta and Philip M. Dearborn, "Federal Grants-in-Aid Soar in the 1990s, But Not for Locals or General Government Purposes," *Intergovernmental Perspective,* Summer, 19:32–33, 1993.

21. Grodzins, *op. cit.,* pp. 89–124.

22. Jack L. Walker, "Innovation in State Politics," in Herbert Jacob and Kenneth Vines, eds., *Politics in the American States,* 2d ed., Little, Brown, Boston, 1971, pp. 354–387.

Chapter 4

1. For an argument that liberalism is not quite so dominant in its hold on the American people and that illiberal behavior is quite predictable, see Rogers M. Smith, "Be-

yond Tocqueville, Myrdal, and Hartz: The Multiple Traditions in America," *American Political Science Review* 87:549–566, 1993.

2. Donald J. Devine, *The Political Culture of the United States,* Little, Brown, Boston, 1972, p. 284.

3. Herbert McCloskey, "Consensus and Ideology in American Politics," *American Political Science Review,* 58:361–382, 1964; James W. Prothro and Charles W. Grigg, "Fundamental Principles of Democracy," *Journal of Politics,* 22:276–294, 1960.

4. John L. Sullivan, James Piereson, and George E. Marcus, *Political Tolerance and American Democracy,* University of Chicago Press, Chicago, 1982.

5. James L. Gibson, "Political Intolerance and Political Repression during the McCarthy Red Scare," *American Political Science Review,* 82:511–529, 1988.

6. See Smith, *op. cit.*

7. Benjamin I. Page and Robert Y. Shapiro, *The Rational Public,* University of Chicago Press, Chicago, 1992; Richard G. Niemi, John Mueller, and Tom W. Smith, *Trends in Public Opinion,* Greenwood Press, New York, 1989. For a rather different conclusion, see William G. Mayer, *The Changing American Mind,* University of Michigan Press, Ann Arbor, 1992.

8. James A. Stimson, *Public Opinion in America,* Westview, Boulder, Colo., 1991, p. 118. And see Mayer, *op. cit.*

9. James A. Davis, "Changeable Weather in a Cooling Climate Atop the Liberal Plateau," *Public Opinion Quarterly,* 56:261–306, 1992.

10. Robert H. Durr, "What Moves Policy Sentiment?" *American Political Science Review,* 87:158–170, 1993.

11. Arthur H. Miller, "Political Issues and Trust in Government," *American Political Science Review,* 66:951–988, 1974.

12. Arthur H. Miller, "Is Confidence Rebounding?," *Public Opinion,* 6:20:1983. Updating this analysis further is Richard G. Niemi, John Mueller, and Tom W. Smith, *Trends in Public Opinion,* Greenwood Press, New York, 1989, chap. 4.

13. William H. Flanigan and Nancy H. Zingale, *Political Behavior of the American Electorate,* Allyn and Bacon, Boston, 1987.

14. Niemi, Mueller, and Smith, *op. cit.,* p. 315.

15. *Ibid.*

16. Paul R. Abramson, Brian D. Silver, and Barbara A. Anderson, "The Effects of Question Order in Attitude Surveys: The Case of the SRC/CPS Citizen Duty Items," *American Journal of Political Science,* 31:900–908, 1987; Warren E. Miller, Arthur H. Miller, and Edward J. Schneider, *American National Election Studies Data Sourcebook, 1952–1978,* Harvard University Press, Cambridge, Mass., 1980.

17. Ronald I. Inglehart, *Culture Shift,* Princeton University Press, Princeton, N.J., 1990.

18. See, for instance, Robert Heilbroner, *An Inquiry into the Human Prospect,* Norton, New York, 1974; Mancur Olson, *The Rise and Decline of Nations,* Yale University Press, New Haven, 1982; Paul Kennedy, *The Rise and Fall of the Great Powers,* Random House, New York, 1987.

19. Seymour Martin Lipset and William Schneider, *The Confidence Gap,* Free Press, New York, 1983.

20. M. Stephen Weatherford, "Economic Conditions and Electoral Outcomes," *American Journal of Political Science,* 22:917–938, 1978.

21. Steven J. Rosenstone, "Economic Adversity and Voter Turnout," *American Political Science Review,* 26:42, 1982.

22. *Ibid.,* p. 26.

23. John M. Ostheimer and Leonard G. Ritt, "Abundance and American Democracy," *Journal of Politics,* 44:365–387, 1982.

24. Albert Somit and Steven A. Peterson, "Political Socialization's Primacy Principle," *International Political Science Review,* 8:205–214, 1987.

25. M. Kent Jennings and Richard Niemi, *Generations and Politics,* Princeton University Press, Princeton, N.J., 1981.

26. Steven A. Peterson, *Political Behavior: Patterns in Everyday Life,* Sage, Newbury Park, Calif., 1990.

27. Steven A. Peterson, "Church Participation and Political Participation," *American Politics Quarterly,* 20:123–139, 1992.

28. Michael X. Delli Carpini, *Stability and Change in American Politics,* New York University Press, New York, 1986. And see M. Kent Jennings, "Residues of a Movement: The Aging of the American Protest Generation," *American Political Science Review,* 81:367–382, 1987.

29. David G. Barnum, "The Supreme Court and Public Opinion," *Journal of Politics,* 47:652–666, 1985; Beverly Blair Cook, "Public Opinion and Federal Judicial Policy," *American Journal of Political Science,* 21:567–600, 1977; Beverly Blair Cook, "Judicial Policy over Time," *American Journal of Political Science,* 23:208–214, 1979; James Kuklinski and James Stanga, "Political Participation and Government Responsiveness," *American Political Science Review,* 73:1090–1099, 1979; Thomas R. Marshall, "Public Opinion, Representation, and the Modern Supreme Court," *American Politics Quarterly,* 16:296–316, 1988; Thomas R. Marshall, "Public Opinion and the Rehnquist Court," *Judicature,* 74:322–329, 1991.

30. Larry M. Bartels, "Constituency Opinion and Congressional Policy Making," *American Political Science Review,* 85:457–474, 1991; Robert J. Erikson, "Constituency Opinion and Congressional Behavior," *American Journal of Political Science,* 22:25–36, 1978; C. L. Herrera, R. Herrera, and Eric R. A. N. Smith, "Public Opinion and Congressional Representation," *Public Opinion Quarterly,* 56:185–205,

1992; Warren E. Miller and Donald E. Stokes, "Constituency Influence in Congress," in Angus Campbell *et al., Elections and the Political Order,* Wiley, New York, 1966; Alan Monroe, "Consistency between Public Preferences and National Policy," *American Politics Quarterly,* 7:3–19, 1979.

31.   Robert S. Erikson, "The Relationship between Public Opinion and State Policy," *American Journal of Political Science,* 20:25–36, 1976; Anne H. Hopkins, "Opinion Publics and Support for Public Policy in the American States," *American Journal of Political Science,* 18:167–178, 1974; R. L. Sutton, "The States and the People," *Polity,* 5:451–476, 1973; Ronald E. Weber and William R. Shaffer, "Public Opinion and State Policy Making," *Midwest Journal of Political Science,* 16:685–699, 1972.

32.   Marshall, "Public Opinion, Representation, . . ."

33.   Monroe, *op. cit.*

34.   William Mishler and Reginald S. Sheehan, "The Supreme Court as a Counter-majoritarian Institution," *American Political Science Review,* 87:87–101, 1993.

35.   Gerald C. Wright, Jr., Robert S. Erikson, and John P. McIver, "Public Opinion and Policy Liberalism in the American States," *American Journal of Political Science,* 31:980–1001, 1987.

36.   Benjamin I. Page and Robert Y. Shapiro, "Effects of Public Opinion on Policy," *American Journal of Political Science,* 77:175–190, 1983.

37.   Sidney Verba and Norman H. Nie, *Participation in America,* Harper & Row, New York, 1972.

38.   Norman H. Nie *et al.,* "Participation in America," paper presented at the American Political Science Association meeting, Chicago, 1989.

39.   Lester W. Milbrath and M. L. Goel, *Political Participation,* 2d ed., Rand McNally, Chicago, 1977.

40.   Lawrence Bobo and Franklin D. Gilliam, Jr., "Race, Sociopolitical Participation, and Black Empowerment," *American Political Science Review,* 84:377–393, 1990. Among older blacks, the same phenomenon occurs. See Steven A. Peterson and Albert Somit, "The Political Behavior of Older American Blacks," *The Gerontologist,* 32:592–600, 1992.

41.   Steven J. Rosenstone and John Mark Hansen, *Mobilization, Participation, and Democracy in America,* Macmillan, New York, 1993.

42.   Verba and Nie, *op. cit.*

43.   *Ibid.,* p. 274.

44.   *Ibid.,* p. 318. For an update of their findings, see Sidney Verba *et al.,* "Citizen Activity: Who Participates? What Do They Say?" *American Political Science Review,* 87:303–318, 1993.

45.   Jeffrey M. Berry, K. S. Portney, and K. Thomson, "Directions for Democracy," paper presented at the Southern Political Science Association meeting, Atlanta, 1988.

46. Margaret M. Conway, M. L. Wyckoff, E. Feldman, and D. Ahern, "The News Media in Children's Political Socialization," *Public Opinion Quarterly,* 45:164–178, 1981.

47. Roberta Sigel and John W. Cohen, "Following the News," paper presented at the Midwest Political Science Association meeting, Chicago, 1983.

48. James M. Carlson, "Crime Show Viewing by Preadults," paper presented at the American Political Science Association meeting, Denver, 1982.

49. Michael J. Robinson, "Public Affairs Television and the Growth of Political Malaise," *American Political Science Review,* 70:409–432, 1976.

50. Arthur H. Miller, Edie N. Goldenberg, and Lutz Erbring, "Type-Set Politics," *American Political Science Review,* 73:67–84, 1979.

51. Shanto Iyengar, Mark D. Peters, and Donald Kinder, "Experimental Demonstration of the 'Not-so-Minimal' Consequences of Television News Programs," *American Political Science Review,* 76:848–858, 1982.

52. Jon A. Krasnick and Donald R. Kinder, "Altering the Foundations of Support for the President through Priming," *American Political Science Review,* 84:497–512, 1990.

53. William W. Lammers, "Presidential Press Conference Schedules," *Political Science Quarterly,* 96:261–278, 1981.

54. Lyn Ragsdale, "The Politics of Presidential Speechmaking," *American Political Science Review,* 78:971–984, 1984.

55. Benjamin I. Page, Robert Y. Shapiro, and Glenn R. Dempsey, "What Moves Public Opinion?" *American Political Science Review,* 81:23–24, 1987.

Chapter 5

1. G. Bingham Powell, *Contemporary Democracies,* Harvard University Press, Cambridge, Mass., 1982.

2. See, for instance, Gerald Pomper, "The Presidential Election," in Gerald M. Pomper *et al.,* eds., *The Election of 1992,* Chatham House, Chatham, N.J., 1993.

3. Barbara Sinclair, "The Emergence of Strong Leadership in the 1980s House of Representatives," *Journal of Politics,* 54:657–684, 1992.

4. Richard Hofstadter, *The Idea of a Party System,* University of California Press, Berkeley, 1970.

5. John H. Aldrich and Ruth W. Grant, "The Antifederalists, the First Congress, and the First Parties," *Journal of Politics,* 55:295–326, 1993.

6. Everett Carll Ladd, Jr., *American Political Parties,* Norton, New York, 1970.

7. V. O. Key, Jr., "Secular Realignment and the Party System," *Journal of Politics,* 21:199, 1959.

8. Ken Kollman, John H. Miller, and Scott E. Page, "Adaptive Parties in Spatial Elections," *American Political Science Review,* 86:929–937, 1992.

9. John G. Geer, "Critical Realignments and the Public Opinion Poll," *American Journal of Political Science,* 53:434–453, 1991.

10. W. Phillips Shively, "From Differential Abstention to Conversion: A Change in Electoral Change, 1864–1988," *American Journal of Political Science,* 36:309–330, 1992.

11. Walter Dean Burnham, "The Changing Shape of the American Political Universe," *American Political Science Review,* 59:7–28, 1965.

12. Ladd, *op. cit.;* James L. Sundquist, *Dynamics of the Party System,* Brookings Institution, Washington, D.C.: 1983.

13. Sundquist, *op. cit.*

14. Kristi Andersen, *The Creation of a Democratic Majority, 1928–1936,* University of Chicago Press, Chicago, 1980; Robert S. Erikson and M. Kent Tedin, "The 1928–1936 Partisan Realignment," *American Political Science Review,* 75:951–962, 1981; V. O. Key, Jr., *The Responsible Electorate,* Vintage Books, New York, 1966.

15. Everett Carll Ladd, Jr., "Like Waiting for Godot: The Uselessness of Realignment for Understanding Change in Contemporary American Politics," *Polity,* 22:511–525, 1990.

16. Jack Dennis, "Public Support for the Party System," paper presented at the American Political Science Association meeting, Washington, D.C., 1986.

17. Larry J. Sabato, *The Party's Just Begun,* Scott, Foresman, Glenview, Ill., 1988.

18. Paul Allen Beck and Frank Sorauf, *Party Politics in America,* 7th Edition, HarperCollins, New York, 1992, p. 153.

19. Bruce E. Keith, *et al., The Myth of the Independent Voter,* University of California Press, Berkeley, 1992.

20. See especially Michael B. MacKuen, Robert S. Erikson, and James A. Stimson, "Macropartisanship," *American Political Science Review,* 83:1125–1142, 1989. See also Herbert F. Weisberg and Charles E. Smith, Jr., "The Influence of the Economy on Party Identification in the Reagan Years," *Journal of Politics,* 53:1077–1092, 1991.

21. For an update on Axelrod, see Gerald Pomper, "The Presidential Election," in Gerald M. Pomper, *The Election of 1992,* Chatham House, Chatham, N.J., 1993.

22. Robert Axelrod, "Presidential Election Coalition in 1984," *American Political Science Review,* 80:281–284, 1986.

23. Herbert McCloskey, Paul J. Hoffman, and Rosemary O'Hara, "Issue Conflicts and Consensus among Party Leaders and Followers," *American Political Science Review,* 54:406–427, 1960.

24. Jeanne Kirkpatrick, *The New Presidential Elite,* Russell Sage, New York, 1976; Everett Carll Ladd, Jr., *Where Have All the Voters Gone?,* Norton, New York, 1977.

25.   John S. Jackson III, Barbara Leavitt Brown, and David Bositits, "Herbert Mc-Closkey and Friends Revisited," *American Politics Quarterly,* 10:158–180, 1982.

26.   Nelson W. Polsby and Aaron Wildavsky, *Presidential Elections,* 8th ed., Free Press, New York, 1991, p. 33.

27.   James L. Gibson, Cornelius P. Cotter, John F. Bibby, and Robert J. Huckshorn, "Whither the Local Parties?" *American Journal of Political Science,* 29:139–159, 1985.

28.   John F. Bibby, Cornelius P. Cotter, James L. Gibson, and Robert Huckshorn, "Parties in State Politics," in Virginia Gray, Herbert Jacob, and Kenneth N. Vines, eds., *Politics in the American States,* Little, Brown, Boston, 1982; James L. Gibson, Cornelius P. Cotter, John F. Bibby, and Robert J. Huckshorn, "Assessing Party Organizational Strength," *American Journal of Political Science,* 27:193–222, 1983.

29.   For more detail, see Larry J. Sabato, *The Party's Just Begun,* Scott, Foresman, Glenview, Ill., 1988.

30.   Gary C. Jacobson, *The Politics of Congressional Elections,* 3d ed., Harper-Collins, New York, 1992, p. 76.

31.   John P. Frendreis, James L. Gibson, and Laura L. Vertz, "Local Party Organizations in the 1984 Elections," paper presented at the American Political Science Association meeting, New Orleans, 1985.

32.   William Crotty, "Party Effort and Its Impact on the Vote," *American Political Science Review,* 65:439–450, 1971; Phillip Cutright and Peter Rossi, "Grass Roots Politicians and the Vote," *American Sociological Review,* 63:171–179, 1958.

33.   Joseph Schlesinger, "The New American Political Party," *American Political Science Review,* 79:1152–1169, 1985. For an update, see Samuel C. Patterson, "Partisanship in the New Congress," *Extension of Remarks,* June:7–8, 1993.

34.   Daniel S. Ward, "The Continuing Search for Party Influence in Congress," *Legislative Studies Quarterly,* 18:211–230, 1993.

35.   Edward G. Carmines and James A. Stimson, "The Two Faces of Issue Voting," *American Political Science Review,* 74:78–91, 1980; Edward G. Carmines, Steven B. Renten, and James A. Stimson, "Events and Alignments," in Richard G. Niemi and Herbert F. Weisberg, eds., *Controversies in Voting Behavior,* Congressional Quarterly Press, Washington, D.C., 1984. And see Edward G. Carmines and James A. Stimson, *Issue Evolution,* Princeton University Press, Princeton, N.J., 1989.

36.   Martin P. Wattenberg, *The Decline of American Political Parties,* Harvard University Press, Cambridge, Mass., 1986.

37.   J. Merrill Shanks and Warren E. Miller, "Policy Direction and Performance Evaluation: Complementary Explanations of the Reagan Elections," *British Journal of Political Science,* 20:143–235, 1990.

38.   Wattenberg, *op. cit.*

39.   Morris Fiorina, *Divided Government,* Macmillan, New York, 1992.

Chapter 6

1.   Steven J. Rosenstone and John Mark Hansen, *Mobilization, Participation, and Democracy in America,* Macmillan, New York, 1993; Raymond E. Wolfinger and Steven J. Rosenstone, *Who Votes?,* Yale University Press, New Haven, 1980.

2.   Howard Reiter, *Parties and Elections in Corporate America,* St. Martin's, New York, 1987. And see Francis Fox Piven and Richard A. Cloward, *Why Americans Don't Vote,* Holbrook, New York, 1988.

3.   Paul R. Abramson and John H. Aldrich, "The Decline of Electoral Participation in America," *American Political Science Review,* 76:502–521, 1982.

4.   Steven J. Rosenstone and John Mark Hansen, *Mobilization, Participation, and Democracy in America,* Macmillan, New York, 1993, pp. 130–131.

5.   G. Bingham Powell, Jr., *Contemporary Democracies,* Harvard University Press, Cambridge, Mass., 1982.

6.   Gary Jacobson, *The Politics of Congressional Elections,* HarperCollins, New York, 1992, pp. 12–15.

7.   John F. Bibby, *Politics, Parties, and Elections in America,* Nelson-Hall, Chicago, 1987.

8.   E.g., see Barbara Norrander, "Ideological Representativeness of Primary Voters," *American Journal of Political Science,* 33:570–587, 1989.

9.   Bibby, *op. cit.* And see Barbara Norrander, "Nomination Choices: Caucus and Primary Outcomes, 1976–1988," *American Journal of Political Science,* 37:343–364, 1993.

10.   Priscilla L. Southwell, "The 1984 Democratic Nomination Process," *American Politics Quarterly,* 14:75–88, 1986.

11.   Benjamin Ginsberg and John Green, "The Best Congress Money Can Buy," paper presented at the American Political Science Association meeting, Washington, D.C., 1979.

12.   Richard L. Hall and Frank M. Wayman, "Buying Time: Moneyed Interests and the Mobilization of Bias in Congressional Committees," *American Political Science Review,* 84:797–820, 1990.

13.   Thomas K. Patterson and Robert D. McClure, *The Unseeing Eye,* Putnam, New York, 1976.

14.   For instance, see Charles K. Atkins and Gary Heald, "Effects of Political Advertising," *Public Opinion Quarterly,* 40:216–228, 1976.

15.   Edie Goldenberg and Michael W. Traugott, *Campaigning for Congress,* Congressional Quarterly Press, Washington, D.C., 1984.

16.   Arthur H. Miller and Michael MacKuen, "Learning about the Candidates," *Public Opinion Quarterly,* 43:326–346, 1979.

17. Lee Sigelman and Carol K. Sigelman, "Judgments of the Carter-Reagan Debate," *Public Opinion Quarterly,* 48:624–628, 1984.

18. Arthur H. Miller and Stephen A. Borelli, "Explaining Policy and Performance Evaluations in the Electorate," paper presented at the American Political Science Association meeting, Chicago, 1987.

19. William G. Mayer, "The 1992 Election and the Future of American Politics," *Polity,* 25:461–474, 1993. For more detail, see William G. Mayer, *The Changing American Mind,* University of Michigan Press, Ann Arbor, 1992. On the development of a conservative mood, see James A. Stimson, *Public Opinion in America,* Westview, Boulder, Colo., 1991.

20. Stimson, *op. cit.*

21. Miller and Borelli, *op. cit.,* pp. 8–9.

22. J. Merrill Shanks and Warren E. Miller, "Alternative Explanations of the 1988 Elections," paper presented at the American Political Science Association meeting, Atlanta, Georgia, 1989.

23. Mayer, "The 1992 Election . . . ," *op. cit.*

24. Kathleen A. Frankovic, "Public Opinion in the 1992 Campaign," in Gerald Pomper, ed., *The Election of 1992,* Chatham House, Chatham, N.J., 1993, p. 130.

25. Gerald M. Pomper, "The Presidential Election," in *ibid.* See also Paul J. Quirk and Jon K. Dalager, "The Election: A 'New Democrat' and a New Kind of Presidential Campaign," in Michael Nelson, ed., *The Elections of 1992,* Congressional Quarterly Press, Washington, D.C., 1993; Mayer, "The 1992 Election . . . ," *op. cit.*

26. George A. Chressanthis and Stephen D. Shaffer, "Major-Party Failure and Third-Party Voting in Presidential Elections, 1976–1988," *Social Science Quarterly,* 74:264–273, 1993.

27. Barbara Hinckley, *Congressional Elections,* Congressional Quarterly Press, Washington, D.C., 1981.

28. Hinckley, *op. cit.*

29. George Serra and Albert Cover, "The Electoral Consequences of Perquisite Use: The Casework Case," *Legislative Studies Quarterly,* 17:246, 1992.

30. Paul Feldman and James Jondrow, "Congressional Elections and Local Federal Spending," *American Journal of Political Science,* 28:147–164, 1984.

31. Gary Jacobson, *op. cit.*

32. Martin Thomas, "Electoral Proximity and Senatorial Roll Call Voting," *American Journal of Political Science,* 29:96–111, 1984; Sunil Ahuja, "Electoral Status and Representation in the United States Senate," *American Politics Quarterly,* 22:104–118, 1994.

33. L. Marvin Overby, "Political Amateurism, Legislative Inexperience, and Incumbency Behavior," *Polity,* 25:401–420, 1993.

34.   John B. Gilmour and Paul Rothstein, "Early Republican Retirement: A Cause of Democratic Dominance in the House of Representatives," *Legislative Studies Quarterly,* 18:345–366, 1993.

35.   Donald R. Kinder and D. Roderick Kiewiet, "Sociotropic Politics," *British Journal of Political Science,* 11:129–161, 1981.

36.   Samuel Kernell, "Presidential Popularity and Negative Voting," *American Political Science Review,* 71:44–66, 1977.

37.   Gary Jacobson, *The Electoral Origins of Divided Government,* Westview, Boulder, Colo., 1990, p. 45.

38.   Morris Fiorina, *Divided Government,* Macmillan, New York, 1992. For one study that attempts to test these assumptions, see R. Michael Alvarez and Matthew M. Schousen, "Policy Moderation or Conflicting Expectations," *American Politics Quarterly,* 21:410–438, 1993.

39.   David R. Mayhew, *Divided We Govern: Party Control, Lawmaking, and Investigations, 1946–1990,* Yale University Press, New Haven, 1990.

40.   Lilliard E. Richardson, Jr., and John M. Schieb, II, "Divided Government and the Supreme Court," *American Politics Quarterly,* 21:458–472, 1993.

41.   Anthony Downs, *An Economic Theory of Democracy,* Harper & Row, New York, 1957.

42.   Benjamin I. Page and Richard A. Brody, "Policy Voting and the Electoral Process," *American Political Science Review,* 66:979–995, 1972.

43.   Gerald M. Pomper with Susan M. Lederman, *Elections in America,* Longman, New York, 1980.

44.   *Ibid.* And see Ian Budge and Richard Hofferbert, "Mandates and Policy Outputs: U.S. Party Platforms and Federal Expenditures," *American Political Science Review,* 84:111–131, 1990.

45.   Thomas, *op. cit.*

46.   Douglas A. Hibbs, Jr., and Christopher Dennis, "Income Distribution in the United States," *American Political Science Review,* 82:467–490, 1988.

47.   Robert X. Browning, "President, Congress, and Policy Outcomes," *American Journal of Political Science,* 29:197–216, 1985.

48.   Hibbs and Dennis, *op. cit.* And see John T. Williams, "The Political Manipulation of Macroeconomic Policy," *American Political Science Review,* 84:767–795, 1990; Alberto Alesina and Howard Rosenthal, "Partisan Cycles in Congressional Elections and the Macroeconomy," *American Political Science Review,* 83:373–398, 1989.

Chapter 7

1.   Robert Dahl, *Who Governs?,* Yale University Press, New Haven, 1961.

2.   E. E. Schattschneider, *The Semisovereign People,* Holt, New York, 1960, pp. 7–18.

3.   See Jack L. Walker, Jr., *Mobilizing Groups in America*, University of Michigan Press, Ann Arbor, 1991, pp. 29–38, 62–64.

4.   Theodore J. Lowi, *The End of Liberalism*, 2d ed., Norton, New York, 1979.

5.   *Ibid.*, p. 93

6.   Mancur Olson, *The Rise and Decline of Nations*, Yale University Press, New Haven, 1982.

7.   Ralph Nader, *Unsafe at Any Speed*, Grossman, New York, 1965.

8.   Rachel Carson, *Silent Spring*, Houghton Mifflin, Boston, 1962.

9.   Mancur Olson, *The Logic of Collective Action*, Harvard University Press, Cambridge, Mass., 1971, pp. 1–3.

10.   David B. Truman, *The Governmental Process*, Knopf, New York, 1951, pp. 264–270.

11.   Randall B. Ripley and Grace A. Franklin, *Congress, the Bureaucracy, and Public Policy*, rev. ed., Dorsey, Homewood, Ill., 1980, pp. 101–104.

12.   Robert Heineman, *Authority and the Liberal Tradition*, 2d ed., Transaction, New Brunswick, N.J., 1994, pp. 158–161.

13.   Graham Wootton, *Interest Groups*, Prentice-Hall, Englewood Cliffs, N.J., 1985, pp. 127–130.

14.   James Q. Wilson, "Mr. Clinton, Meet Mr. Gore," *Wall Street Journal*, October 28, 1993, p. A22.

15.   *U.S. v. Harriss* (347 U.S. 612 [1954]).

16.   *Buckley v. Valeo* (424 U.S. 1 [1976]).

Chapter 8

1.   *Congressional Quarterly Weekly Report*, April 13, 1985, p. 687. *CQ* notes that part of this discrepancy can also be attributed to the fact that some Democrats are elected from urban districts that have very low voting turnout.

2.   Thirteen of the new black Representatives and six of the new Hispanic representatives won in districts specifically drawn to increase minority representation.

3.   Stephen Hess, *The Ultimate Insiders: U.S. Senators in the National Media*, Brookings Institution, Washington, D.C., 1986, pp. 30–36.

4.   Rudolf Engelbarts, *Women in the United States Congress, 1917–1972*, Libraries Unlimited, Littleton, Colo., 1974, p. 23.

5.   Two useful works on the GAO are Frederick C. Mosher, *The GAO: The Quest for Accountability in American Government*, Westview, Boulder, Colo., 1979, and Wallace Earl Walker, *Changing Organizational Culture: Strategy, Structure, and Professionalism in the U.S. General Accounting Office*, University of Tennessee Press, Knoxville, 1986.

6.   Each house in Congress has a parliamentarian and parliamentarian assistants. One of these people is always on the floor to advise the presiding officer on points of order. These people also help the membership generally with questions about procedures.

7.   See Julie Rovner, "After Fiery Debate, Senate Passes AIDS Bill," *Congressional Quarterly Weekly Report,* April 30, 1988, pp. 1167–1169.

8.   *Congressional Quarterly's Guide to Congress,* 2d ed., Congressional Quarterly Press, Washington, D.C., 1976.

9.   See David E. Rosenbaum, "Michigan Democrat Presides as Capital's Grand Inquisitor," *New York Times,* September 30, 1991, pp. A1, A12.

Chapter 9

1.   Thomas Cronin, *The State of the Presidency,* Prentice-Hall, Englewood Cliffs, N.J., 1980, p. 192.

2.   John E. Mueller, *War, Presidents and Public Opinion,* Wiley, New York, 1973.

3.   Aaron Wildavsky, "The Two Presidencies," in Aaron Wildavsky, ed., *Perspectives on the Presidency,* Little, Brown, Boston, 1975.

4.   Barbara Kellerman, *The Political Presidency,* Oxford University Press, New York, 1984, chap. 5.

5.   David McKay, "Presidential Strategy and the Veto Power: A Reappraisal," *Political Science Quarterly,* 104:3, 1989.

6.   Donald F. Kettl, *Deficit Politics,* Macmillan, New York, 1992, chap. 2.

7.   Samuel Kernell, *Going Public: New Strategies of Presidential Leadership,* Congressional Quarterly Press, Washington, 1992.

8.   Paul Brace and Barbara Hinckley, "The Structure of Presidential Approval: Constraints Within and Across Presidencies," *The Journal of Politics,* 53:4, November 1991.

9.   Charles W. Ostrom, Jr., and Dennis M. Simon, "Promise and Performance: A Dynamic Model of Presidential Popularity," *American Political Science Review,* 79:2, June 1985.

10.   Richard Neustadt, *Presidential Power,* Harcourt, Brace & World, New York, 1960.

11.   Richard Waterman, *Presidential Influence and the Administrative State,* University of Tennessee Press, Knoxville, 1989.

12.   Benjamin Page and Mark Petracca, *The American Presidency,* McGraw-Hill, New York, 1983, p. 169.

13.   Richard A. Watson and Norman C. Thomas, *The Politics of the Presidency,* Congressional Quarterly Press, Washington, D.C., 1988.

14. Arthur Schlesinger, *The Imperial Presidency*, Houghton Mifflin, Boston, 1973.

15. Lance LeLoup, *Budgetary Politics*, King's Court Communications, Brunswick, Ohio, 1986, p. 134.

16. Schlesinger, *op. cit.*

17. Bob Woodward and Carl Bernstein, *The Final Days*, Simon and Schuster, New York, 1976.

18. Clark R. Mollenhoff, *The Man Who Pardoned Nixon,* St. Martin's, New York, 1976.

19. Clinton Rossiter, *The American Presidency*, Harcourt, Brace & World, New York, 1960.

20. Neustadt, *op. cit.*, chap. 1.

21. Calvin Mouw and Michael MacKuen, "The Strategic Configuration, Personal Influence and Presidential Power in Congress," *Western Political Quarterly*, 45:2, September 1992.

22. Cronin, *op. cit.*, chap. 7.

23. Irving Janis, *Victims of Groupthink*, Houghton Mifflin, Boston, 1952.

24. Waterman, *op. cit.*

25. Neustadt, *op. cit.*, p. 77.

26. Watson and Thomas, *op. cit.*, p. 501.

27. Cronin, *op. cit.*, p. 22.

Chapter 10

1. Hans Gerth and C. Wright Mills, *From Max Weber: Essays in Sociology*, Oxford University Press, New York, 1958.

2. Mancur Olson, *The Logic of Collective Action,* Harvard University Press, Cambridge, Mass., 1971.

3. James Q. Wilson, ed., *The Politics of Regulation*, Basic Books, New York, 1980.

4. Eugene Bardach, *The Implementation Game,* MIT Press, Cambridge, Mass., 1977; Jeffrey Pressman and Aaron Wildavsky, *Implementation*, 2d ed., University of California Press, Berkeley, 1979.

5. Louis M. Kohlmeier, Jr., *The Regulators: Watchdog Agencies and the Public Interest*, Harper & Row, New York, 1969; Richard A. Harris and Sidney M. Milkis, *The Politics of Regulatory Change: A Tale of Two Agencies*, Oxford University Press, New York, 1989.

6. Dennis Dresang, *Public Personnel Management and Public Policy,* Little, Brown, Boston, 1984, p. 28.

7. *United States Statistical Abstract,* Government Printing Office, Washington, D.C., 1992, pp. 330, 333.

8. Steven W. Hays and T. Zane Reeves, *Personnel Management in the Public Sector,* Allyn and Bacon, Boston, 1984.

9. Woodrow Wilson, "The Study of Administration," *Political Science Quarterly,* vol. 2, June 1887.

10. Judith Gruber, *Controlling Bureaucracy: Dilemmas in Democratic Governance,* University of California Press, Berkeley, 1987.

11. George Berkley, *The Craft of Public Administration,* Allyn and Bacon, Boston, 1984, p. 140; *Washington Post,* September 23, 1993, p. A23.

12. Allen Kneese, *Measuring the Benefits of Clean Air and Water,* Resources for the Future, Washington, D.C., 1984.

13. Anthony Downs, *Inside Bureaucracy,* Little, Brown, Boston, 1967.

14. William Niskanen, *Bureaucracy and Representative Government,* Aldine-Atherton, Chicago, 1971.

15. B. Dan Wood, "The Dynamics of Political-Bureaucratic Adaptation," *American Journal of Political Science,* 37:2, May 1993. Cathy Marie Johnson, *The Dynamics of Conflict between Bureaucrats and Legislators,* Sharpe, Armonk, N.Y., 1992; Susan Hunter and Richard W. Waterman, "Determining an Agency's Regulatory Style: How Does the EPA Water Office Enforce the Law?," *Western Political Quarterly,* 45:2, June 1992.

16. Samuel P. Huntington, "The Marasmus of the ICC: The Commission, the Railroads and the Public Interest," *Yale Law Journal,* 61:4, 1952.

17. Marver Bernstein, *Regulating Business by Independent Commission,* Princeton University Press, Princeton N.J., 1955.

18. Hugh Heclo, "Issue Networks and the Executive Establishment," in Anthony King, ed., *The New Political System,* American Enterprise Institute, Washington, D.C., 1978.

19. Francis E. Rourke, *Bureaucracy, Politics and Public Policy,* Little, Brown, Boston, 1984.

20. Olson, *op. cit.*

21. Terry M. Moe, "The New Economics of Organization," *American Journal of Political Science,* 28:4, November 1984; John Brehm and Scott Gates, "Donut Shops and Speed Traps: Evaluating Models of Supervision on Police Behavior," *American Journal of Political Science,* 17:2, May 1993.

22. Moe, *op. cit.*

23. Gary J. Miller, *Managerial Dilemmas: The Political Economy of Hierarchy,* Cambridge University Press, Cambridge, England, 1992, chap. 9.

24. Frederick Mosher, *Democracy and the Public Service*, Oxford University Press, New York, 1982.

25. *New York Times*, August 19, 1987.

26. New York State Department of Environmental Conservation, Memorandum #87–14: Source Separation and Recycling, June 15, 1987.

27. Charles Peters, *How Washington Really Works*, Addison-Wesley, Reading, Mass., 1993.

Chapter 11

1. An explanation of Supreme Court citations is appropriate at this point. In these citations, the first number is the volume number and the second is the page number on which the case begins. In cases since the late 1800s, these numbers for the official Court citations are separated by the initials *U.S.* designating the government's printing of the decisions. Before this, the names of the Court's reporters were used. Thus in this citation Cranch was the Court reporter, and the case can be found in volume 1 at page 137. There are also two major private publishers of Supreme Court decisions: West Publishing Company in St. Paul, Minnesota, and The Lawyers Co-operative Publishing Company in Rochester, New York. Instead of the initials *U.S.*, West uses a *S. Ct.* citation and the Lawyers Co-operative uses *L. Ed.* (for volumes since the mid-1950s, *L. Ed. 2d.*) These editions of the Supreme Court's decisions include law notes, case summaries, and other information not included in the official Supreme Court reports.

2. George R. Metcalf, *From Little Rock to Boston*, Greenwood Press, Westport, Conn., 1983, pp. 197–220.

3. B. Guy Peters, *American Public Policy*, 2d ed., Chatham House, Chatham, N.J., 1986, p. 86.

4. William H. Rehnquist, *The Supreme Court*, Morrow, New York, 1987, pp. 289–290.

5. Carl Brent Swisher, *Stephen J. Field*, Archon Books, Hamden, Conn, 1963, pp. 443–444.

6. William B. Lockhart, *et al.*, *The American Constitution*, 6th ed., West, St. Paul, Minn., 1986, p. 264.

7. See Samuel J. Konefsky, *The Legacy of Holmes and Brandeis*, Collier Books, New York, 1961.

Chapter 12

1. Charles O. Jones, *An Introduction to Public Policy*, Brooks/Cole, Monterey, Calif., 1984, p. 25.

2. Matthew Crenson, *The Un-Politics of Air Pollution*, Johns Hopkins University Press, Baltimore, 1971.

3. David R. Morgan and Robert E. England, "White Enrollment Loss," *American Politics Quarterly*, 12:241–264, 1984.

4. Paul E. Peterson, *City Limits*, University of Chicago Press, Chicago, 1981. While this formulation is directly applied to local government, Peterson also notes its applicability to state and national decisions and the interactions among the various levels of government.

5. The diagram is based on Charles O. Jones, "The Policy Process," paper presented at the Northeastern Political Science Association meeting, Newark, N.J., November, 1993.

6. Jones, *op. cit.*, p. 38.

7. John W. Kingdon, *Agendas, Alternatives, and Public Policies*, Little, Brown, Boston, 1984, p. 106.

8. Anthony Downs, "Up and Down with Ecology—The 'Issue Attention' Cycle," *The Public Interest*, 28:38–50, 1972.

9. Kingdon, *op. cit.*, p. 207.

10. E. E. Schattschneider, *The Semi-Sovereign People*, The Dryden Press, Hinsdale, Ill., 1975, p. 69.

11. Charles Lindblom, "The Science of Muddling Through," *Public Administration Review*, 19:79–88, 1959.

12. Steven A. Peterson, "Why Policies Don't Work," in Elliott White and Joseph Losco, eds., *Biology and Bureaucracy*, University Press of America, Washington, D.C., 1984.

13. Kingdon, *op. cit.*, p. 209.

14. Eugene Bardach, *The Implementation Game*, Cambridge, Mass., MIT Press, 1977.

15. Jeffrey Pressman and Aaron Wildavsky, *Implementation*, University of California Press, Berkeley, 1973.

16. Graham Allison, *Essence of Decision*, Little, Brown, Boston, 1971.

17. George C. Edwards III, *Implementing Public Policy*, Congressional Quarterly Press, Washington, D.C., 1980.

18. Erwin L. Levine and Elizabeth M. Wexler, *PL 94-142. An Act of Congress*, Macmillan, New York, 1981.

19. For instance, see Carol H. Weiss, "Utilization of Evaluation" and "The Politicization of Evaluation Research," in Carol H. Weiss, ed., *Evaluating Action Programs*, Allyn and Bacon, Boston, 1972.

Chapter 13

1.   Mancur Olson, *The Rise and Decline of Nations,* Yale University Press, New Haven, 1982; Alan Schick, "The Distributive Congress," in Alan Schick, ed., *The Distributive Congress*, American Enterprise Institute, Washington, D.C., 1983.

2.   Lance T. LeLoup, *Budgetary Politics*, King's Court Communications, Brunswick, Ohio, 1986.

3.   Richard Hula, ed., *Market-based Public Policy,* Macmillan, New York, 1987; E. S. Savas, *Privatization: The Key to Better Government*, Chatham House, Chatham, N.J., 1987.

4.   James A. Buchanan and Richard E. Wagner, *Democracy in Deficit: The Legacy of Lord Keynes*, Academic Press, New York, 1977.

5.   Milton Friedman and Walter Heller, *Monetary vs. Fiscal Policy*, Norton, New York, 1969.

6.   Douglas A. Hibbs, *The Political Economy of Industrial Democracies*, Harvard University Press, Cambridge, Mass., 1987, chap. 4.

7.   Stephen Marris, *Deficits and Dollars: The World Economy at Risk*, Institute for International Economics, Washington, D.C., 1985.

8.   Council of Economic Advisers, *Economic Report of the President: 1994*, Government Printing Office, Washington, D.C., 1994, pp. 240–243.

9.   Frank Levy and Richard C. Michel, *The Economic Future of American Families: Income and Wealth Trends*, Urban Institute Press, Washington, D.C., 1991, chap. 7.

10.   Paul Craig Roberts, *The Supply Side Revolution*, Harvard University Press, Cambridge, Mass., 1984.

11.   David Stockman, *The Triumph of Politics: How the Reagan Revolution Failed*, Harper & Row, New York, 1986.

12.   Bob Woodward, "Bickering While Rome Burns," *Washington Post*, October 19, 1992, p. 8.

13.   John T. Wooley, *Monetary Politics: The Federal Reserve Board and the Politics of Monetary Policy*, Cambridge University Press, New York, 1984.

14.   Greg B. Markus, "The Impact of Personal and National Economic Conditions on Presidential Voting, 1956–1988," *American Journal of Political Science*, 36(3):829–834, August 1992.

15.   Council of Economic Advisers, *Economic Report to the President January 1993*, Government Printing Office, Washington, D.C., 1993, p. 115.

16.   *Ibid.*

17.   Lester C. Thurow, *Head to Head: The Coming Economic Battle Among Japan, Europe and America*, Morrow, New York, 1992.

18.   Edward Tufte, *Political Control of the Economy,* Princeton University Press, Princeton, N.J., 1978; James E. Alt and Alec Crystal, *Political Economics,* University of California Press, Berkeley, 1983.

19.   Joseph A. Pechman, *Who Paid the Taxes, 1966–1985?,* Brookings Institution, Washington, D.C., 1985; Bureau of the Census, "Measuring the Effect of Benefits and Taxes on Income and Poverty: 1989," *Current Population Reports,* Series P-60, No. 169-RD, September 1990.

20.   Richard C. Michel, "Economic Growth and Income Equality Since the 1982 Recession," *Journal of Policy Analysis and Management,* 10:2, Spring 1991.

21.   Howard E. Schuman, *Politics and the Budget: The Struggle Between the President and the Congress,* Prentice-Hall, Englewood Cliffs, N.J., 1988.

22.   Peter G. Peterson and Neil Howe, *On Borrowed Time: How the Growth in Entitlement Spending Threatens America's Future,* Institute for Contemporary Studies, San Francisco, 1988.

23.   Joseph White and Aaron Wildavsky, *The Deficit and the Public Interest,* University of California Press, Berkeley, 1989.

24.   Donald F. Kettl, *Deficit Politics,* Macmillan, New York, 1992, chap. 1.

25.   *Ibid.*

Chapter 15

1.   Thomas A. Bailey, *A Diplomatic History of the American People,* Prentice-Hall, Englewood Cliffs, N.J., 1980; Walter LaFeber, *The American Age: U.S. Foreign Policy at Home and Abroad Since 1750,* Norton, New York, 1989.

2.   Alexander L. George and Richard Smoke, *Deterrence in American Foreign Policy: Theory and Practice,* Columbia University Press, New York, 1974.

3.   See Graham T. Allison, "Conceptual Models and the Cuban Missile Crisis," *American Political Science Review,* 64: 689–718, 1969.

4.   George and Smoke, *op. cit.*

5.   Ole R. Holsti and James N. Rosenau, "The Structure of Foreign Policy Attitudes Among American Leaders," *Journal of Politics,* 52:1, February 1990.

6.   John Lewis Gaddis, *The United States and the Origin of the Cold War, 1941–1947,* Columbia University Press, New York, 1972.

7.   Neil Sheehan, *A Bright Shining Lie: John Paul Vann and America in Vietnam,* Vintage Books, New York, 1988; David Halberstam, *The Best and the Brightest,* Random House, New York, 1969.

8.   Seymour Hersh, *The Price of Power: Kissinger in the Nixon White House,* Summit Books, New York, 1983; Stanley Hoffman, *Primacy or World Order: American Foreign Policy Since the Cold War,* McGraw-Hill, New York, 1978.

9.   Joan E. Spero, *The Politics of International Economic Relations*, St. Martin's, New York, 1981.

10.   Seyom Brown, "U.S. Policy Toward the Post-Soviet States," in Robert J. Art and Seyom Brown, *U.S. Foreign Policy: The Search for a New Role*, Macmillan, New York, 1993.

11.   William W. Kaufman, *Glasnost, Perestroika, and U.S. Defense Spending*, Brookings Institution, Washington, D.C., 1990; Sam Nunn, *Nunn: 1990: A New Military Strategy*, Center for Strategic and International Studies, Washington, D.C., 1990.

12.   Bruce Stokes, "Export or Die," *National Journal*, January 2, 1993.

13.   Saadet Deger and Ron Smith, "Military Expansion and Growth in Less Developed Countries," *Journal of Conflict Resolution*, 27, June 1983.

14.   Mitchell Reiss, *Without the Bomb: The Politics of Nuclear Nonproliferation*, Columbia University Press, New York, 1988.

15.   Richard Rosecrance, *The Rise of the Trading State: Commerce and Conquest in the Modern World*, Basic Books, New York, 1986.

16.   Joseph M. Grieco, *Cooperation Among Nations: Europe, America and Non-Tariff Barriers To Trade*, Cornell University Press, Ithaca, N.Y., 1990.

17.   Hans Morgenthau, *Politics Among Nations: The Struggle for Power and Peace*, Knopf, New York, 1973, p. 4; A. F. K. Organski, *World Politics*, Knopf, New York, 1958.

18.   Adam Przeworski, *Democracy and the Market*, Cambridge University Press, New York, 1991; Georg Sorenson, *Democracy and Democratization*, Westview, Boulder, Colo., 1993.

19.   James Schlesinger, "Quest for a Post Cold War Foreign Policy," *Foreign Affairs*, 72:1, 1993.

20.   Jessica Tuchman Mathews, "Environmental Policy," in Robert J. Art and Seyom Brown, *op. cit.*

21.   Alexander L. George, *Presidential Decisionmaking: The Effective Use of Information and Advice*, Westview, Boulder, Colo., 1980; I. M. Destler, Leslie H. Gelb, and Anthony Lake, *Our Own Worst Enemy: The Unmaking of American Foreign Policy*, Simon and Schuster, New York, 1984.

22.   Graham Allison, *Essence of Decision*, Little, Brown, Boston, 1971.

23.   Henry Kissinger, "Domestic Structure and Foreign Policy," in James N. Rosenau, ed., *International Politics and Foreign Policy*, Free Press, New York, 1969, p. 268.

24.   Nathan Miller, *Spying for America: The Hidden History of U.S. Intelligence*, Paragon House, New York, 1989.

25.   Arthur M. Schlesinger, Jr., *The Imperial Presidency*, Houghton Mifflin, Boston, 1989.

26.   Thomas E. Mann, ed., "Making Foreign Policy: President and Congress," *A Question of Balance: The President, the Congress and Foreign Policy*, Brookings Institution, Washington, D.C., 1990.

27.   Duane M. Oldfield and Aaron Wildavsky, "Reconsidering the Two Presidencies," *Society*, 26:5, July/August 1989.

28.   Roger Hilsman, *The Politics of Policy Making in Defense and Foreign Affairs: Conceptual Models and Bureaucratic Politics*, Prentice-Hall, Englewood Cliffs, N.J., 1987.

GLOSSARY

Absolute position   Justice Hugo Black's view that all speech and written expression are protected by the First Amendment.

Access   The term used to describe an interest group's ability to contact and influence government decision makers.

Accusatorial system   In contrast to the European continent's inquisitorial system of criminal procedure, the American accusatorial system has protections designed to keep the defendant from being forced to aid in his or her prosecution.

Adversary process   The basic form of the American legal process which strives for a balanced contest between the parties to a case on the theory that from such a contest the truth will emerge.

Affirmative action   A policy in which schools, governments, and businesses make a special effort to recruit women and members of minority groups who are underrepresented in their organization.

Agency capture   A regulatory agency originally established to protect consumer interests is "captured" by the industry it is supposed to regulate.

Agenda setting   Deciding what issues to discuss seriously; deciding what to decide about. When applied to the media, agenda setting refers to the power of the media to define the important issues of the day.

Anti-Federalists   Those who opposed the Constitution during the ratification battle. Anti-federalists later moved into the Jeffersonian Democrat-Republican Party.

Appropriations committees   The House and Senate Appropriations Committees consider only legislation providing funding for programs.

Articles of Confederation   The United States' first constitution as an independent state. It emphasized states' power and legislative dominance.

Authorizing committees   Those standing substantive committees, e.g., Agriculture, Labor and Human Resources, that consider legislation establishing and renewing programs.

Bill of attainder   Prohibited by the Constitution, a bill of attainder is a legislative, as opposed to a judicial, finding of guilt.

Bipartisanship   The idea that Republicans and Democrats should put aside partisan differences, especially on foreign relations, where Americans share a common interest.

Block grants-in-aid   Grants-in-aid that allow funds to be distributed among programs within a general area such as law enforcement and education.

Bureaucracy   A form of organization defined by hierarchical structure, formal rules, and specialization.

Categorical grants-in-aid   Grants-in-aid for narrowly defined purposes accompanied by specific standards that must be met by the recipient.

Certiorari, writ of   A discretionary writ, which the Supreme Court grants if it wishes to consider a case on appeal.

Checks and balances   The structural feature of the Constitution that gives each branch power to check other branches of government.

Civil Service   The government personnel system which requires that potential government employees demonstrate their competence through appropriate testing. Once employees are hired, they may not be fired for political reasons.

Class action suit   A case brought before the courts on behalf of the plaintiff and all others similarly affected by the challenged law or governmental action.

Clear and present danger test   A judicial standard first enunciated by Justice Oliver Wendell Holmes that holds that speech normally protected by the First Amendment can in certain circumstances create a "clear and present danger" and thus be subject to prosecution.

Clientele group   The group, usually organized, served by an agency's program.

Cloture   An extraordinary majority—on substantive legislation, 60 votes—that enables the Senate to end a filibuster.

Cold war   The post World War II period of intense competition between the United States and the Soviet Union, featuring an expensive military buildup and efforts to extend political influence around the world.

Collective benefits   Benefits such as clean air or military security which, if provided for some citizens, must be provided for all citizens.

Common law   The historical basis of the Anglo-American legal systems which utilizes judicial decisions as the basis for legal principles.

Concurrent majority   John C. Calhoun's idea that government decisions should require the agreement of a majority of those composing each affected interest.

Concurring opinion   A separate judicial opinion that agrees with the majority opinion but utilizes different reasoning.

Conference committees   Ad hoc groups appointed from the House and Senate to work out the differences in the two chambers' versions of a specific bill.

Containment   A United States foreign policy objective of preventing the Soviet Union from extending its influence into other areas of the world.

Cost benefit analysis   An effort to evaluate the worth of a public program by comparing the cost of the resources used to the benefits which users of the program gain.

Critical elections   Those elections or election periods during which underlying political coalitions change, ushering in a new party era.

Dealignment   Periods of time when party declines as a guide for the electorate and in which party loses some of its ability to structure political discourse.

Delegate   A representative or senator who believes that it is his or her job to carry out the explicit will of the people.

Deterrence   The military doctrine that a strong military buildup and a clearly demonstrated willingness to use military weapons would deter political adversaries from launching an attack.

Differential access   A situation in which some groups have a natural advantage in being heard by government agencies, as is the case with veterans groups and the Department of Veterans Affairs.

Discharge petition   A procedure by which the House or Senate can require a committee to discharge a bill for further consideration.

Divided government   The situation that exists when different parties control different branches of government.

Dual federalism   A constitutional doctrine from the late 19th century until 1937 that limited national power with the claim that the states retained certain areas of reserved powers that could not be regulated through national action.

Electoral College   The mechanism by which the president and vice-president are selected; each state gets the number of electoral votes equal to the number of U.S. senators plus members of the House of Representatives from the state.

Elitism   The idea that a small number of individuals dominate all major political and social institutions and control the political decision-making process.

Entitlement   A program such as social security in which benefit payments to qualified citizens are enacted in law. The level of benefits cannot be altered through the annual budgetary process.

Equity law   A form of law which allows courts to undertake actions in the interest of fairness not possible under the more rigid common law.

Errand running   Office holders who respond to personal problems of their constituents, intervening with government to help them. Helps create the incumbency effect (see p. 388).

Ex post facto law   Prohibited by the Constitution, an ex post facto law makes an act a crime after it has occurred or increases the penalty for a crime after it has been committed.

Exclusionary rule   A judicial rule that requires that evidence illegally obtained against an individual may not be used in any criminal prosecution against that person.

Expressive conduct (symbolic speech)   Behavior that claims to be a form of expression protected by the First Amendment from prosecution.

Federalism   The sharing of power between two levels of government within the same geographic area.

Federalists   Supporters of the constitution during the ratification battle and the name given to one of the first two political parties.

Fighting words doctrine   Court position that holds that some violent, aggressive forms of expression do not merit protection under the First Amendment.

Filibuster   A parliamentary device in which opponents of a bill exploit the Senate's right of unlimited debate by holding the floor until the bill's supporters agree to drop the proposal.

Fiscal policy   A policy of adjusting federal government taxing and spending levels to stimulate a sluggish economy or to reduce inflationary pressure.

Flexible response   The military doctrine calling for the buildup of conventional arms and small nuclear weapons to provide the United States with military alternatives to all-out nuclear war.

Forma pauperis, In   A writ granted by courts, usually to state and federal prisoners claiming to be too poor to afford normal legal expenses, allowing them to proceed with an appeal.

Free rider problem   A problem of groups, most clearly stated by Mancur Olson, in which those who do not join a group still benefit from its activities, as, for example, the higher wages that nonunion workers gain because of union efforts.

General schedule   A system that classifies most civil service jobs into eighteen grades according to level of difficulty and responsibility.

Germaneness, rule of   The fact that, unlike the House, the Senate has no rule of germaneness allows legislation under consideration on the Senate floor to be amended with entirely unrelated proposals.

Gerrymandering   The drawing of legislative district boundaries to favor a specific interest.

Glasnost   A Russian term associated with the dismantling of the Soviet Union in 1991. It refers to broadening participation in political life.

Habeas corpus, writ of   A writ requiring that after a reasonable period of time a prisoner must be either charged with a crime or released. Today it is often used by convicted prisoners who claim that they are being held unconstitutionally because of errors in their prosecution.

Hearings   The legislative stage at which a committee or subcommittee takes testimony from witnesses on legislation or an issue.

Impeachment   A constitutionally prescribed means of removing presidents or civil officers and judges from office in which the House of Representatives impeaches (brings charges) and the Senate tries and convicts.

Implementation   That part of the policy process when decisions have been made and government employees must now put them into effect.

Impoundment   Refusal of the president to spend sums of money appropriated by Congress.

Incrementalism   Slow change in existing laws, based upon "tinkering" with the status quo.

Incumbency effect   The high reelection success rate of incumbents, based on "scaring off" strong potential opponents, high name recognition, errand running, and bringing government funds into their districts.

Independent counsel (special prosecutor)   An individual appointed on a temporary basis by a special judicial committee to investigate particular allegations of criminal activity within the executive branch of the national government.

Initiative   Some states provide for initiative, whereby if enough signatures get onto petitions, a legislative proposal will be brought before the people of the state for a referendum (see referendum on p. 391).

Inner ring   These are the leaders of the journalistic pack; *The New York Times, Washington Post, LA Times,* CNN, the three TV networks, *Time, Life, U.S. News, The Wall Street Journal,* for example.

Interest group liberalism   Theodore Lowi's idea that American politics is dominated by special interests, each pressing self-serving claims which government is unable to resist.

Iron triangles (cozy triangles, subgovernments)   Relationships that develop among agencies, their clientele groups, and legislative committees that form political bases for agencies.

Isolationism   The dominant principle of foreign policy prior to World War II. Isolationism maintained that the United States should avoid entangling alliances with European powers.

Issue networks   Competitive interaction among numerous and diverse interest groups, government agencies, and members of Congress who are interested in and knowledgeable about a policy issue.

Joint committee   A congressional committee composed of members from both the House of Representatives and the Senate.

Judicial review   The power of a court to declare unconstitutional a law or executive action.

Laissez-faire   The idea that government should play a minimal role in the economic and social life of society.

Lame duck president   A president who loses some of his authority in dealing with members of Congress and career civil servants because he cannot or will not run for reelection.

Liberalism   A political perspective which emphasizes the individual, natural rights, and materialism.

Markup session   A meeting in which a subcommittee or committee considers changes in a bill before it.

Marshall plan   A large foreign aid program which helped European nations to recover from the devastation of World War II.

Massive retaliation   The post World War II military doctrine which pledged that the United States would respond to serious acts of provocation by the Soviet Union with an all-out nuclear retaliatory attack.

Mobilization of bias   The idea that a small elite decides policy, not by winning debates over policy alternatives but by deciding what issues will be brought up for discussion; central in agenda-setting stage of the policy process.

Monetary policy   The policy of adjusting the supply of money and interest rates to stimulate a sluggish economy or to reduce inflationary pressure.

Mutual assured destruction (MAD)   After the Soviet Union developed a strong nuclear capability in the 1960s, both the United States and the Soviet Union could absorb a nuclear attack and still launch a massive retaliatory strike. Therefore, either side attacking first would guarantee its own destruction.

National Security Council   A permanent group of advisers who provide the president with advice in dealing with foreign emergencies and national security.

Nuclear proliferation   The spread of the capability to make nuclear weapons from six nations in 1990 to approximately thirty nations in the mid 1990s.

Participatory democracy   In smaller political communities, a system in which individual citizens play an active role in debating and deciding the important political issues of the day.

Party in government   The role of party on those holding positions in government.

Party in the electorate   The impact of political party (especially party identification) on the electorate and citizenry.

Peak association   A form of interest group organization that represents several separate interest groups, e.g., the AFL-CIO representation of member unions.

Peremptory challenges   Challenges, specified in number, that either side in a trial may make without cause to prevent individuals from the jury pool from being seated as jurors.

Perestroika   A Russian term associated with the dismantling of the Soviet Union in 1991. It refers to dismantling the centrally planned economy and introducing free market economic principles.

Pluralism   The idea that many citizens have some influence on the political issues important to them, but little influence on most issues.

Police power   The inherent power of states to act on behalf of the health, welfare, morals, and safety of their citizens.

Policy communities   Groups of people and organizations with a common policy interest who draw up proposals and try to get these onto the agenda.

Political efficacy   The feeling by a person that he or she can influence government and that government will respond.

Political participation   Activities carried out by people to influence government, such as voting, contributing money to a political cause, or taking part in a protest.

Political resources   Assets, such as organization, knowledge, money, and large numbers, which are convertible into influence in deciding political issues.

Political socialization   The process by which people come to learn about politics; it is lifelong and not restricted to childhood and adolescence.

Postmaterialism   The view that citizens emphasize self-fulfillment over material support. Characteristic of those who are better educated and better off financially.

Preferred freedoms doctrine   The view that the freedoms in the First Amendment hold a "preferred" position relative to other freedoms in the Constitution and thus deserve heightened judicial protection.

Primary   Elections in which the voters select who will run for office in the general election on the party labels.

Privatization   Transferring from government agencies to private firms responsibility for providing services such as prison operation and building maintenance.

Problem recognition   The process by which government and the people come to realize that a problem might be serious enough for government to consider taking action on it.

Program evaluation   The process by which programs are examined to see how well they work.

Progressive taxation   As earner income increases, the amount which the earner is taxed relative to income increases. The federal income tax is mildly progressive.

Public opinion   Attitudes and more general orientations by the people toward their government and the political world.

Public policy   What government does; decisions made by government officials.

Recall   Special elections called to see if the people wish to remove an officeholder from office.

Referendum   Special elections in which the people vote to approve or disapprove a legislative proposal; in a sense, the people become citizen legislators, taking over some legislative functions.

Regressive taxation   As earner income increases, the amount which the earner is taxed relative to income decreases. Taxes on gasoline and tobacco are regressive because the tax paid by rich and poor consumers is identical.

Representative democracy   A system in which voting citizens elect representatives to debate policy issues, enact legislation, and see that bureaucrats implement the laws correctly.

Revenue sharing   A general form of fiscal aid from the national government to the states and localities that was initiated under the Nixon administration and terminated under the Reagan administration.

Reverse discrimination   The claim that affirmative action programs may deny white males the equal protection of the laws.

Select committee   A temporary congressional committee with jurisdiction over a narrowly specified subject area.

Senatorial courtesy   A Senate practice wherein the Senate will reject a presidential nomination if it has not been approved by the senator (s) from the president's party in the state in which the position, e.g., judgeship, is located.

Separation of powers   Dividing the legislative, executive, and judicial powers among three different branches of government, thus separating those three powers.

Single-issue group   A group organized around a single, usually noneconomic, issue such as abortion or capital punishment.

Socialization of conflict   A view of government suggested by E. E. Schattschneider which depicts government as an extension of conflicts appealed to it by private interests.

Spoils system   The tendency of newly elected presidents in the early 19th century to replace incumbent government workers with their own political supporters.

Standing   The requirements that a party must meet in order to be qualified to bring a legal action in a particular court.

Supply-side policy   The policy of reducing tax rates in the hope that a tax cut will stimulate economic activity and generate enough additional tax revenue to pay for the original tax cut.

Test case   A case brought by a group before the courts because it possesses facts that increase the likelihood of a decision favorable to that group.

Trustee   A type of representative who believes that it is his or her job to use judgment and wisdom in making decisions—even if this means going against the will of the people.

Turfing   Jurisdictional conflict among government agencies and among presidential advisers who compete for control of programs.

War Powers Resolution   An act authorizing Congress to require that the president withdraw troops from combat overseas after 60 days in the absence of a formal declaration of war.

Whips   Officers for the minority and majority parties in each house of Congress who assist the leaders in assembling voting support for issues.

Index

CPSIA information can be obtained
at www.ICGtesting.com
Printed in the USA
FFOW02n1536280617
37283FF